The Farmerfield Mission

*A Christian Community in
South Africa, 1838–2008*

FIONA VERNAL

OXFORD
UNIVERSITY PRESS

OXFORD
UNIVERSITY PRESS

Oxford University Press is a department of the University of Oxford.
It furthers the University's objective of excellence in research,
scholarship, and education by publishing worldwide.

Oxford   New York
Auckland   Cape Town   Dar es Salaam   Hong Kong   Karachi
Kuala Lumpur   Madrid   Melbourne   Mexico City   Nairobi
New Delhi   Shanghai   Taipei   Toronto
With offices in
Argentina   Austria   Brazil   Chile   Czech Republic   France   Greece
Guatemala   Hungary   Italy   Japan Poland   Portugal   Singapore
South Korea   Switzerland   Thailand   Turkey   Ukraine   Vietnam

Oxford is a registered trade mark of Oxford University Press in the
UK and certain other countries.

Published in the United States of America by
Oxford University Press
198 Madison Avenue, New York, NY 10016

Library of Congress Cataloging-in-Publication Data
Vernal, Fiona.
The Farmerfield mission : a Christian community in South Africa, 1838–2008 / Fiona Vernal.
p.   cm.
Includes bibliographical references.
ISBN 978-0-19-984340-4
1. Wesleyan Methodist Church of South Africa.
2. Wesleyan Methodist Church—Missions—South Africa—Eastern Cape—History.
3. Eastern Cape (South Africa)—History. 4. Eastern Cape (South Africa)—
Church history. I. Title.
BX8321.V47   2012
266.716875—dc23   2012000444

1 3 5 7 9 8 6 4 2

Printed in the United States of America
on acid-free paper

*To my mother, who dared to dream of an education for all her children;
and sacrificed everything to make it happen*

and

*Robert C-H. Shell, who represents the best academic mentor
a student could ask for*

CONTENTS

PART THREE

ACKNOWLEDGMENTS

This book is the outcome of trying to track slaves in the Eastern Cape to decipher what role missions and missionaries played in helping them to refashion their lives during those heady days of the 1830s and 1840s when many got a taste of freedom for the first time. The result of my lofty goal was a hitchhike to Farmerfield with the man without whom none of my oral histories would have been possible: my research assistant Cecil Nonqane. Then, in 1998, only the cows grazing at the estate and the whitewashed Methodist Church provided a hint of the lives imagined and lived at the mission farm. Cory Library's records of Farmerfield helped me fill in the gaps and I discovered a heterogeneous community of Africans whose stories proved as fascinating and eventful as the path from slavery to freedom. My journey then led to Mimosa Park, near King Williams Town, where the descendants of Farmerfield's residents had sought to rebuild their lives since the apartheid government dumped them there in 1962. Their resilience and faith provides the next chapter in the quest for autonomy that defined Farmerfield's existence and I thank them for opening up their homes and hearts to me and letting me share in their sorrows and their joys.

I have incurred many intellectual debts to my professors at Princeton including Barbara Browning, Steve Kotkin, Nell Painter, Robert Shell, Robert Tignor, and Kitsi Watterson. At Yale, Linda Colley, Robert Harms, Paul Landau, Michael Mahoney, Lamin Sanneh, Sandra Sanneh, and Robin Winks provided top-notch training. Robert Shell awakened my interest in South African history at Princeton University and provided unending support and encouragement over the past twenty years. Robert Tignor pushed me beyond my South African partiality. Paul Landau provided critical advice that led to my interest in the history of missions and made sure my stumbling did not result in a fall. Thanks go to Robert Ross for providing the crucial information at short notice that relieved me from a state of panic over reconstructing the early population of Farmerfield, and for taking on the role of my mentor. To my colleagues at Kalamazoo who provided a forum for me to share my ideas, and my current colleagues at the University of Connecticut, I appreciate the support and hospitality you have shown me. For this, I am especially grateful to Marigene Arnold, Charlene Boyer-Lewis, Kiran Cunningham, Ahmed Hussen, and James Lewis; at UCONN: Chris Clark, Brendan Kane, Charles Lansing, and Amii Omara-Otunni. The revisions to the manuscript are a reflection of the feedback of my original dissertation group: Amy Chazkel, Michael Cohen, Jay Garcia, Tori Langland, and Mark Overmyer-Velázquez; the aid of my research assistants Rachel Traficanti, Sheena Williams and Joe Turecek; and the crucial assistance provided by Robert Harms, Paul Landau, Lamin Sanneh, Alan Kirkaldy, Rodney Davenport, Clifton Crais, J. B. Peires, and Robert Ross at various stages of the drafting and rewriting process as well as the reviewers for Oxford University Press.

Library staffs are academics' secret weapons in all our research endeavors. Many thanks to the staffs of the Cape and Pretoria state archives who endure the countenances of their foreign researchers with grace. Moore Crossey at the Sterling Memorial Library at Yale managed to exhibit more excitement about my sources than even I possessed and ordered anything and everything I requested. The staff at the South African Library in Cape Town, especially Marius Fortune and John Dwyer, were so effective that they started anticipating my requests and suggesting sources that had not yet come across my radar, while Melanie Guestyn was gracious in providing images. I kept the staff at the Cory Library busy for almost a year and they were indefatigable in all their efforts to assist me, especially: Sandy Shell, Victor Gacula, and Zwelli (Jackson Vena), the current head of Cory, Jeff Peires and Fleur Way-Jones at the Albany Museum; in the Geography Department, John Keudler and John Landman prepared my maps; cartographer Alice Thiede patiently rendered the final maps for the book. Cecil Nonqane, Sabata Mageza, and Decemba sacrificed many weekends, and most likely car parts, to accompany me to Mimosa Park and Farmerfield to conduct interviews, and Patty Jeppson graciously shared her archaeological work on Farmerfield with me.

In South Africa, the warmth and hospitality of my hosts and friends made it difficult to go home each time. The first time I set foot in Cape Town, Christopher Saunders went above and beyond as one accommodation plan after another fell through. Many thanks to Julia Wells, Virginia Wells, Cecil and Constance Nonqane, and Jane and Korwa Adar, who provided the warmth of their company, their home, and their family. They surrounded me with as much love and support as a sojourner far from home could wish. Many thanks go as well to Virginia Wells, who lent a sympathetic ear for a young mother and offered advice about ways of being a woman in the world. Pamela Ndinisa became the best second mother a girl could want and continues to volunteer in that role. My wonderful friends Stella Dhlomo, Stephen Hinana, Mphikeleli Mnguni, Mbuleli Mpokela, Babalwa Sishatu in Cape Town, Khayelitsha, Johannesburg, and Grahamstown provided company, inexpensive accommodation, and many laughs.

Some people have been along on this journey since I lived in Trenton and I thank Stan Johnson for being the consummate intellectual and for pushing me to set high goals. John Templeton at Princeton and James Chambers, formerly of

COLLEGBOUND, are both engaged in quiet revolutions involving college admissions and educational advocacy of which I am a proud beneficiary. In their deeds they pay tribute to the legacy of Ruby Bridges, Addie Mae Collins, Denise McNair, Carole Robertson, and Cynthia Wesley.

To my cheerleaders, I thank you all for being in my corner and encouraging me. Maya Angelou's crowded stage metaphor rings true here: Nana Amos, Jen Archey, Espelencia Baptiste, Kristen Bilotta-Brzozowski, Wiebe Boer, Ruramisai Charumbira, Wayne Dennis, Mila Davis, Yudyssa and Jesse Fernandez, Anne Guernsey, Tracey Harris-Dowdell, Inocencia Jayaratne, Carol Johnson, Edgar Johnson, Dennis Jones, Roger Levine, Essie Lucky-Barros, Dodie Mcdow, Sheridan Quarless-Kingsberry, Shilpa Patel, the dearly departed Brenda Lee Rios and her daughter Rita Vazquez, Jon Rapping, Denise Russell, Joshua Schreier, Yvette Simms, Geraldine Simpson, Brenna Smith, Marjorie Smith, Maureen Stewart, Kate Steinway, Sheena Williams, and Winsome Watson. The unflinching support of the best friend anyone could ask for, Lavonda Rowe, and Hector Brown, the brother I never had, have been my life blood. Then and now both have anticipated my needs and kept me grounded and focused like no one else.

My mother inspired me to come this far and provided unending love and support while the rest my family endured many bouts of separation for me to complete this book. I would like to thank all of the Browns and Wrights for helping me on this journey. The other half of my heart, Robert, has been on this journey all along. I thank you for persevering with me through the ups and downs. I truly could not have done this without you. At this stage I say that if you believe, no proof is necessary; and if you do not believe, no proof is possible. My little angels, Josh, Cameron, and Katya provided me with the many laughs and reality checks I needed to make it through this process.

This book has been generously funded by a Fulbright scholarship, the Andrew Mellon Foundation, the Social Science Research Council (SSRC), the Yale Program in Agrarian studies, the Yale Center for International and Area Studies, now the Macmillan Center, and generous faculty research grants at Kalamazoo College and the University of Connecticut.

No casual visitor ends up at Farmerfield accidentally unless Eastern Cape farms, local Methodist churches, and government land reform experiments feature prominently on their itineraries. Nestled in a picturesque, secluded valley fourteen miles (twenty-two kilometers) southeast of Grahamstown in the Eastern Cape, South Africa, the former Methodist mission farm can inspire any tourist brochure. It would have to be a day trip, however, as there are no "guest" accommodations and getting there requires travel beyond the national roads. After leaving the main N2 highway that joins various Eastern Cape locales to the rest of the Cape and KwaZulu-Natal provinces and driving six more miles (nine kilometers) on a noisy, gravel road, Farmerfield slowly comes into view. Fifty-six newly built government houses, their roofs gleaming in the sunlight depending on the time of day, are set off on either side of a lane that ends with the school and church. Then, the ascent to Farmerfield begins on an unpaved path that spells bad news for impractical shoes or car chassis, axles, and tires. With their horses and ox wagons, the nineteenth-century denizens of Farmerfield probably had a much easier time navigating its dirt and gravel roads. Only the four-wheel-drive vehicles of safari fame would suit a contemporary sojourner.

My initial trip to Farmerfield in 1998 revealed an unassuming landscape: aloes in full bloom in the most spectacular shades of red, orange, and yellow; a few cows grazing lazily; segments of the Assegaibos River gathered in pools or sometimes rivulets here and there, but dry in most other places; undulating hills dotted with thornveld, whose patchwork appearance seemed as if the bushes spurned any long-term commitment to the land. At its zenith Farmerfield's original expanse was 6,000 acres (2428 hectares) the standard size for many white farmers making their way to the region in the nineteenth century. One such farm came on the market in the 1830s, and the Wesleyan Methodist Missionary Society (hereafter WMMS) purchased the land for evangelical purposes and renamed it Farmerfield. Rather than accommodate one farmer, however, dozens of African families lived at Farmerfield, one hundred at its peak in 1838. Despite its status as a showcase for the best of Methodist evangelism and early African assimilation of Christianity, Farmerfield's population waxed and waned. Throughout the nineteenth century, periodic war and natural disasters like locust infestations and drought devastated pastoral farming and crippled agricultural productivity.

Although new residents filled the ranks of the population throughout the twentieth century, black communities like Farmerfield faced an increasingly hostile legal landscape as South Africa transitioned from the segregation to the apartheid era. Surrounded by a sea of white farms, the Farmerfield mission was an anomaly and a threat to apartheid racial sensibilities. The Methodist Church kept the government at bay from the 1930s to the 1950s, seeking residential exemptions for Farmerfield's residents. But it was a war of attrition involving endless paperwork, as apartheid bureaucrats sought parity between the letter of the law and the loopholes that still allowed enclaves of black communities to exist among white ones. Enervated by paperwork and frustrated by their own attempts to manage Farmerfield, Methodist Church authorities eventually lost this epic battle when the apartheid government rezoned the land for white occupation. In 1962 the apartheid regime unceremoniously dumped the last eighteen families in the middle of a forest in their putative Xhosa ethnic homeland hundreds of miles away.

A cursory physical survey of contemporary Farmerfield on the eve of land resettlement reveals some modern, granite headstones, rocks and bricks from older graves, and a few stones left over from homes razed in 1962. The only imposing physical element is the Methodist Church, a white-washed rectangular building, fifty feet long and thirty feet wide, built in 1844. A prototypical crenellated roof, a green door with glass panels, and arched windows accent the façade of this Gothic Revival stone church. Upon closer inspection, however, the church's poor upkeep becomes readily apparent. The green paint on both the door and windows is chipped, revealing the brown wood underneath. Cardboard makes a jarring replacement for a broken window pane on the front door, while another broken pane remains agape. The orange-red mud creeping up at the base of the church seems almost decorative compared to the three nondescript brown steps visitors mount to get inside. The altar has seen better years and the roof is in serious need of repair. Plastic chairs supplement the worn and sometimes rickety benches as needed; and it is doubtful anyone could fall asleep or even nod off on them when listening to a sermon.

The Methodist Church stands alone as a crucible—as vestige, witness, preserver, and facilitator—of a different past for this land. Farmerfield held multiple and overlapping, symbolic meanings as a specific type of space: land confiscated from Africans by the Cape Colony; a farm, a residential community; a Methodist religious enclave; an area for blacks to access land in an otherwise white farming community; a labor reserve for whites to procure African labor; a rural reserve populated by the surplus population of the elderly and children; and a "black spot" razed to accommodate apartheid's racial and ethnic sensibilities. In the residential space of Farmerfield, Africans of different ethnic backgrounds pursued their own ideas about how to live as Christians against the backdrop of contentious debates in missionary societies about strategies to implement their evangelical and civilizing goals. Through the behavior of Farmerfield's African residents, Methodist missionaries attempted to test, legitimize, and vindicate their projects to encourage socioeconomic and religious reform in African societies amid opposition and disdain in colonial, imperial, and indigenous political circles. In the end, Farmerfield's experiment demonstrated how colonial and then apartheid policies could stymie African economic self-sufficiency and development. As a religious experiment, however, Farmerfield showcased the malleability and vitality of Christianity in African cultural contexts.

The only consistent presence at Farmerfield in the 1990s was its minister, Napthali Mbozanani, an elder Malawian national who clearly neither preached nor experienced American-styled prosperity gospel. He had the demeanor and carriage of Alan Paton's Stephen Kumalo in *Cry, the Beloved Country*.[1] Mbozanani was keen on demonstrating his fluency in the local Xhosa language and reminding occasional visitors that Christianity remained the defining characteristic of Farmerfield. Christianity originally brought him to, and has kept him at, Farmerfield as its minister, far from his native country. Were it not for the church, Farmerfield's landscape would mirror that of the neighboring farms and seem mostly inconspicuous except for what it revealed about contemporary Eastern Cape flora and farming endeavors. The landscape's silence was artificial, however, the result of apartheid social and racial engineering policies that labeled the mission a "black spot" in a white area and demarcated it for exclusive white occupation. Residents recounted in vivid details where and how they washed clothes, planted mealies, joined wedding parties, held prayer meetings, took shortcuts to fetch wood and water, grazed cattle, picked aloes, collected dung to smear the floors, led funeral processions, hid *abakweta* lodges for young male initiates, collected prickly pears, buried their dead, lingered to talk with friends from neighboring farms after church services, and first caught the eye of a smitten future husband or wife. Apartheid elided the history of a dynamic, enduring community whose four generations of residents weathered natural disasters as well as church and government bureaucracies to maintain one of the longest running, continuous missions in the history of South Africa.

A Christian legacy now defines contemporary land claims and resettlement at Farmerfield, with its former residents using a language of religious commonality to justify the restoration of land to dispossessed members of the community. The meticulous documentation of the Methodist Church has facilitated the land claim, as it has many of the assertions in this book. Looking backward to Farmerfield's past in the 1830s and forward to its postapartheid reincarnation, I am aware of the limits of historical thinking and reconstruction so deftly demonstrated by cognitive psychologist Sam Wineburg and historian David Lowenthal.[2] Yet I am also inspired when historian S. D. Goitein states, in his magisterial overview of

Jewish life in the Mediterranean, that it was "the privilege of the historian to conceive the accidental past of ever present life."[3] In the South African context, writing the history of Farmerfield involves far more than addressing historians' blind spots. Apartheid's recent past, and before it colonialism's, have meant eliding other stories—other histories—by those who commanded the power to dispossess Africans and then tell narratives of "empty land." Addressing apartheid and colonial legacies encompasses far more than free and fair elections and political freedom, therefore; it must also involve rewriting historical narratives, writing different kinds of textbooks, and teaching other histories to address the erasures like those evident in my first visit to Farmerfield. Through birth, marriage, and death registries, Methodist annual reports, diaries, travelers' accounts, government documents, reports from criminal and civil authorities, and interviews, this portrait of Farmerfield's history reinscribes the many incarnations of an important Eastern Cape community. It is a story of Africans making mission Christianity their own; enduring the economic and social ravages of colonialism and apartheid until 1962; using their historical connection to the Methodist Church and to Christianity to regain land; and launching the Farmerfield experiment anew, while navigating the meaning of postapartheid land access and citizenship in South Africa.

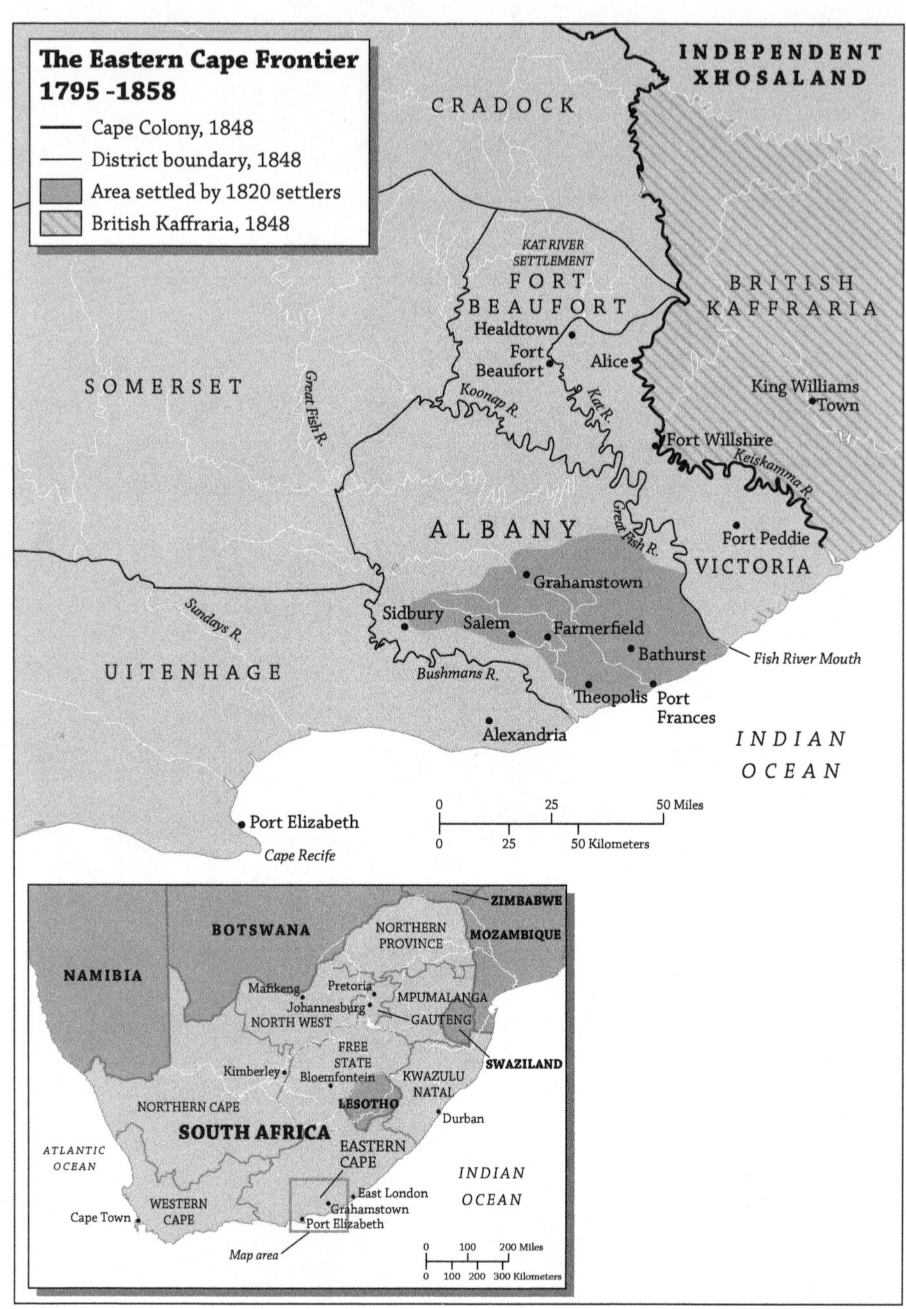

Map 1 The Eastern Cape Frontier, South Africa, 1795–1858. Based on J. S. Bergh and J. C. Visagie, *The Eastern Cape Frontier Zone, 1660–1980: A Cartographic Guide for Historical Research* (Butterworths: Durban, 1985); John Arrowsmith frontier map, 1851. Courtesy of Rhodes University, Geography Department.

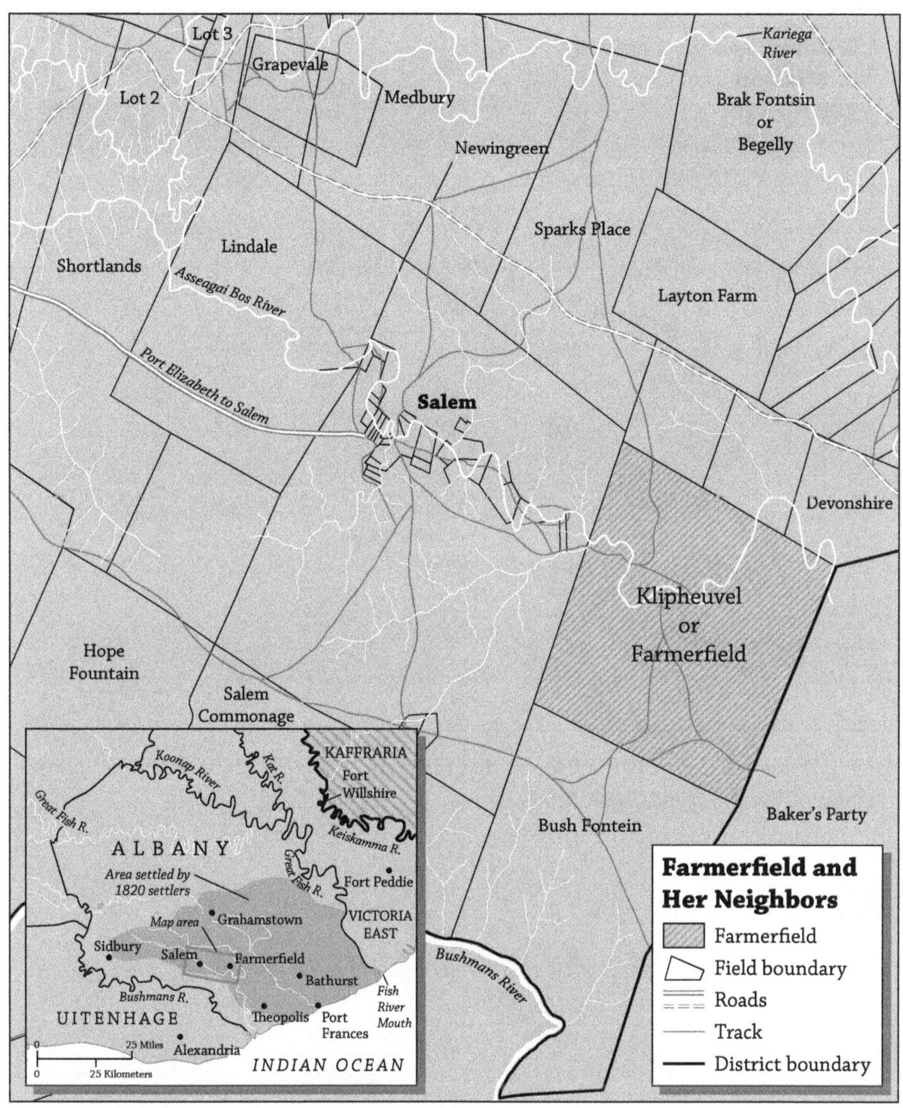

Map 2 Farmerfield and her Neighbors, inset from Albany Divisional Map, 1899. Courtesy of Rhodes University, Geography Department.

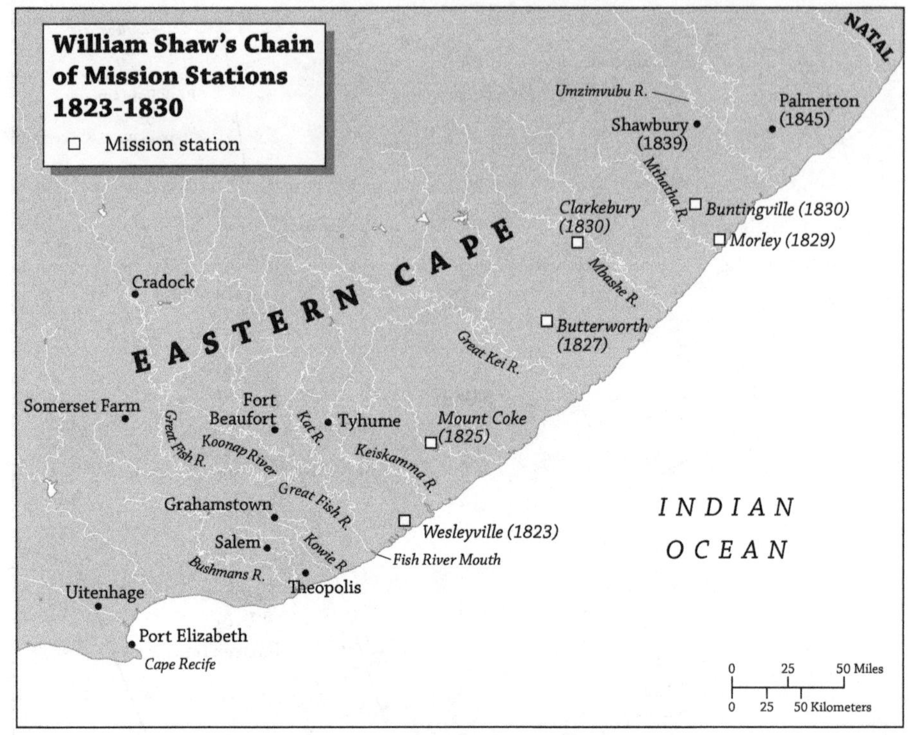

Map 3 William Shaw's Chain of Methodist Missions, 1823–1830. Based on W.B. Boyce, Memoir of the Reverend Shaw, 1874.

The Farmerfield Mission

Introduction

The Farmerfield Mission explores the history of Farmerfield, a residential Christian community in South Africa established for Africans in 1838 by Methodist missionaries, destroyed in 1962 by the apartheid government when it was zoned as an exclusive area for white occupation, and returned to the descendants of the community under South Africa's land reform program in 1999. As a farm, a residential site, a Christian community on a violent colonial frontier, and a "black spot" in a white area during the apartheid era, the history of the Farmerfield mission links the broad narratives of colonialism and Christian evangelism with the case study of a particular African Christian community. Farmerfield's genesis and evolution thus provide a distinct lens through which to view broader nineteenth- and twentieth-century debates about the African vernacularization of Christianity and assimilation of cultural norms associated with European colonial culture. In this Eastern Cape enclave, Africans cultivated a vital, mature African Christianity within the Methodist evangelical tradition long before the much vaunted era of African-initiated or independent churches (AICs).

For more than a century Farmerfield's residents and missionaries engaged each other in what John and Jean Comaroff have characterized as a "long conversation" about the form and content of African Christianity and the meaning of daily life through several critical epochs of South African history. The liberal humanitarianism that held sway in many missionary and abolitionist circles in the fervent decade of the 1830s gradually waned. By mid-century, missionary societies with deep historical roots in South Africa had grown pessimistic and disenchanted as they assessed their failures and reexamined their evangelical priorities. Farmerfield's African residents faced a major threat as their economic fortunes declined and Methodists considered closing the mission. Meanwhile, white consolidation of their hold on land and political power in the Eastern Cape continued apace. South Africa began its transition from an agrarian to an industrial economy and completed the conquest of independent African polities. The early decades of the twentieth century witnessed government intervention to systematically destroy African farming endeavors and subsidize white farming enterprises. In the segregation and apartheid eras Farmerfield's designation as a rural reserve and a "black spot" brought heightened government surveillance.

Despite the Methodist Church's attempt to shield the mission from the onerous demands to register annually, the government finally expelled all of the residents in 1962. Farmerfield's former residents then the joined millions of other dispossessed people living out ignominious elderhoods on the brink of economic disaster while raising a generation of young people whose political and economic aspirations the government tried to thwart at every turn. In the postapartheid era, Farmerfield's former residents resettled the land and attempted to discern and engage the meaning of citizenship, community, and contemporary Christian identity.

Imperial, Evangelical, and Abolitionist Intersections

The debate over African socioeconomic and religious improvement that unfolded at Farmerfield has had a long history and has spawned legions of cautionary tales. From martyred missionaries and ill-fated expeditions to short-lived missions and thwarted African protégés, a host of individuals and interest groups—black and white—pursued grandiose ideas about developing the human and natural resources of Africa.[1] Africans, missionaries, philanthropists, metropolitan governments, colonial administrations, white settlers, and a range of personalities in the colonies and in Great Britain created and participated in a marketplace of competing ideas and policies involving, inter alia, legislative remedies, model peasant communities, Christian evangelization, and commercial projects. Some ideas suffered from a poverty of imagination, where even the best outcomes conceived for Africans placed them on inferior socioeconomic and political planes in relation to whites. In other instances, ignorance, misinformation, poor planning, disregard for indigenous knowledge systems, and blatant racism stunted the potential of other schemes.

Perhaps more than any other two external developments, antislavery and evangelicalism and the important ideological cross fertilizations between them, contributed in profound ways to shaping the late eighteenth- and early nineteenth-century discourses about African social and economic improvement.[2] In a world where the French and Haitian Revolutions raised crucial questions about the meaning of liberty and equality, antislavery and evangelicalism gained significant momentum and engaged these themes in both metropolitan and colonial public discourses.[3] The efflorescence of missionary organizations, the abolition of the oceanic slave trade, and the implementation of measures to reform then abolish slavery linked diverse audiences, constituencies, and activists across the Atlantic world. With a spiritual and vocational call to go forth and spread the gospel to far-flung corners of the globe, Christian missionaries found their potential constituencies filled with the ranks of slaves, former slaves, and various indigenous inhabitants in the throes of colonial conquest. Some missionaries became or supported abolitionists and many abolitionists promoted Christian evangelism as part of the revolution in character, morals, and culture they hoped to instill in slaves and peoples of African descent. Whatever their particular stance, missionaries had to deal with hostile planters, at worst; or colonial elites ambivalent about the radical implications of spiritual equality even as they embraced Christianity's language of obedience and subservience as a part of their ideological and disciplinary arsenal. Many missionaries and abolitionists promoted a liberal humanitarian platform that reached its height in the 1820s and 1830s. Farmerfield was one outcome of missionaries' attempts to remake African societies using missions as laboratories to create the peasant idylls that featured so prominently in both missionary and abolitionist visions of post-emancipation and African societies.[4]

The convergence of antislavery and mission narratives indelibly bound tales of benighted, savage, "heathen" Africans without proper knowledge of God and civilization to images of slavery and the slave trade as inhumane, evil, and immoral. For example, while antislavery activists decried the reputed state of immorality slavery engendered by preventing slaves from marrying legally and encouraging illegitimate births, missionaries in Africa condemned polygyny as an institution promoting African men's sexual licentiousness and laziness. Antislavery, evangelical, and travel literature riveted imperial audiences with titillating, scandalous tales about "heathen" customs and the evils of slavery, as historians Susan Thorne and Michael Ledger-Lomas have demonstrated.[5] This literature offered redemptive stories of baptisms and conversions as a reminder to sponsors and readers of their central role. Missionaries and antislavery activists marketed humanitarian, evangelical, and even commercial undertakings as a way to accomplish twin goals: rescue and reparations for Africans on the one hand, and spiritual, moral, and economic development on the other hand. In the 1790s, antislavery activists touted the potential of Sierra Leone as a settlement of repatriated former slaves and peoples of Africans descent using the oft-quoted trifecta of "Christianity, commerce and civilization." A century later, as the scramble for Africa unfolded, despite significant disillusionment with the liberal humanitarian platform that had supported the Sierra Leone, antislavery, and missionary projects, the three C's had lost little of their discursive power. European imperial authorities and their subjects, travelers, abolitionists, and missionaries thus participated in a vast network of ideas and discourses about Africa and retooled "Christianity, commerce and civilization" to support new nineteenth-century imperial and evangelical priorities.

Missions, Empire, and African Agency

Whether advanced by some abolitionists as a means to accomplish their own ideological ends, or spread by missionaries as their primary agenda, Christian evangelism required attention to mercurial political landscapes. The metropolitan, colonial, and indigenous contexts all influenced the mechanisms and strategies missionaries used to promote Christian evangelism as part of a broader project to facilitate African socioeconomic and religious improvement. Recent scholarship on missions and empire draws on the work and intellectual legacies of scholars like Robin Horton and Lamin Sanneh.[6] Horton and Sanneh have long inspired scholars to think in broad historical terms about world religions and the multiple contexts in which Africans vernacularized Christianity. In addition, historians like Terence Ranger and Richard Elphick have been particularly mindful of giving religion its rightful due in historical analyses by paying attention to both the instrumental aspects of religion as well as matters of faith—whether in the precolonial, colonial, and postcolonial eras.[7]

The intersections of imperial, colonial, and subaltern subjectivities provided both an early, conventional analytical axis and a site of current reconsiderations of empire and missions.[8] While historians Norman Etherington and Elizabeth Elbourne could bemoan the voids in the historiography of missions in Africa up to the 1980s and early 1990s, some of the lacunae have since been addressed.[9] The history of missionary endeavors in Southern Africa, like those the WMMS undertook at Farmerfield, for example, is now in 2012, a rich, established, subfield of mission history with some of the most dynamic recent work coming from southern and west African case studies, as well as works pairing anthropological and historical methodologies.[10] Building on an earlier era of scholarship examining colonialism and the missions, the new historiography emphasizes a host of important arenas. In addition to delineating the local, regional, ethnic, and gender dimensions of missionary activities in southern and west Africa, the recent scholarship has also explored the roles of particular missions, missionary societies, and missionary personalities.[11]

Despite the common analytical axis of missionary complicity in maligning many African cultural traditions and facilitating colonial rule, the new literature on missions and empire revisits the imperial angle and the theme of missionary involvement in original ways. These works delineate how local imperatives in Africa influenced missionaries' agendas in Britain while underscoring how the intellectual, economic, and cultural backgrounds of the missionaries shaped their local interactions with Africans. Acknowledging the pivotal role Christianity played in the "civilizing" process that accompanied the extension of colonialism, commerce, and capitalism in Africa, the Comaroffs' magisterial work, for example, casts its anthropological lens at both the Nonconformist missionaries in South Africa and their Southern Tswana hosts. The Comaroffs' ethnographic analysis highlighted missionaries' status as powerful agents of cultural imperialism and as a specific strata of British society whose own social and economic worlds, and not just their race, informed their cultural myopia and evangelical strategies. While no scholar could ever claim that missionaries have been left out of the historiography, the Comaroffs' work, more than any other, has reminded us of the need to understand the backgrounds of specific missionaries, in this case British Nonconformists.

Just as African cultural and indigenous religious traditions shaped Tswana reception and assimilation of the missionaries and their message, so too did missionaries' own cultural, social, and economic ideals influence their civilizing and evangelizing goals. Despite the meager financial resources and personnel at their disposal, Nonconformist missionaries marshaled the symbolic, cultural, and ideological foundation of British imperial discourse to support their evangelical mission. Lest we think they propagated these discourses only in African contexts, however, Susan Thorne has reminded us that the local evangelical drives among the poor and working classes of Europe intersected closely with endeavors and rhetoric in Africa.[12] In tabulating their work among London's poor, for example, the missionaries' metrics involved more than noting how many people attended services and how many sick and dying they visited. Missionaries also took stock of: "fallen females rescued or reclaimed," "unmarried couples induced to marry," and "drunkards reclaimed." They engaged in efforts to "urge those who are living in neglect of religion to observe the Sabbath and attend public worship."[13] Evangelicals also pursued various strategies for sustaining Christianity among the urban and middle classes in Europe to combat irreligion, reinforce the position of Protestantism, and expand support for the missionary cause.[14] Combined with evangelicals' efforts overseas, missionaries conceived of nothing less than an international community of congregants and converts, united by their redemption from sin by Christ's death.

The new historiography thus engages the large narrative of colonialism's intersection with evangelicalism in meaningful ways and underscores how these narratives worked out in different local contexts. But the "local" turns on more than the Africa-Europe axis to include expansive investigations of the regional and ethnic dimensions that are important in disaggregating the term "African." In this regard, the notion of ethnogenesis has also been among the most fruitful areas of inquiry by providing discrete anthropological and historical case studies of particular African groups and polities, for example the Tswana, the Yoruba, and the Khoekhoe. West African case studies like J. D. Y. Peel's recent magnum opus, *Religious Encounter and the Making of the Yoruba*, for example, build on a rich tradition of scholarly work on the intersections of Christianity and colonialism in Nigeria while asking crucial questions about the making of Yoruba identity. Literacy among the Yoruba, for example, played an instrumental part in defining the concept of community by integrating new concepts based on Christian religious affinities and technologies with indigenous Yoruba frameworks for organizing their societies.

Paul Landau's follow-up to his study of the Ngwato Kingdom, *Popular Politics in the History of South Africa*, is a timely reconsideration of how identities are mobilized in the precolonial and colonial eras, the use of Christianity as a tool in this process as Africans came into contact with the Christian message and its emissaries, and the triumph of ethnicity as the primary way of thinking about African identities. Elizabeth Elbourne examines both the British and South African context of evangelicalism and also engages the theme of ethnogenesis to produce an authoritative account of Khoekhoe encounters with Christianity, and the malleable uses of Christianity to both mobilize the weak and to entrench the position of the strong. Dutch settlers at the Cape, and later, their white counterparts throughout other parts of Africa and the Caribbean, used Christianity to exclude the Khoekhoe from colonial civil society even as missionaries preached a radical message of spiritual equality.[15] Peel, Landau, and Elbourne's analyses add historical depth to our understanding of the intellectual, political, and religious histories of precolonial and colonial African societies and polities while they inform our understanding of how the enduring encounter between Africans and Christianity has delineated contemporary narratives of ethnic and national identity.

Given the penchant for hagiography in earlier assessments of missionary personalities and the reinforcement of the concept of a missionary "colossus," the historiography has also revisited the careers of influential missionary figures to reveal the specific content of their liberal and paternal agendas and to explore the source of their cultural hubris, myopia, or sympathies.[16] The careers of Johannes Van der Kemp, David Livingstone, John William Colenso, and James Read, to name a few, bear witness to the many instances in which white missionaries veered from or complicated the official transcripts of imperial discourse. For some missionaries, Southern Africa was one posting among several in their spiritual portfolios; for others it became their permanent home. In these local assignments many found new vocations in political and humanitarian advocacy. No single model of missionary activity, therefore, captures the complexity and ambiguities of evangelical work in colonial settings. Some missionaries remained accidental tourists, attempting to reproduce England or other European models in miniature. Others found their own faith severely tested and left Africa as pessimists; still others developed idiosyncratic interests in indigenous systems of thought, beliefs, performance, language, and medical knowledge.

Whether it was advocacy for African political and economic rights, the promotion of African agency in the administration of the church, or the flouting of racial boundaries in marriage and sexual relations, the behavior of individual missionaries challenged the sedate stance of their parent missionary societies. Missionaries reinforced common racial stereotypes, yet at times also subverted colonial policies and local social mores. Instead of the caricatured figure of the colossus, the aggregate picture that emerges is one of missionary personalities who derived their status from the power of their ideas, the radical implications of their convictions in a colonial context, and the far-reaching or limiting consequences of their visions for Africa and Africans. These engagements with the individual biographies and careers of missionaries challenge any facile arguments about missionary complicity in colonialism.

Farmerfield was not without its own influential personality in the form of its founder, William Shaw, the superintendent of Wesleyan Missions in South Africa. The story of Farmerfield's rise, demise, and reincarnation is indelibly bound to the vision and actions of William Shaw in his lifetime, and after his death, with his legacy. Shaw's life as a settler and missionary, his vision of a Methodist sphere of influence, and his legacy, informs our understanding of Farmerfield, Methodism, and the intersection of colonialism and evangelism in a particular locale. Both Shaw's white settler and African constituencies revered him. Although he nurtured grandiose dreams for Christian evangelism in general and Methodism in particular, he did not see himself as a colossus. He pinned his model of race relations and evangelism on fidelity to the white settlers he relied on for support and the Africans whose Christian allegiance he sought—a tenuous balance in most cases. William Shaw's career and his project at Farmerfield reveal how thorny it was to manage whites and blacks as part of the same religious community when spiritual egalitarianism bore little relation to social, economic, and political practices. Farmerfield's political longevity is a testament to Shaw's skill as local superintendent of the WMMS in convincing local whites on a war-torn frontier to tolerate, or perhaps accept, Africans they distrusted as neighbors, economic competitors, and spiritual compatriots.

Engaging new perspectives on missionary personalities has also required some attention to the institutional frameworks within which they worked, with missionary societies creating certain cultures all their own. Missionary societies have been keen on documenting their own histories long before historians ever attempted to do so. While Nonconformist British missionaries have received the lion's share of analyses in Southern Africa, Patrick Harries and Alan Kirkaldy have enhanced our understanding of the contributions of Swiss and German missionaries to wider European imperial discourses about Africa and to the importance of African intermediaries and collaborators. Even with no formal colonies, the stories Swiss missionaries told about Africa shaped metropolitan identities and influenced their perceptions of everything from African religious systems to their social structures and physical landscapes. Meanwhile, Kirkaldy demonstrated that even when German missionaries encountered Africans already exposed to Christianity, they shunned these individuals as potential evangelical partners, refused to build on gains they had already made, and attempted to impose their doctrinaire brand of Christian theology. In whatever era missionaries entered the mission field, and whether they encountered Africans already exposed to Christianity, they imagined themselves front and center of evangelical efforts. Tremendous devotion and faith led hundreds of missionaries from all European national backgrounds to participate in evangelical causes whose success eventually made them redundant once indigenous churches were planted. Many remained ambivalent about the bureaucratic and professional maturity of indigenous churches and intervened to curtail independent expressions of Christianity but eventually had to yield to the realities of indigenization.

For the German missionaries, attempting to control the path and content of Christian evangelization among the VhaVenda was one way to remain relevant. Yet whatever their stance on indigenization, it was not a process they could completely control. The documentation of practices they tried to eradicate and initiatives they stifled, for instance, suggested Africans had already created alternative narratives in their encounters with Christianity. In the realm of literacy, however, missionaries held distinct advantages. Missionaries not only narrated their own histories in letters and diaries, they created registries of African societies, thereby contributing significantly to the fields of linguistics, science, anthropology, and history. Missionaries' sense of purpose and faith as well as their intellectual agendas and tools, indelibly shaped their identities, their religious vocation, and the histories they made.[17]

Despite the specter of imperial domination that often accompanied Christian evangelization and its assumptions of European cultural and moral superiority, the belief that anyone could become a Christian lay at the very heart of the missionary enterprise. As the hallmark of Christianity's universality and its adaptability to various cultural settings, "translatability" also empowered Africans and allowed them to assimilate Christianity. This way of looking at Christianity allows historians to focus on both the conscious and unconscious actions of missionaries and Africans as well as on the specific characteristics of Christianity that determined its adaptability.[18] Before Sanneh introduced the concept of translation as a vehicle for understanding how "any language could be made the bearer of the Word of God . . . and any culture could become a Christian culture," historians had acknowledged the importance of translation as a means of reducing African languages to writing and fueling Christian evangelism.[19] Yet they also emphasized how, as language became one of the primary markers of cultural identity, translation and vernacularization encouraged tribalism.[20] According to Landau, the "epistemological triumph" of the notion of tribe limits the way we understand African identities and political mobilization in the precolonial and colonial eras.[21] "Translation" has now entered the lexicon of mission history, connoting the translation of the Bible into African vernaculars and the ways in which various African (and other) cultures assimilated Christianity. These flexible meanings of "translation" have been crucial for understanding developments from millenarian Christian movements and independent churches to the uses of Christianity as a tool for political and ethnic mobilization.

Anyone using missionary sources acknowledges the tenacious problem of trying to distill African voices from missionary tomes and letters and to assess the numerous African-initiated or independent churches as well as, for the most recent period, "new religious movements."[22] Between these two poles, a vibrant area of the historiography has been a reconsideration of the unsung lay agents whose pioneer efforts contributed significantly to some of the early successes missionaries attained and to the "translatability" and indigenization of Christianity throughout Africa. The Khoekhoe, given their early exposure to Christianity at Moravian and LMS missions, became lay agents par excellence and played crucial roles as interpreters and guides to missionaries from a variety of missionary societies using Cape Dutch as a lingua franca.[23] Throughout the nineteenth century other colonial and missionary projects would turn to South Africans from a variety of backgrounds to assist them with their evangelical endeavors elsewhere in Africa.[24] Missionaries from all backgrounds expressed both gratitude and unease in their reliance on African interpreters. From their desire to control how the Christian message was distilled and their concerns about whether uneducated assistants could convey their messages to their paternalistic and sometimes hostile views of "native agency," most missionary societies had to confront their own linguistic shortcomings by using locals.

Paul Landau's monograph, *The Realm of the Word*, for example, systematically injects African agency into the analysis of Tswana encounters with Christianity in the Ngwato kingdom.[25] Landau traces the intersection of politics, kingship, gender, and Christianity and demonstrates how the Tswana king used his new faith to consolidate power by disseminating the Word to the peripheries of the kingdom.[26] Africans indeed were able to make Christianity their own and in this process, African missionaries (*baruti*) played pivotal roles. By focusing on the agency of the *baruti*, Landau shows that it is precisely because of the omission or discounting of Africans' early contributions to evangelism that the rise of African independent churches appears as a radical break with the missionary past. The establishment of independent churches only institutionalized the roles Africans had played all along in the evangelizing process and gave them their own forum for practicing more creative forms of Christianity. At Farmerfield and other missions, lay agents played a crucial role in preaching and teaching their counterparts at the mission and in the local area. Furthermore, they exhibited a degree of agency that was absolutely necessary for Africans' long-term assimilation of Christianity no matter how grudgingly missionaries admitted this.

African agency has struck several chords in the historiography in addition to documenting the roles of Africans in disseminating Christianity and working in a host of capacities to sustain the long-term evangelical cause. The concept of agency has also prompted scholars to investigate broad themes of class and gender among white and black missionaries and lay agents as well as among the recipients of the message who had diverse motivations for experimenting with Christianity and just as diverse reactions. These analyses have examined black and white women's spirituality and their participation in the missionary enterprise. White women's multifaceted roles as missionary wives and daughters and as "civilizing influences" have become a prolific area of research. Some of these analyses have also been paired with critical assessments of African women in their evangelical capacities as well as their roles as models of new womanhood and domesticity based on monogamous marriages.[27] Cultivating new concepts of African womanhood required a complementary focus on the making of African manhood and the alternative models of masculinity Christianity offered. In peasant settlements like Farmerfield, the ideal unit was a woman who had taken her rightful place in the home, a man who had assumed duties for agricultural production, and children who were receiving an education in day schools. None of these radical transitions occurred without struggle. African women and men became embroiled in cultural conflicts with missionaries over the very meaning of gender roles in marriage, work, and family life and over who had the authority over households. Many missionaries downplayed the tensions and underscored any instance of victory without taking note of how many times they had to declare a truce or capitulate.

African men, especially in their role as missionaries, also faced conflicts, as white missionaries refused to derogate power to them. Roger Levine has produced a long overdue biography of Jan Tzatzoe, whose self-invention took place at the intersection of mission, settler, and African politics and demonstrates the crucial role Tzatzoe played as "the vanguard of an African intellectual tradition born in the colonial encounter."[28] Combined with early works such as Wallace Mills's exploration of the role of Xhosa clergy, Donavan Williams's biography of Tiyo Soga, Catherine Higgs's biography of D. D. T. Jabavu and Terence Ranger's examination of the Samkange family, these studies of elite Christian men, women, and families add an additional foundation to our understanding of the role of Christianity in cultivating an African intellectual, economic, and political elite. These directions in the historiography reveal Africans' challenge of navigating two cultural spheres and adjusting to new notions of masculine and feminine subjectivities as well as new political and economic cultures.[29]

Questions about the relationships between metropole and colony, indigenization, and the making of an educated African Christian elite have, perforce, privileged analyses of the social and economic context of evangelization. Neither missionaries nor the scholars who study them can maroon issues of faith from their socioeconomic context. Peel, for example, has rightly asserted that no matter the context, any history of missionary endeavors has to address matters of faith and religious change. Yet, without autobiographies, conversion narratives, or other written sources, accessing African expressions of faith and engagement in spiritual and intellectual inquiry at Farmerfield can only be read through the behavior of the missions' successive residents. Even with a creative reading of the available sources, where one can impute certain motives and beliefs from behavior, forms of worship, language, and hymnody, the content of an individual's relationship with God remains obscure. While *The Farmerfield Mission* pursues an analysis of the form, content, and iteration of mission Christianity at Farmerfield, it does so by accepting the faith of Farmerfield's residents at face value. What Farmerfield missionaries glossed over as "apathy" or "nominalism" among the mission residents can hardly serve as a diagnostic window into the hearts and minds of Africans. None of the class leaders and preachers at Farmerfield left any record of their discussions and deliberations with their charges.

Farmerfield produced no Tiyo Soga or Jan Tzatzoe—African Christian elites who became famous abroad and at home as symbols of African agency in the missionary enterprise.[30] What Farmerfield did produce, however, was a steady stream of young people whose success in school and interest in the ministry guaranteed their exit from Farmerfield as they sought opportunities to get a higher education and to train for the ministry, then move around a wide-ranging Methodist circuit throughout the country. In turn, others educated in Methodist institutions took up temporary posts at Farmerfield as teachers, preachers, and later, ministers. Farmerfield's history allows a *longue duree* analysis of how the fortunes of the mission waxed and waned as the contours and structure of Methodist missionary strategies and bureaucracy also changed. Although Farmerfield's missionaries would have been loath to admit it, so much of what contributed to their religious perceptions was the eventual failure of generations of tenants to live up to their secular expectations. Missionaries' lofty goal of a "civilized" lifestyle was difficult to achieve and preserve against the backdrop of a harsh colonial world, persistent subsistence crises, school fees, the cost of clothing, and the ongoing fees associated with church membership.

In practice, conflation of the goals of the evangelical enterprise with the civilizing mission meant that from the outset, the missionaries attempted to change more than the souls of Africans, making the analysis of religious change at Farmerfield as critical as understanding the vast social, economic, and cultural changes associated with Christianity. Rather than "winning souls in spiritual or verbal battles," the Comaroffs assert that missionaries attempted to change the Southern Tswana by "inculcating the everyday forms of the colonizing culture."[31] As Thomas Beidelman argued in an early case study on Tanzania, missionaries aimed at the "colonization of the heart and mind as well as body."[32] With indigenous African communities in flux across South Africa in the nineteenth century, what makes Farmerfield so instructive—and constitutes the stance of this book— is that even at an idealized mission, Africans seldom experienced Christianity as only a religious encounter and rarely experienced mission life only in the purview of their souls, minds, or conscience. The socioeconomic and political context continued to inform the religious lives Africans led and the religious associations they made.

Those Africans who participated fully in intellectual and religious discourses concerning sin, eternal damnation, or salvation often compared their own systems of explanation, prediction, and control and found them to be equally as plausible as the missionaries', as David Chidester, Peires, Horton, Peel, and others have demonstrated in different African contexts.[33] Africans matched wits with the missionaries, challenged the literalness of the Bible, redeployed missionaries' arguments against them, and began separating Christian teachings from the European cultural garb that missionaries used to propagate it. When historian Steven Shapin pinpointed how social and economic facts came to support claims to "truth," he could just as easily have been talking about missionaries as about the creation of the figure of the honorable, truth-bearing "gentleman." "It was a matter of interpretive cultural practice," Shapin argued, "to read those facts as warrants for truth."[34] Missionaries promoted as Christian doctrine and as "truth" what were, in fact, their own cultural ideals and religious interpretations. Their "truths" gained legitimacy from the relative power of the European culture supporting their claims. Yet, as long as Christian faith was about the "evidence of things not seen," and as long as Protestantism privileged a personal relationship

with God, the ultimate power lay with the believer.[35] Africans had long vernacularized Christianity before they indigenized it and throughout this process Christianity remained open to interpretation. Missionaries had to find solace in
acknowledging that the European cultural moorings of the evangelism they practiced was a local iteration of the religion. No matter how crucial they assessed
their own pioneer efforts to be, Christianity's ultimate malleability and translatability in any cultural context and the autonomy of an individual's relationship
with God eventually made white missionaries redundant.

Farmerfield and the Eastern Cape

The book envisions Farmerfield at the center of a concentric circle, an uneven
collaboration between missionaries and Africans to maintain a community geographically and symbolically situated within the wider circle of the Eastern Cape.
As a part of this distinct region, the history of Farmerfield engages with the rich
historiography of the Eastern Cape that has catalogued the unending cycle of warfare and intermittent violence between white settlers and Africans on a turbulent
frontier.[36] This literature features epic and seminal accounts of the Xhosa polities
and chiefs who felt the brunt of dispossession and the profanation of Xhosa indigenous authority.[37] Early interventions also sought to explain key themes that
anchored later works: the distinct worldviews that emerged in the Eastern Cape
among the British emigrants who settled there in 1820, the oscillations of British
policies in a region they saw as an unruly frontier, and the impact of Eastern Cape
politics on the liberal humanitarian agenda that had found its most powerful
evocation and success in the antislavery movement.[38]

Building on this important lattice, more recent work by historians Clifton
Crais, Alan Lester, Tim Keegan, and Richard Price, for example, have explored
how competing discourse networks emanating from the imperial, colonial, and
indigenous realms contributed to the forging of white settler and African identities in the nineteenth-century Eastern Cape.[39] Britain as metropole, the Cape
and its eastern districts as a colonial enclave, and the various indigenous Xhosa
polities that felt the worst of the dispossession in the Eastern Cape, receive distinct treatments based on these scholars' vantage points. Crais and Keegan weave
the story of late slavery with the narrative of the economic displacement of the
Dutch by British settlers in the Eastern Cape, antislavery, and African resistance.
Rather than see the triumph of white settlerdom and the dispossession of Africans
as the inexorable coda to the British and Dutch colonial encounters, Crais and
Keegan show how Africans lived and competed as members of imperial and
African polities and how white settlers came to define their own identities as
imperial subjects and colonial masters. Against a backdrop of violence and a
discourse of racial exclusiveness, white settlers tried to recreate Africa and
Africans in their own image. Lester also examines the competing discourses of

humanitarianism, colonial "governmentality," and settler capitalism to explore the making of white settler identity and the fashioning of the Eastern Cape in relation to other enclaves of the British Empire such as the Caribbean, New Zealand, and India, for example. Even as whites cemented their political and economic power, tensions within and between discourses created uneven colonial and imperial landscapes of compromise and deferred colonial projects.[40]

Although Lester engages the theme of subaltern resistance to colonialism, especially to explain the disenchantment with liberal humanitarianism, a rather oblique sense of alternate Xhosa discourses remains. Despite their power, humanitarianism, "governmentality," and settler capitalism also competed with indigenous worldviews and discourses. As Etherington has noted, other discourses of land, cattle, witchcraft, chieftaincy, and power exerted a tremendous influence on how the Xhosa responded to "colonialism and its forms of knowledge."[41] Lester's study is thus best paired with J. B. Peires and Les Switzer's engagement with these themes as well as Crais's early work *The Politics of Evil*, an original exploration of the intersection of occult conceptualizations of power and their meanings and manifestation in people's lives in South Africa.[42] In the tradition of metropolitan scholars now reconsidering the imperial world from different colonial terrains, British historian Richard Price makes the case for the import of the Eastern Cape as Britain's testing ground for how to deal with Africans and as another graveyard where the bones of liberal humanitarianism are buried. Price demonstrates that even in the colonial backwater of the Eastern Cape, the texture of domination proved no less insidious and the discourse and knowledge was contradictory as any other place that may have had most-favored colony status. Colonial settlers, administrators, and Africans shaped each other indelibly. Taken together, these new interventions stand as instructive reminders of the multiple loci and antecedents of racial and class amalgamation and domination in modern South Africa, in the aftermath of slavery and before the mineral revolution.[43]

Methodists and Farmerfield

Regional conflict in the Eastern Cape gave a particular arc to the colonial encounter. Before race relations hardened and the Xhosa felt the worst of the Eastern Cape's brand of settler colonialism, William Shaw and his colleagues were laying the foundation for another important part of the region's identity—as the center of Methodism. Like their LMS and Moravian predecessors, Methodist missionary enterprise took place in the context of broader colonial and imperial trends. In nineteenth-century South Africa, Methodist missionaries and their potential African converts found themselves at the cusp of broad debates drawing on the legacy of antislavery humanitarianism and the Evangelical Revival. Working in the Cape Colony guaranteed a certain tempestuous climate and these debates refracted differently depending on whether or not missionaries were situated among groups like Khoekhoe and slaves living in de facto and de jure slavery, respectively, who had borne the brunt of the colony's labor needs since the seventeenth century. These debates resounded quite differently for groups like the Xhosa whose colonial encounter had not yet destroyed their polities, alienated their lands, or challenged their cultural practices and beliefs. African reception of the missionary message and the "civilizing" enterprise behind Christian spiritual doctrines equally depended on the local contexts. Neither in theory nor practice did Christian evangelism remain hermetic, as shifts in both metropolitan and local politics vindicated or repudiated certain policies and ideas. Some Africans ignored or challenged Christian doctrines; others experimented with its spirituality, forms of knowledge, doctrines, and lifestyles in creative ways.

For missionaries working among these disparate groups, these debates also proved consequential for the success of their strategies in particular geographical locations—in situating themselves among Africans as well as the local white settler population. The establishment of Moravian and LMS sphere in the Cape Colony proper, influenced William Shaw's choice of the Eastern Cape frontier as a site for Methodist work to avoid duplication. Shaw also targeted relatively weakened polities, shown historically to be more receptive to missionaries. Where the LMS and Moravian doctrines shaped Khoekhoe and slave perceptions of Christianity, Shaw hoped to create specifically Methodist allegiances among independent African chiefdoms beyond the Cape's frontier. The WMMS, meanwhile, attempted to strike a delicate equilibrium between building support for Methodism among local whites in the Eastern Cape and promoting the importance of African missions.

Strategically, the Moravians opted for a quietist approach while the LMS missionaries embroiled themselves in local political and economic conflicts, earning them a reputation as "negrophiles." LMS advocacy for the Khoekhoe led to charges of interference in the social order and disruption of proper labor relations. Scholars such as Robert Ross and Elizabeth Elbourne in their analyses of Khoekhoe encounters with Christianity show how their early history of colonial subjugation and the destruction of their culture influenced the alacrity with which they assimilated the religion. Elbourne also effectively demonstrates how local conditions on the ground informed metropolitan perspectives; and how the political currents of evangelicalism in Great Britain shaped the fortunes of the Khoekhoe and the agendas and advocacy of the LMS missionaries who proselytized among them and took up their political cause. Like their Yoruba counterparts, the Khoekhoe used their new faith to challenge their subjugation and push for respectability and spiritual and social equality, although their national projects proved far less successful.[44]

For Methodists, evangelizing along the Cape's eastern frontier soon meant working in a war-torn region among Africans, some of whom remained committed to fighting to the death for their political independence no matter how many previous defeats they had suffered. Therefore, once deployed in controversial mission fields like South Africa, missionaries who had shunned formal political activism as a matter of principle or policy found it near impossible to remain aloof from colonial politics. However missionaries distilled their allegiance to the humanitarian and philanthropic ideas behind the antislavery movement and then later criticisms of imperial policies, they all had to address the disorder colonial policies unleashed upon their potential converts and the implications for the future of their evangelical work.

Although colonial violence, dispossession, and displacement initially generated multitudes of desperate people seeking assistance from missions, these circumstances were hardly the clarion call missionaries wanted their converts to associate with the coming of Christianity. Granted, some missionaries privately or quietly welcomed the destruction of African political independence as a boon to their own influence, even ascribing to providential intervention the incorporation of formerly independent African chiefdoms into the Cape Colony. Others went overboard and advocated war and violence as the only path forward; indigenous societies had to be broken and war was an effective way to recast African society in a Christian mold.[45] Yet protracted wars of dispossession in the Eastern Cape destabilized missions. Short-term boosts in mission populations and even the successful proselytization of particular ethnic groups whose desperation made them embrace missionaries actually militated against the long-term goals of cultivating a vital, mature, self-sustaining African engagement with Christianity. Moreover, after initially waxing eloquent and downright romantic about the importance of developing a cadre of African ministers, lay preachers, and teachers—known otherwise in the missionary lexicon as "native agency"—some missionaries expressed ambivalence when these hopes of indigenization came to fruition.

By the 1830s and 1840s Africans faced a rising tide of corrosive colonial policies that led to the usurpation of land and the erosion of local political authority. Meanwhile, Christian evangelical proselytization continued to profane sacred local beliefs and traditions and encouraged some individuals to experiment with new lifestyles and beliefs. Perceived missionary complicity in facilitating these developments threatened the longevity and legitimacy of missionary work and the vitality and maturity they sought in their converts. The emissaries of the WMMS in South Africa, while evangelizing among independent Xhosa chiefdoms, tried to chart a path between what they saw as the political meddling of the LMS that led to acrimony with local whites, and the quietism of the Moravians. It was an ambitious political balance almost impossible to maintain. Local Xhosa chiefs watched as missionaries erected one, then two, and eventually six Methodist missions amid or near their chiefdoms.

African leaders willingly granted the missionaries land on which to build and welcomed the superintendent of Wesleyan Missions, William Shaw, and his Methodist colleagues as potential diplomatic arbiters in their dealings with the colonial government. Yet, most remained wary of Christianity and the European cultural accoutrements missionaries propagated in their civilizing mission. Missionaries pursued their faith as exclusive truth claims, teaching as Christian doctrine their own cultural practices and interpretations of appropriate clothing, architectural styles, gender roles, and marriage. As long as the missions welcomed individuals whom Africans considered the detritus of their own society, their presence would be tolerated. When more and more of their subjects moved to the chain of six Methodist stations and expressed a deeper interest in Christianity, however, many African chiefs and household heads confirmed their suspicions that missionaries acted as the cultural arm of a colonial phalanx intent on undermining their political stability and integrity while converting their subjects to new ways of life and a new religion. Although the missionaries cast their mission stations as havens from the secular politics of the colonial world and disavowed any involvement in colonial policies, Africans burned the chain of missions when war broke out in 1834, demonstrating the missionaries' failure to convince the majority of Africans that Christian evangelism bore little relation to colonialism.

Violence and insecurity dissipated human and financial capital and wreaked widespread physical destruction at pioneer Methodist missions in the 1830s and 1840s. But the Methodists and missionaries in general had even more nettlesome trends to worry them. The evangelical and antislavery legacy had contributed a potent ideology based on a civilizing discourse centered on the assimilation of European cultural norms. The marketplace of ideas about how best to effect socioeconomic change among Africans shared a homogenous vision with antislavery agendas about the redemptive power of Christian faith in the afterlife and the transformative power of a Christian lifestyle in this life. War threatened the legitimacy of these ideas and also highlighted more significant problems than the binary gulf between Christian and "heathen" lifestyles. Although more sanguine sentiments about African potential gave way to pronounced pessimism centered on the shortcomings of former slaves and other colonial subjects who waged war against their subjugation, a host of Christian missionary organizations still propagated with gusto the civilizing discourse that had featured so prominently in the new lifestyles antislavery activists had envisioned for former slaves throughout the British Empire and for Africans. Still, the divergence between ideology and practice troubled even the most optimistic missionaries.

The far-reaching changes missionaries suggested Africans make in their housing, gender relations, marriage, clothing, manners, and work ethic remained lofty ideals. In practice, Methodist missionaries tolerated shallow adherence to these lifestyle changes at their six missions, as did other missionary societies. Facing widespread opposition and sometimes disdain from Africans, many Methodist missionaries had opted for evidence of a modicum of civilized dress and accepted a basic interest in the Christian faith as a minimum standard for mission residence. Most missionaries compromised on their high standards as a matter of strategy and expedience to generate African interest in Christianity. The denouement of missionary experiments in social improvement and religious change, when calibrated using European guidelines about the preferred form and content of Christianity, led to continual disillusionment and at times exasperation throughout the nineteenth century.

Having pioneered mission stations to attempt to shield their adherents and converts from wider "heathen" influence and to focus on their civilizing experiments, many missionaries now bemoaned the shortcomings of this strategy; yet could do little to improve on it. The embryonic and fitful progress of Christian evangelism had almost dictated "missions" as a first tentative step. Farmerfield, founded on the model of a vital and mature African engagement with Christianity rather than the superficial commitment evident at pioneer missions, evolved as an important bellwether in this regard. Designed as a corrective to the recurring trend of "nominalism," the Farmerfield mission represented a concerted effort by the WMMS to address the persistent deficiencies in the existing model of missions. The lived experience of Farmerfield's African residents charts, for four generations, how the debates and experiments in African socioeconomic and religious improvement unfolded against the backdrop of volatile political landscapes and missionary agendas. Shifting the focus from missionary strategies to the origins of Farmerfield in the request African congregants made to William Shaw reveals another critical angle for assessing African assimilation of Christianity.

While missionaries bemoaned the slow pace of conversions and cultural assimilation at their missions, Africans became more knowledgeable about missionary agendas and grew savvy in their interactions with missionary personalities. African chiefs had always sought diplomatic ties with missionaries for their connections to the colony and to Great Britain. Those considered marginal, social misfits, or outsiders likewise accepted missions. But now ordinary Africans sought missionary assistance and used their potential conversion as leverage to secure their own interests beyond temporary sanctuary from the war that had razed the pioneer missions. Farmerfield emerged only after Africans from the pioneer missions reminded William Shaw that while they had taken temporary refuge in Grahamstown, the closest colonial city to their former homes, they wanted to resettle where they had more economic options to live independently. Moreover, these congregants, while committed to Christianity, remained open to its denominational or theological content. When Shaw advised his African congregants to return to the pioneer missions and rebuild, they instead requested that he establish a new mission for them on the colonial side of the border among the white settler community. Thus began a novel turn in Methodist mission when Shaw purchased a 6,000-acre farm, named it Farmerfield to honor one of the treasurers of the WMMS, Thomas Farmer, and invited African Christians to apply for residence and land access. Rather than settle "any rambling native" who expressed a rudimentary interest in Christianity at Farmerfield, however, William Shaw screened and recruited residents he termed "a select class of natives." From a heterogeneous mix of former slaves and Africans from beyond the Cape's colonial borders, William Shaw selected for residence those who expressed a serious commitment to Methodist evangelism and possessed the economic means to lead lifestyles commensurate with the European "civilizing mission." An idealistic and strict convergence of the civilizing and evangelical missions took root from the moment Farmerfield's first denizens began relocating to the new mission.

Yet the creation of Farmerfield involved far more than William Shaw's simple compliance with his congregants' needs. While impressed by their dedication to maintaining a Christian lifestyle, Shaw believed his congregants manipulated their Christian status to pressure him, saying as much in his autobiography. When Africans pressed him about creating a new mission, he equivocated, delayed his response, and again redirected them to the pioneer stations being rebuilt. In reassessing the status of Methodist evangelism in the aftermath of the recent 1834–35 War of Dispossession and weighing his congregants' request, William Shaw had considered the physical destruction of the mission properties as well as the problem with mission settlements as they were conceived and executed by his and other missionary organizations. With a decade of experience in the mission field, Shaw now found some of his grander ambitions for Christian evangelism tempered by ongoing violence between Africans and white settlers, African mistrust of missionaries, and a shallow engagement with the tenets of Christian teachings and lifestyle among early converts.

Despite some misgivings, Shaw remained committed to the conventional model of missions and the WMMS supported his rebuilding efforts. He thus had no plan to create an African mission in the colony when his strategic interests still rested on currying favor with African chiefs. An African mission on the colonial side of the border promised no great conversion of African chiefs to impress metropolitan audiences and the WMMS. Nor did Shaw believe his congregants had reached a level of spiritual maturity commensurate with navigating residence at a new mission in the middle of a white colonial constituency. Despite championing the concept of "native agency," Shaw grew concerned about this particular instance of African initiative. That Africans should now determine the strategic location of a Methodist mission and decide its primary purpose granted them too much agency in shaping the WMMS agenda. Moreover, would a white settler community still recovering from recent war welcome a new settlement of Africans as their neighbors, economic competitors, and spiritual compatriots—especially a community that defined economic independence as avoiding labor for whites?

Although metropolitan directives and agendas guided missionary ambitions, as historian Andrew Porter has demonstrated, local conditions shaped what missionaries could achieve on the ground.[46] Even with a basic knowledge of Christianity, those Africans interested in Christian missions not as a temporary retreat but as a serious attempt to fashion new lives for themselves now had enough clout to know that missionary societies would vie for their allegiance. Shaw's dilemma captures one crucial aspect of the encounter between Africans and their missionaries and its denouement at Farmerfield. Even if Methodist congregants did not share Shaw's vision about the importance of locating missions in African chiefdoms, they made their own strategic calculations about their worth as potential converts and church members in relation to their status as laborers. Africans knew their value as spiritual commodities to fill the columns of Christian statistical registers, diaries, and letters. As a result, they sought out any missionary society willing to assist them, and not just the Methodists. Africans also knew that whatever reservations local white settlers had about their status as refugees on the colonial side of the border, their presence would be tolerated as long as they provided labor.

Africans feared their sojourn to the colony would culminate in a life of servile labor for white settlers. Exposure to missions and Christianity taught them that they could at least maintain their access to arable land and perhaps aspire to a measure of prosperity and economic independence. The African refugees who approached Shaw used their clout as Christians to forge a third, more palatable option aside from working in the Eastern Cape for whites, or returning to their former chiefdoms and missions. If African Christians now leveraged their status for their own agendas, they did so by obeying the main dictates of mission Christianity and challenged missionaries to prove their assertions that their spiritual and material needs mattered as much to the WMMS as those of their white constituencies.

Despite acceding to his congregants' request, Shaw had resolved the problem of regaining the leverage he had lost in the negotiation phase. He mediated his congregants' newfound influence with an innovative concept and design for Farmerfield distinct from the chain of six pioneer Methodist missions established between the 1820s and 1830s. For Shaw, the civilizing mission was a sine qua non of evangelism. With Farmerfield's residents having produced mixed results at their pioneer missions, William Shaw hoped they could demonstrate the African capacity to lead civilized and Christianized lifestyles and thus silence some of the critics of missionary work. Given the local denominational competition among missionary societies, Farmerfield's African residents had grown keenly aware of their leverage and status as converts or potential converts and used it to influence Shaw on a matter that was ultimately economic. Grahamstown's Methodist chapel could have accommodated their spiritual needs, but Africans now learned that those needs could not be assessed in a vacuum because long-term residence in areas demarcated for Africans meant accepting immiseration and subservience as a part of normal life. The stakes for Shaw and for his congregants thus diverged. In the new mission blueprint, the individual and collective behavior of Farmerfield's future residents proved consequential for the broader European assessment of African character, of nascent African Christianity, and of appropriate metropolitan support for overseas missions. Farmerfield's Methodist residents, who chose to experiment and commit to a Christian lifestyle before the war, now faced four options: continue with that experiment in a new locale; return to the old missions; return to their chiefdoms; or settle for a life of colonial servitude.

By locating the mission on the colonial side of the border and populating it with experienced African Christians, Shaw crafted Farmerfield as a crucial departure from the blueprint of pioneer missions. Rather than welcoming almost anyone who expressed even a shallow interest and tolerating numerous "heathen" residents as the pioneer missions had done, Shaw screened Farmerfield's residents for their commitment to Christian teachings and lifestyle. He required that potential residents submit an application and provide character references about their integrity and industry. Shaw embarked on a new mission experiment to cultivate a vital, mature African engagement with Christianity. *The Farmerfield Mission* thus argues that Farmerfield's origins in the initiative of African congregants, its strict rules of residence, its location amid a competing white farming community, and its recruitment of "a select class of natives," changed the tenor and direction of African evangelism as William Shaw had envisioned it earlier in the 1820s and represented a distinct, enduring turn in Methodist evangelical strategies.

Four generations of Farmerfield residents debated Methodist missions about the content and character of African Christianity and fought to maintain their economic independence against the rapacious tide of African dispossession and immiseration unfolding across the South African landscape. As Farmerfield's successive missionaries implemented William Shaw's new vision of a vital, mature African Christianity, its African residents faced scrutiny and criticism about their commitment to a Christian lifestyle, their desire to focus on their own economic endeavors rather than provide labor exclusively to their white neighbors, and their fidelity to certain banned cultural rites like male circumcision or the exchange of bridewealth. From its foundation in 1838 to its destruction in 1962, the nature of the religious encounter between African congregants and missionaries thus involved negotiation and dissimulation, deference and defiance. Farmerfield's residents confronted a host of disconcerting realities, many of them rooted in continued colonial violence and dispossession that by the late nineteenth century led to widespread economic malaise. These challenges, many times degenerating into war, forced the WMMS and its agents in South Africa to question how to properly situate themselves politically among the colonial government, white settlers, and the African communities they proselytized.

The political question was critical for the Methodists in the Eastern Cape, which more than any other denomination then operating at the Cape looked to local British colonial settlers to staff and provide financial and moral support for African missions. At Farmerfield, older generations died and new generations moved in, often bearing no familial relation to former denizens. But what they all shared was a religious commonality and communality that no matter how ideologically diluted by the twentieth century, still sustained a vision of Farmerfield as first and foremost an African Christian space. By the time of its destruction in 1962, Farmerfield had long taken on the characteristic features of an impoverished, rural African community, making it one of many such enclaves in a harsh political environment moving toward social engineering policies that supported putative ethnic and racial purities.

What Farmerfield contributes to imperial and South African history is a panoramic overview of a multiethnic African community whose lifespan segued with and contributed to crucial developments in mission and colonial discourse as well as apartheid-era racial engineering. Farmerfield captures how, in the heady decades of the 1820s and 1830s, one African community participated in the marketplace of ideas about African social and economic improvement and gained enough clout as Christians to survive until 1962. In that marketplace, antislavery activists, missionaries, and philanthropists drew on Christian evangelism as a fundamental guarantor of the socioeconomic and cultural changes they propagated in the civilizing mission to Africa. In cultivating a vital, mature engagement to Christian evangelism in general and Methodism in particular, Farmerfield's successive African residents used the tools of faith, literacy, education, and their bonds to a powerful evangelical organization to secure their long-term interests. Meanwhile, Farmerfield's Methodist missionaries found themselves protecting Africans against the worst ravages of colonialism and apartheid while waxing ambivalent about the implications of their message of spiritual agency, racial equality, and political pragmatism. Despite the awe and power associated with colonial authority and missionaries, in the most important realms of this encounter, it was ultimately Africans' own acceptance and assimilation of Christianity that determined ultimate success and long-term commitment to Christianity as a faith and lifestyle.

The question of whether Africans can make Christianity their own is one that has been answered with a resounding yes in the last few decades, given the rapid growth of Christianity in former European colonial haunts now referred to as the global south. Farmerfield's history encapsulates one early nineteenth-century experiment to test this proposition in the heady days of the 1820s and 1830s, when antislavery activities and missionaries dominated the debate on African development. The twentieth-century denouement of the mission experiment at Farmerfield diverged from the much-celebrated instances of African-initiated or independent churches. Rather, Africans' practice of a vital, mature African Christianity grew organically from their experience of colonialism and Christian evangelism in the nineteenth-century Eastern Cape. Christianity at Farmerfield emerged from pioneer Methodist evangelism and even as Africans asserted their right to maintain their fidelity to their African cultural moorings, the residents maintained a commitment to the basic tenets of Methodism.

Farmerfield's history contributes to the historiographical latticework by reaffirming the importance of discrete historical case studies, personalities, and locations in informing the way historians should think about and reassess the meaning of colonialism and evangelism as discourses and as lived experiences for missionaries, their multiple white constituencies at home and abroad, and their African congregations. Moreover, Farmerfield's longevity and legacy allows for a new look at the emergence of a vital, mature African Christianity within a missionary framework and not only in African independent churches. The evolution of Christianity at Farmerfield also demonstrates how the stakes of Christianity changed in the colonial and apartheid era. Far from the purview of missionaries and for almost four decades without formal white oversight, many of Farmerfield's former residents built a new Methodist spirituality. Many still attended church and proudly identified themselves members of a Christian collective. Even as they disavowed the drinking and smoking of some of their neighbors as unchristian behavior, the moral judgment was not paired with any secular threat to lose their access to land. They proclaimed the right for individuals to live by their own moral compass, as the ultimate judgment lay between that person and God. Religious freedom now meant Christian faith without fundamentalism or dogmatism; it now meant one could be as secular and irreverent as one saw fit without forfeiting the claim to be Christian in the broadest sense of the term. Economic freedom now incorporated multiple notions of land access—leasing and subleasing—without a romantic attachment or an ideological commitment to farming. What remains in the new iteration of Farmerfield is an affirmation of Christian affiliation and commonality as a way to legitimize access to land and a flexible interpretation of what it means to be an African Christian.

Chapter Overviews

The first three chapters of the book form a unit exploring the expansion of missionary work to the Cape Colony in the wake of the eighteenth-century Evangelical Revival that regenerated Protestantism in Europe, gave rise to Methodism, and sparked the creation of numerous evangelical missionary societies and led to the creation of a chain of pioneer Methodist stations in the Eastern Cape, South Africa, between 1823 and 1833. Chapter 1 places the Evangelical Revival in a European context, outlines the birth and significance of Methodism, and explores how these developments were manifested in formation of missionary societies to spread the Gospel to Africa. The Evangelical Revival overlapped chronologically and ideologically with the growth in momentum of the antislavery movement in the 1790s. Missionaries undertook a zealous evangelical scheme to Africa as a program of moral and humanitarian reparation for the slave trade. They also transferred many of the ideas behind amelioration and emancipation to their blueprints for mission stations. In this context, the book highlights how Sierra Leone emerged as an early prototype of an African settlement centered on agricultural industry and Christianity, a model that missionaries of all denominations tried to emulate in some format throughout the nineteenth century. The final part of the chapter outlines how the social geography of the Cape Colony delimited pioneer missionary work between 1799 and 1834, particularly the work of the London Missionary Society. The chapter argues that the early evangelical work of the LMS, by fusing African political advocacy with evangelism, left a legacy the WMMS tried to distance itself from when they arrived on the scene in the 1820s.

Chapter 2 examines pioneer Methodist evangelism at the Cape and the establishment of a chain of mission stations among Africans living beyond the borders of the Cape Colony. Proselytizing at a time when Africans still maintained their political independence from the Cape Colony and when the social and economic fabric of their societies remained intact, missionaries made little impact on Africans, who responded to the Christian message with a mixture of curiosity and disregard. Similar to other mission settlements throughout Africa, missionaries received a mélange of political refugees, social pariahs, and other individuals on the fringes of African societies. Despite gaining some converts, missionaries saw more evidence that Africans flocked to the mission for material gains without being certain of their spiritual engagement with Christianity. The book asserts that while missionaries accepted this as an inevitable characteristic of pioneer work, they grew increasingly impatient with the persistence of what they called "nominal" Christianity. Furthermore, the slow pace at which Africans were willing to change their circular huts, adopt European clothing instead of bedaubing themselves with red ochre, and assume European methods of agriculture also led missionaries to complain about "incipient" civilization. By the 1830s, when the small number of converts seemed incommensurate with the great missionary zeal and effort expended, missionaries were ready for a new strategy.

Chapter 3 explores the circumstances surrounding the creation of the Farmerfield mission station and argues that Farmerfield was novel in two ways. First, the mission was the initiative of Africans who made a request to local Methodist missionaries in Grahamstown to establish a mission for them within the borders of the Cape Colony. Having already established a chain of missions between the 1820s and 1830s, the Methodists had no plans to create new settlements on the colonial side of the border until Africans approached them. Second, Farmerfield represented a new phase in Methodist pioneer work. Capitalizing on the African request, the Methodists decided that Farmerfield would be created as a corrective to the problems of "nominal" Christianity and incipient civilization. The missionaries attempted to populate Farmerfield with experienced African Christians who owned property in the form of cattle, sheep, or goats. With these twin goals in mind, the stage was set for a new experiment in Methodist evangelical strategy: an exclusive African peasant community as the embodiment of a vital African Christianity and mature civilization.

The second unit of the book analyzes the social, economic, and religious history of Farmerfield from 1838 to 1884, when the WMMS considered terminating the mission. The book now examines the creation of the Farmerfield mission in 1838, the African residents' social and economic milieu, and early missionary acclaim over the settlement. Chapter 4 explores the extent to which Farmerfield was imagined as, and became, an economic enterprise where Africans engaged in peasant farming while providing labor to local whites. The book argues that in the early decades of the settlement, Farmerfield provided one example of the rise of a successful African peasantry that negotiated the limits of arable farming by engaging in a three-part strategy of laboring for whites while practicing arable farming and pastoralism and self-employment in various trades. The book demonstrates how Farmerfield's peasants rose in the 1840s, long before the process was duplicated on a wider scale in the Cape Colony, and declined just when other peasants began experiencing prosperity elsewhere in the Colony. I paint an economic mosaic of the African residents to demonstrate how their activities departed from or converged with the missionary vision of the estate, and to explore the viability of the missionary model of a laboring agricultural peasantry.

Chapter 5 examines the religious component of Farmerfield's design to trace how the African residents actually lived as Christians versus the expectations missionaries had of them. I argue that missionaries commended the Christian character of the residents in the early decades of the settlement, although expressing some reservations about evidence of occasional declension in religious piety. Furthermore, as a settlement peopled by African Christians, Farmerfield's residents stood in stark contrast to other Africans living in the vicinity on white farms. Farmerfield's residents themselves served as evangelists to fellow Africans, fulfilling one of their designated roles as "native agents" of Christianity. The final part of the chapter argues that the accusation of "nominal" Christianity and incipient civilization that the Wesleyan Methodist Missionary Society and white missionaries leveled at the settlement in 1884 was not borne out by the missionaries' own evidence and rather served as a pretext for justifying the termination of the mission.

Chapter 6 explores the review of 1884, when the WMMS considered expelling the residents and dissolving the mission. I argue that the criticism of the mission was symptomatic of a general dissatisfaction with the pace of evangelical work in the Cape Colony, the relatively small number of African converts to mission Christianity compared to the overall population, and displeasure with the growing number of Africans adopting unorthodox, syncretic versions of Christianity. The missionaries glossed over the economic decline of the settlement as part of their criticism of Christianity at Farmerfield. Yet I argue that although the economic decline was real, the review demonstrates that the missionaries took umbrage at any signs that Africans challenged missionary paternalism and missionary interpretation of Christianity. Africans indeed questioned the sanctity of freehold tenure as the only guarantor of perpetual land access and asserted their right to the land by long-term occupancy as well as usufruct rights. Moreover, they guarded their discretion to use the land in the way they saw fit, whether it was leaving it fallow or sharecropping with individuals who lived off the estate. I also argue that it was the same strand of missionary paternalism that finally led to the decision to retain the mission. To avoid complicity in alienating lands from Africans when the colonial government was stripping them of their land rights throughout the colony, the missionary society voted to give the mission a second chance to live up to its blueprint.

The third unit of the book analyzes the community's reincarnation between the 1880s and the 1950s and its destruction by the apartheid government in 1962. By then the mission had a different generation of residents assuming occupancy, some of whom were related to the original inhabitants. The population also received a significant influx of new individuals as missionaries renewed their plans to revamp William Shaw's vision for Farmerfield, this time with colonial exploitation more rapacious. What distinguished this period was the rising tide of colonialism as Britain gained a dominant foothold in the emerging mining industry and used this clout to unite disparate territories into a single political and economic unit. Yet the goals of the missionaries maintained the same plan for creating a laboring Christian peasantry and the land available at Farmerfield took on a relatively higher value as Africans throughout the region lost even more land.

Chapter 7 explores how the tenants fared after the mission was long past its heyday and when the local missionaries continued to ponder the least conniving way to get rid of it. The chapter shows that rather than try to live up to missionary expectations, Farmerfield tenants continued to assert their independence in the economic and religious realms, sometimes contravening mission rules to do so. I also maintain that the vulnerability of both arable and pastoral agriculture already demonstrated in the early years of the settlement became the leading factor once again in its further decline. Between the 1880s and the 1950s, Farmerfield took on characteristics of other African reserves whereby the majority of the population were the elderly, women, and children. As Farmerfield lost its luster, the missionaries saw this as an opportunity for the mission to die a natural death and therefore capped the population. Each time a tenant died the missionaries allowed no new tenants to take his place. As the tenants of the 1880s grew older and their younger family members migrated in search of better opportunities presented by the mineral revolution of the 1860s and 1880s, the missionaries considered selling off small portions of the estate and circumscribed the residents to smaller pieces of land. They pursued this strategy throughout the 1920s and 1930s, as Africans elsewhere throughout the country confronted soil erosion, further land dispossession, and the subsequent collapse of many African farming enterprises.

In apartheid South Africa, areas reclassified as "black spots" designated any Africans living on such land as "squatters." The government then forcibly relocated these "squatters" according to their particular ethnic affiliation, accomplishing, in the case of Farmerfield, the expulsion many missionaries wanted in the preceding decades. Chapter 8 discusses the government declaration of Farmerfield as a "black spot" in a white area. I retrace how the tenants first heard the news, how they perceived the impending termination of the settlement, how an alternative place was found for settlement, and how they fared in the new location called Mimosa Park. The chapter emphasizes the importance of understanding how the experience at Farmerfield shaped the perceptions and experience of Mimosa Park and impacted the sense of "community," one of the many historical perspectives on African communities that got lost as apartheid generated its own internal refugee crisis.

Chapter 9 explores the reclamation and resettlement of Farmerfield between 1990 and 2008. Former tenants and their descendants at Farmerfield, as well as thousands of other dispossessed litigants throughout South Africa, reclaimed their land via new Land Claim Courts more than thirty years later. Their memories and reflections serve as a vital source for reconstructing particular experiences of migration, dispossession, and reclamation in contemporary South Africa. The chapter addresses how the remaining Farmerfield families viewed the process of land reclamation, their perceptions of the "new" Farmerfield, and their nascent plans now that they have regained access to the land. Postapartheid resettlement at Farmerfield captures some of the stark challenges of restoring agricultural land to people, many of whom are too old to resume subsistence agriculture and too impoverished to attempt commercial agriculture. Meanwhile, their children, grandchildren, and other descendants express little interest in agriculture as a viable economic endeavor in contemporary South Africa. In a political climate where the clamor for land reclamation as restorative justice is strong but government action is slow, the restitution of Farmerfield's lands highlights the shortcomings and possibilities of the land reform process.

Farmerfield's historical trajectory reinforces and celebrates the legacy and longevity of an African Christianity that has survived against the odds of colonialism and apartheid. Yet this new version of Farmerfield faces serious economic and social obstacles. Whereas Farmerfield was once enmeshed in antislavery and evangelical discourses, its most current iteration is immersed in several key debates in postapartheid political discourse: the relationship between poverty and economic development; the role of civil society and nongovernmental organizations; strategies for recuperating or pioneering effective leadership models; the relationship between communalism and land access/rights; and the meaning of citizenship and community in postapartheid South Africa.

PART ONE

‖ 1 ‖

Genealogies

The Evangelical Revival, Methodism, and Pioneer Mission Work in the
Cape Colony, 1790s–1820s

The Evangelical Revival, Methodism, and Antislavery

Before embarking on her landmark trip to Africa in 1893, Mary Kingsley sought advice from her friends and colleagues, who redirected her to missionary literature as a font of expert advice about the "dark continent."[1] By the 1890s, missionary societies of every ilk could be found in Africa. By the late nineteenth century, the journals of missionaries like John Philip, David Livingstone, and Robert Moffat, as well as excerpts of their reports published in evangelical periodicals, suffused the genre of travel literature. Missionary literature informed ordinary people about far-flung places in the British Empire, allowing them a vicarious experience of the adventures, romance, and challenges of pioneer missionary work. As historian Susan Thorne has noted of missionary literature and propaganda, "The attractions of foreign missionary intelligence were considerable in an age before alternative means of enlightenment, entertainment, and even assembly were widely available."[2]

Missionary literature explained how and why funds were needed and allowed the poor and middle classes to see how the accretion of their small sums advanced a worthy moral cause. According to Kingsley, these missionary reports expounded on "how necessary it was that their readers should subscribe more freely, and not get any ideas in their heads about obtaining an inadequate supply of souls for their money." Although she admitted that missionary literature provided useful information about African socioeconomic and political conditions, Kingsley was amused by how often missionaries "wrote their reports not to tell you how the country they resided in was, but how it was getting towards being what it ought to be."[3]

Although she was primarily discussing West Africa, Kingsley's musings apply to the genre of missionary literature in general. Inherent in missionary narratives

31

was the penchant to romanticize the pioneer aspects of evangelical work and to justify progress and their budgets in relation to a persistently low and often suspicious number of "native converts." A century before foreign missionary literature riveted British audiences, the Evangelical Revival laid the foundations for the creation of new geographic foci of religious literature, mainly Asia, the Caribbean, and Africa. For Africa and the Caribbean, the Evangelical Revival overlapped with the most ambitious human rights endeavor undertaken to end the traffic in slaves and bring the institution of slavery to an end. These two powerful ideological movements at times pursued similar agendas and shared personnel with missionary organizations. Some missionaries worked closely with abolitionists, if not becoming abolitionist themselves, while Christian teachings and lifestyles featured prominently in the reforms abolitionists advocated for slave societies as well as indigenous communities in Africa.

The nascent missionary activity underway in the 1790s in the Cape Colony was a product of the Evangelical Revival that had swept Europe several decades earlier in the eighteenth century.[4] The first wave of Reformation zeal that had given birth to Protestantism had fallen into a lethargic rhythm desperately in need of reinvigoration by the late eighteenth century. Protestantism, now "settled down into well-established patterns controlled by state authorities and served by a well-educated clergy," had become too "bureaucratized and bereft of religious enthusiasm."[5] The tradition of religious dissent that defined the Reformation had lost its popular appeal and its evangelical zeal.[6]

As the Protestant Reformation had challenged the Catholic Church, so too did the Anglican Church, as the established Church of England, face dissent in a wave of protest in the seventeenth century that called for more far-reaching reforms and religious toleration.[7] Throughout Europe, the clamor for religious toleration fell on deaf ears. In this period, the Puritans escaped religious persecution by fleeing to America, and the French Huguenots sought refuge elsewhere in Europe, as well as in America and the Cape Colony.[8] Weakened evangelical fervor, discrimination and religious persecution in the form of harassment, and legal battles and imprisonment sapped Protestant dissent of its momentum in the seventeenth and early eighteenth centuries.[9] By the 1720s the initial Reformation movement's demand for an unmediated relationship with God was injected with a call for a more individual and heartfelt spiritual experience that focused on personal salvation and piety in daily life. In Germany this spiritual rebirth took the form of Pietism, a movement that was the basis for the first short-lived Moravian missionary venture in the Cape Colony in 1732 and again in the 1790s.[10] In Britain, the Evangelical Revival flowered through multiple Protestant denominations, including the Anglican Church in Britain, but the most profound expression of this call for spiritual regeneration was found in Methodism.

Methodism developed in the crucible of eighteenth-century revivalism and capitalized on the plea for reawakened faith and religious zeal. More than any other Protestant group (for example, Quakers, Baptists, and Puritans), of the established dissent tradition, Methodism answered the call for a more profound and pious religious experience. From its humble beginnings in the 1730s as a small group of Oxford men meeting for religious study and discussion, Methodism grew into a powerful revival movement that breathed new life into religious dissent and the search for a meaningful spiritual experience. John Wesley, the founder of Methodism, initially began as an ordained minister in the Anglican Church. Though Methodism remained a movement within the Anglican Church during his lifetime, his religious tenure in the Anglican Church did not provide the religious experience he desired. In his search for a fulfilling spiritual experience, Wesley sought a balance between faith and devotion. He formulated guidelines to observe in his daily life to maximize the time he dedicated to spiritual introspection and religious work. When John Wesley joined his brother Charles and the handful of others from Oxford who had formed a club to explore and study Christianity, he recommended that they adopt the rules he used in his own daily life.[11] The group members were derisively called "Methodists" for the discipline they practiced in their daily lives and religious studies, and the appellation stuck with them.

Wesley's spiritual quest culminated in his conversion at a religious gathering in 1738 when he was overcome with a profound assurance that faith was the path to salvation. His brother Charles had undergone a similar experience a few days previously. The Wesley brothers resolved to share their spiritual epiphanies and blueprint for a Christian lifestyle with the rest of the world. Conversion, as a radical alteration of spiritual consciousness, was an essential part of this blueprint along with prescriptions for observing piety in daily life. John Wesley and the cohort of preachers that quickly multiplied throughout England traveled around preaching to ordinary folk in their houses, barns, in the open air, and wherever they could get people to assemble and listen to them—scenes reminiscent of early missionary work in Africa. In the process, they converted thousands of souls to the cause of Methodism. While the Methodists did not officially break with the Anglican Church until 1784, Methodism was outgrowing the Church of England and becoming recognized as an established denomination rather than a sect. In a series of conferences between 1744 and 1747, Wesley and some of his preachers laid out the doctrines of Methodism and consolidated these into an organized belief system.

Methodists used simple techniques that proved brilliant in their organization and effectiveness. Itinerant preaching and by extension, the charismatic revivalist assemblies they sparked, defined the hallmarks of eighteenth-century Methodism; both proved to be valuable missionary tools for appealing to the masses. Itinerancy emphasized the importance of the domestic missionary project and encouraged the creation of a cohort of local preachers everywhere the message was spread.[12] Lay agency underpinned evangelical revivalism and remained an essential part of Methodism even with increasing professionalization of the clergy after the 1790s. The development of several institutions such as the class meeting and the "love feast" fueled the sense of Christian fellowship and gave ordinary people a voice and agency in their own salvation. The division of congregations into smaller units or classes gave Methodism a crucial self-regulatory element and provided a crucible for cultivating the leadership skills of the lay clergy. Congregants met to pray, read together, examine each other's knowledge and understanding of the faith, and help each other to answer questions about salvation, faith, and Christian behavior. The class leader provided an important contact point from among one's peers to whom spiritual, liturgical, and other issues could be addressed. Combined with the "love feasts" where congregants shared a meal and testified about their spiritual experiences, the class meetings reinforced the bonds linking a community of believers.

John Wesley expanded on the embryonic form of the Oxford meetings to create one of the most enduring features of Methodism.[13] The class meeting created a forum for ordinary folk to share their experiences as Christians, to take responsibility for their own salvation, and to themselves get involved in the organizing. Sunday schools, which expanded rapidly after the 1780s, built on the earlier charity school efforts that preceded them to provide a vehicle for literacy as well as religious instruction.[14] Itinerant preaching, love feasts, class meetings, and Sunday schools empowered common people, who in seeking their own salvation, learned how to read and to discipline themselves, became class leaders and local preachers, and gained the respect of their spiritual compatriots.[15]

Perhaps the most powerful idea of Methodism, and of Christianity in general, was that "all have sinned and come short of the glory of God."[16] Methodism emphasized spiritual egalitarianism. Everyone—whether one was the king of England, the wealthiest aristocrat, the humblest peasant, or the most exploited worker—had sinned and had an equal chance of salvation.[17] While spiritual equality certainly could not alleviate material and political inequality, it was a powerful idea in a context where even the established Anglican Church reflected the contemporary political and economic hierarchy. Against the backdrop of the social and economic dislocations of the Industrial Revolution, Methodism provided a potentially powerful salve to mitigate some of the worst aspects of industrialization. For the lower classes dealing with the impact of enclosures and the dissolution of older forms of community, subsistence, and authority, Methodism provided other worldly hopes to which they could aspire, as well as a schema for creating some order and purpose in their earthly lives beyond the realm of labor. Methodism afforded a measure of predictability, stability, and control, created new forms of community and sociability, cultivated networks of mutual aid and assistance, and developed new rituals in which congregants could participate.

Methodism's appeal was not limited to the poor working classes, however, for its emphasis on industry and frugality were among the very traits that made working-class labor pliable. Some members of the English middle class appreciated the ideological quiescence Methodism possibly encouraged in the lower classes, even as they, too, found some resonance with various aspects of its message of personal salvation and leading a respectable life of hard work, sobriety, charity, morality, and religious devotion. Although historian E. P. Thompson criticizes Methodism for its role in making the working classes more submissive, and encouraging acquiescence to political and economic inequality through its otherworldly orientation, he presents a balanced picture of its malleability.[18] "Methodism obtained its greatest success," he observed, "in serving simultaneously as the religion of the industrial bourgeoisie . . . and of wide sections of the proletariat."[19] Notwithstanding Methodism's complicity in legitimizing the social economic and political hierarchy, its basic tenets carved out a realm of spiritual agency that held meaning and significance in people's social and communal lives beyond their class status.

By the 1790s Methodism had developed into a distinct movement that could claim the allegiance of approximately 54,000 people in England.[20] Methodism did not saturate religious enthusiasm or evangelical zeal, however. As with all evangelical movements, Methodism experienced its own growth and declension as it matured and became institutionalized and bureaucratized. As the lines between ministers and laymen were more clearly demarcated, and as Methodism settled into an establishment, it lost some of its evangelistic fervor and its popular appeal to the masses.[21] By the time these trends in Methodism became evident in the 1790s, however, it had created an important legacy and honed an excellent administrative structure and evangelical methods that were adopted in various guises by the wider Evangelical Revival that took off in the 1790s.[22] The older established dissent movement also experienced the revivalism that had had its most profound articulation in the creation of Methodism as a new denomination.

The Evangelical Revival of the 1790s witnessed a rapid proliferation of missionary societies with the professed aim of extending evangelism to the rest of the world, particularly India, the Caribbean, and Africa. The Baptists created their missionary body in 1792. Several denominations (Congregationalists, Anglicans, and Methodists) came together in 1795 to found the London Missionary Society (LMS).The Glasgow Missionary Society (GMS) was founded in 1796. In 1799 many of the Anglican supporters of the LMS switched allegiances when their own society, the Church Missionary Society (CMS), was formed. Although the Wesleyan Methodist Missionary Society (WMMS) was not founded until 1813, Methodism itself was a missionary movement. Perhaps to a much greater extent than the other denominations, Methodism was a missionary movement on two fronts. While the Methodists were extending their evangelical work to the Caribbean in the 1790s and to the Cape Colony in the 1820s, they were simultaneously engaged in a domestic missionary effort in England. In fact, some of the greatest gains for Methodism in England coincided with the proliferation of missionary societies in the 1790s.[23] The creation of the WMMS in 1813 gave an organizational form to the missionary characteristics already inherent in Methodism.[24]

Perhaps one of the most significant developments from this new wave of evangelism that enveloped established Protestantism was the acknowledgment that missionary proselytization was needed on both the domestic and international fronts.[25] The evangelical imperative resounded as much in Britain as in Africa and the rest of the "heathen" world. Therefore, the upsurge of Protestant revivalism and missionary societies was further accompanied by three parallel and related developments instrumental in the expansion of missionary work throughout Europe and to Africa: first, the development and expansion of Sunday schools;[26] second, the expansion of itinerant preaching to bring the message to the masses;[27] and third, the growth and maintenance of a charitable, philanthropic spirit that became even more pronounced in the late eighteenth and nineteenth centuries.[28] Itinerant preaching and Sunday schools became part of a broader strategy to capture the hearts and souls of people outside the established church and "heathens" not yet convinced of the need for personal salvation through Christian faith.

The period that gave birth to missionary organizations also nurtured important intersections between the local and the international efforts. The rhetoric of darkness, idleness, indolence, and immorality resounding in the missionary enterprise in Africa in the late eighteenth and nineteenth centuries echoed the idioms used to talk about the poor and working classes in Britain.[29] Undoubtedly, cultural and racial prejudices informed the white missionaries' negative perceptions of Africa; yet similarly negative appraisals were forthcoming on the local front. Despite sharing a common denominator of race with the poor and working classes, missionaries accused this population segment of complacency and impiety, as well as immorality and indolence.[30] The discourse defining the moral and religious campaigns to change the lifestyles and work habits of the poor and working classes was assimilated into the missionary project in Africa.

The creation of missionary societies as a direct outgrowth of the Evangelical Revival provided a stimulus to Christian missionary work that brought Protestantism to cultures different from the European framework that gave birth to it. When Protestantism went beyond the boundaries of Europe, the issues of cultural relativism and spiritual egalitarianism were drawn in sharp relief to the purported universalism of the Christian faith. The centuries of struggle for religious toleration in Europe did not usually encourage religious pluralism in other cultural contexts, yet the most spectacular growth in Protestantism in the nineteenth century took place outside of Europe. Whether it was in Asia, the Caribbean, or Africa, most white missionaries assumed that either their potential converts were devoid of religious beliefs, or that their religious traditions, at best, were inferior to Christianity. In most cases, the religious rituals and beliefs that white missionaries encountered outside of Europe were cited as empirical evidence of superstition and primitivism, and therefore of the need for Christian evangelization. No matter how uncivilized, degenerate, or primitive missionaries assumed non-Western people to be, they at least acquiesced to the fundamental belief that everyone had an equal chance of deliverance from sin. As historian Andrew Walls pointed out, the "spiritual parity of the unregenerate of Christendom and the 'heathen' abroad had important missionary consequences."[31]

Protestantism's encounter with non-Western culture transferred the issue of spiritual egalitarianism into the midst of contentious local conflicts that were far more incendiary than the notion of spiritual leveling between social classes in Britain.[32] When viewed in the colonial context of slavery and racial domination in the United States, the Caribbean, or the Cape Colony, for example, the idea of spiritual equality raised serious alarm. Some slave owners were absolutely galled by the idea of spiritual equality and opposed the Christianization of their slaves.[33] The Christian missionary connection to the antislavery movement troubled slave owners throughout the Atlantic world and the possibility of seeing their former slaves in heaven was more than some could bear.[34] The convergence of evangelism with the growth of Sunday schools, missionary societies, and philanthropy in the 1790s created an atmosphere where the plight and relative equality of slaves, Africans, and the poor and working classes in England were discussed using the similar language of moral development. Antislavery sentiment was a common link that bound these late eighteenth-century developments together. The Evangelical Revival brought evangelism, Sunday schools, and missionary societies to Africa as programs of moral and humanitarian reparation for the slave trade; and much of the concern about the indolence and immorality of the working class provided a framework for delimiting the African capacity for improvement.

Missionary Evangelism and Africa in the Late Eighteenth Century

By the 1790s, when missionary societies planted their outposts in Africa, Europeans had developed their familiarity with the continent primarily through travelers' accounts and the slave trade. It was a cursory knowledge at best and developing a better understanding of Africa required missionaries to become amateur anthropologists of sorts. Much of the criticism of the slave trade highlighted the horrors of the Middle Passage by which Africans were brought to the Atlantic world and blamed the avarice and guile of European traders and planters for the rapacious traffic in human beings. Yet the culpability did not rest solely with Europeans.[35] Some segments of the African population, too, participated in and benefited from the slave trade.[36] Moreover, although Africa was seen as a victim of the slave trade, by the late eighteenth century, the immorality and barbarism of slavery and the slave trade came to be associated with Africans themselves and the millions of slaves transported to or born in the Atlantic world.[37] Britain's remedy for addressing the deleterious effects of the slave trade required an agenda with three tasks: first, to redress European complicity in the exploitation of Africa and assuage national guilt;[38] second, to provide an alternate form of trade so that Africans would be less inclined to participate in the slave trade; and third, to promote the moral regeneration that Africa needed after centuries of practicing slavery and exporting slaves.

Between the 1780s and the 1830s, as pioneer evangelical work grew at a rapid pace in Africa and the Caribbean, the antislavery cause captured the imagination of the British public and developed into a popular, contentious political issue.[39] In the crusade to end the slave trade and to exorcise the legacy of slavery in Africa, the abolitionist cause found an important ally in religion. Missionaries were among the vanguard of the movement into the interior of Africa and consequently served as an important network of support and information about slavery and the slave trade in Africa and the Atlantic world.[40] This same corpus of information about the evils of the slave trade reinforced the need for a Christian mission to Africa as Britain's moral compensation for participating in the slave trade, while economic reparations would come by encouraging more "legitimate" forms of commerce.[41] Antislavery and Christian missionary work thus proceeded in tandem and lent tremendous support to each other.[42] As Boyd Hilton asserted, the antislavery movement was the "supreme example of the politics of atonement, and provided public evangelicalism with its most potent *raison d'être*."[43] The decade of the 1780s was particularly fruitful in bringing abolition to the forefront of humanitarian causes. The Abolition Society was founded in 1787, with the Methodists and Quakers among the most steadfast of its religious supporters.[44] Heightened parliamentary lobbies and public campaigns for eradicating the slave trade ensued, followed in the next three decades by legislation to finally end the oceanic slave trade in 1807, to ameliorate the condition of slaves in the 1820s, and to abolish the institution of slavery in British territories in 1834.[45]

The intersection of antislavery and evangelicalism had its most symbolic expression in the creation of a settlement for freed slaves in Sierra Leone in 1787.[46] Sierra Leone epitomized the abolitionist goal for an Africa based on legitimate commerce and Christianity, while many in England hoped it would serve as an outlet to get rid of some of the thousands of blacks freed by a legal judgment in 1772 that ostensibly emancipated slaves who were on British soil. Sierra Leone's appeal on so many fronts shows that, as historian C. A. Bayly put it, "Commerce, religion, and domestic social control marched hand in hand."[47] Rather than the thousands of blacks anticipated, only a few hundred signed on. Disease and storms delayed their departure and lowered their morale. The first convoy arrived safely in Sierra Leone in May 1787, but within ten months, death had whittled down the intrepid group of 411 people to only 130. It was only later in 1792 and again in 1800 that the population increased when the settlement received another contingent of free blacks from Nova Scotia. After 1808, slaves who were confiscated and freed from illegal slave ships augmented the settlement. As a settlement of freed slaves, Sierra Leone was most important for planting the antislavery movement onto the African continent itself. This crucial step provided legitimacy to the international antislavery movement and gave Africans an audible voice in their own liberation.[48] As a Christian settlement, Sierra Leone symbolized the "first success story of the modern missionary movement."[49]

The nascent settlement based on freedom, agricultural industry, and Christianity spread by African agents held much potential for what could be achieved in the rest of Africa.[50] As historian Lamin Sanneh so aptly stated, the settlement was "an experiment compounded of the elements of historical tragedy, economic exploitation, foreign paternalism, religious idealism and the dream of an African utopia."[51] The idea of a model Christian community informed the missions established by voluntary missionary organizations from the late eighteenth and throughout the nineteenth century. With the heterogeneity of Sierra Leone's population, its emphasis on industry, and the centrality of Christianity as a unifying and liberating identity, the country became the prototype for mission settlements in the Cape Colony and elsewhere in Africa.

As with most great ideas, however, the objective of making Sierra Leone a model African Christian settlement was difficult to implement. The various missionary denominations that marked out their sphere of influence in Sierra Leone believed that African leadership and control would evolve only after a certain period under European tutelage. They remained ambivalent about African agency, especially in the form of an independent indigenous church. Notwithstanding the opposition or the lukewarm reception of some missionaries, west Africa, by virtue of the tremendous influx of black missionaries from Sierra Leone and the Caribbean into that region made early advances in this regard.[52] For example, between the 1860s and 1870s the Church Missionary Society took steps to hand control over to local black clergy in Sierra Leone.[53] The black missionaries who were responsible for evangelizing many of their brethren exerted and received a level of independence that their counterparts found was more difficult to duplicate elsewhere on the continent. Yet even this flowering of indigenous agency was not the prologue to the new Africa that it was intended to be. Fundamental doubts settled in about the capacity of Africans to "develop," and the late nineteenth century was characterized by an upsurge of European imperialism, spurred on by a new era of scientific racism. Critics of the missionary project in Africa questioned the authenticity and vitality of African Christianity. The rapacious conquest of African territories in the late nineteenth century tempered the robust process of indigenization and agency witnessed in the Sierra Leone experiment.

The issues of agency, Christian identity, and agricultural industry delineated in the creation of the Sierra Leone settlement were transferred and reshaped in the missionary enterprise in the Cape Colony when Moravians resumed, and LMS missionaries initiated, evangelical work there in the 1790s. The Methodists joined the fray in the 1820s and within a decade created a chain of mission settlements where missionaries and their potential converts engaged in what Jean and

John Comaroff have called, a "long conversation" about the meaning of Christianity and civilization. What links the idea of Sierra Leone with the contemporaneous missionary project in the Cape Colony is the creation of local mission settlements as part of a distinct evangelical strategy. As with Sierra Leone, mission settlements in the Cape Colony were held out as paths to African renaissance and development.

Missionaries tried to create a world apart—cells of industrious African Christians that could be showcased as examples to other Africans, financial supporters, and to any potential detractors who doubted the effectiveness of missionary work. These communities, like Sierra Leone, would demonstrate both the African capacity for development and Christianization as well as the missionary's role in facilitating this process. As Andrew F. Walls noted, Sierra Leone was the "triumphant demonstration of the repeated missionary assertion that given the same opportunities, Africans were as capable of 'improvement' as anyone else."[54] Such optimistic and idealistic plans were tempered by a profound ambivalence about the true meaning of African agency, the vitality of African Christianity, and about Africans themselves as colonial subjects pushing for the rights of citizens. Like their historical antecedents among the Native American communities in colonial America, for example, these mission communities met with mixed success and sometimes downright failure.[55] In the Cape Colony and the Caribbean, local settler concerns about controlling their slave and African laborers and maintaining a social hierarchy based partly on slavery and religion muddied the issue of Christianizing slaves and Africans.[56]

The second half of this chapter outlines the social geography of the Cape Colony and highlights the activities of the LMS between the 1790s and the 1830s. LMS evangelism left a contentious political legacy that informed the strategies of later entrants to the mission field, such as the Methodists. The strengths and shortcomings of LMS missions provided ammunition to those who stressed the futility or dangers of missionary work. Since the Methodists tried to distance themselves from the LMS, an overview of the early models available to them to craft their own evangelical strategies is important. The LMS model influenced the chain of Methodist stations in the Eastern Cape and the political stance of local Methodist missionaries. Shortcomings in these pioneer missions, in turn, influenced the creation of Farmerfield mission station as an important departure from the conventional mission blueprint.

The Cape Colony in the Age of Revolution:
A Social Geography

By the 1790s, when revolution engulfed Europe and organized missionary activity began at the Cape, the colony was transitioning from almost a century and a half of rule under the Dutch East India Company (VOC) to British rule.[57] When the revolution that convulsed Europe spilled over into the Cape, the colony became one of several Dutch territories that the British captured during the Napoleonic Wars to foil French expansion and to secure the Cape's strategic position as a route to Asia.[58] Under Dutch rule (1652–1795) the Cape had transformed itself from a refreshment station for ships to a thriving slave colony with the largest white settler population in Africa. During the early years of its rule, the VOC encouraged some of their employees to settle as farmers so that they could supply the necessary provisions that were not forthcoming from the local population.[59] Throughout the eighteenth century, as many of these settlers turned to stock farming, they slowly expanded the northern and eastern borders of the colony. Whites in various settlements on the existing frontiers of the colony, for example in Stellenbosch and Swellendam, declared frequently that their existing land grants were insufficient. For example, in 1775 residents of the district of Swellendam asserted, "That unless this district spreads further to the east and northerly, the inhabitants will not be able to procure for themselves or children any more farms."[60]

The development of stock farming spurred white settlers to move into the Cape interior, where they combined stock farming with hunting and sometimes illicit trading with Africans in the interior.[61] Those who settled closer to Cape Town and its environs became wheat and wine farmers, agricultural activities that required the importation of a heterogeneous mix of thousands of slaves from Indonesia, Ceylon, Mozambique, Madagascar, and India.[62] While the turn to slave labor was occasioned by the directive that the indigenous people at the Cape should not be enslaved, the first group of indigenous people the Dutch encountered soon came to occupy a position akin to slavery and worked alongside the imported slaves doing some of the same work. Thus, legal fiat did not prevent the subjugation of the indigenous people whom the Dutch first encountered when they came and settled at the Cape from 1652 onward.

By the 1790s the two most important divisions among whites at the Cape lay between the Dutch and British sectors of the population. One section of the existing white population was an amalgam of Dutch settlers with small contingents of people of German or French origin.[63] These early white settlers were the majority of the wine and wheat farmers who dominated the southwestern region of the Cape and the majority of stock farmers who blazed trails into the interior in the eighteenth century.[64] The early Dutch settlers at the Cape and their descendants were called "Boers," meaning "farmer" in Dutch; later in the nineteenth century they adopted an Afrikaner identity, reflecting the development of a distinct culture and heritage, and underscoring the politicization and differentiation of their identities from the British. The British at the Cape consisted primarily of the military and colonial officials, administrators, some traders and missionaries, and later on in the 1820s, unsuspecting colonists who were settled along the eastern borders of the colony as a human bulwark against African expansion.

The Africans

The Khoekhoe and San are indigenous to the region that encompassed the Cape Colony and were the first group of Africans the Dutch encountered when they set up their small refreshment station in 1652.[65] While the Khoekhoe were primarily pastoralists and the San were hunter gatherers, the socioeconomic boundaries between the two were neither static nor linear. As historian Richard Elphick noted, the relationship between the Khoekhoe and San "entailed war, trade, clientage and intermarriage."[66] Historians have collectivized both groups generally as the "Khoesan."[67] The term whites used for the Khoekhoe, "Hottentot," carries no uncertainty in its derogatory connotation, as it came to symbolize "irredeemable savagery and the very depths of human degradation."[68] Historians have completely abandoned the use of the term altogether. Throughout this book, the terms Khoekhoe and Khoesan will be used to identify these two particular groups of indigenous people of the Cape Colony; the terms "Bushman" and "Hottentot" will only be used in direct quotations.[69]

As they expanded north and east in the Cape Colony, white settlers encountered other groups of Africans whose cultures and languages differed from the Khoesan. Whereas the Khoesan spoke "click" languages (called such because of their use of implosive consonants) that constituted their own language family, Africans north and east of the Cape spoke languages related to the larger family of Bantu languages spoken in much of sub-Saharan Africa.[70] The Xhosa, who were the subject of intense Methodist evangelism in the Eastern Cape (and explored in more detail in Chapter 2), belong to the Nguni language family along with the Zulu, the Swazi, and Ndebele. The 1820s and 1830s witnessed the creation of new identities and the division of existing groups into more discrete categories. In the 1820s the term Mfengu was attached to Africans cast as refugees fleeing violence.[71] Historians have sought the origins of this violence in a host of arenas. From environmental stressors and intense competition over resources to the rise of the Zulu Kingdom and the effects of the slave trade in the Delagoa Bay area, historians have reexamined the evidence to explain the nature and range of regional conflict and population dispersals in the 1820s and 1830s.[72] Whatever the origins of the violence and migrations, it is clear that dispossession by white settlers compounded the hardships of various population groups and the label of "Fingoes" aggregated people from a variety of backgrounds. The Mfengu were among the most important refugee groups to emerge from this period given the subsequent efforts to create a specific historical narrative for them as a distinct ethnic group "liberated" by the British from the "oppression" they endured when they sought refuge with the Xhosa. The Mfengu, resettled in Eastern Cape locales in 1835, came to be represented as British loyalists because of their military support in the various outbreaks of wars after 1835. Missionaries and the colonial government painted the Mfengu as more receptive to Christianity and the accoutrements of European civilization than their African counterparts.

As historian Timothy Stapleton noted, "the Fingoes became loyal colonial soldiers, prosperous peasant producers, and devout Christians."[73]

The Sotho-Tswana linguistic category covers a range of people who were also dispersed during the upheavals of the 1820s. Previously conglomerations of people speaking closely related languages and sharing a common culture and ancestry, the Sotho-Tswana became more distinct in the 1820s and 1830s when war and land alienation spurred migration and squeezed people from the lands they used to occupy.[74] Throughout the nineteenth century mission stations at the Cape Colony were constituted of amalgamations of these various groups, making for polyglot, heterogeneous communities, perhaps on an unprecedented scale at the Cape. Farmerfield, for example, had a motley group of ex-slaves, Sotho-Tswana, Xhosa, and Mfengu residents. War and migration brought disparate groups together in mission communities where missionaries hoped they would reconstitute their identities based on a common culture of Christianity.

The terms white colonists used to designate the Africans they encountered as they expanded north and east in the Cape varied tremendously before the orthography of each language was standardized. Whether the Africans they encountered along and beyond the borders of the Cape were Xhosa, Zulu, Sotho-Tswana, or another ethnic group, whites sometimes indiscriminately resorted to the term "Kaffir," which means "infidel" in Arabic, to identify them—with varied spellings such as Kafir and Caffre. Later they glossed these groups as "natives" and as "Bantu." When specific ethnonyms were used, they were further glossed as "Bechuana" for Tswana, "Basuto" for Sotho, "Xosa" for Xhosa, and "Fingo" for Mfengu. Whites were also fond of affixing the suffix "land" to ethnonyms to designate geographical location, hence: "Fingoland," "Bechuanaland," and "Xhosaland," to name a few. In addition, the term "Kaffir" gave rise to such generalities as "Kaffraria" and "Kaffirland" to demarcate the land or place where "Kaffirs" lived. In this book, the term "African" will be used to refer to all indigenous people in South Africa, while specific references to ethnic identities and geographical locations will be used in the relevant contexts.

For the purposes of this book, perhaps the most important distinctions between the Khoesan and other Africans that whites encountered at the Cape lay in the extent of the socioeconomic, demographic, and political collapse of the Khoesan in the wake of colonization. By the time white settlers engaged the Xhosa in their first frontier conflict in the 1770s, the Khoesan had endured more than a century of white contact, conflict, and subordination that many of them experienced as a catastrophic transformation of their way of life. An economy based on pastoralism, and hence frequent mobility in search of water and pasture, inhibited the development of strong politicized centers of power, and made wealth in cattle highly susceptible to drought, disease, war, and theft.[75] In the geopolitical struggles over access to pasturage, hunting grounds, and water resources, whites invariably came out the victors.[76] Economic subordination had brought many into the service of white farmers, where, as Elphick pointed out, "their expertise in the training and handling of draught animals prepared them for plowing and driving wagons on arable farms, while their skills in the management of flocks and herds ensured their importance to white graziers."[77] The slow yet progressive dwindling of herds, the whites' monopolization of the best pasture lands, incorporation into the colonial economy under unfavorable circumstances, and the smallpox epidemic in 1713 devastated the Khoekhoe. These catastrophic developments differentiated the experiences of the Khoesan from other groups of Africans at the Cape by the close of the eighteenth century and rendered them extremely vulnerable. Missions played an important role in helping the Khoesan to reconstruct their material livelihood and adjust their worldviews to make sense of their experiences, in much the same way that slaves in the New World, former slaves in Sierra Leone, or Britons in the throes of the industrial revolution had to do.[78]

Africans on the eastern and northern frontiers of the Cape Colony did not experience the demographic and cultural catastrophe that characterized the Khoesan interaction with the Dutch. The Khoesan encounter approximates the experiences of Native Americans in colonial America and represents an extreme form of the sort of subordination and assimilation that exemplified the colonial enterprise all over the world. Africans on the eastern frontier and interior of the Cape Colony proved to be formidable military foes, refusing to accept colonial domination as a fait accompli even when defeat on the battlefield and land confiscation suggested otherwise. As white colonists pushed the official eastern borders of the Cape Colony in search of land, laborers, and water, they came into contact with the Xhosa, who were undertaking a complementary expansion westward toward the colony. By the 1770s the Fish River became a major scene of conflict, both as a literal site of endemic warfare and a glaring symbol of failed colonial policies. Both the Dutch and British governments unsuccessfully tried to administer the river as a no man's land.[79] For a century, the Xhosa, other African groups, and whites met on the battlefield in a series of nine wars of dispossession. Yet even when their traditional leaders had been killed, exiled, or deposed, and their powers profaned or otherwise undermined, the Xhosa maintained the integrity of their cultures and of their languages.

While the Xhosa and the colonists were engaged in the third War of Dispossession, the Zulu kingdom had risen from its infancy and through a series of intermittent battles had established itself as a formidable kingdom by the 1820s. Historians have debated how much the Zulu polity contributed to creating the waves of refugees streaming into the Cape Colony in the 1820s, yet all agree that political upheavals dispersed Africans throughout southeastern Africa. Some of these refugees, including the Mfengu, having experienced deep inroads into their political and material security, turned to missionaries and the colonial government for assistance and in the process redefined the Mfengu identity ascribed to them as refugees. Alliance with the colony in subsequent wars, as well as their relationship with missionaries, generated an enduring stereotype of the Mfengu as British loyalists par excellence, and the various resettlement schemes the British devised for them were lauded as examples of British philanthropy and goodwill toward a downtrodden people. Sotho-Tswana-speaking peoples also scattered throughout the Cape Colony, a tremendous boon to mission stations that received a huge influx of people seeking temporary and permanent refuge from the ravages of war.

In sum, the Cape population consisted of whites divided primarily between those of Dutch and British backgrounds. Centuries of assimilation and contact as well as miscegenation with Khoekhoe and slaves produced Africans relegated to a "Coloured" group whose identity became more distinct and politicized after the emancipation of slaves in 1834. An important group of Khoekhoe had mixed with the Xhosa and came to be called Gonaqua. Other Africans were divided primarily by their ethnolinguistic classification. The Xhosa, primarily, and the Mfengu, Sotho, and Tswana formed a polyglot community at Farmerfield in the nineteenth century. By the 1860s and 1880s, however, economic opportunities associated with the discovery of gold and diamonds led to the out-migration of many inhabitants and to the homogenization of Farmerfield as primarily a Xhosa and Mfengu community.

Christianity at the Cape and Pioneer Missionary Efforts

Despite the heterogeneity of the African populations at the Cape, colonial rule generated a striking concordance of activities and policies that delimited their experiences of disruptive and sometimes violent encounters. The Cape Colony stood apart from other areas in Africa in that it was under continuous Dutch rule from 1652 until 1795, when the British captured it as a spoil of the Napoleonic Wars. Most other areas in Africa, by contrast, did not experience formal colonialism until the surge of late nineteenth-century imperialism. As white settlement progressed steadily, most groups of Africans made the transition from hearing about white encroachment to experiencing it directly. In the many decades before the Moravians and the LMS undertook pioneer work at the Cape, Christian evangelical work among the Khoekhoe and slaves was minimal and nonexistent among other Africans on the borders of the Cape Colony. The Dutch Reformed Church (DRC), as the established church of the colony, exercised control over religious expression at the Cape and did little to attract any particular group of Africans to convert.[80]

The Calvinist doctrine of the Reformed Church, with its emphasis on the notion of an elect group that had a special contract with God, played an integral part in demarcating racial difference at the Cape, though historians disagree on just how much it encouraged the development of a distinct Afrikaner identity, and how much it facilitated the hardening of race relations, especially on the frontier.[81] At the most basic level, the DRC reinforced the difference between Christian and "heathen," and as the refreshment station matured into a colony, the term "Christian" was used interchangeably with "European."[82] As theologian Jonathan Gerstner noted in an exploration of Christianity during the Dutch era at the Cape, the Dutch Reformed Church "contributed greatly to the formation of a distinctive identity among the white settlers and to their conviction of superiority to indigenous peoples and slaves."[83]

The DRC did little to alter or mitigate the beliefs and attitudes that underpinned the local settler use of Christianity to demarcate themselves as white, superior, and dominant. At the Cape the evolution of the beliefs that Christianity conferred certain civic and legal rights on the worshipper, and that a correlation existed between baptism and civil liberties, did much to inhibit the baptism and Christian instruction of slaves. Slaves with some white ancestry were sometimes proffered this privilege. Slave children satisfied these criteria in greater numbers than adult slaves.[84] White attitudes toward slaves were extended to the rest of the African populations they encountered. Beyond their pastoral work with local white settlers, the Dutch Reformed Church did little to evangelize the population of the Cape Colony. Consequently, the field for missionary enterprise remained wide open.[85] The Moravians, under George Schmidt, initiated missionary work at the Cape among the Khoekhoe in 1737 and established the first mission station with eighteen Khoekhoe at Baviaanskloof, later renamed Genadendal in 1805. Local Cape settlers did not subscribe to the idea of universal redemption and the DRC clergy disapproved of Schmidt's work. When Schmidt proceeded to baptize his initial batch of five converts, he was banished from the Cape in 1744.

In the 1790s the Moravians (United Brethren) resumed their efforts and the London Missionary Society (LMS) initiated missionary work in a colony now under British control. In the 1820s the WMMS and the (Scottish) Glasgow Missionary Society (GMS) commenced their pioneer work.[86] Despite the ardor and commitment that heralded missionary work at the turn of the nineteenth century, the Cape Colony was a challenging field for missionary work. By the 1820s the Colony had developed into a racially stratified society where whiteness came to be firmly associated with Christianity and moral and spiritual superiority over Africans. Missionaries from all denominations found themselves in the midst of a protracted and increasingly aggressive colonial encounter that devastated the Khoekhoe and was now engaging other Africans on the borders of the Cape Colony. By the time missionary societies began work at the Cape, therefore, the general outlines of the conflict over land alienation, access to and mobility of labor had already been set. These struggles had already passed the threshold of becoming the most contentious political issue on the eastern frontier of the colony. Between 1799 and 1802, the overlapping of a Khoekhoe rebellion with the third War of Dispossession between the Xhosa and the colonists invoked the worst fears about Africans uniting to fight against colonialism.[87]

Ultimately, the rebellions on both fronts proved unsuccessful in changing the status quo. Land alienation continued apace and the economic subordination of the Khoekhoe and Xhosa persisted. Politically and socioeconomically weakened, most of the Khoekhoe within the colony were still drawn or forced into Dutch colonial society as farm laborers and servants. Others continued to serve in the special regiment designated for the Khoekhoe, the Cape Corps.[88] Mission stations provided some with an alternative place of residence. The settlement of some of the former rebels at the newly established Bethelsdorp mission of the LMS riled many colonists who did not want the mission to harbor individuals who were so willing to bear arms against them.

Neither the resumption of missionary work at Baviaanskloof (Genadendal) nor the creation of the Bethelsdorp mission in 1802 started on a sanguine note. In the early years of its existence, white farmers believed Bethelsdorp, as well as the Moravian station of Genadendal, would allow Khoekhoe to avoid farm labor. The journals of the Moravian missionaries H. Marsveld, D. Schwinn, and J. C. Kühnel are filled with testimonies of the various methods whites used to dissuade the Khoekhoe from going to mission stations. While visiting the old grounds of the previous Moravian mission in 1792 the "Hottentot" guide told the missionaries that the local farmers had warned individuals that the missionaries would at first be "friendly, but if they went to them, several others would come and sell them as slaves to Batavia" (Indonesia).[89] As they settled into the daily task of reestablishing the mission, the missionaries found many of the farmers inhospitable and unwilling to sell them vegetables.[90] As the mission attracted more Khoekhoe, farmers continued to use manipulative and sometimes cruel tactics to prevent their workers from going to the mission. According to the missionaries, one farmer kept the two-month-old baby of one of his workers to prevent the mother from going to the mission station. In another case, a young man was beaten for asking to go to the mission when his contract expired.[91] Others claimed that they were told the missionaries were teaching about the devil.[92]

The belief that missionaries would take away their laborers was the source of much farmer hostility toward the missions in their early years, but this specific animosity to the mission abated somewhat when they realized that economic impoverishment still pushed many Khoekhoe into the labor market. Notwithstanding the reassurance white farmers received that they would still have access to workers, the issue of labor remained contentious. The existence of mission communities mediated the power white farmers had over the mobility of their African laborers. The issue of control and supply of labor had become even more pressing after 1808 with the abolition of the oceanic slave trade.[93] Moreover, although many mission residents still worked on white farms, they used the mission stations to either evade the most onerous aspects of their labor contracts or to periodically avoid labor for whites altogether.[94] An alternative place of residence also gave male laborers far more control over their wives and daughters, who were usually used as leverage in labor contracts.[95] Missionary critique of the terms of labor contracts executed between white farmers and their laborers also enraged white settlers. The missionaries inveighed against the farmers' practice of giving their laborers alcohol in lieu of wages, a practice called the *tot* system that contributed to alcoholism. They also pinpointed the heightened use of incentives such as tobacco and alcohol as harmful to the overall interests of the Khoekhoe.[96]

Khoekhoe participation in Christian rites and adoption of some aspects of white lifestyles slowly challenged one of the prime markers whites used to distinguish themselves from their Khoekhoe and slave laborers. Christian conversion, along with the ability to read and write, had some leveling effects in putting Khoekhoe, slave, and other laborers on the same spiritual plane with their masters, if not in daily practice, then in principle.[97] Local settlers did not welcome this wave of missionary zeal that attempted to make Africans literate and Christian. For example, many white farmers in the vicinity of the second incarnation of the Moravian settlement did not want their laborers to withdraw periodically from farm labor, much less learn how to read and write.[98]

In an environment where Christianity served as an important marker of identity and superiority and where whites did not have to even profess their faith to be considered Christian, it is not surprising that some were not pleased that missionaries were paying so much attention to people they considered beneath them. The Moravian missionaries asserted that since some of the farmers were several days' journey from the closest church, they "begrudge the Hottentots hearing the word more often (than they do)."[99] Moreover, since many of the white farmers and their children only possessed a modicum of education, it is not surprising that many would resist missionary labors among the servile population.[100] As the Moravian missionaries pointed out in 1792, "Many Christian children do not know a single letter and grow old unable to read the word of God."[101]

In the early phase of LMS work, a few missionaries went beyond the call for spiritual egalitarianism. They flouted the racial and social hierarchy by getting sexually involved with and marrying African women. For example, Johannes Van der Kemp, the first superintendent of LMS missions in South Africa who established the Bethelsdorp mission, married a young slave girl; that she was fourteen years old and forty years his junior caused some alarm, and her slave status made his actions even more controversial. His colleague and successor, James Read, followed suit and married a sixteen-year-old Khoekhoe girl in 1803. In local circles, Van der Kemp and Read's marriages caused some consternation about formal interracial unions. Yet interracial sexual encounters were certainly not odd in a colony where sexual unions between colonists, Khoesan, and slaves had occurred for more than a century by the 1790s, when missionaries arrived on the scene. The mixed-race individuals resulting from these unions were usually incorporated into the group with the lower status, or formed an intermediary group.

The establishment of circuit courts to hear Khoesan complaints against the farmers, through Van der Kemp and Read's initiative, heightened the existing tensions between the LMS missionaries and the local whites enraged by these actions. Despite few convictions being obtained, the mere existence of these courts spawned further animosity toward the LMS missionaries. Although these developments cemented for the missionaries a reputation as "negrophiles," the era of marriages across the color line was a relatively short-lived phase that was no longer common by the 1820s. When James Read had an extramarital affair and impregnated a young woman in his congregation, argued historian Julia Wells in an excellent overview of the scandal, his imbroglio provided the perfect pretext for the LMS to redirect the course of LMS missionary work at the Cape.[102] Although some advocacy for the rights of Africans continued, the LMS capitalized on Read's behavior to reassert clearer boundaries between white missionaries and African congregants. Hearings, reprimands, demotions, and a general reconfiguration of LMS mission work followed on the heels of the sexual scandals that rocked the LMS missionary establishment in the Cape Colony. What remained of the earlier phase of LMS work was a strong tradition of advocacy for civil liberties that escalated in the 1820s and coincided with the robust antislavery movement in Britain.

Even with the reorganization of missionary work, prominent LMS missionaries in the 1820s continued to portray the Khoekhoe as a downtrodden group of indigenes, while local white settlers continued to view the Khoekhoe primarily as potential laborers and the missionaries as meddlers. In the early decades of missionary work, the slaves and Khoekhoe who later constituted the "Colored" population were accorded a sympathetic audience with the missionaries, which was extended to the international humanitarian cause in the 1820s. It was an international audience they never had before, or since. LMS missionaries spoke about, wrote about, and tried to effect legal redress for the ill treatment of the indigenous population at the Cape. Efforts to emancipate slaves and the Khoekhoe from the yoke of Dutch servitude were included in the general British antislavery cause. As the only British colony on the African continent with a system of slavery akin to the institution practiced in the Atlantic world, the Cape Colony endured the suppression of the slave trade and the amelioration and eventual abolition of slavery at the same time as the Sierra Leone experiment.[103] Cape slaveholders experienced the antislavery movement, and the attempts to emancipate the Khoekhoe from virtual serfdom, as an assault on their way of life. They complained that they were under siege and expressed as much furor about antislavery as their counterparts did in other British slave colonies. Any white person at the Cape displeased with the importation of humanitarian sentiments via imperial edicts could vent their dissatisfaction on the local missionaries who advocated for ameliorating the condition of slaves and the Khoekhoe.

When, in 1819, John Philip assumed the helm of the LMS as the new superintendent, Cape settlers were introduced to yet another prominent missionary personality whose political advocacy riled them. Philip, a Scottish minister, worked diligently to remove the legal barriers that prevented Khoekhoe from maintaining control over their mobility and selling their labor on the market as free agents.

Philip's advocacy was one that emphasized the importance of the civilizing mission in addition to the evangelical imperative. The Khoekhoe, as the quintessential victims of white domination, were to be given an equal opportunity for personal salvation; in the process they would also adopt a relatively civilized lifestyle they had not been afforded after more than a century of contact with the Dutch. Even though he represented a new era of LMS missionary policy, Philip came to be reviled as much as, if not more than, James Read.

Various missionaries at the Cape, even when they disagreed on whether Christianity should precede or accompany civilization, agreed that the Dutch had contributed little to any civilizing effect—whether by conscious effort or cultural osmosis. The British viewed the Dutch as comparatively poor instruments of the civilizing mission. To make matters worse, some of the Dutch in the outlying areas were even thought to be in danger of "going native" themselves and were in need of their own civilizing mission. Philip's fundamental belief that civilization should accompany Christianity can be seen in light of the experiments such as Sierra Leone that held out a particular model of progress and improvement for Africa as a whole. Now that the LMS had stamped out James Read's brand of "going native," it could pursue a much more straightforward transfer of European culture and civilization to the Cape through missionary work.

Philip and other missionaries demonstrated tremendous optimism and ardor in their belief that Africans could be elevated to some level of civilization through a modicum of education and Christianity. Africans would take bold steps toward civilization if they were allowed to sell their labor on the open market, own property, adopt Western-style housing, Christianity, clothing, and notions of cleanliness, and acquire basic literacy. These were among the accoutrements of civilization that Philip propagated in his book, *Researches*.[104] Philip's appeals to the humanitarian-minded British public and to colonial officials coincided with the government promulgation of legislation to emancipate the Khoesan from virtual serfdom. Ordinance 50 of 1828 was intended to liberate the "forlorn remnants of the former possessors of South Africa" by eradicating the legal restrictions to land ownership and repealing the pass laws that inhibited mobility and bolstered the virtual enslavement of the Khoesan.[105] In 1834 the British emancipated slaves in their territories, usually with the proviso of a mandatory four-year apprenticeship period. In the Cape Colony, slave-owners and others who used Africans as laborers were dealt an additional blow when not only slavery was abolished, but their attempts to reinstate vagrancy laws for the Khoesan were forestalled.

The passage of these legislations was a triumphant moment for missionaries and other members of Cape society with humanitarian outlooks. It was a moment full of possibility for former slaves and Khoesan, and full of euphoria for humanitarians. The people who were to be the main beneficiaries of these legislations understood their significance insofar as it affected their material circumstances and their daily lives. In light of the economic subordination and racial discrimination that continued to characterize African experiences, both Ordinance 50 as well as slave emancipation proved limited as measures to radically alter the material circumstances and beliefs that underpinned white predominance at the Cape. Even humanitarians lost some of their euphoria when former slaves did not turn out to be the industrious protégés they had expected. Still, the moment was full of hope and possibility. Perhaps more than any other event that followed the passage of Ordinance 50, the creation of the Kat River Settlement in 1829 seemed to fulfill some of the material aspirations of the Khoekhoe.

Born of the desire to situate another buffer group between colonists and the Xhosa, the Kat River Settlement addressed both the imperatives of frontier policy and the Khoekhoe desire for a measure of land restitution. As commissioner general for the Eastern Districts and architect of the settlement, Andries Stockenström, declared the settlement as the "Hottentot Magna Carta."[106] Stockenström also believed that the settlement would "give practical effect" to Ordinance 50.[107] Thus began an important experiment in the social and economic rehabilitation of the Khoesan through the creation of an independent agricultural community that would showcase what Africans could accomplish if vested with property rights. Experiments like these were going on at various mission settlements within and beyond the borders of the Cape Colony, but all eyes were on the Kat River Settlement.

Between the 1790s and the 1820s, the LMS found it difficult to conduct their missionary work without addressing the social and economic disadvantages their African congregants faced in a racially stratified society. Their political advocacy on behalf of a heterogeneous group of Africans left a legacy of politicized evangelism that marred the perception of missionary work in some Cape colonial circles and distinguished them from other missionary societies at the Cape. When the Methodist missionaries entered the South African mission field in the 1820s, they also found themselves in the unenviable position of mediating between white colonial society and their African congregants. The changing frontier of the Cape Colony, and with it the expropriation of African territory, created waves of refugees that initially flocked to mission stations and swelled their congregations. Once mission stations gained congregants, however, colonial warfare ceased to be a boon to evangelical work, especially when the theater of war spilled over to these locales.

Finding themselves in such a complicated racial and political milieu, Methodist missionaries at the Cape sought a balance between LMS-style political advocacy and evangelism. One response was to avoid duplicating LMS work and explore areas beyond the borders of the Cape Colony that had a small or no missionary presence. As a result of this deliberate policy, the WMMS created a chain of missions in southeastern Africa and with it an important sphere of influence among independent African chiefdoms. This strategy hardly spared them involvement in politics, however. Methodist missionaries not only served as arbiters between African chiefdoms and white colonists, but by inveighing against certain African cultural practices, they found themselves in the midst of political power struggles in the very chiefdoms they tried to convert to Christianity. In the process, mission settlements became separate political entities, in competition with independent African chiefdoms. Chapter 2 now turns to the creation of a chain of Methodist mission stations between 1823 and 1830 as a precursor to the far more ambitious enterprise that became Farmerfield.

Pioneer Models of Methodist Missionary Enterprise

The Chain of Missions and the Albany Settlement, 1820–1838

Genesis

Upon arriving in the Cape Colony in 1820 as minister to a party of British settlers, the future superintendent of Wesleyan missions, William Shaw (see Figure 2.1), predicted an auspicious start for Methodist missionary work. Shaw's optimism was grounded in his own informal survey of local missionary endeavors. Despite the pioneer efforts of the Moravians and the London Missionary Society (LMS) that made South Africa "one of the most intensively 'occupied' fields of Christian mission in the world," Shaw surmised the Cape Colony and its frontiers still held unbounded possibilities for Christian evangelization.[1] Although the LMS and Moravians, with twelve and three mission settlements respectively, had established an important sphere of influence *within* the colony itself, the Cape's eastern and northern frontiers remained relatively untouched. Shaw's gaze was a physically expansive one, encompassing a swath of territory that his political contemporaries later envisioned as the Cape to Cairo route. Shaw further assessed from his vantage point in the Eastern Cape that besides Latakoo, site of early LMS evangelizing efforts from 1801, "there is not a single missionary station between the place of my residence and the northern extremity of the Red Sea; nor are there any people professedly Christian with the exception of those of Abyssinia." After surveying the mission field and reviewing the challenges other missionary societies faced, Shaw selected the Cape's eastern frontier as the best site for a Methodist "chain of stations" (see Map 3).

William Shaw responded with alacrity and creativity to the opportunity presented him. The chain of six mission stations founded through his indefatigable efforts, and those of his Methodist colleagues between 1823 and 1833, carved out an unrivaled sphere of influence for the WMMS in the Eastern Cape. At the outset, however, his plan hinged far more on accident than on design, and his confidence rested on an idea that the Eastern Cape was a tabula rasa, rather than on any grandiose missionary plan. An 1820 British emigration scheme had brought between 4,000 and 5,000 white settlers, including the twenty-two-year-old Shaw, to the troubled eastern frontier of the Cape Colony.[2] Here the 1820 settlers served as human buffers on behalf of the colony, occupying land confiscated from the Xhosa who saw the Eastern Cape territories as their land. Each settler party comprising one hundred or more families was allowed one minister from their own denomination and Shaw had used his contacts to persuade the Missionary Committee of the WMMS to allow him to fill one of these positions.

Shaw and Hezekiah Sephton's party of British emigrants settled in the Salem valley some twenty-five miles south of Grahamstown, itself 400 miles from Cape Town. Salem, Shaw wrote in his journal, "is a delightful valley through which the river [Assegaibos] runs in a curious serpentine manner. There are two or three smaller valleys and in each a few of our people are located"[3] (see Map 1 and Map 3). Between 1811 and 1812, almost eight years before Shaw made this observation, locales near Salem were far from picturesque and romantic. The only river that concerned the colonial government at the time was the Fish River, which was envisioned as a no-man's-land that would keep the Xhosa and whites to their respective side of the border (see Map 1). However, the Fish River having proven to be a wholly ineffective natural barrier, the colonial government sought new ways to deal with what was becoming an intractable problem. The result was a new policy of total war whose aims were not only to push the Xhosa beyond the border of the colony but also to instill "a proper degree of terror" in them. Terror came in the form of a scorched earth policy that burned crops and habitations—creating scores of human and animal refugees in its wake—as well as the new military post of Grahamstown.[4] By 1820 the Cape Colony recruited British immigrants to settle in the Eastern Cape who, unlike the soldiers garrisoned in Grahamstown, understood little of their "human buffer" status when they signed up for passage to the Cape and land.

The soldiers stationed in Grahamstown presented a foreboding and constant reminder of the defensive purpose of the town. The descent of 10,000 Xhosa warriors on Grahamstown in 1819 had demonstrated that even the tactics of total war could not dissuade them of their right to the territory, leading the colonial government to then turn to the creation of human settlements as military buffer zones. Grahamstown, Salem, and other frontier settlements were thus designed to create a human cordon against Xhosa incursions, a fact those in Britain encouraging emigration masked behind more lofty promises of land and new opportunities at the Cape. The defensive purposes of Grahamstown, Salem, and the other frontier settlements remained far from the immediate concerns of the settlers, even as they were front and center of colonial frontier policy.

Even when Shaw and other 1820s settlers later assessed the relationship between their claims in the Albany area and African discontent over losing this territory, it did not change their sense of entitlement to the land, or their indignation when war broke out again in 1834. In the interim between settlement in 1820 and the outbreak of war in 1834, the new colonial population in Albany became the largest concentration of British settlers in any part of the colony. In acclimating to life in the Eastern Cape, the narratives of the 1820s settlers read like scripts from accidental tourists anxious to recreate as much of England as they could on an alien landscape. As part of the Cape Colony's white population, they quickly assimilated the social norms that elevated whites to an elite status above their African neighbors, even when economic circumstances made them far from elite. Three miles from the area Shaw settled was the sheep farm Klipheuvel, part of an earlier attempt to settle Dutch farmers in the area in order to have them serve as a human buffer. Shaw would eventually purchase Klipheuvel in 1838 in order to establish the Farmerfield mission, but at the moment of his settlement in 1820 his gaze and his plans for African missions were centered elsewhere. Since Salem, other settler towns, and the future Farmerfield were located near the border of the Cape Colony and several independent African chiefdoms, the Albany district would be the "key to Caffreland, a country abounding with 'heathen' inhabitants."[5] Shaw would work for fifteen years beyond the Cape colonial frontier before he considered establishing an African mission station a few miles from Salem.

The WMMS, created in 1813, was just a decade old by the time Shaw established his first African mission in 1823, and was still engaged in significant proselytization in its home missions. Although Shaw has his gaze on the African population immediately beyond the border, he firmly believed, as a matter of policy, that it was important to establish support for African missions among the white settler population. Yet evangelism among the white population in Grahamstown and the small settler communities in its vicinity was not without its own challenges. Here the obstacle was not "heathenism" or "barbarism," but secularism. As Shaw lamented in his journal, "the trials, cares and vicissitudes which always attend the first adventures in a New Colony, have unhappily counteracted its influence and too generally produced worldly mindedness—violation of the Sabbath and an awful disrelish for the solemnities of religion."[6]

Shaw also complained about the lack of any minister in town and described both the African and white population as "low in drunkenness, lewdness and other deadly sins." He and a small cohort of local preachers drawn from the white population ministered to small congeries of the English, Dutch, Khoekhoe, and other African populations. Building on the existing cohort of settlers who were already practicing Methodism when they emigrated in 1820, Shaw and his colleagues first erected humble, then more impressive, churches throughout the Eastern Cape. By the time Baptists and Anglicans entered the Eastern Cape, the Methodists had gained the best foothold among whites, wielded the most influence among them, and by the 1840s, had built more churches than any other religious body.[7]

While Shaw was laying the foundations of Methodism in the Albany area, his "eye was constantly fixed on Kaffraria (the area immediately beyond the border of the Cape Colony), as a great field for future missions."[8] However, before he could proceed with his mission to Africans, whom he described as a "'heathen' and barbarous race of people," Shaw wanted to consolidate a white base in Albany. Disagreeing with a few of his missionary colleagues who wanted to focus their immediate evangelical efforts on Africans, Shaw asserted that any work among Africans would be more successful by "having a considerable body of European Christians so near, who would be likely to sympathize with us, and in various ways aid our labors." The LMS missionary Henry Calderwood, whose own society often infuriated local whites, concurred with Shaw on the importance and long-term benefits of linking evangelical work among both the white population in the Cape Colony and the black population within and beyond its borders.[9] As Shaw predicted, the white constituency of the Albany district did indeed become important supporters of Methodist missionary work. Yet this intimacy between Methodist missionaries and the local white settlers sometimes compromised their objectivity when war broke out between Africans and the colonists in 1834, 1846, and yet again in 1850. Just as LMS missionaries had found it difficult to avoid the politics that brought Khoekhoe to their missions seeking refuge, Methodist missionaries found it difficult to isolate their evangelism from frontier politics. The different politics of the two missionary societies thus came to be encapsulated in the contentious relationship between two of the most influential missionaries of the time—John Philip and William Shaw and their constituencies.[10]

In the annals of protestant missionary enterprise, each missionary society has had its institutional reputation and its distinct personalities, some serving as cautionary tales, others as paragons of Christian evangelism. Some of these interpretations bordered on hagiography, with historians' interventions serving as a crucial counterpoint to the official portraits. For many of these missionaries their fame and symbolism were far out of proportion to any actual number of souls converted—David Livingstone being the prime example of a missionary whose influence, personality, and symbolism far outweighed the actual number of Africans won over to Christianity. Both the political landscape and the personalities of the missionaries proved mercurial. Some missionaries' sense of vocation was lost in the field. Having championed his slave congregants in the Caribbean, William Shrewsbury's (see Figure 2.2) posting to South Africa and his interactions with the Xhosa seemed to eventually pulverize any sense of liberal humanitarianism. As Richard Price put it, "The man who had come to Southern Africa as a cultural relativist left South Africa as a hardened racist who rejected the possibility of their [Xhosa] salvation without coercive subjugation."[11] Others, like the LMS Henry Calderwood, also grew disenchanted, but redirected their energies and worked for the colonial government.[12]

Given his seminal role in creating a sphere of influence for Methodism in the Eastern Cape, William Shaw was such a figure. Even with his grandiose ambitions,

Shaw was far from a missionary colossus, though he was certainly a visionary who came to command tremendous respect and moral capital among his missionary colleagues and among local whites who were asked to contribute and support the missionary cause. In a political climate where the activities of the LMS especially had brought controversy and conflict to the missionary enterprise, Shaw's enduring legacy and reputation was a significant achievement. Beyond his important work among white settlers in the Albany area, the makings of Shaw's legacy in pioneering African missions began among the Xhosa.

Encountering Xhosa Society

By June 1823, when the Cape colonial government finally granted William Shaw the approval to pursue an African mission, he had already conducted several evangelical reconnaissance tours of chiefdoms beyond the frontier. During these exploratory visits beyond the Cape frontier, Shaw evaluated African chiefs' receptivity to mission work and assessed whether the existing religious landscape would facilitate or stunt the growth of Christianity. In the estimation of Shaw and his missionary colleagues, African religious beliefs consisted mostly of a rudimentary notion of a high god and superstitious beliefs in witches. When he went to visit a Xhosa prisoner in the Grahamstown jail and asked him questions about God, for example, Shaw used his responses as "melancholy proof of the need his countrymen have of the Gospel." The prisoner declared to Shaw that he heard there was a God, but had never seen him; that he knew nothing about what happens after death.[13] The more Africans he encountered, the more convinced Shaw became that they were bereft of Christian conceptions of God.[14] Reflecting on his pioneer days in the 1820s, Shaw told an investigative committee on aborigines that he found the Xhosa in "an exceedingly ignorant and degraded condition."[15] While Shaw tried to collect as much data on ordinary Xhosa as possible, he fixed his gaze on chiefs whom he determined could be either great enablers of or serious impediments to missionary work. Like generations of white missionaries before him, Shaw realized immediately that securing approval and conversion of African chiefs would enhance the legitimacy of a new faith in the wider community and serve as a boon to the number of congregants filling the pews. And like his predecessors, Shaw found that the strategy of convincing African chiefs to forego the prerogatives of their positions and to proclaim a foreign faith was as an evangelical cul-de-sac.

The Xhosa, by the 1820s, were a loose conglomeration of several autonomous Eastern Cape chiefdoms geographically and politically divided from the eighteenth century in two main branches: the AmaRharhabe in the Ciskei and AmaGcaleka in the Transkei. These chiefdoms vied with each other for power, people, cattle, land, and influence—violating their own rules of succession and seniority when necessary. They drew any other group they saw as potential allies (other

Africans like the Khoekhoe, white settlers, the colonial government, missionaries) into their internal political struggles. At the apex of Xhosa political structure stood the chief, who, as guardian of his people, was responsible for declaring
war, allotting land, resolving disputes, and levying fines. Kinship governed
Xhosa political and social relations from the highest level of the chief down to
his subjects. Xhosa lineages traced descent from a common ancestor along patri-
lineal lines. A number of these lineages sharing a common ancestry comprised a
clan, which observed exogamous rules of marriage. Xhosa chiefs generally origi-
nated from the same royal clan while the rest of the chiefdom descended from
more common clans. The most basic unit of Xhosa social and economic organization was the homestead, usually comprising eight to fifteen individual households. Since marriage outside of the clan dispersed kinsmen all over the
chiefdom, any given homestead had households both related and unrelated to
each other.

As historian J.B. Peires explained, Xhosa households would have "neighbors
who were not clansmen and clansmen who were not neighbors."[16] One of these
household heads, usually the eldest member of the lineage, was selected to represent the interests of the other households in the homestead. As a group, these
men often served as councilors to the chief and acted as intermediaries between
the chief and his subjects. Spiritual matters fell within the direct purview of
household and homestead heads, and were not only an individual concern for
each homestead member. The entertaining new ideas the missionaries introduced
had significant implications not only about the existence of God, but also about
women's roles, agricultural production, marriage patterns, residential rights, and
a host of fundamental issues beyond the spiritual realm.

Although chiefs represented the ultimate authority among the Xhosa,
homestead and household heads maintained a considerable degree of autonomy from the chief, and wielded power in their own domestic spheres.[17]
The need to consult with councilors and secure consent from the wider population limited the autocratic tendencies of Xhosa chieftaincy. When disputes
arose, commoners and councilors had some latitude to vote with their feet, at
times shifting their allegiance to rival chiefs. Despite the limits of their political domination, the power of Xhosa chiefs was conspicuous, both materially
and ritually. Chiefs usually had more wives, ate better food, accumulated more
and better quality cattle than commoners, and lived in larger, more spacious
accommodations.[18] Once Christian evangelism got underway, the tangible
power chiefs held as well as the habitual missionary practice of recruiting political leaders ensured they remained major actors in the battle for control of
sacred power.

The chiefly entourage of wives, children, and subjects had its counterpart at
the household level. Since the survival of the lineage depended on reproduction,
Xhosa society epitomized polygynous marital unions. Ideal households consisted of a senior lineage head, as many wives as he could afford, and his progeny.

In the household, as in wider Xhosa society, gender and age determined who held authority and performed certain tasks. Men wielded power over women and their dependents; the eldest members of society held authority over juniors. Building a home was one of the few tasks where men and women worked cooperatively. Dwellings consisted of beehive-shaped homes built in a semicircle around a cattle-byre and granary. Men focused on creating a framework for the house from tree branches while the women plastered the wall and floors with clay and dung and provided grass thatching for the roof.[19] While it was men's duty to tend cattle, work on animal hides, and make ironware, women made pots and wove baskets. Women's domestic duties included fetching water, collecting firewood, gathering and preparing food, brewing beer, reapplying cow dung to the home, and tending to the children. Besides the periodic heavy work of clearing the land to make way for cultivation, men focused primarily on hunting and pastoralism and left agriculture to women. Women assumed responsibility for the entire cultivation process, from hoeing and planting to weeding and harvesting.[20]

Although important, agriculture played a subordinate role to pastoralism in determining status and affluence in Xhosa society. Wealth and prestige were reflected in the accumulation of large herds of cattle, which the Xhosa used as economic and social currency. Milk and meat comprised the principal dietary staples, skins provided clothing, and dung provided material for building homes. Cattle also underpinned everything from securing cordial relations with the ancestors, to marriage and tributary relationships with the chief. Cattle were used to venerate and appease deceased ancestors, to acquire new wives, to pay fines, to welcome children as new members of the lineage, and to commemorate the transition from childhood to adulthood. Since the transfer of cattle cemented and legitimized marriages, achieving the ideal polygynous household also depended on how much cattle a man had at his disposal; not everyone could afford multiple wives. The acquisition of cattle and wives therefore was a lifelong process.

Initiation rites commemorated the transition from childhood to adulthood. While the similar fanfare of slaughtering cattle, feasting, and dancing accompanied the rites of both sexes among the Xhosa, only the boys endured circumcision. Like male and female circumcision ceremonies throughout Africa, initiates underwent a preliminary period of seclusion, used clay or ochre or other substances to decorate themselves, observed particular food taboos, and employed certain medicines to prepare for and then help heal their excisions. Among the Xhosa, girl's ceremonies *(intonjane)* could be delayed without adverse reactions from the community. In fact, the great expense of slaughtering animals and feeding the many people attending the celebrations led some families to defer girls' ceremonies, sometimes until after marriage. For men, however, circumcision was the sine qua non of adulthood and marriage. An uncircumcised boy could not participate fully in society, as he was not considered a man at all. As the missionary William Clifford Holden, citing J. C. Warner's notes on circumcision, wrote in an exclamatory fashion, "An uncircumcised male, though as old as Methuselah, would still be considered but a boy."[21]

Adulthood conferred the right to participate fully in society and marry. While marriage entailed some special privileges, it placed a demanding set of responsibilities on women and further elaborated the gendered division of labor. Marriage, moreover, demanded changes in social deportment that reinforced a separate spheres ideology for men and women. For example, while the clothing of both Xhosa men and women consisted of hides that covered the private parts, only married women bedaubed themselves with a special mixture of red dye and fat. Distinct dress and hairstyles displayed the special status of married men and women. To show respect (*ukuhlonipha*) for her husband's relatives and men in particular, married women had to observe certain rules of social interaction. For example, social propriety proscribed women from using the personal names of their male in-laws, or words similar to them. Women also had to avoid occupying or using male areas of the homestead.[22]

As documented in other societies throughout Africa, the veneration and propitiation of ancestors featured prominently in traditional Xhosa belief systems.[23] Ancestors, the forebears of the lineage, were believed to be active agents that revealed their pleasure or displeasure in daily life. The Xhosa ancestors manifested their benevolence by providing them with rain, fertility, and abundant harvests. Conversely, the ancestors expressed their dissatisfactions through afflictions like droughts or diseases. Each household made the requisite sacrifice of cattle to invoke and appease their ancestors, while ritual matters pertaining to the chiefdom as a whole fell within the purview of the chief.[24] Households, for example, would focus on sacrifices relating to the fertility of their wives, whereas the chief would make sacrifices to bring rain or success in war. While the historical literature is unanimous on the centrality of ancestors in Xhosa cosmology, the existence of a supreme being bearing parity to the Christian conception of a high God has been the subject of some contention. To the extent that such an omniscient, omnipotent being existed, Xhosa relegated him to the periphery and accorded the foremost, interactive role to their ancestors.[25] This distinction hardly mattered to the missionaries—their God was a jealous one who left no room to share his sacred power.

The Xhosa religious worldview, like many found throughout Africa, depended on a schema of explanation, prediction, and control where little was left to chance. All misfortune had a cause and an agent. Individuals maintained order in this system by observing rituals and taboos and making the requisite sacrifices to propitiate their ancestors. While ancestors demonstrated their discontent by causing affliction or malaise, the concept of evil was generally attributed to the agency of witches and witchcraft. Xhosa society encompassed a number of special agents who combated the problem of evil. Diviners diagnosed the cause of the problem and suggested methods of restoring harmony. Medicine-men or herbalists drew upon their specialized skills and knowledge to provide protection, treatment, and cure. Rain men also featured among the most important ritual specialists since drought was one common way that ancestors showed their displeasure. To expand their worldview or explain events that did not fit into their local cosmology, the Xhosa willingly borrowed concepts or terminology from other Africans such as the Khoesan and subsequently from Christianity.[26] From the outset, therefore, the indigenous knowledge structures of the Xhosa recognized the existence of spiritual forces and remained open to new ideas.

By the time William Shaw approached Xhosa chiefdoms with his evangelical message in the early 1820s, some of them had already had several brief encounters with Christian missionaries. The LMS missionary Johannes Van der Kemp had established the first mission in 1799, which lasted until 1801. Joseph Williams, also from the LMS, made a second attempt in 1816, but died prematurely after only two years. John Brownlee, another LMS missionary, established the Tyhume mission in 1820 under government auspices. Scottish missionaries assumed control of Tyhume when Brownlee left the service of the colonial government to resume his position as an LMS missionary. Surveying these early missionary efforts in southeastern Africa, Shaw observed that the field for Christian evangelism remained wide open because most chiefdoms were still without missionaries. Between 1823 and 1830, Shaw and his Methodist colleagues established a chain of six stations (see Map 2) to fill what they perceived as an evangelical void. The six missions (Wesleyville, Mount Coke, Butterworth, Morley, Clarkebury, and Buntingville) all bore the eponyms of important Methodist personalities and secured a crucial sphere of influence for Methodism in southeastern Africa.

The establishment of one mission station expedited the creation of others in the chain. As news of the missionaries' presence spread, each mission in the chain served as a crucial stepping-stone for the subsequent ones. For William Shaw and his Methodist colleagues, the first mission, Wesleyville, was "a prosperous entrance into . . . 'heathendom.'"[27] Wesleyville served as a pioneer mission to be showcased as a Christian oasis amid "heathenism," as a neutral meeting ground for African chiefs and colonial officials, a rest stop for travelers, and an administrative center from which other missionaries embarked on their assignments (see Figure 2.3). The traveler Andrew Steedman observed that the chain of missions provided "a facility of visiting this interesting country . . . with a degree of security previously unknown." Steedman also lauded missions for facilitating the exploration of Africa, for "with its knowledge, its morality, its religion, and its schools amid a tribe of men before unknown," mission stations were "beyond comparison the best key for unlocking the mysteries of Africa, the most important conquests that can be made within its immense boundaries."[28]

The Chain of Stations

To secure land for establishing a mission, Shaw and other missionaries had to make formal requests to various chiefs. While some chiefs acceded to the request or even invited the missionaries before they asked, the process required diplomacy and patience. The circumstances surrounding the establishment of Wesleyville, Mount Coke, and Butterworth, the first three links in the chain, reveal how much the initial experience of the missionaries depended on the discretion of the chiefs. Chief Phato, who along with his brothers Kama and Kobe ruled the Gqunukhwebe chiefdom, proved receptive of missionary overtures. The inaugural Methodist mission, Wesleyville was established among them in 1823. Similarly, the chief Dushane received the missionaries into his territory and granted permission to establish Mount Coke, the second link in the chain.[29]

To reach Phato's chiefdom, Shaw had to travel through the territory of the chief Ngqika, whom the Cape government had elevated to the position of paramount chief of all the Xhosa and considered an ally. Ngqika shared the government's concerns about whites and Africans closely interacting with each other and possibly causing conflict by disregarding colonial boundaries. By the time he received William Shaw's request, his power was severely undercut and he relied on the colony to reinforce his authority. He therefore equivocated about allowing the missionary entourage to proceed through his chiefdom to Phato's. Trying to understand Ngqika's motivations, a "chagrined" and uninformed Shaw was satisfied to declare, "Why should we be astonished? Gaika [Ngqika] is a 'heathen.'"[30] Ngqika's initial reluctance gave way, however, and he granted permission for Shaw and his companions to proceed through his chiefdom.

In the third mission, Butterworth, Shaw encountered more than hesitation from the chief in that area, Hintsa. Chief Hintsa questioned the prudence of allowing missionaries in the middle of his polity; he avoided the missionaries when he could, vacillated when Shaw and others approached him directly in April 1825 and December 1826, and remained recalcitrant about giving his approval for much of 1825 and 1826. Frustrated with Hintsa's delaying tactics, yet receiving no explicit sign of disapproval, the missionaries commenced their work in July 1827 without his permission.[31] A week later when Chief Hintsa approached the area where the missionary William Shrewsbury was holding service, the congregation dispersed for fear that the chief would make reprisals against them for attending services before he had given his official permission. Hintsa "traveled past without casting his eyes toward our dwelling, and affected to treat us with the utmost indifference and even contempt," Shrewsbury reported.[32] When Shrewsbury visited the chief a few days later, Hintsa "pretended that he had not heard a word concerning our mission up to that hour."[33] The standoff continued until early August 1827 when Hintsa finally sanctioned Butterworth, the third Methodist mission in the chain (see Figures 2.4 and 2.5).

The establishment of Wesleyville, Mount Coke, and Butterworth, the three missions amid Xhosa chiefdoms, highlight the difficult position in which African rulers found themselves. African chiefs were wary of white colonial encroachment, which had already led to armed conflict and resulted in land alienation. Between 1779 and 1819, five wars had already ensued. The last of these wars dealt the Xhosa great defeat when some 10,000 warriors descended on Grahamstown in 1819 in daylight. Even at the beginning of the nineteenth century before warfare and land alienation seriously threatened the Xhosa polities, a white colonial administrator admitted that in their interactions with Africans, whites often employed tactics of "deceit" and "depravity."[34] Despite missionary attempts to dissociate themselves from the Cape government and colonial policies, African chiefs in particular remained suspicious about their allegiances. The handful of missionaries who acted as paid agents of the government reinforced this association.[35] Though they remained circumspect about the missionaries' political stance, African chiefs acknowledged the secular benefits that accrued from having a resident missionary and feared the outcome of rejecting them overtly. They could use missionaries as intermediaries, translators, scribes, informants, and as advocates. Although official instructions from most missionary societies warned against political involvement, the strained relations between the colony and its border chiefdoms thrust most missionaries into the role of liaisons and inevitably politicized their evangelism.[36]

Once they surmounted the initial difficulties of negotiating with African chiefs, the Methodists began creating the basic infrastructure for evangelism to proceed. Before they settled among Xhosa chiefdoms, most Methodist missionaries knew that they would have to introduce the Christian lexicon, and in most instances they acknowledged this as an inevitable feature of pioneer work. One of the first tasks Methodist missionaries faced was determining how Xhosa religious structure facilitated or impeded the reception of Christianity. One anonymous observer proclaimed what was probably the typical missionary perception of the Xhosa society. "It can scarcely be said that the Kaffirs are destitute of religious ideas, and yet it must be allowed that they exist in almost the feeblest and most imperfect degree imaginable."[37] The notion of a high or supreme God so central to Christianity only found a vague equivalent among the Xhosa.[38] Of all the features of Xhosa society, the belief in witchcraft as the source of evil and death elicited the most invective from missionaries and other observers of Xhosa society. Rather than assimilate Xhosa concepts and personification of evil with Christian notions of sin and the devil, however, missionaries treated Xhosa religious beliefs and rituals as barriers to the successful dissemination of Christian ideas and lifestyles.[39] Assessing the overall religious and moral character of the Xhosa, Samuel Young proclaimed, "Where there is much superstition and cruelty, there is moral darkness, and an absence of moral feeling and principle. The Kafirs have no Bible, no Sabbath, no ordinances, no ministers, no means of grace; they were truly without God and without hope in the world, deeply degraded by sin and glorifying in their shame."[40]

Those most intimately associated with Xhosa religious and ritual practices, such as rain men and diviners, came under special attack from missionaries who labeled these individuals as "quacks" and "witchdoctors." Missionaries argued that rainmakers and diviners were the linchpin in "one of the most oppressive and cruel systems of superstition and sin."[41] The conflicts that arose between rain men and missionaries took shape in conversations and sometimes in physical confrontations where each tried to discredit the other by bringing rain. Beyond public confrontations, missionaries used the construction of watercourse and dams and other means of irrigation as leverage in their contestation with rainmakers.[42] In drought-ridden areas where pasture and water for cattle were so crucial, the missionaries' perceived power to bring rain through prayer or produce other sources of water attracted some of the earliest converts. In one confrontation with the Methodist missionary William Shaw, the rainmaker exclaimed that after he had made all the requisite sacrifices and preparations, the church bell interfered with the rain. As soon as the rain was ready to fall, the rainmaker asserted, "that thing which you have brought into the country and set up on a pole . . . goes tinkle, tinkle, tinkle; and immediately the clouds begin to scatter, they disappear and no rain can fall."[43] Shaw accused the rainmaker of lying and warned that perhaps God was punishing them with drought because they put their faith in man's power rather than His. The conversation drew to a close and only after a prayer meeting and subsequent rainfall could Shaw claim a clear victory. Shaw noted that his encounter with the rainmaker discredited rainmaking in the local Wesleyville area.[44]

Similarly, a protracted drought at the Butterworth mission settlement between 1828 and 1829 disgraced many of the local rainmakers, who subsequently fled the area.[45] These confrontations between rain men and missionaries were the typical, caricatured anecdotes missionaries recounted in their journals and letters as a symbol of the conflict between Christianity and "heathenism."[46] Wesleyville residents and those in the drought-stricken area were certainly grateful for the rain, but Shaw and others were overly confident in their methods. Deriding cultural traditions and dishonoring rainmakers were quick victories. But, while they impressed large crowds of people, in the larger battle they won relatively few converts during the pioneer evangelical phase.

Beyond acknowledging the authority of chiefs, white missionaries approached Xhosa society with disdain and condescension and held on to a rigid, dogmatic view of Christianity that alienated the vast majority of people. No area of Xhosa social, economic, and religious organization escaped missionary scrutiny. Whether they were describing Xhosa religious ideas, the treatment of women, initiation rites, economic livelihoods, the cosmetic use of red ochre to bedaub the body, or the construction of homes, missionaries from all denominations registered strong and often negative reactions and filled their journals and letters with vituperative commentary. The geometry of Xhosa homesteads, for example, made a lasting impression on missionaries, and became one symbol of the struggle between European notions of civilization and Xhosa society. "The Kafirs worked in circles;

their huts, their fireplaces, their kraals or villages were all circular," the Reverend Whiteside wrote in his chronicle of Methodism in South Africa.[47] An annual report from the 1850s, whose content reflected the chaos and havoc of the 1850–53 War of Dispossession, did not hesitate to note a particular triumph at Buntingville. "There is not a round house on the station, nor would it be an easy task to get any of the people here to live in a round house again—their present houses are so much more convenient."[48]

Describing the location of the first Methodist mission station, the Methodist missionary Stephen Kay declared, "The site of the mission village is a low rocky ridge with a beautiful valley at its base." When his gaze expanded immediately beyond the mission village, however, to the chief's homestead, Kay found no such admiration. To him the chiefly quarters appeared to be "filthy, shattered and exposed huts; their appearance at a distance is not unlike that of so many ant-hills."[49] Even when missionaries praised the skill it took to construct rain-proof homes, their observations still revealed a measure of disdain and sarcasm. After delineating "the strong framework of their simple mansion," and expressing amazement at how women carried bundles of thatch that were "enough to break the neck of ordinary persons," the missionary William Holden was quick to add a barrage of sarcastic comments. "There is more room and convenience in these simple abodes than any ordinary observer would suppose," Holden began, "for in addition to rats, they are the sleeping places of the small calves, young goats, and a number of dogs and cockroaches[.]"[50]

Polygyny, circumcision, and bridewealth also received an inordinate amount of criticism from missionaries. Reacting to a conversation in which his informant explained that he had used all of his cattle to acquire wives, the Methodist missionary John Ayliff resorted to the New Testament to express how polygyny marred its African practitioners. They were, Ayliff declared, in the "gaul [gall] of bitterness and in the bond [of] iniquity!"[51] Polygyny, William Clifford Holden and a host of missionaries of various denominations believed, was a pretext for male indolence, allowing men to treat women as beasts of burden and satisfy their voracious sexual appetites. Polygyny "affords full scope for the unbridled passions of selfishness and lust to revel in," Holden asserted, and "secures unbounded license to sensual indulgence." The exchange of cattle for wives, Holden continued, relegated women to the position of slaves.[52] To compound matters, men left most of the agricultural work to women. In the missionaries' estimation, this sexual division of labor was the pinnacle of African men's laziness and women's oppression.

Throughout much of the nineteenth century, missionaries continued to depict African women as beasts of burden and promoted Christianity and civilization as a corrective to the disorderly model of domestic life where women played such a central role in food production. The emancipation of African women would remove them from the "lowest possible state of degradation in which they were doomed to the drudgery of building, digging, sowing [and] reaping," and elevate them to the "comforts of social life . . . as wives and mothers . . . attending to household duties almost exclusively."[53] Shaw's introduction of the plow at Wesleyville became one of the more popular anecdotes told in missionary circles. Robert Young, a Scottish missionary, wrote that the plow represented the "grey [sic] dawn of agriculture in Kafirland, and a happy omen for the future release of the women from such drudgery as had heretofore invariably been their lot."[54]

Most aspects of Xhosa social economic organization reinforced the missionary belief that Christianity and civilization had to march hand in hand for Christianity to succeed. Even when they did not explicitly support Christian evangelization, other voices like those of white settlers, government officials, and even temporary sojourners to the Cape added to the chorus the need for Africans to be civilized on the European model. The cosmetic use of red ochre came to represent the struggle between Christianity and "heathenism" as the missionaries saw it. Beyond the conventional dichotomy of believer/nonbeliever, the terms "Red" and "School" entered the lexicon as a dramatization of the division between Christianity and Xhosa tradition. Those Xhosa who continued to smear themselves with red ochre were contrasted to others who adopted Christian ways and attended the schools that missionaries established as one of the crucial "civilizing" arms of the evangelical enterprise. Throughout the nineteenth and twentieth centuries the glossary of words grew, symbolizing the deep transformations and bifurcations that Christianity, education, and colonial rule wreaked in Xhosa and other African societies. Some of these terms include kholwa (believers), amaqaba (those who smear themselves with red ochre), abantu ababomvu (red people), amaqoboka (those who have a hole—those who have opened a hole in the society), abantu basesikolweni (school people), and abantu becawe (church people).[55] Of all the terms, the "red" associated with red ochre came to be used in a colloquial sense by the Xhosa, travelers, and anthropologists as an index of Xhosa traditionalism.[56]

The integration of Xhosa religious, cultural, political, and economic life led most missionaries to the realization that their vision of evangelical success depended on dismantling many aspects of Xhosa society. Even some Methodist missionaries wary of the deleterious effects of colonial policies on Xhosa society eventually welcomed the subjection of Xhosa to British rule. As David Chidester pointed out, missionaries "nearly all turned to advocate various instruments of economic, social and political, or military coercion to create the necessary conditions for Christian conversions."[57] If Africans adopted the superstructure of British law and authority and adopted inter alia European methods of agriculture and dress, then the sort of Christianity missionaries envisioned could take root more easily amongst them. For most Xhosa and other Africans with their chiefdoms still intact, the adoption of Christianity was tantamount to cultural suicide. Even under the best of circumstances, the missionary perception of African cultural practices still made allegiance to Christianity a potentially subversive act.[58] Like many other African societies, missionaries did not make great headway with Christianity until the political, economic and social structures of Xhosa society deteriorated under the pressure from colonial conquest.

For the Xhosa and other Africans, deterioration meant a succession of wars with the Cape Colony in the first half of the nineteenth century (1819, 1834–35, 1846–47, 1850–53) that resulted in widespread land dispossession, social dislocation, and diluted power of Xhosa chiefs. These violent encounters happened alongside missionary attempts to undermine particular aspects of Xhosa culture (polygyny and witchcraft, for example) that conflicted with their vision of Christianity. Although these wars initially disrupted missionary work and created disillusionment among some missionaries, in the long run war could be a boon to the missionary effort. Hundreds of Xhosa flocked to the mission stations as places of refuge out of desperation and poverty. With each successive war, British authorities annexed more Xhosa territory to the Cape Colony. In the aftermath of the 1846–47 war, after parceling out land to loyalists and white settlers, the remaining Xhosa chiefdoms were placed under British authority as the new entity of British Kaffraria. In this new colonial order, white magistrates usurped some of the power that previously fell under the jurisdiction of chiefs.[59] In addition, the British administration added another layer to its blueprint for checking the power of chiefs by making them salaried employees of the colonial government, thus compromising their legitimacy.

By the middle of the nineteenth century, few Xhosa chiefdoms were spared the cultural and political assault of the Cape Colony and Christian missionaries. Unwilling to forfeit their cultural and political integrity, the Xhosa engaged in another protracted war between 1850 and 1853. This time they joined forces with other Africans, particularly those of the Kat River Settlement who also suffered the economic deprivation that accompanied land alienation. A bitter struggle with the Colony for self-preservation led to eventual defeat. The Xhosa lost even more territory while the Kat River settlement was sold off to white settlers. An epidemic of lung sickness that decimated cattle herds plunged Xhosa society into a severe economic and political crisis whose resolution required more drastic measures beyond the usual military confrontation. The solution unfolded between May 1856 and June 1857 as thousands of Xhosa obeyed a prophetic call to slaughter their herds and destroy their crops. This ritual purification would usher in a new era when the ancestors so central to Xhosa well-being would return and bring new cattle herds with them. At least 35,000 people died from starvation and some estimates range as high as 50,000.[60] Thousands of refugees descended upon the Cape Colony and sought out mission settlements to alleviate poverty and starvation. Christianity did not make significant progress among the Xhosa until they suffered this tragic economic and cultural coup de grace.

The prophetic visions that underpinned the cattle killing combined Xhosa beliefs about ritual sacrifice and purification as well as Christian ideas of death and resurrection. The incorporation of certain Christian symbols, imagery, and concepts provides one index of which aspects of Christianity the Xhosa melded into their worldview to explain and redress their disastrous experience of colonialism. In the first half of the nineteenth century, Xhosa society confronted new forms of colonial warfare that were nothing short of destructive. Colonial troops laid waste to Xhosa land through scorched-earth policies, burning crops and homesteads and seizing thousands of cattle in retribution. At the end of each war, the colony punished the Xhosa by expelling them from their lands. In the context of such disasters new prophets arose, sometimes adopting conciliatory approaches to deal with the perceived crisis, other times making militant proclamations about driving the white man into the sea. Whatever the spectrum of these forecasts, the prophetic visions that molded Xhosa responses to colonial encroachment provides important instances of how Africans made use of Christianity in ways that were meaningful and instrumental for them. Once Africans were exposed to Christian evangelism, white missionaries could not control how they interpreted and appropriated the message; nor could they prevent the emergence of African religious figures and prophets who had far more legitimacy and made more headway in attracting other Africans to Christianity. So many of the early advances made in Christianity happened outside of the dictates of what white missionaries were trying to accomplish.

Pioneer Methodist Evangelism

In the thirty-four years between the foundation of the first mission at Wesleyville in 1823 and the end of the cattle killing in 1857, Methodist missionaries made great strides in creating the infrastructure of missionary evangelism among the Xhosa. They built churches and schools and established small outstations. They hired interpreters to assist them with their sermons and with the translation of the gospel into the vernacular. They established a store filled with the sort of clothing and implements they hoped the Xhosa would use. The missionaries structured their time around day and evening services, prayer meetings and intermittent periods of preaching throughout the week, class meetings, catechism, Sunday schools, and day schools. In these venues and through these mediums, the Methodists introduced the general narrative of Christianity. They preached about the creation, Adam and Eve, the fall of man, the death and resurrection of Christ, heaven and hell, the immortality of the soul, sin, repentance, and the gamut of Old and New Testament teachings.[61]

Two of the hallmarks of Methodism, whether in the context of the Evangelical Revival in Europe or pioneer evangelism in the South Africa, are its grassroots appeal and origins. So much of the daily work of spiritual communion and pastoral care fell to laymen. This structure allowed ordinary people in the role of class leaders and local preachers to play important roles in evangelizing and guiding spiritual affairs in their communities. Moreover, it addressed the staffing shortages that all missionary societies eventually confronted. Expounding on this feature of Methodism in his testimony before the committee on aborigines, Shaw told the commissioners, "In the religious society to which I belong, it is part of our system everywhere to employ the natives who we deem qualified to teach and we are accustomed to sending these persons around the villages on a regular plan for the purpose of imparting instruction."[62] By giving Christianity an African face, white missionaries dealt with the practical issue of personnel shortages. Using African missionaries potentially gave Christianity more legitimacy. Reflecting on the importance of African agents, Samuel Young declared, "The Kafirs themselves became the instruments of relating scriptural facts, and communicating gospel truths throughout the length and breadth of their country."[63]

Since the preaching at the mission premises was so localized, the missionaries adopted an additional strategy for getting the gospel out to more people. They visited neighborhoods beyond the mission premises and established outstations connected to the main mission. While he was stationed at Wesleyville, for example, William Shaw traveled beyond the confines of the station, sometimes being absent from the mission premises for several days at a time; as did his successor, Samuel Young.[64] While at Butterworth, Reverend Shrewsbury itinerated once per month, preaching to groups of four, six, twelve, or twenty people.[65] This was one crucial way of getting the message to people who could not or would not come to the mission. For others who still did not get to hear the missionaries preach, the gospel spread as gossip.

The missionaries themselves, their message, daily activities, and idiosyncrasies were objects of curiosity. Their reputation sometimes preceded them when they went to outlying areas beyond the mission so that they undoubtedly became the subject of many conversations as well as the butt of many jokes. Africans were "great disseminators of the news of missionary endeavors," Samuel Young noted in his journal.[66] The introduction of the plow, for example, drew huge crowds. During this pivotal event at Wesleyville, William Shaw noted, "There was no small stir among the great numbers of the people, who although they had heard of such an implement, had never seen its operation. As soon as it began to get fairly at work," Shaw continued, "the people looked on with great surprise, and followed up and down the field muttering all manner of exclamations expressive of their astonishment." Later that same day one chief exclaimed that, "This thing that the white people have brought into the country is as good as ten wives."[67] Whatever relationship the missionaries wanted to draw between Christianity and civilization, and in this case farming implements, most Xhosa could accept the material gains without spiritual engagement. They could acknowledge the efficiency of the plow and use it without converting to Christianity. Thus, even though the missionaries' skills and accoutrements could be impressive, it was not enough to make people want to convert.

Even when they were invited or allowed into African chiefdoms with little opposition, the strategies missionaries employed ensured that early evangelism elicited much argument from and reluctance on the part of the Xhosa. The vast majority of Xhosa among whom the missionaries established residential stations showed no lasting interest in becoming full-fledged members of the Methodist

Church. While hundreds of people heard about Christianity in the decades between the 1820s and 1850s and became more familiar with its lexicon and its imagery, few people were willing to take the significant step of conversion and renouncing those features of their cultural and religious practices that conflicted with mission Christianity. Of those who did, it is sometimes difficult to disaggregate their material interests from their spiritual commitment. The historical literature provides overwhelming evidence that the material benefits missionaries provided and the perceived diplomatic advantages of associating with missions generated more interest in Christianity than any initial attraction to the message of spiritual salvation.[68] To elucidate this point, a distinction between the attitudes of African chiefs versus the rest of the population is instructive because African leaders often had far more to lose by converting to Christianity and few chiefs ever became full-fledged members of mission churches. In his chronicle of exemplary Christians in South Africa, historian Horton Davies declared that the African Christian ruler was a "rare phenomenon" and was hard pressed to find more than one African chief to include in the monograph, *Great South African Christians*.[69]

By railing against certain features of Xhosa society, missionaries threatened to tear the fabric of society apart and undermine the power of Xhosa and other African chiefs. Disavowing ancestors, discrediting rainmakers as legitimate practitioners, questioning the rationality of witchcraft, and casting polygamy as a sin directly challenged the material and ritual basis of chiefly power. Whether in the pioneer phase of Methodist evangelism in the 1820s and 1830s or in the late nineteenth century when other denominations augmented missionary work among Africans, few chiefs could accept the risks of Christian conversion.[70]

Though they stopped short of becoming full-fledged members of Christian churches, African chiefs acknowledged the secular benefits of associating with missions. On his missionary tour of the Cape Colony, the Quaker missionary James Backhouse commented on the motivations of the chiefs Faku and Ncapai [Ncaphayi] for requesting missionaries to come to their territory. Backhouse noted, "They [the chiefs] saw that to have missionaries gave them importance with other tribes and nations, and opened communications, by which they learned what was going on in other parts of the world."[71] One of the main concerns of the chiefs and their counselors was that the missionaries would dissipate their power by acting as an alternate authority. When Shrewsbury met with Hintsa in December 1826, for example, "One old man, with the sagacity of an experienced politician, asked several questions as to the tendency of the Christian religion to support or weaken the authority of the chief and those who held subordinate authority under him." Shrewsbury responded by assuring him that Christianity would buttress the principle of people to "reverence rulers for the Lord's sake."[72] Even as late as 1850, several decades after pioneer work had begun, government officials were still warning missionaries that they were not allowed "territorial supremacy or imperium in imperio within the chiefs' allocated land."[73] And in the 1880s, the missionary Alan Gibson noted that the persistence of the mission station as a system of evangelization still encouraged the missionary to rival the local chief by acting like a "headman [by] granting permission to settlers . . . giving out gardens [and] settling disputes[.]"[74]

Among the Xhosa chiefs, the Methodist missionaries claimed one major victory for Christianity in the early nineteenth century. After creating Wesleyville in 1823, one local chief, Kama, began attending services regularly and taking a keen interest in the Christian message (see Figure 2.6). When Kama finally decided to be baptized in 1825, Shaw was overcome with emotion. Among the annals of Methodist work, Kama's conversion overshadows the experience of the more ordinary converts because of his authoritative position in Xhosa society. The missionary William Holden wrote a seventy-three page monograph on Kama. Methodist literature constantly refers to his conversion, monogamous marriage, and loyalty to the colony as one of the greatest examples of missionary success.[75] Although they hoped that other chiefs would follow Kama's actions, the Methodists would be disappointed. Xhosa chiefs and their families attended church services and some encouraged their children to take advantage of the educational services. Some chiefs opted to send their children to be educated in the Cape Colony.[76] Other chiefly progeny ended up in Cape schools voluntarily.[77] Still, others ended up in the colony for education under some duress. Several children and grandchildren of Xhosa chiefs, like Emma Sandile for example, were sent to Cape Town's Zonnebloem College in the aftermath of the cattle killing where they were held as virtual hostages.[78] Still others ended up in Europe where they experienced the African version of the "black man's grave" and succumbed to long bouts of poor health and sometimes death, most notably the grandchildren of the Xhosa chief Maqoma.[79]

Missionaries had to be satisfied with the mutual display of deference that characterized their relationships and interactions with Xhosa chiefs. Although Kama was the only chief considered a Christian, the missionaries capitalized on any inkling of interest that other chiefs showed. If they could not get chiefs to convert, they would encourage the chiefs to at least endorse the presence of the mission in a public way. The first missionary meeting at Wesleyville, for example, was a crucial public display of chiefly approval and a symbolic boon for the missionaries. The assembly at the missionary meeting consisted of some 600 to 800 people including important figures like chiefs and colonial government officials.[80] Reverend Shrewsbury's observations on the advantage of having the chiefs Hintsa, Ngqika, Bhuru, and Ndlambe supporting missions were also true on this occasion. He asserted:

> if it can be brought about for the chiefs in such a solemn and public manner unanimously to concur in their sanction of the preaching of the gospel, the issue will be of the greatest importance, and nothing more will be wanting to place all our present and all our future missions throughout the whole country, in a legal point of view, on the best footing possible.[81]

With no other chiefly conversions forthcoming, the missionaries and chief tacitly accepted the limits of their authority. The missionaries accepted that the chiefs were the head of the polities where the mission stations were established. The chiefs accepted the authority of the missionaries on the premises of the mission primarily in reinforcing basic rules such as attending church and wearing clothing, for example. Even with these implicit rules of distinct authoritative realms, however, many chiefs reminded their subjects that they were still a part of a Xhosa polity even on the mission station. For their part, the missionaries went beyond the confines of the mission, preaching against practices that buttressed the chieftaincy. Despite ample warnings about not treating the mission as a state within a state, missionaries acted like de facto chiefs on the mission premises. They allocated land, determined residence, and treated the mission inhabitants like subjects.[82]

The rank and file of Xhosa society, just like its leaders, also exhibited skepticism about Christianity. Far from receiving the gospel with "a meek and lowly mind," the Xhosa were "much more ready at raising objections against divine truth," the missionary William Shrewsbury noted in his journal. His colleague William Shaw proclaimed that they:

> disputed every inch of ground with us; they were willing to go into inquiry but we found them very different in that respect to the Hottentots in the colony, who always receive with implicit credit what is stated to them by their teachers. The Caffres exhibited considerable powers of mind, and were not willing to receive any dogma until it was proved to their satisfaction.[83]

The Xhosa bombarded the missionaries with questions and engaged them in protracted debates about Christianity. Some individuals asked whether God had any cattle, what kind of cattle they were, and whether He had a wife. Others asked why Eve did not question Adam about his origins, whether Adam and Eve were still alive, and if Satan had a wife. They also asked the name of the forbidden tree, what sort of food was eaten before Adam sinned, who was Mary's father, and what was the color of the first man. One man wondered if he would become immortal if he stopped sinning and asked why he could not go to Heaven without having to die first. Still others pushed the practical issue of why God did not kill Satan and spare everyone else the trouble of having to repent of their sins. Samuel Young received questions about where God stood when he made the earth and what happened to people who had died without being Christians.[84]

William Shaw received queries that challenged God's purported omnipotence and questioned the need for missionaries. On various occasions, Africans asked him and his colleagues why God had not converted the devil; why old people who had lived their whole lives without God now needed him; and why, if God were so powerful, did He not just change the people without having to employ missionaries?[85] Sometimes the questions were filled with a mixture of comedy and sarcasm. When Reverend Shrewsbury told Chief Ndlambe that Christians "leave the world happy and rejoicing in hope of the glory of God," the chief asked whether it was "possible that any man can leave this fine grass and cattle rejoicing."[86] LMS missionary Henry Calderwood noted that opposition to missionaries and their message took various forms. "Sometimes opposers meet you simply with silent disdain; sometimes with an infidel argument," he observed, "and at other times there seems a general combination to secure that the word of God shall not even be spoken in a particular locality."[87]

While some missionaries welcomed the opportunity to explain Christian doctrine in detail, others grew exasperated. William Shrewsbury in particular wrote constantly of the "difficulties" he encountered when trying to assemble people and of the "idle" questions they asked.[88] For William Shaw the queries demonstrated the urgent need for missionary work. Unlike Reverend Shrewsbury, who saw the questioning as irksome, Shaw welcomed the questions in the spirit of genuine curiosity on the part of the people who were asking them.[89] William Shrewsbury, on the other hand, seemed completely irritated by the questions, viewing them in so many instances as acts of defiance. These kinds of questions added to the frustrations of the missionaries, for while they welcomed queries about God, some questions evinced the underlying fact that so many of the people whom they were trying to convert still found Christianity unappealing. Once serious debates ensued, some Christian teachings seemed as implausible and impractical as the missionaries made rainmaking and witchcraft out to be.

Members of Xhosa society demonstrated their reluctance in other symbolic ways. At the beginning of pioneer work, some people treated religious gatherings with an irreverence that annoyed the missionaries. "Our public services were occasionally disturbed by whispering and bursts of laughter or jocular remarks amongst the hearers," the missionary Stephen Kay stated.[90] On some of his itineration beyond the mission, William Shaw complained that people were as "careless and inattentive as any I ever saw."[91] William Shrewsbury was particularly aggrieved by nudity and complained that whenever the missionaries asked Africans in the congregation to cover themselves, it only elicited "laughter and merriment." On such occasions Shrewsbury could not help but think "on happy England, and on British Christians and on the high privileges we have with them enjoyed, and on the solemn devotion we have witnessed in the multitudes that there keep that holy day," and contrast it with the irreverence he experienced among the Xhosa. In Britain Shrewsbury described the missionary experience as having "eaten the fruits of paradise" whereas his work among the Xhosa was likened to barrenness; "here we plow up a wilderness," he wrote to the parent missionary society in England.[92]

The landscape of some of the pioneer missions also provided an index of missionary successes and failures. Although William Shrewsbury noted some "comfortable dwellings" at Wesleyville three years after it was established, most of the people who chose to live at the mission station had not erected homes on the British model. "Most of the natives still reside in their smoky habitations without much clothing," Shrewsbury observed disdainfully.[93] On a tour of the Cape Colony, one traveler noted that even in the 1830s, the Xhosa still preferred their conventional homes. At Wesleyville he declared, "Scattered in various directions towards the rear may be seen a number of old Caffer huts, for the construction of which the natives still manifest a strong and decided preference."[94] The same observation held at a pioneer Scottish mission where the traveler J. W. D. Moodie noted, "Most of the habitations of the Kaffres on the establishment were the common bee hive huts used by the rest of their nation."[95] At some of the other missions in the chain, the landscape also revealed that Africans did not always gloss the concepts of civilization and Christianity the way that missionaries did. At the Morley mission, for example, the missionary James Backhouse noted with pride the wattle and daub cottage of his interpreter, complete with chimney and window, but quickly added that most of the homes on the mission were the conventional ones.[96] At Clarkebury, missionaries cited the small number of church members and the disproportionate number of traditional homes as symptomatic of their marginal impact on Xhosa architectural tastes as a whole.[97]

From the missionaries' perspective, perhaps the most potent sign of African disinterest or irreverence toward Christianity was the persistence of practices like circumcision, polygyny, and witchcraft accusations after many years and countless sermons preaching against their sinfulness. The peremptory manner in which missionaries dealt with Xhosa culture as well as some of their preaching about sin, hell, fire, brimstone, and damnation, did little to endear Africans to Christianity. While most of the missionaries were guilty of employing the full hyperbolic arsenal of Christianity when discussing their work among Africans in general and the Xhosa in particular, some of them were overly dramatic. Most talked about "heathenism" and sin, while a few of them tended to wax theatrical about "whoredom" and "fornication." William Shrewsbury, whom Hildegarde Fast has described as "an extremist in his own culture," fits this description well.[98] He was aggrieved about everything from the slow pace of the work to what his congregants did not wear. "I go and preach to companies of 4, 6, or 12 naked men without the smallest sense of decency or shame and half naked women." The "licentiousness of the people," he complained in 1828, "exceeds all description. The men are all naked without the least sense of shame. . . . Were it not that I desire to promote the salvation of their souls, I would not dwell among such wretched people another hour, and much less bring up my family amongst them."[99] Two years later Shrewsbury's perception of his potential congregants remained unchanged. Writing from the Mount Coke mission station in 1830, Shrewsbury insisted that the "old habits of thieving, dissimulation, and impurity remain unabated."[100]

Undoubtedly the strict nature of mission life alienated individuals who did not agree with the missionaries about what actions constituted sin. Visiting mission stations beyond the borders of the colony, J. W. D. Moodie "could not help remarking the gloomy and desponding expression which pervaded the countenances of the people; there was no singing—no dancing—and none of the buoyancy of spirits and animation which characterize the Kaffir race in general." Few missionaries would concur with Moodie's observation that the gloomy aura of the mission "cannot for a moment . . . be the effect of true religion, which by purifying the heart, elevating the sentiments, and providing the highest motives of action, should rather fill the soul with cheerfulness, and promote innocent hilarity."[101] Yet as the missionary experience demonstrated throughout the nineteenth century, the strategy of casting customs as aberrant, sinful, and immoral won few converts to Christianity.

Despite the creation of mission stations, schools, and outstations, and the employment of some Africans to assist in spreading the Gospel, many factors militated against missionary success. Missionaries complained of difficulties in reaching remote or isolated Xhosa homesteads and problems with interpreters. Shrewsbury's experiences highlight some of the frustrations missionaries faced during the early stages of their work. In 1828 he complained, "The scattered state of the population and their roving habits, with their national and individual sins, seem to pose insurmountable obstacles to a general spread of the gospel amongst the people."[102] In a letter to the WMMS in England, Shrewsbury complained that missionaries must "travel a great many miles in a day and preach many sermons to make up the total amount of hearers that would be considered in England only a village congregation."[103] Once the missionaries could reach and assemble people to hear the message, their concerns shifted to their relative fluency in Xhosa, the use of interpreters, and the translation of the Bible into the vernacular.

One of the most powerful legacies of Christianity, and the key to its successful dissemination, is vernacular translation.[104] Before missionaries could express any triumphs about becoming proficient in Xhosa or translating the gospel, however, they had to perform through the medium of interpreters.[105] Through their early exposure to Christianity in the late eighteenth and early nineteenth centuries, the Khoekhoe served as important middlemen in the process of evangelization. They acted as interpreters and guides to the missions and also featured prominently among the early Christian converts living at mission stations beyond the borders of the Cape Colony.[106] But despite the instrumental role of interpreters, the translation of the Gospel was not always a straightforward process. Reverend Shrewsbury complained that potential problems could arise when fluency in a language was not necessarily combined with literacy:

A missionary sits down with his interpreter, who cannot read a single line of the word of God in any language, and perhaps his knowledge of divine things is very imperfect and some of his notions erroneous. He opens the sacred volume and has to translate that into barbarous Dutch, that his interpreter may comprehend its meaning; and then his interpreter tells him how that barbarous Dutch ought to be worded in the

Caffre language. And thus every verse being [a] double translation, not only is the progress exceedingly slow, but it may be several instances, after all care and caution have been employed, the genuine sense is not given, or in only a very imperfect manner. With this translation the missionary stands up to read a portion of the word of God for his interpreter cannot read it. And here a defect in the pronunciation of words, entirely dissimilar in their sound to any in his own language, occasions a further deterioration of his labor.[107]

Commenting on this laborious method of translation, Moodie stated that the translators had "a very imperfect knowledge of their meaning, and often make sad blunders, which are not likely to escape the notice of the shrewd Kaffres."[108] The translation of portions of the gospel addressed some of the problems Shrewsbury highlighted. Moreover, missionaries of different denominations made a concerted effort to produce Xhosa grammar guides and dictionaries to facilitate their evangelical work. Despite the combined efforts of all the missionary societies, progress was slow, leading Shrewsbury to exclaim rather melodramatically in 1830 that, "If this people [Xhosa] are to gain knowledge by translated work, centuries will pass away and leave them a semi-barbarous people still."[109]

Even later in the nineteenth century, with a well-established grammar and dictionaries and Bibles translated into Xhosa, the complaints about interpreters remained a common refrain of missionaries from various denominations. Alan Gibson, for example, made the following pronouncement on the relative utility of working with interpreters: "It is difficult to say which affords greater facility for misconstruction and misapprehension," he began, "employing an interpreter or preaching in Kaffir before the language has been fully mastered. In either case ludicrous or terrible mistakes may arise[.]" Gibson recounted an example of confusion between the homonyms foul and fowl and the rather hilarious implications of delivering a sermon about foul words and a foul heart. The interpreter rendered the first part of the analogy as, "If a man speaks like a fowl," and Gibson had to hastily correct him before he told the people that they would have fowl hearts.[110] Gibson's colleague Godfrey Callaway experienced a similar mishap. Trying to ascertain the sex of an infant presented for baptism, Callaway mistakenly asked the congregation if the child was an "umfazi" or an "indoda," only realizing later that he had asked if the child was a married man or a married woman.[111] The translation of the Bible in the Xhosa vernacular was itself an astounding linguistic and cultural achievement, yet in the early phase of evangelical work, true vernacularization of Christianity was a process that the Xhosa themselves had to undertake willingly and thus the missionaries had no choice but to wait.

Whatever the missionaries' concerns about converting chiefs, gaining fluency in Xhosa, and translating the Bible into the vernacular, the relatively small number of converts was perhaps the most discouraging index of evangelical progress. Although William Shaw was proud of the introduction of the plow at Wesleyville, by the time he left in 1830 only forty of the 300 people living on the mission station were church members. At Buntingville, another mission in the chain, only seventy-five of the 600 residents in the 1830s were members of the church.[112] Though missionaries liked to view the mission station as a Christian island in a sea of "heathenism," even the composition of the mission itself reminded them that Christianity still stood at the periphery of Xhosa society. Shrewsbury, lamenting the piecemeal nature of conversion, stated that while "individuals are becoming truly penitent for sin and believing in Jesus . . . there is scarcely any apparent change in the national character or improvement in the entire body of the people."[113] Writing from the Mount Coke mission station a few years later in 1830, Shrewsbury exclaimed pessimistically, "I do not expect to see the Gospel have such widely-extended success in Southern Africa for many years to come, unless it please God to pour out his spirit in an extraordinary manner upon the people."[114]

Conversion was no small affair. For the chiefs, it threatened the symbolic and ritual basis of their power and signified an abandonment of the customs and lifestyle of the people. For the rank and file it also meant turning their backs on cultural practices and beliefs that had shaped their upbringing before the missionaries arrived. Christian converts at times faced considerable social pressure and ridicule from their peers and family members. The missionary John Appleyard explained to one visitor to Mount Coke that, "out of the numbers of Kafirs who now hear the sound of the gospel[,] a very small proportion will openly profess belief, even if they are in some measure favorably disposed towards the truth, because by that open profession they lose caste among their people, and become very subject to deep humiliations and severe trials."[115] Similarly, Reverend Shrewsbury stated in 1829, "When individuals who hear the word preached begin to manifest the smallest concern for salvation, their friends and kindred cry out against them with much bitterness of spirit." Some people were accused of becoming "mad" when they showed any interest in Christianity and it required a certain amount of bravery for some to take the initial steps to convert.[116] As Reverend Shrewsbury pointed out, "those who do not reside upon the station have not yet the courage to brave the frowns of the world, and thus sustain the loss of their worldly all, which would probably follow" from converting to Christianity.[117] This made for great narratives of Christian martyrdom to rivet imperial audiences, but yielded few converts.

Even "native agents," those Africans who played such a crucial role in catechizing their countrymen and gave some legitimacy to Christianity, experienced difficulties. The missionaries vaunted these agents as paragons of missionary success and in most instances cited the agents' crucial work in interpreting sermons and scriptures and acting as local preachers and missionaries. While this sort of "native agent" was crucial in disseminating the Christian message, this does not necessarily mean they were immune from some of the challenges that white missionaries faced. Their peers often doubted their sincerity. When Joseph Xakala attempted to respond to a man who complained that God had given white people the "Book" and had not done so for black people, the man retorted, "A few months ago you were one of our great dancers, and were confirming us in all our old customs; and do you now set about teaching us this new religion; what is come to you?"[118] Those Africans not convinced by Christianity were willing to challenge "native agents" in the same way that they raised their objections to what white missionaries taught.

For those who showed some initial interest in Christianity, the process of becoming a Methodist church member was quite rigorous, the rules of Christian living were strict and sedate, and a Christian lifestyle could be expensive. One man living at the Butterworth mission station was at a loss for how to deal with his multiple wives. He eventually brought one wife and three children to Butterworth and left the other in the village. He continued to be married to both and to act as husband to both, remaining conflicted about his new religion versus his lifestyle. Although he eventually settled at Butterworth with one wife and solemnized their marriage in a Christian ceremony, his was obviously a difficult situation experienced by many converts. Shrewsbury does not mention what became of the other wife, but undoubtedly for others in a similar conundrum, a resolution was not easy and they could not simply abandon their other wives and children in favor of monogamy.[119]

William Shrewsbury prohibited people at his mission from participating in marriage celebrations because in his view the dancing and other aspects of the festivities were "filled with fornication, whoredom and uncleanliness."[120] Even when converts were committed to the more staid Christian ceremony, they had to forego participation in the weddings of their non-Christian family members. In addition to disavowing practices like polygyny or circumcision, potential converts had to undergo catechism. This period of instruction could last six months and even longer. Once the catechumen had satisfied the missionaries that he had a sound knowledge of Christian principles, he or she underwent a public baptismal ceremony and became a member of the church. In December 1826 Shrewsbury noted that missionaries baptized five people at Wesleyville after a six-month trial period—Thomas, Lydia, Mary, Beki, and Mephibosheth.[121] They joined the fourteen other members of the church. Of several hundred people living at the mission, only a handful were willing to undergo or passed the rigorous and sometimes protracted process of becoming a member of the Methodist Church.[122]

Church members had to attend weekly class meetings where they shared their experiences with each other and asked and answered questions about their faith. As members of the church they were constantly reminded about the parameters of proper Christian conduct. These class meetings, an institutional part of Methodism, became the primary avenues for missionaries to assess the maturation of Christianity among the select few who became converts. In many instances the missionaries still expressed disappointment. They also complained about the "nominal" nature of African allegiance to Christianity and questioned the piety of African converts. The rudimentary nature of education also made missionaries wonder about scriptural depth and mastery, which in their view, was pivotal to understanding Christianity. The first class meeting at Wesleyville was held on March 22, 1825, with six men and women. After the second class meeting the following week, Shaw declared that his African catechumens were "weak in faith, and very ignorant, and must be treated with much tenderness and forbearance."[123] Decades later, his colleague expressed similar reservations about African Christians. "Of those brought to a profession of Christianity," Appleyard told a visitor to Mount Coke, "a very small proportion appears to be really under the spiritual power of the gospel."[124]

Reverend Shrewsbury echoed the concerns of numerous missionary societies when he complained that many of the early converts at Wesleyan missions were "poor and men of little or no outward influence."[125] As the historical literature has demonstrated, the social and economic composition of early mission settlements often differed from what missionaries preferred.[126] Converts to Christianity were far from the ideal candidates (chiefs, councilors, and other people of influence) missionaries desired. Rather, some of the early converts were social pariahs and impoverished people who sought out the mission for assistance. Other people used the mission as temporary refuge from famine, violence, or witchcraft accusations and these were hardly the paragons of Christianity that the rest of the Xhosa would emulate. A gathering of converts at the Wesleyville mission station provides a limited yet important insight into the experiences of some of the early converts. Samuel Young, William Shaw's successor at Wesleyville, excerpted the testimony of approximately twenty men and women at a time when the membership of the church had grown to forty.[127] These members included a chief and commoners of varying backgrounds. Interestingly, some of the people who eventually converted in the 1820s and 1830s had heard about Christianity before the Methodists began their pioneer work, but had not taken any significant steps to affiliate themselves with the religion. The testimonies also highlight the sort of language the converts used to describe their experiences.

Chief Kama had welcomed William Shaw into his kingdom and after his conversion the missionaries used him as a paragon for other chiefs to follow in adopting Christianity and practicing monogamy. Martha Qotije started thinking about sin when she visited the Wesleyville mission station and now she "greatly lamented the badness of her heart [.]"[128] Jantije Nookqa had served in the capacity of interpreter for a missionary in the Cape Colony and in the process had "received much light." Yosef Wesley had also been exposed to Christianity in the Cape Colony but had not taken an earnest interest until he came to Wesleyville. Titus Dubula (who eventually relocated to Farmerfield) had come to Wesleyville seeking beads and afterward had accompanied William Shaw's wagon to Grahamstown. He was influenced by the word of God on this journey and testified that "he was now ready to wish that God would take him to heaven lest he should fall from his steadfastness." Sarah Nokyelo had been exposed to Christianity at Bethelsdorp, an LMS mission, but "did not receive it in her heart" until she came to Wesleyville.[129]

Maria Nomali had also heard the "word" in the Colony but had not converted until she came to Wesleyville. Similarly, Lydia Midi had "heard the gospel in the colony, but without much impression." After a bout with illness, she became concerned about her soul and converted.[130] Hlebikazi (who eventually relocated to Farmerfield), still a catechumen, found refuge at Wesleyville while escaping warfare. She was afraid to go to the church because of the weeping she heard during services, but now she "wept over her own bad heart [.]"[131] Maninji, also a catechumen, had overheard a sermon while she stood under the church window and "felt deeply affected by hearing of the love of Jesus for sinners [.]"[132]

These early converts were the "first fruits" of Methodist evangelism among the Xhosa. Although they were all testifying about their experiences at a Methodist mission established in a Xhosa area, the converts were not all Xhosa. Mission settlements commonly had heterogeneous population.[133] At the Butterworth mission station, the description of the first four baptismal candidates provides insights into the varied background of early African Christians. Simon Xila, the first resident of the Butterworth mission, was a slave from Batavia who had escaped to "Kafirland" to avoid ill treatment from his master and had lived there for almost thirty years. By the time he was baptized in 1828, Simon was almost seventy years old. Shrewsbury described the next candidate, Esther Tonis, as "an elderly Namacqua woman, while the remaining two Xhosa candidates were Joseph Qakala and John Patross, aged forty and thirty-six respectively."[134]

Missionary Assessments

In the decade between 1823 and 1833, William Shaw and his missionary colleagues created a chain of six mission stations that established an important Methodist sphere of influence beyond the borders of the Cape Colony. The important Methodist personalities who lent their names to these mission settlements had their names emblazoned on maps from that era, and recorded in travelers, and missionary journals. Stretching approximately 200 miles along the eastern frontier region beyond the Cape Colony, the chain of stations presented a cartographic victory over "heathenism." But maps mask, they certainly lie, and at times they reveal far more about the idea of a place than about the place itself. What the maps concealed was the arduous process of establishing these pioneer missions and the nature of African resistance to these efforts.

From the outset missionaries had to contend with the politics associated with the distrust of whites as well as the politics within African chiefdoms, both of which sometimes compromised their evangelical work. Many Africans viewed missionaries as potential agents of the colonial government and while they welcomed some of the material and secular benefits associated with missions, remained skeptical of their motives. Missionaries intentionally and inadvertently

Table 2.1 **Pioneer Missions and African Church Membership, 1823–33**

Pioneer Mission	*Date Established*	*Membership, 1832*	*Membership, 1833*
Wesleyville	1823	65	66
Mount Coke	1825	18	7
Butterworth	1827	22	22
Morley	1827	28	24
Clarkebury	1830	12	12
Buntingville	1830	5	No figure given

Source: WMMS Synod Minutes, Albany District Meeting, 1833, 1834.

reaffirmed some of these suspicions when they acted as arbiters between the colonial government and African political leaders. Politics within the chiefdom also limited the expansion of Christianity because most African chiefs viewed conversion as a certain sort of political suicide and were unwilling to forego the prerogatives of chiefly power to become Christians. Moreover, African chiefs grew concerned that mission stations served as alternate residences for their subject and that white missionaries acted as rival authority figures.

Missionary attitude toward Xhosa cultural traditions and social customs also ensured that missions remained politicized for much of the nineteenth century. The attack on circumcision, bridewealth, and polygyny alienated the vast majority of the Xhosa. Missionaries challenged everything from Xhosa sexuality and notions of respect to the sexual division of labor. All of these characteristics of nineteenth-century missions among the Xhosa, for the Methodist as well as other missionary societies, created a particular trend: the vast majority of people who attended church did so without becoming registered church members and the number of Christians at the mission was usually far out of proportion with the total population of the mission station. As Table 2.1 shows, between the commencement of Wesleyville in 1823 and the establishment of Buntingville in 1830, the number of church members was relatively low in relation to the actual number of residents on the mission. This was true of pioneer Methodist missions between the 1820s and the 1830s, and remained a distinguishable feature at many mission stations even in the latter part of the nineteenth century.

Despite the relatively small number of converts and the many challenges missionaries faced, their long-term impact on Xhosa society was significant. As John and Jean Comaroff and Hildegarde Fast have noted in their assessments of missionary endeavors in South Africa, the small number of converts did not detract from the overall importance of the mission enterprise. As Fast asserted, missionaries were the:

harbingers of the future order which . . . was to transform the surrounding communities. Economically, the stations modeled the capitalistic relations which were to profoundly affect the pastoral societies of the Xhosa and politically the authority of the white missionaries over black Christians became the paradigm of white-Xhosa relations, and the missionary-colonial tie was to play an important role in depriving the Xhosa of their independence.[135]

It was as emissaries of European culture and its concomitant colonial and capitalist ideologies that missionaries effected such far-reaching economic, linguistic, and cultural changes in the African societies they encountered. This impact was cumulative and insidious, however, and the juggernaut itself was not that Xhosa society changed or incorporated Christianity and European cultural norms into their worldviews, but that the cultural and spiritual assault missionaries made was paired with persistent political violence and economic dispossession from the colonial government and white settlers. By the time Methodist missionaries could claim evangelical success, Xhosa political and economic independence was shattered and these political and economic debilities were not a coincidental part of the increased interest in Christianity and missions.

In general, refugees, outcasts, or the dregs of society featured prominently among early mission converts. Over time, even as more Xhosa became interested in Christianity, the transition and its costs were still steep. Eventually these Christians became part of a nascent class of elite Africans whose education, minimal though it was, and whose familiarity with colonial society, placed them in much better circumstances to cope in the new society shaped by war, land alienation, and racial discrimination. This new social class of African Christians acquired a certain status, respectability, and privilege that improved their own and their children's life chances as they were drawn into the wider colonial nexus. However, this outcome and this assessment was hardly discernible in 1823 when the first mission was founded, or even by 1830 when the last chain in the mission was inaugurated.

A similar argument could be made on the missionary side. Missionaries in the field hardly saw themselves as any type of colossus. Righteous, embattled, and steadfast, certainly; but omnipotence they reserved for the God whose work they were carrying out. The early experiences of Shaw and his colleagues in the field demonstrated that pioneer evangelism was a gargantuan task that, from the perspective of those working on the ground, seemed to be going at a tortoise's pace with minimal returns—if those returns were counted solely in the number of registered church members. Missionaries certainly calculated that changing the economy, and the needs and the wants of the Xhosa, would draw them into the wider colonial network and make their exhortations about labor and civilization more effective, but they had little influence over the strategic use of economic dispossession or political violence to hasten their work. What political and economic subjugation clarified to the Xhosa was that living in and navigating white colonial society required new tools, new ideologies, and new ways of being—many of which were linked to Christianity and missions. By the time Xhosa began educating their children and pushing for higher education, however, it still could not be said that these developments were solely a reflection of mass conversion to Christianity. The charitable, relief, and educational services that missionaries provided was integrated with evangelical work, and produced mixed results. The question of what it meant to be an African Christian was far from a settled one among the missionaries.

The 1834–35 war punctuated an important decade of pioneer Methodism among Africans and brought many of these earliest converts from the chain of stations and other Africans into the Cape Colony seeking refuge. Grahamstown, a nascent frontier town in the Eastern Cape, received many of these refugees who then turned to William Shaw to create a mission for them. Chapter 3 now turns to the story of Grahamstown's African population and its important link in the eventual creation of the Farmerfield mission station as a novel turn in pioneer Methodist missions. Escaping the limitations they faced in Grahamstown was one of the primary motivations of Farmerfield's first African cohort. A critical mass of Africans exposed to Christianity and mission rhetoric capitalized on their privileged position as Christian recruits to advocate for an African mission—not beyond the borders of the frontier as the Methodist missions were during the era of pioneer missions, but within the Cape Colony. The result was the first exclusively African Methodist mission founded amid a white community. Let us see how these events unfolded in Grahamstown between the 1820s and 1830s and led to the creation of Farmerfield.

Bringing the Chain of Missions Back to the Eastern Cape

A Novel Turn in Methodist Missions

African Initiatives and Missionary Visions

In 1838 various African members of the Methodist Church in Grahamstown approached William Shaw, the general superintendent of Wesleyan missions, about finding a suitable place for them to resettle. In the African locations demarcated on the outskirts of Grahamstown, residents did not have legal titles to assert inalienable access to their residential and garden plots and their land allotments were insufficient for grazing and farming. A steady influx of refugees after the war of 1834–35 placed additional pressures on the already circumscribed African habitations, thereby exacerbating land shortage and creating a squatting problem in town.[1] Because of insecure tenure and inadequate access to land, some of the African church members considered going to mission settlements where they could keep cattle, have access to farming land, and continue to attend church.[2] William Shaw acceded to the congregants' appeal by purchasing a farm approximately nineteen miles outside of Grahamstown and establishing the Farmerfield mission station.

This chapter examines the circumstances that led to the African congregants' request by looking at how and why these Africans ended up in the Eastern Cape and often found themselves in dire economic conditions. The origins of Africans in the Eastern Cape and the challenges they faced is explored alongside the growth of the Eastern Cape, particularly Grahamstown, as a part of a contested frontier zone, a center of Methodism, and a regional trade emporium. The creation of the Farmerfield mission highlights two important developments that distinguished this settlement from pioneer missions. First, whereas William Shaw had established a chain of mission stations based on his own vision for evangelizing Africans beyond the borders of the Cape Colony, the original idea of Farmerfield came from African initiative. Instead of waiting for a missionary to solicit amongst them, the congregants assessed their own needs as African Christians and requested a mission. Despite missionary concerns about the relatively small number of converts, sustained missionary presence at the Cape and beyond its borders made Africans keenly aware of the secular and spiritual benefits of mission lifestyle. I argue in this instance that the congregants' request highlights this awareness, while the missionary response underscores concerns about the latent rivalry among the various Christian denominations in the Eastern Cape.

The second way in which Farmerfield was different from pioneer Methodist mission settlements was its geographical location. Rather than choosing a mission amid or adjacent to an African chiefdom as the previous Methodist missionaries had done, the congregants sought one within the established borders of the Cape Colony. Such a mission would land them squarely in the middle of a white community, a residential scheme that diverged sharply from William Shaw's original evangelical goals. An African community amid a white one veered from Shaw's plans of having a strategic chain of missions among African chiefdoms stretching from the Cape colonial borders through to Natal. After contemplating that his Methodist congregants could choose another Christian denomination, however, Shaw reconsidered. He decided to capitalize on this instance of African initiative to promote his vision of a mission station composed of industrious African Christians living in symbiosis with surrounding white farmers. This chapter looks at how such a momentous initiative evolved from the leverage Africans gained as Christians in the Cape Colony. Farmerfield then developed into a concrete plan to advance Methodist evangelism among Africans in the Eastern Cape and to ameliorate the miserable living conditions and dire circumstances in which many Africans lived by the 1830s.

Grahamstown and the Eastern Cape Frontier Zone

The city of Grahamstown figures prominently in the origins of Farmerfield. Founded in 1812 as a military post near the eastern boundary of the Cape Colony, Grahamstown immediately took on the important identity of a defensive frontier town. As such, its earliest population consisted mainly of military personnel. The town itself was named to commemorate Lieutenant Colonel John Graham, whom the colonial government entrusted with the task of using any necessary tactics to oust Xhosa chiefdoms from the area called the Zuurveld between 1811 and 1812.[3] By 1812 the Cape Colony had engaged Africans in four wars of dispossession, the last of which attempted to reinforce a territorial division between African chiefdoms and the colony. Access to the grazing lands of the Zuurveld, as well as disputes about where colonial and African boundaries lay, ushered in the creation of Grahamstown as a military bulwark against Africans.

On account of political rivalry and splintering among the Xhosa, the Zuurveld had become the western boundary of an advancing group of Xhosa chiefdoms with permanent settlements established by the 1760s. For the advancing guard of white colonists coming from the opposite direction, the Zuurveld became their eastern boundary and a contested territory.[4] "In this way," wrote the historian Hermann Giliomee, "two cultures, which both valued land as a means of production and cattle as a source of wealth and prestige were brought together in a single area."[5] Moreover, as Giliomee pointed out, "the opportunities each saw for supplementing stock through raiding and trading, became both bonds and sources of conflict[.]"[6] The 1811–12 War of Dispossession created a territorial division predicated on the belief that the Fish River, forming a partial boundary of the Zuurveld itself, was a natural line of demarcation. The Fish River was an easily recognizable barrier that would keep Africans in the right proximity from the colony and whites within the official borders, thereby avoiding more costly warfare on the frontier.[7] Yet this boundary created problems from the outset. Moreover, in the 1770s white colonists had appealed to the colonial government to meet their needs for pasture by extending the borders of the colony to the Fish River.[8] By 1778 the colonial government had concluded an agreement with some African chiefdoms whereby the Fish River would indeed constitute the official border.[9]

Between 1811 and 1812, the colonial government justified the expulsion of Africans from the Zuurveld and beyond the Fish River by acting on the belief that the Fish River was the official and sacrosanct eastern border of the Cape Colony. In the short term, colonel Graham and his military force were successful in driving the Xhosa from the Zuurveld. He and his military force used nothing less than a scorched earth policy, burning the dwellings and destroying the crops of the Xhosa. The destruction of material and human life in this new strategy of total war was an altogether novel and traumatic experience for the Xhosa.

While on a tour of the missions in the colony approximately a year after the expulsion, the Reverend John Campbell passed through an area the Xhosa used to occupy. During a part of his journey he observed:

> [W]e came in sight of a beautiful valley between the mountains, of about four miles extent. The sides of the mountain were covered with Caffre gardens, among the trees, from whence they had lately been driven by the military. The skeletons of many of their houses remained, and some tobacco was still growing; but all their corn fields were destroyed. The hills were covered with trees to the top, and were divided by the course of a river. Formerly the whole was covered with Caffre villages, but now there is not a living soul, but stillness everywhere reigns.[10]

Despite Colonel Graham's military success between 1811 and 1812, frontier security continued to worry the colonial government as Africans defiantly crossed the demarcated boundaries. Moreover, the sense of injustice they had suffered as well as the material need for access to the Zuurveld hindered the secure, peaceful denouement colonial officials had in mind. Within five years of the establishment of Grahamstown, the Xhosa descended on the town and proved to colonial government that their frontier policy was completely ineffective. It was the fifth outbreak of war on the Eastern Cape frontier.

Although the Xhosa were defeated, the fifth War of Dispossession in 1819 lent further urgency to the issue of frontier defense. Immediately after the war, the colonial government alienated approximately 4,000 square miles of land to create a neutral zone between Africans and the colony. Moreover, two new settlements were established to serve as human buffers against the Xhosa. The first was the 1820 emigration scheme that brought between 4,000 and 5,000 British emigrants to settle in the Zuurveld, now renamed Albany.[11] A Scottish settlement was also envisioned—rife with stereotypes of warlike Scottish Highlanders as the ideal neighbors to thwart any potential Xhosa uprising. What emerged instead in 1829 was the Kat River settlement, which served the dual purposes of protecting the colony as well as providing land restitution for those Khoekhoe who chose to emigrate to the new community (see Map 1). The commissioner general for the Eastern Districts and architect of the settlement, Andries Stockenström, asserted that, "no better defense against the Kaffirs (in case of necessity) does exist than such a community of Hottentots, attached to the soil by the right of property, would be."[12]

Though only implemented in the 1820s, the call for the creation of human settlements to act as barriers against Africans was made even before the Xhosa were cleared out of the Zuurveld between 1811 and 1812 or descended on Grahamstown in 1819.[13] Despite military successes over the Xhosa, these human buffers provided no effective measures in maintaining long-term peace or securing the frontier. Since both the Kat River and the Albany settlement, as the emigrant British community was called, encompassed lands the Xhosa had previously occupied, they were destined to remain at the forefront of grievances over access to land and the stability of the frontier. It is against the backdrop of these struggles over land and attempts to maintain peace between whites and Africans on the frontier that the city of Grahamstown and various new settlements came into being.

Grahamstown and the other towns and villages that constituted the Eastern Cape remained, throughout much of the nineteenth century, crucial theaters of confrontation between various groups of Africans and white settlers. Long before the mineral revolution and the South African War, colonial officials made and sometimes sullied their careers over the issue of securing the Eastern Cape frontier. In its physical proximity to Xhosa chiefdoms, Eastern Cape towns, and Grahamstown in particular, concerns about security were characterized by a certain frontier hysteria that historian Basil Le Cordeur argues often escalated into psychosis.[14] Given these features of the area, it was all the more surprising that the same developments contributing to violence and security led to the creation of an

African community amid a predominantly white one as well as renewed attempts to attract even more white settlers.[15]

In the 1820s and 1830s the Eastern Cape experienced ripple effects from the protracted and violent encounters between whites and Africans. Intermittent streams of refugees flocked to the area. Drought, food shortages, and violent struggles for political ascendancy between and within African chiefdoms compounded the hardships Africans experienced and also spurred temporary migrations into the Eastern Cape. Africans came into the Eastern Cape and into frontier towns like Grahamstown as refugees seeking work, food, and temporary succor. Although we do not know what these early African residents thought of the new Eastern Cape landscape populated by whites, some of the Xhosa among them must have been pained to become refugees in areas they formerly occupied. Imagining these scenarios as he watched wagons come from the interior, Cowper Rose noted that the "dark train of natives" now "look[ed] upon that which the white men have taken from them." An African chief, Mdushani [Mdushane], who had attacked Grahamstown before, most tellingly expressed that with the growth of the town, "the *kraal* was now too large to be attempted."[16] For some of those who had not experienced colonial encroachment firsthand, it was evident that what had happened to the Xhosa of the Zuurveld and of the now neutral or "ceded" territory could certainly become their own fate; Perhaps it did not augur well that, according to Cowper Rose who visited in the 1820s, the prison was the "handsomest building, and the most necessary" structure.[17]

Besides the military presence, Grahamstown itself was unimpressive, both its landscape and its inhabitants. Cowper Rose, who seemed to have a rather humorous penchant for insulting everyone and everything, described the town as a "large, ugly, ill-built straggling place." Of the residents, Rose noted with much humor "a strange mixture of lounging officers, idle tradesmen, (merchants, I beg your pardon), drunken soldiers and still more drunken settlers."[18] When most of the original cordon of 1820s British settlers decamped from their land allotments and filtered into town, few were inspired by what they saw.[19] For example, the settler Jeremiah Goldswain, (who had significant spelling issues) upon visiting Grahamstown in the early 1820s, wondered if the place should indeed be called a town since "thear ware not more than twentey or twentey five Houses in it that was worthey to be caled Houses."[20] Another settler, Thomas Philipps, also noted in May 1820 that there were no more than "twenty good houses in it."[21]

The more missionary-minded of the settlers expressed less consternation at the material deficiencies of Grahamstown's landscape than at the seemingly spiritual barrenness of the town. Given missionaries' stance on temperance, the drunkenness was particularly alarming. In December 1820 William Shaw had exclaimed, "Alas in Graham's Town there is no *Minister*, not even for the Europeans and both classes [of Europeans and Africans] are generally speaking sunk low in drunkenness, lewdness and other deadly sins."[22] Fellow settler and missionary colleague, John Ayliff, expressed similar concerns about the "Beastly" intoxication and "Sin of drunkenness" he often witnessed in Grahamstown.[23] Missionaries and temporary sojourners voiced concerns about the moral and economic fate of new settlers within the framework of irreligion, immorality, and economic distress.

The ranks of 1820s settlerdom also shared missionaries' anxieties, but addressing religious and moral fortitude would mean little if not coupled with immediate plans to avoid economic disaster. The settlers, who were described in a contemporary newspaper retrospective on Salem as "men and women who gave up their country to hack out a place for civilization in the midst of the African wilderness," had to develop new economic strategies beyond agriculture to support the lifestyles they had envisioned.[24] Roughly divided into cohorts reflecting the British poor, working classes, and elite hierarchy, the impoverished emigrants now had to worry about a degree of social and economic leveling they had not anticipated.[25] In addition to their economic woes, settlers also grew concerned about isolation from the refinements of "civilized" society and the alarming implications for white women who now had to engage in backbreaking labor without proper help.[26] Women, if they were not before, had to be and became, more self-conscious about the critical roles they played in upholding the standard of a "civilized life within their own circles and promoting it in the other; a role missionary wives and daughters long had to assume."[27]

From these vantage points, the Eastern Cape and its new detachment of white settlers hardly seemed the crucible for the making of a new elite that would contribute significantly to the entrenchment of modern racial and class domination in South Africa. Accomplishing white domination was a protracted, uneven process. It required settlers to redefine themselves in relation to the Africans in their midst, ensure they had an adequate supply of land and access to laborers, and wage war when necessary to defend their way of life in the Eastern Cape. As the settlers reoriented their economic strategies toward new patterns of trade, production, and consumption, they soon took what they believed to be their rightful place among the pantheon of elite white settlerdom throughout South Africa and the rest of the British empire.[28] Despite the unsatisfactory assessments of Grahamstown in the early 1820s, settlers continued to migrate to town, and the city grew rapidly.[29] The population increased and the residents erected new houses. As the status and wealth of the Eastern Cape settler elite grew, some of those who maintained farms in the more outlying rural areas also kept a house in town.[30] Consonant with the more modern city the settlers had in mind, the prison military barracks was among the more imposing new structures.[31] As early as 1826 the material and religious growth of Grahamstown was apparent to first-time visitors. William Shrewsbury, a British Methodist minister who arrived at the Cape in 1826, was quite impressed by the town he saw a few years after Goldswain recorded his initial, unremarkable impressions:

> The houses, the farm-yards, the cross-barred gates, the inhabitants in
> manners, dress and appearance are thoroughly English, and while look-
> ing at every object I met, and the field of oats and barley, and the gardens
> with abundance of vegetables of the same kind as I met with in my native
> country, it almost seemed a reverie to conclude that I was in Africa.[32]

Well beyond Goldswain's earlier pronouncement, Grahamstown by the late 1820s was becoming "England in miniature," as Reverend Shrewsbury put it.[33]

The town blossomed into a commercial entrepôt, a center of Methodism, unofficial capital of the Eastern Cape, and the second largest city in the Colony besides Cape Town.[34] "The local government being placed here with a considerable number of military, and several merchants . . . having taken up their residence in the place," James Backhouse, a Quaker on a missionary tour of the Colony noted, Grahamstown "gained an importance such as its locality did not promise."[35] The streets, Backhouse further observed in 1838, "are regularly laid out; and the houses are neat, and white, or yellow."[36] Moreover, unlike the thatch roofed houses that dotted the town's landscape in the 1820s, the houses in Grahamstown were now "usually covered with slate, or zinc obtained from England."[37] Grahamstown's landscape told the story of the rapid move to the level of civilization that was deemed appropriate for white settlers. Just as missionaries assessed their progress among the Xhosa based partly on the changes in the physical landscape, so too did visitors and settlers gauge the growth of Grahamstown in terms of its architecture and how closely it resembled England.

Grahamstown's socioeconomic growth paralleled similar developments in the religious realm. Far from the religious barrenness William Shaw complained about upon arriving at the Cape in 1820, Grahamstown soon boasted several denominations including Baptists, the Dutch Reformed Church, Episcopalians, and Methodists. Shaw immediately began preaching in the Albany area and some of the settlers who were previously Methodist laymen in Britain undertook similar roles as local preachers and class leaders in the new settlement.[38] By November 1822 the first Wesleyan chapel, begun in 1821, was opened for church service, presaging Grahamstown's significance as a center of Methodism. At the end of December another chapel was opened for services in Salem, one of the 1820s settler villages approximately nineteen miles outside of Grahamstown, where Shaw lived. The Methodists thus established themselves as the most influential denomination among white settlers in the area. William Shaw and his colleagues erected first humble, then more impressive, churches throughout the Eastern Cape. Although various denominations operated in the area, the Methodists gained the best foothold among the white settlers, wielded the most influence on them, and by the 1840s had already built more churches than any other religious body.[39]

In addition to the semipermanent population of soldiers garrisoned in town, Grahamstown's inhabitants consisted of British settlers who had migrated to the Cape in the 1820s and part of the Dutch population who had not migrated into the interior during the Great Trek. By the 1830s at least 4,000 whites, mostly British, lived in Grahamstown, the highest concentration of British settlers in any part of the Colony.[40] These white settlers by the 1830s and 1840s had become farmers, merchants, mechanics, carpenters, butchers, bakers, masons, shoemakers, shopkeepers, traders, and tailors, along with a few attorneys, clerks, druggists, wagon makers, painters, blacksmiths, wheelwrights, sawyers, and seamstresses.[41] These were the kinds of respectable occupations that characterized a burgeoning middle class.

By the 1830s an increasingly heterogeneous mix of Africans augmented the population of Grahamstown and its vicinity. A cross section of the baptismal registry of the Methodist Church in Grahamstown between the 1820s and the 1830s, for example, shows the African population as comprising slaves, ex-slaves, Khoekhoe, Sotho-Tswana, Xhosa, and Mfengu.[42] The origin of these populations in the Eastern Cape and in Grahamstown was partly related to the displacement that various groups of Africans experienced in the 1820s and 1830s. Historians attribute the sources of the intermittent and violent upheavals of the 1820s to the rise of the Zulu kingdom, the demands of slave trading in the Delagoa Bay area, and the steady white encroachment on African lands. The result was a dispersion of people into southeastern Africa. Many of these people came to or were resettled in the Eastern Cape. These Africans came into the colony seeking refuge, work, and a chance to rebuild their lives. In these quests, their motivations, if not their life chances, were similar to those of the British settlers who came in the 1820s also seeking opportunities to start anew.

The slaves and ex-slaves were a motley group, some imported into the colony from places as far flung as Asia and East Africa, others born at the Cape. Some had been "prize Negroes" taken by the British naval squadron from illegal slave ships and brought to the Cape. Some of these "prize Negroes" worked at the nearby Somerset Farm (see Map 3), a government institution that produced food for the military, and migrated to Grahamstown when the farm was broken up in 1825.[43] Eventually some of the descendants of Khoekhoe and former slaves assimilated into the "Colored" category, but in the 1830s, the two groups were still considered distinct. Some of the Khoekhoe present in Grahamstown served there as a special military corps, and after they demobilized, remained in town. Many of these military men had had previous experience at the various Moravian or LMS mission stations in the Colony. They maintained their affiliation to the LMS missionaries in Grahamstown and in Theopolis—a nearby LMS mission located approximately twenty-five kilometers away from town (see Map 1).[44]

The Mfengu, Xhosa, Sotho, and Tswana were among the groups who were forcibly brought, or voluntarily came, into the Eastern Cape seeking refuge in the 1820s and 1830s. The sixth outbreak of war between particular Xhosa chiefdoms and the colonists between 1834 and 1835 compounded the privation many Africans already faced. By now Africans were becoming more and more familiar with the characteristics and outcome of colonial warfare against them. Once again mixed detachments of white and Khoekhoe soldiers destroyed residences, burned crops, seized cattle, and expelled Africans from their lands. Women and children were also detained and brought into the colony, while desperation and hunger brought another steady stream of refugees into the Eastern Cape. Some of these refugees were individuals who had been living at Methodist mission stations beyond the borders of the Cape Colony.

Grahamstown itself offered these Africans little in the way of permanent refuge. The small plots of land on which some Africans settled were far from ideal in their location or productive potential. As historian J. B. Peires observed in his seminal work on the Xhosa, "From the 1830s, the black quarter or 'location' sited on communal waste or old burying ground—became a familiar feature of the eastern Cape country town."[45] Even the Khoekhoe serving in the colonial forces had inadequate accommodations. The Khoekhoe regiment was housed in barracks in town, while their wives and children sought whatever employment and housing was available in town or the surrounding locations.[46] The Khoekhoe location, according to missionary visitor James Backhouse, was "a disgrace to Grahamstown." Backhouse asserted that this "disgrace" was not only limited to the physical appearance of the location but to the character of the people as well:

> In this place [the location] . . . more than fifty families were living in miserable huts, or in the most wretched hovels. Some of them were constructed of fragments of rush mats, sugar bags and old clothes, thrown over a stick, stuck in the ground in a sloping direction, and eked out at the bottom with stones or the skulls of bullocks. Most of the inhabitants were filthy in their persons; but they were easy, contented, and indisposed to work, beyond what was absolutely necessary to get them a little tobacco and the meanest fare; themselves were in rags, and their children naked. Several of them were living in concubinage, and spent much of their small earnings in brandy.[47]

The Khoekhoe location was, in short, a missionary nightmare. Backhouse and Shaw, the Methodist minister and superintendent, were far more pleased with the Tswana and Mfengu areas. Shaw noted, "More than half of the natives live in separate settlements on the eastern side of the town, where their beehive huts or other dwellings (for some have erected comfortable cottages) occupy building lots assigned to them by the Government."[48] The rest of the population lived on the premises of their employers as servants and laborers, or squatted any place they could. No matter how desperate the circumstances of the refugees filtering into the area, these miserable living conditions hardly afforded long term succor.

Farming on any self-sufficient scale on these allotments was virtually impossible and grazing was out of the question. Africans could keep a few head of cattle if they were employed on white farms. Yet their employers had no desire to facilitate a situation that allowed Africans to accumulate enough property in cattle and possibly seek a more independent existence. Whenever they accumulated enough to avoid subservience on white farms, Africans voted with their feet and settled on the fringes of any land accessible to them in the Eastern Cape. Moreover, since some were mistreated or paid low wages, they reserved the right to seek better working conditions. Whites interpreted any African reluctance to work for them as indolence and insolence.

Like their counterparts in industrial Britain, local settlers complained about the intractability and shortage of labor and sought measures to compel Africans to do work that they now thought was beneath them as whites. Britons, some who only a few years before had been among the very poor and unemployed in England, "did not retain any inclination to work" after resettling at the Cape and accused Africans of being lazy and fickle.[49] Indeed the labor shortage in the Eastern Cape was real and the prohibition of slave labor in the British settlements deprived settlers in that part of the colony of the slave labor that was otherwise legally available up to the end of apprenticeship in 1838.[50] The settlers explained away their difficulties in procuring labor by appealing to and reinforcing the existing stereotypes of Africans. When considering proposals for easing the labor shortage in the Eastern Cape, local colonial officials affirmed that previous attempts to induce Africans to remain in long-term, continuous employment had been unsuccessful because of the "difficulty of reconciling the savages to habits of regular industry."[51] After seeking temporary relief in the Eastern Cape, many of the laborers showed "apathy and a disinclination to work," and sought more independent options.[52]

Historian Clifton Crais had noted the existence of a few such semi-independent settlements in the 1820s and 1830s as testimony to African attempts to avoid economic marginality and limitations on their mobility.[53] Everywhere Africans tried to eke out an independent existence they incurred the ire and jealousy of local white farmers and the displeasure of government officials anxious to maintain peace. A heterogeneous group of Africans flocked to these fledgling villages from Grahamstown. While there were some individual successes, these communities were unable to assert themselves as independent, long-term peasant entities. Africans continued to work intermittently on white farms or in town.[54] Given the limitations of these early hamlets, it is not surprising that mission settlements featured into African strategies to mitigate their landlessness, economic deprivation, and dependence on whites. Many individuals filtered back into Grahamstown as a temporary sojourn until they could find a better place to go.

Grahamstown's African residents were far from settled or prosperous in relation to whites. Heterogeneity and close contact between Africans and whites in Grahamstown did little to increase understanding between the various groups or generate any sense of security across the frontier. What the convergence of whites and Africans in the Eastern Cape generated was a proliferation of stereotypes and caricatures of Africans centered on continuums of savagery and civilization, capriciousness and predictability, docility and bellicosity. A heterogeneous populace did not contribute to any sense of Grahamstown being a cosmopolitan city composed of diverse groups comfortably interacting, learning, or borrowing from each other. After a decade of serving as human buffers along the frontier, white settlers in the Albany area had formed strong, negative opinions about frontier policy and about the Africans they encountered. They employed Africans in the capacity of servants and laborers and their perceptions of Africans were partly shaped by these daily interactions and the overall difficulty in getting Africans to "evince a good disposition," and to be "docile and tractable."[55]

White views were also shaped and hardened by the very real experiences of cattle raids and physical danger. Africans were portrayed as inveterate cattle thieves with an insatiable desire and almost pathological need to plunder. Nowhere is this more apparent than in the local newspaper established in the 1830s, the *Graham's Town Journal*. News features and editorials in the newspaper abound with words like "plunder" and "depredations" to describe the plight of the whites on the frontier. Africans were described in the pages of the journal as "hordes" and "savages," always on the brink of "irrupting." The *Journal* helped to promote an atmosphere of hysteria and anxiety already fueled by rumors of possible African uprisings against the Cape Colony; as well as fears that conflicts between Africans would spill over into Albany, sending intractable refugees into the area. One settler, Thomas Stubbs, recorded the "uproar" on the frontier between 1827 and 1828 when Grahamstown received word that "a nation of cannibals" was destroying other African polities close to the frontier, while the commissioner general of the area recorded the many instances in which these alarmist fears of the settlers were ungrounded.[56]

In such an environment, settlers demonstrated some uneasiness in their interactions with Africans. Every time theft of cattle was reported or war was imminent, settlers undoubtedly wondered if the Africans in their employ would turn against them. Even Andries Stockenström, who demonstrated tremendous objectivity in his views of relations on the frontier, asserted that the Xhosa, "if they were sure of success would rise to a man, and cut the throat of every white male and female, whom they could overtake."[57] These insecurities were also fueled by the continued reliance on an African corps for their protection. They feared that the military regiment of Khoekhoe soldiers in town would abscond and unite with other Africans against them. Referring to the regiment as a "corps of demi-savages," Thomas Philips, an influential 1820 settler, asserted that it was crucial for whites to be "prepared against any mischief which may arise from the Force [the military] being any other than European."[58]

Settler concerns about the Khoekhoe transcended unease about their loyalty as part of a military corps. As discussed in Chapter 1, some whites viewed the various mission settlements established for the Khoekhoe throughout the colony as refuges for the idle who did not want to work. Even for the 1820s settlers new to the colony, the Khoekhoe were now stereotyped as among the laziest of workers. Colonial officials and local settlers anxious to alleviate the labor shortage in the Eastern Cape blamed the chronic problem on the "vagrant disposition of the Hottentots and other natives who have hitherto been in the service of the farmers."[59] Commenting on the local Theopolis mission station, Mrs. Philipps, wife of the settler Thomas Philipps, wrote that the "institution seems of little or no use to the Men and Women, excepting the aged who are not able to work. The others are most of them idle, and it is a receptacle for them if they do not choose to work or remain in their places, and they are not obliged to work, or go out to Service unless they like it."[60] These views were not only evident in settler diaries or frontier newspapers. Whites throughout the colony shared similar opinions about the mission stations within the borders of the Colony. For example, when the Cape newspaper the *South African Commercial Advertiser* ran a series of columns early in 1824 on the progress at the mission settlements established for the Khoekhoe, one correspondent replied that the positive assessments were quite incredulous and he was more inclined to believe earlier assessments of the missions as "receptacles of idleness, filth, canting fanaticism, and squalid poverty."[61]

These negative assessments and stereotypes were applied to the Khoekhoe as well as other groups of Africans. Given the frequent clashes between the colonists and the Xhosa, this group on the immediate borders of the colony was considered among the most warlike. Positive portrayals were reserved for the Tswana who had come from much farther in the interior. When determining which group would be ideal as laborers, the Tswana usually came out on top.[62] Mrs. Philipps, assessing the Tswana servants in her employ in 1826, stated, "Our Bechuanas continue to improve greatly and nothing of the Savage remains, a milder set of People I never saw from the beginning, and they are strictly honest."[63] On the Mfengu dispersed throughout the Eastern Cape in the 1820s and 1830s, Mrs. Philipps wrote that they were "a most interesting People, mild in their manners, and naturally good humored and happy dispositions." Moreover, she pointed out that since the Mfengu were "very superior to the Hottentots," she was certain they would make "valuable servants."[64] Of the Khoekhoe, Mrs. Philipps was unimpressed as she thought they made poor servants because they "never will stay long anywhere."[65] Her husband was of the opinion that the Khoekhoe, especially those who had intermixed with slaves or whites were, "like the half-castes in all countries . . . cunning and presuming."[66]

The diverse confluence of Africans in Grahamstown presents a daunting challenge when trying to ascertain identity politics among the Khoekhoe, Xhosa, Sotho-Tswana, and Mfengu. The regiments of Khoekhoe soldiers who were used against other Africans in the numerous wars of dispossession during the nineteenth century certainly complicate any assessment of unity. Moreover, the same is true of some Mfengu groups who after the 1835 war fought on the side of the colony, as well as particular Xhosa chiefdoms that had remained loyal or neutral.[67] In addition to these fractured loyalties, the variety of languages spoken by these groups of Africans also revealed the difficulties of forging common bonds. By the 1830s, language and physical features were among the key markers whites used to distinguish various groups of Africans from each other. Mrs. Philipps, for instance, described the Mfengu as a "remarkable, fine, tall, handsome people, very different and very superior to the Hottentots, but [who] like them have the same flat noses and hair . . . and skin much blacker."[68] Undoubtedly, language also helped Africans to identify each other while reinforcing differences between them in certain situations.

Despite linguistic heterogeneity and some divided interests, Africans in the Eastern Cape sometimes converged in mixed settlements as an underclass seeking refuge and independence. One settlement under a former Tswana chief, Damon, consisted of Tswana-speaking peoples in addition to Khoekhoe, ex-slaves, and Xhosa, reflecting the variety of the African populations in the Eastern Cape.[69] That such a diverse group of people came together to avoid the most onerous aspects of working for whites is testimony to the ability of Africans to unite around a common cause whatever their ethnic affiliations. These early ethnically mixed, polyglot communities, however, failed in securing any permanent settlements for Africans within the borders of the Cape Colony. If Africans were going to remain in the Albany area, they would have to accept the limited residential and economic opportunities available for them. However "good humored" or "mild" some settlers assessed their servants to be, employment was often intermittent, remuneration low, and land access wholly inadequate. Service for white employers in Grahamstown and on surrounding farms was rarely a path to economic independence and material prosperity for Africans. As much as Mrs. Philipps was delighted to see "so many little black creatures [the school children at the Theopolis mission] brought into a state of civilization and improvement," she only envisioned that their education and civilization would make them "useful as Servants."[70] The congregants who approached William Shaw to found a mission for them must have surveyed their situation and come to the conclusion that given the lack of opportunities for self-sufficiency, Grahamstown could only be a temporary sojourn for them.

Acceding to the Congregants' Request

By the late 1830s, the Albany area was a religious smorgasbord. One consequence of this was the drift toward segregated worship. Whereas various communities had worshipped together when Grahamstown was in its nascent stages of development, now each segment of the population splintered off to their own denominations with services conducted in a variety of languages to suit the distinct needs of each congregation. Whites in Grahamstown's polyglot population cordoned off more and more areas of their lives into distinct spaces, in their religious lives as well as their social and economic lives.[71]

The plurality of religious denominations reflected wider gulfs between blacks and whites, while it also engendered a sort of competition for souls. This is perhaps the only agenda Africans could influence. Missionaries went to Africa to minister to the "heathen" and to found African missions, not to write home about their white congregations. Undoubtedly, the Cape's white population had its fair share of "heathens" and the irreligious. In fact, many individuals in Britain believed that missionaries could proselytize at home without going to far-flung corners of the globe to find converts. But at the Cape, as elsewhere in Africa, missions were an African affair. Whatever else the missionaries may have had difficulty in communicating, this much was clear to their potential African congregants, who used this to their advantage.

In his correspondence about the origins of the Farmerfield mission, William Shaw provides some evidence that the pioneering phase of missionary work had resulted in certain expectations and perceptions of white missionaries. Africans viewed missionaries in a variety of different roles: as diplomatic arbiters, as sources of information, and as influential individuals who played roles akin to African chiefs. Missionaries were the guardians of a special knowledge (Christianity). They secured access to fertile lands that they then allocated like chiefs and welcomed individuals seeking refuge from the dictates of life in an African chiefdom. First informally, then legislatively, missionaries tried to have African Christians exempted from customary law.[72] In short, missionaries set themselves up and acted as alternatives to African chiefly power, leading to warnings from the colonial government about acting as "imperium in imperio."[73]

Since the missionaries set themselves up as redeemers of "heathens," ordinary Africans decided to test the truth of this stance. Africans used their expectations of missionaries as part of a conscious strategy to maintain autonomy and gain access to land. The Grahamstown congregants not only asked for material assistance, but also reminded the Methodist missions that they had a choice of denominations. According to Shaw, the congregants pointed out:

> As the London and Moravian Missionary Societies (either by receiving grants from the government, or purchasing with their own funds) had provided land for the occupation of the people of this class who had attached themselves to those societies respectively; so they have a claim upon us for a similar provision of their wants.[74]

William Shaw had received several requests for missions in the 1820s and 1830s and was thus accustomed to African initiative. Shaw had capitalized on some of these requests to further his own desire to establish a chain of missions, and thereby a powerful Methodist sphere of influence. What was so different about the request of the Grahamstown congregants was that they made Shaw aware that missionaries were being called upon to make their rhetoric real and effective. Shaw, therefore, believed that the activities of other missionary societies:

> forced the measure upon us [Methodists], unless we had been willing to
> sacrifice the fruit of much diligent and successful missionary labor
> bestowed upon this class of peoples. And it was not to be supposed that
> we could willingly submit to see the people whom we have instructed
> withdrawn from our care by temporal advantages which the arrange-
> ments of other societies present to their acceptance.[75]

Ultimately, the missionaries had to accept that Africans sought missions for spiritual as well as material needs. Just as missionaries were willing to unite their
spiritual message of Christianity with the material demands of civilization, so too
were the congregants willing to point out that they could not maintain a proper
spiritual state when they faced such material deprivation in the Eastern Cape.

The Africans in Grahamstown had seen and heard about mission settlements
as places to gain access to land because some had previously lived at other settlements. In addition, the LMS and Wesleyan missionaries were popular and well-
known. The congregants certainly believed the Methodists could do something
for them. What might William Shaw offer instead of an essentially grim situation
in town? The Grahamstown congregants sought a place where they could establish
permanent residence, maintain a measure of economic independence, and pursue
a Christian lifestyle. In lieu of the freehold tenure they could never gain in the
Eastern Cape, the congregants decided that engaging in rent tenancy contracts at
a mission would be far more advantageous to them than any temporary labor
contract they might arrange with whites. Contractual arrangements with the
Methodist Church required a specific set of rules they were already familiar with
as congregants in that Church. For the heterogeneous group of Africans, their
quest for economic independence meant, in principle, that they were ready to
accept several basic proscriptions for being a Christian: attend church, engage in
monogamous marriage, abstain from alcohol, and refrain from initiating young
men into adulthood through the rite of circumcision. In short, the Grahamstown
congregants, as Christians, already had an idea of what was expected of them.

The congregants made their request in the context of a Methodist revival in
Grahamstown that brought 300 new members into the church between 1837 and
1838. Of the 300 church members, somewhere between one hundred and 130
people fell into the category of Xhosa, Mfengu, ex-slaves, and Tswana, while
whites constituted the remainder.[76] Coming on the heels of the 1834–35 War of
Dispossession that destroyed several of the missions in the Methodist chain and
sent Africans scattering into the colony, this religious revival had overjoyed Shaw
and his colleagues. In addition to the revival, Methodism among Africans received
further reinforcements by the creation of an educational institution, the Watson
Institute, and a vernacular newspaper, *Umshumayeli Wendaba*, during the same period of revival. The Watson Institute trained Africans to become teachers and schoolmasters and was an important part of the Methodist plan to implement the principle
of "native agency." *Umshumayeli Wendaba* provided a forum for literate African

Christians to communicate with each other and for missionaries to disseminate Christian news and teachings. For example, the newspaper ran an article on Chief Phato's noteworthy proclamation of the Sabbath as a holy day in 1833 (although they glossed over Phato's refusal to convert like his brother Kama) and on the momentous conversion of Kama, as well as featuring stories on Adam and Eve.[77]

Despite these auspicious developments in Methodism in general and for African Methodists in particular, Shaw was hesitant about establishing a new mission. Believing the request an imposition, if not an outright manipulation, Shaw responded equivocally and tried to persuade the church members to stay in Grahamstown. Methodists established mission settlements for Africans exclusively beyond the borders and wanted to maintain that trend. With no chiefdoms in the Albany area, Shaw had not envisioned creating a mission close to Grahamstown or the general Albany area. The only local mission was Theopolis, established by the LMS specifically for the Khoekhoe population within the area. Whereas the LMS and the Moravians had established their sphere of influence among the Khoekhoe through the creation of mission settlements for them, the most ambitious plan Shaw had in mind was the African population in the Albany area frequenting the local Methodist chapels. Under Shaw's leadership, the Methodists had secured a stronghold among Africans in the Albany area without creating a special mission for them. An African mission in Grahamstown was impossible because of the land constraints; one amongst the white farming communities would be an anomaly since it was never part of a blueprint for the Methodist chain of missions.

Shaw considered the possibility of his congregants soliciting other missionary societies and concluded that he was unwilling to "sacrifice the fruit of much diligent and successful missionary labor [already] bestowed on this class of people."[78] Since he was unable to guarantee church members the ability to practice the agricultural lifestyles they wanted to pursue in Grahamstown, Shaw was finally "constrained to yield to the wishes of the people."[79] He purchased the farm Klipheuvel, one of the many sheep farms that had come on the market with the out-migration of Dutch farmers from the Cape Colony[80] (see Map 3). Shaw renamed the farm "Farmerfield" as a tribute to one of the treasurers of the Wesleyan Missionary Society, Thomas Farmer.[81] The appeal of the African congregation in Grahamstown presented Shaw with the opportunity to respond creatively to what Africans needed instead of relying solely on his personal vision for a chain of stations.

Although initially reluctant to form a new mission, Shaw eagerly developed a scheme to make the Farmerfield mission the pinnacle of missionary work, an emblematic departure from other pioneering missions. Within months of the request, African initiative once again gave way to grand evangelical aspirations. Shaw used this opportunity to reflect on LMS missionary work as well as fifteen years of his own experience as a missionary. What had been accomplished in the five decades between 1790 and 1838? The LMS, by championing the cause of the Khoekhoe and other Africans, had become totally embroiled in politics and had fallen into disrepute among many settlers. The Methodists had set their sights beyond the conflicts in the Colony and established a chain of missions that stretched hundreds of miles into Natal. Shaw, while critical of frontier policy, was also careful to avoid accusations made against the LMS that they portrayed Africans as innocent victims and whites as rapacious aggressors. Shaw declared to a colonial official in Britain in the aftermath of the war of 1834–35:

> I profess myself, and am very well-known to be, a devoted friend of the native tribes; but I will not be a party in the advocacy of their rights, on principles which involve an aggression on the character and claims of others. . . . I cannot perceive that true philanthropy requires me to blacken my white friends, for the purpose of making my black friends white.[82]

In addition to proclaiming his sympathy with the colonists' view of the frontier problem, Shaw also wanted to make sure that his mission would avoid the accusations leveled at the LMS stations that they were "asylums for the extremely poor and the incorrigibly idle."[83]

Shaw instead wanted a mission that was a culmination of all he had learned about the pitfalls of missionary experiments in the Cape Colony. He could, however, find no one mission or African settlement that he thought an unqualified success. While many of the LMS mission stations were included in the general dissatisfaction with pioneer missions, perhaps the most important model that Shaw wanted to differentiate Farmerfield from was the Kat River settlement. The establishment of the Kat River settlement for the Khoekhoe in 1829 was perceived as perhaps the last attempt to prove once and for all whether the Khoekhoe were redeemable. Andries Stockenström, then the lieutenant governor of the eastern portion of the Cape Colony who advised the government to establish the community, believed that the settlement would "give practical effect" to Ordinance 50, the "Hottentot Magna Carta" that removed the legal restriction on the mobility and freedom of the Khoekhoe.[84] The Kat River was specifically sited on land confiscated from the Xhosa, another buffer settlement that showed how philanthropy and frontier defense could march hand in hand.

Envisioned as a model of agricultural industry, the Kat River settlement encompassed some sixty square miles of land divided into residential, agricultural, and grazing plots. While not established as a mission per se, many individuals from mission stations, especially Theopolis and Bethelsdorp, moved to the settlement. The settlement of 900 individuals in 1830 had burgeoned to 1,500 by 1832 and more than 2,000 in 1835.[85] Like previous settlements or missions before it, the Kat River attracted a heterogeneous group of people seeking access to land and better places to live; like its predecessors, it also faced a tremendous amount of pressure on its carrying capacity. With poverty, overcrowding, discrimination, and undercapitalization militating against the settlers' best efforts, the Kat River certainly was not the panacea for Khoekhoe landlessness and economic marginalization that many had imagined. Though the settlement could not fulfill everyone's aspirations for self-sufficiency and political empowerment, its existence held out hope for many people. In the middle of 1832, an article appeared in the *Graham's Town Journal* expressing optimism about the progress of religion, education, and agricultural production at the settlement:

> It is the germ from where will spring all the blessings of religious and social order and the means by which the cloud of prejudice still hanging over them will at length be dissipated. . . . The whole colony has watched with much interest this experimental test of the capability of the colored classes to exercise the duties devolving on denizens having a direct and positive interest in the soil they occupy. . . . They have been found equal to every exigency, and it must now be admitted, that a large measure of success had at longth [*sic*] crowned their efforts.[86]

Soon after the appearance of this article, the *Graham's Town Journal* featured many editorials expressing skepticism about the potential of the Kat River as an industrious agricultural settlement. Rather than acknowledging the disadvantages the Kat River settlers faced vis-à-vis whites, these editorials attributed the problems at the settlement to indolence and drunkenness.

In 1832 the journal reported several instances of desertion by slaves and other laborers and imputed that these individuals were heading to the Kat River.[87] Kat River was thus subjected to the same criticism leveled at mission stations throughout the colony since the beginning of missionary work in the 1790s. One farmer responding to the encouraging picture painted of the settlement replied sarcastically that the correspondent had only taken "a peep for the first time at romantic glades and sylvan glens," and was hardly in a position to assess the overall progress of the settlement. This farmer asserted instead that the settlement was "justly regarded by the idle, profligate and by delinquents of every magnitude as the most perfect place of sanctuary which the globe affords."[88] Shortly before this exchange, someone had sent in a sardonic quip describing the settlement as "a newly formed Garden which being afterwards neglected soon becomes a wilderness where every wholesome plant is in danger of being choked and destroyed by noxious weeds."[89]

The crescendo of criticism and defense of the Kat River settlement carried on unabated throughout the *Graham's Town Journal* in the 1830s. Once again, a promising settlement came under fire for harboring individuals who preferred not to work for whites and who, even when given land, supposedly could not prove themselves worthy of the philanthropic and religious energies spent on them. Therefore, by the time William Shaw was considering what kind of model he wanted to emulate for Farmerfield in 1838, the Kat River was perhaps the most important settlement he wanted to distinguish his mission from. Shaw believed that the population of the Kat River was too large and the method for allowing residence too open-ended.[90] He wanted a model mission that would combine the best of agricultural industry with the loftiest evangelical goals for a community of African Christians. At that moment he did not think the Kat River reflected these characteristics.

Farmerfield was not the first attempt to "establish agricultural settlements of devout Christians," as historian Crais has noted. These experiments were common among humanitarians and many missionaries at the Cape. The idealism surrounding the creation of the Farmerfield mission in 1838 echoes back to the optimism about the Sierra Leone settlement in the 1780s. Thus, in many ways Shaw was attempting to refine a familiar model of African development centered on Christianity. Shaw aimed at making this mission more effective than every single model of African settlements that preceded it.[91] No segment of the Cape population—African or white—would find anything to criticize about Farmerfield. The missionaries, the African residents, white settlers, and the colonial government would all be pleased with this mission. Since the mission's motto would be, "If any will not work, neither he ought to eat," indolence would not be tolerated.[92] White colonists would not complain about the availability of labor since the mission was in the midst of a white community and would therefore be accessible. The local mission residents would know that seasonal labor was expected of them and since they also needed some cash, both parties would benefit from this arrangement. Africans would have access to land and therefore have a real opportunity to prove that they could be industrious. They would also have access to the missionaries for their religious and educational needs. If both Africans and whites benefited from this arrangement, then there would be no need for African discontent or white criticism.[93] While Shaw acknowledged that these were rather utopian ideas, he nonetheless hoped this refined model of Farmerfield would represent a novel turn in missions.

From Sheep Farm to Mission Station: Klipheuvel Becomes Farmerfield

Farmerfield, situated in the Albany district on the eastern frontier of the Cape Colony, consisted of 6,000 acres of land that was once a sheep farm belonging to a Dutch farmer. The sheep farm, Klipheuvel, was the conventional size of farms allotted to Dutch settlers. The transition from its use as a sheep farm to its position as a mission settlement highlights the different perceptions of white and African land needs. A farm slated for the use of one white farmer was now purchased, subdivided, and deemed to be sufficient for the needs of approximately one hundred Africans families.[94] The carrying capacity of Farmerfield, like other mission settlements in the Cape Colony, therefore, was inherently limited. Consequently, mission residence for Africans could only provide partial refuge from land shortage. Nevertheless, Shaw and his future mission residents hailed this as an exciting beginning.

Between 1838 and the early months of 1839 William Shaw finalized the purchase of the farm and drew up plans for the physical layout and management of the estate. His plan included a screening process for potential residents that would not "allow any rambling native who thought fit to come and squat down among his countrymen on the Station, under professions, real or feigned, of a desire to receive religious instruction [.]"[95] Rather, Shaw rented the land on a yearly basis at a rate of one pound sterling per household to those individuals who, "either by means of the stock which they brought with them, or by well-known habits and occupations, possessed the means of supporting themselves by honest industry."[96] Shaw did not have a problem finding Africans who fit this description. By the time he signed the deed on May 28, 1839, he had received a deluge of applications from individuals eager to secure a spot at the mission.[97] As Shaw noted in his journal, "There were speedily as many applicants for admission as the extent of the land would allow us to accommodate."[98] Each household, upon paying one pound, gained access to residential plots as well as land suitable for farming and grazing. Farmerfield thus began on an auspicious design.

By the 1830s many of the heterogeneous mix of Africans who made their way into the Eastern districts of the Cape Colony seeking relief from misfortune and economic deprivation found that the town could offer only temporary succor. Some work was available in the Eastern Cape, but an increasing number of Africans found that laboring for whites held out little hope for reconstructing their lives on the model they desired. Attempts to establish independent communities in the Eastern Cape underscores how important it was for Africans to maintain a peasant option, defined in the broadest sense as some sort of access to agricultural and grazing plots that allowed opportunities to increase their herds and produce food. Increasingly, people turned to the Methodist Church, trying out all avenues that could possibly be of assistance, whether psychologically or materially. In Grahamstown some Africans were able to use their position as congregants of the Methodist Church to ask that the WMMS establish a mission for them as they had witnessed elsewhere in the Cape Colony. These individuals self-consciously used their position as Christians to ask the Church to intervene in a more concrete way in order to ameliorate the difficulties they encountered in Grahamstown.

Farmerfield's congregants struck a bargain to live as industrious Christian peasants who would follow the model Shaw envisioned of their living among whites in a mutually beneficial relationship. Shaw's plan was a grand one, and one of his greatest accomplishments after establishing a chain of missions beyond the Colony. Chapter 4 turns to the first fifty years of the Farmerfield settlement, highlighting the experiences of its early residents. The chapter explores how a mission designed to alleviate some of the economic burdens Africans faced was transformed into a labor regime for local white settlers. From such a perspective, it is possible to gauge the extent to which the lived experiences of the people of Farmerfield veered from their own goal for independence and Shaw's vision of an ideal mission station.

PART TWO

‖ 4 ‖

"A Selected Class of Natives"

Economic Visions and Realities of the First Fifty Years of the
Farmerfield Mission Station

By the early months of 1839, the general superintendent of Wesleyan Missions in South East Africa, William Shaw, had completed his screening of applicants for residence at Farmerfield. As outlined in his selection criteria, the vast majority of these residents was either Christian already, or had indicated they were making preparations for baptism and other requisite steps in adopting a Christian lifestyle. If these applicants also possessed sheep, cattle, goats, horses, and wagons, they were even more welcomed to the mission as these assets provided concrete evidence of material wealth and potential industry. These two prerequisites of Christian affiliation and property ownership shaped the development of Farmerfield both as an imagined and an actual community. As Shaw stated in his journal, he purchased the farm to "establish a selected class of natives thereon."[1]

Farmerfield's design merged spiritual and secular concerns in an evangelical and economic coupling far beyond anything the Grahamstown congregants had articulated in their request. What the African congregants deemed an important step in securing access to residential, arable, and grazing land as well as religious instruction, the missionaries further elaborated into an ambitious strategy to create a labor reserve populated exclusively by African Christians. Religious philanthropy and an economic labor regime marched unabashedly together on a plan William Shaw believed was a novel direction and design for mission settlements. In this living embodiment of the idea that Christianity and civilization should proceed together, Shaw identified work as a crucial part of the civilizing process. This chapter explores the extent to which Farmerfield was imagined as, and became, an economic enterprise, while the subsequent chapter explores the religious component of the design.

This chapter makes two arguments relating to Farmerfield's residents as a "selected class" of Africans. First, William Shaw defined "class" in a way that addressed

107

both African economic impoverishment and white labor shortages. The residents at Farmerfield constituted a special group or "class" of African Christians selected for their industry; this industry, when applied to their own agricultural pursuits at Farmerfield, would demonstrate how an African mission should operate as an economic establishment. By employing European agricultural techniques and technological implements, and by growing crops for the market, Farmerfield's residents would become an empowered peasantry. The residents would demonstrate the mechanics and benefits of the European civilizing mission on an economic scale. Second, as the only Methodist African mission established amid a white community, (see Map 3), Farmerfield's residents were earmarked as a special "class" of laborers that whites could and should be able to employ. This two-pronged design addressed both how an African mission should work on a local, self-contained economic scale, as well as the structural role Africans were expected to play in the wider economy.

This chapter asserts that the central ideological linchpin that held this design together was African capacity as laborers. African economic empowerment came with the proviso that any quest they undertook to be industrious, to produce for the market, or grow a wider range of crops, would be delimited by the socioeconomic and political imaginations that always saw white over black and begrudged any real challenge to this order. To explore the development of Farmerfield both as an idea of an empowered peasantry working in symbiosis with whites and as a living community, the first part of the chapter turns to the mechanics of establishing the mission and moving to Farmerfield. The next section briefly surveys early missionary acclaim over the settlement. The last part of the chapter paints an economic mosaic of the early residents to capture some aspects of how the early settlers fared at the mission, and how their economic endeavors deviated from or converged with the missionary idea of Farmerfield.

Moving to Farmerfield

Although there were as many applicants as the carrying capacity of the farm would allow, people did not move en masse to the mission as soon as land was available. Some people began settling in at Farmerfield between January and April 1839, even before the formal deed was signed in May, while others who had secured their spots came at different times throughout 1839 and into the early 1840s. People delayed in relocating to Farmerfield for a variety of reasons, including taking time to organize transportation and settle preexisting labor contracts. In June 1839 James Cameron, one of the ministers who frequently preached at Farmerfield in the early period of the settlement, encountered one of the Grahamstown congregants and his family moving to Farmerfield via an ox-wagon.[2] For this and the vast majority of families, the physical removal by ox-wagon was the primary means of travel. If they owned their own ox-wagon, it was a straightforward trip with a young man or the wagon owner leading the oxen while the women and children traveled with the personal belongings inside the wagon. If the wagon had to be hired, it was an added expense for individuals who already had to worry about the cost of rent and grazing fees. This expense probably factored into some delays in settling at Farmerfield.

If Farmerfield tenants hired or owned an ox-wagon, how arduous was the removal to the mission station? In his 1842 overview of the eastern districts of the Cape Colony, Robert Godlonton, editor of the *Graham's Town Journal*, assured potential emigrants that ox-wagons were "far superior, both in point of workmanship and durability, to the vehicles used for a similar purpose in any part of England." Moreover, Godlonton asserted that the flexibility and strength of these wagons made them suitable for the roughest terrain and when outfitted with a span of ten to twelve oxen, they could carry between 2,000 and 3,000 pounds. Finally, the arc-shaped roof of the wagon, covered with the same material used for sails, provided ample protection from wind, rain, or sun.[3] Ox-wagons proved to be relatively dependable means of transportation to make the task of moving a bit easier.

In addition to the potential logistical delays of hiring a wagon, some of the individuals accepted for residence had to fulfill their previous labor contracts before they moved to Farmerfield. William Shaw preferred for residents still employed as farm laborers and servants to give notice to their employers about changing residence and leaving their current jobs. Given his background as an 1820 settler and superintendent of Wesleyan missions, Shaw was well known throughout the Albany area. He would not have wanted Farmerfield's ambitious design to be shrouded in accusations about harboring deserters or encouraging laborers to leave their white employers, a charge leveled at many of the pioneer mission settlements in the Cape Colony. Ex-slaves in particular were vulnerable when their apprenticeship expired in December 1838 because some of them experienced opposition from their former owners when they wanted to leave.[4] By February 1839, at least five or six former slaves had applied for a spot at Farmerfield, yet had not moved to the mission. Shaw indicated that some of these individuals were unable to extricate themselves immediately from their previous labor arrangements to take up residence at the mission because they were "working at their trades, or as laborers in Graham's Town and its neighborhood."[5] Another reason why ex-slaves did not flock to Farmerfield in droves was the creation of an additional Methodist mission called Haslope Hills. Although a heterogeneous mix of individuals sought residence at Haslope Hills, William Shaw had earmarked the mission specifically to accommodate former slaves at around the same time as the creation of Farmerfield.[6] Haslope Hills thus had important ramifications for the post-emancipation population distribution at Farmerfield. Since so many former slaves chose Haslope Hills, Farmerfield's population came to reflect an even greater proportion of Africans originating from the chiefdoms beyond the borders of the Cape Colony than otherwise would have been the case. This feature helped to further distinguish Farmerfield from other missions in the Cape Colony, which were largely populated by individuals of Khoekhoe descent who were eventually merged with former slaves into one broad category of "Colored."[7]

The Cape colonial government was very concerned about how the distribution and migration patterns of former slaves would affect labor shortages in the Cape Colony and whether missionaries intentionally persuaded them to come to mission stations such as Farmerfield and Haslope Hills. Indeed hundreds of former slaves had flocked to the various missions within the borders of the Cape Colony and in March 1839 the government issued a circular to missionaries inquiring about the number of ex-slaves at their respective stations.[8] It is from Shaw's response to this government inquiry that we know some details about his intentions for Farmerfield and about its early population.[9]

In Shaw's reply to the government circular, we find, for example, that many Tswana-speaking residents were less encumbered than ex-slaves in moving to Farmerfield. They responded with alacrity to the opportunity and were among the first batch of residents at the mission. By April 1839, thirty-nine of the first fifty-four people living at Farmerfield were Tswana, while the remainder were Xhosa and Mfengu. The early population at Farmerfield reflects how much the Tswana presence had grown in the Eastern Cape by the 1830s. Moreover, some individuals who identified themselves as Tswana, having migrated to the Eastern Cape under extremely unfavorable war conditions in the 1820s and 1830s, had recovered enough to acquire a relatively favorable economic status. As a result, whites sometimes stereotyped Tswana individuals as the more industrious segments of the African population in the Eastern Cape. Of the first fifty-four residents at Farmerfield, twelve were men and forty-two were women and children.[10]

As individuals made their way to Farmerfield between 1839 and the early years of the 1840s, the mission scene was a hive of activity. Ox-wagons conveying goods and people traversed the pathways between Farmerfield, the surrounding neighborhoods, and Grahamstown. Hundreds of cattle, goats, sheep, and a few horses made their way to Farmerfield under the guidance of men, young and old. For the yearly rent of one pound, ten shillings, each tenant was allowed to run sixteen head of cattle on the estate; any number above sixteen obliged the tenant to pay two pounds in rent. The possession of a wagon and oxen incurred an additional charge of ten shillings.[11] Upon arrival the tenants registered their names with William Shaw and his assistants, and in return received grazing and residential land lots. Individuals then set about the task of constructing kraals (byres) for housing their animals and temporary lodgings for themselves. Within weeks the mission premises became more and more familiar as people sought and gathered mud to build more permanent houses, limestone to whitewash them, and thatching for the roofs. From the outset, tenants were reminded of the sort of housing that was becoming of Africans Christians. Lest they should revert to their former architectural styles and betray the civilizing mission, tenants were apprised that under no circumstances could these houses be "Kafir or Beehive huts" (see Figure 2.3). Rather, their houses should be constructed in the manner of a "decent cottage or round house." Moreover, these houses had to be whitewashed at least once per year and had to be kept "clean and orderly."[12]

Although the missionaries pointed out whenever they could that square houses were the pinnacles of what they considered civilized housing, they were willing to compromise and allow tenants to construct round houses. The Methodist missionary Henry Dugmore provides some clues about the links missionaries drew between housing, cleanliness, and the adoption of European clothing as accoutrements of a civilized lifestyle at the mission. Writing in response to an 1848 government circular soliciting advice about the "moral and social improvement" of Africans, Dugmore based his recommendations on his personal experience as a missionary and what he had witnessed at other Wesleyan mission settlements. Describing the Mfengu, for example, Dugmore emphasized:

> Could they be induced generally to abandon their grass huts, and adopt a kind of dwelling more favorable to habits of cleanliness, it would greatly tend to promote the use of European apparel. It would indeed render it necessary. The [conventional] huts are so low, and so hot and smoky, that European clothes can scarcely be worne [*sic*] in them . . . The use of walled houses would necessitate the use of more clothing, at the same time it would enable the wearer to preserve it . . . A step has been taken in this matter on several of the Wesleyan stations in the interior, by requiring people to build huts, *circular* indeed but *walled*, being plastered and wattled.[13]

Not only did these whitewashed, circular huts represent progress, but Dugmore also pointed out that these sorts of houses were "felt by the people to be within their ability to make, and thus little difficulty is found in inducing them to erect them."[14] The whitewashed structures found at Farmerfield in the early 1840s represented exactly the civilizing trend missionaries wanted to initiate and maintain as part of the plan for uplifting Africans.

In addition to house construction, the residents busied themselves with the more mundane tasks of locating firewood and finding the easiest route to the river to fetch water for cooking and washing. They also erected a temporary building for church services, enclosed their lands to mark the boundaries of their allotments, and made paths from their houses to various spots on the mission. They prepared for the agricultural season by plowing the land, sowing seeds, and planting crops such as wheat, barley, Indian corn, potatoes, onion, peas, and beans, as well as a host of fruit trees. Since no money was yet forthcoming from their crops, the main avenue for earning cash was by transporting goods and people in ox-wagons; as well as by churning butter and gathering firewood to sell on the market at Grahamstown.[15]

The physical layout of Farmerfield reflected the ethnolinguistic heterogeneity of the population that had settled in the Eastern Cape by the 1830s. As in his congregations in Grahamstown, William Shaw had to accommodate a diverse population speaking in varied fluencies of English, Dutch, Xhosa, and Tswana at Farmerfield. The visiting Quaker missionary, James Backhouse, asserted that Farmerfield was divided into four villages because the "different habits of these classes [ethnolinguistic groups] seemed to make such a separation necessary." Shaw, however, suggested that language was the underlying factor in creating distinct villages when he declared that, "There was considerable difficulty at first in managing their affairs, and in imparting religious instruction to such a diversified people, using such a variety of languages."[16] The first area was apportioned for the Xhosa and Mfengu, while a second was demarcated for the Tswana. Emancipated slaves and "Prize Negroes"—slaves taken from illegal slave ships by the British Navy after the abolition of the slave trade in 1808 and landed at the Cape— occupied a third section.[17]

William Shaw slated the fourth division of the mission for the Watson Institute, an industrial and educational experiment spearheaded by the Methodists and later duplicated by the colonial government. Envisioned by Wesleyan missionaries earlier in 1834 in Grahamstown, the Watson Institute was the first Methodist school of industry at the Cape. War disrupted Shaw's plans for the Institute and he relocated it to Farmerfield after 1838. [18] In addition to the industrial pursuits the missionaries planned for the African students, they also calculated on the school advancing their evangelical and civilizing goals much farther than did the existing mission schools.[19] William Shrewsbury, one of Shaw's missionary colleagues, stated that by establishing such a school in Grahamstown, "It would cut off, in a great measure, intercourse with 'heathen' parents, and by constant intercourse with the English would facilitate the acquirement of the English language and general literature."[20] Moreover, once these young students gained fluency in English, they "would facilitate the labors of future missionaries by furnishing them with interpreters . . . without being necessitated, as is now the case, to learn the Dutch language."[21]

Daniel Roberts, who worked with William Shaw at the first Methodist mission station, Wesleyville, was selected as the teacher and manager of the Watson Institute. Roberts was the son of one of the 1820s settlers. After teaching in Salem, where he was also educated, he relocated to the Theopolis mission and then Wesleyville in 1826 to assist with the pilot school that William Shaw had created.[22] Having worked at Wesleyville since 1826, Roberts was familiar with Xhosa society, spoke Xhosa, and was the ideal man for the job. In 1838, upon his additional appointment as manager of the mission, he and the young men of the Watson Institute relocated from Grahamstown to Farmerfield.[23]

When he visited Farmerfield in 1839, James Backhouse noted that the Watson Institute consisted of "a few youths, rising towards manhood, some of whom were the sons of native Chiefs [and] were instructed in English, Dutch and Sichuana

[Setswana], and Caffer [Xhosa], with a view to their being employed as schoolmasters at Missionary Stations."[24] Some of the young men at the school, Backhouse further asserted, "had made good progress and were pious."[25] The school was designed to be self-supporting and was the embodiment of what Shaw and other missionaries hoped was a new African manhood centered on Christianity and industry. By welcoming the sons of influential African chiefs, Shaw hoped that this new generational spin on cultivating African leaders would be more successful than the failed attempts to convert African chiefs (see Chapter 2). Late into the nineteenth century, other missionaries and popular colonial figures like Sir Frederick Lugard (former governor of Hong Kong and Nigeria) would continue to doubt the prudence of secular and religious instruction for adults "wedded to custom and prejudice," and pin their hopes on the youth.[26] The Methodist missionaries were not alone in devising schemes to try to change African societies through the progeny of chiefs and other influential persons in African societies.[27]

Since Shaw had succeeded in getting only one chief, [William] Kama, to convert to Christianity, he hoped that the next generation of young men of chiefly stock would exhibit more than a "nominal" interest in Christianity. These young men would learn from an impressionable age that as heads of household, they and not their womenfolk were supposed to engage themselves in agriculture and industry and take care of the material needs of their families. While Roberts played the role of teacher, manager, and catechist, the young male students kept a correspondingly demanding schedule trying to become new icons of Christian African manhood:

> The lads of the Watson Institution devoted a certain part of each day in school, and the remainder to industrial pursuits, which, by enabling them to raise a large portion of the food required for the establishment, and also some surplus produce for sale . . . considerably reduced what would have been the unavoidably heavy expense of the Institution.[28]

These young men of the Watson Institute would serve as models for other young people at the mission to emulate, especially because the chiefs' sons held some sway over their peers. By moving another ambitious scheme to Farmerfield, Shaw placed even more pressure on the mission to live up to his grandiose expectations. By intercepting the future leaders of chiefly descent at an early age, these young men would form the core of an indigenous leadership that would, in turn, evangelize and educate their own people.[29] Moreover, these young men would learn that as men and heads of household, they had a specific role to play, namely supplanting women in agriculture. By merging the pilot industrial school with his model of a mature, vital African Christianity, Shaw crafted Farmerfield as an ideal and early example of Methodist evangelical and educational work.

Established after the 1834–35 War of Dispossession, the Watson Institute provided another testing ground for schemes for African social, economic, and moral improvement. The educational, economic, and evangelical goals of the school formed the kernels of what missionaries from all denominations recommended to the government in the late 1840s.[30] The fourteen missionaries who responded to the government circular on the civilization of Africans acknowledged that adult and youth education had to proceed on a different plan. From a practical perspective it was simply easier for young people to learn a language and a new way of life. Youth, after all, were far more malleable and impressionable and would exert an important influence as the rising generation of Africans. The missionaries recommended the expansion of regular mission schools, as well as the creation of seminaries for building a cohort of African teachers and religious leaders.[31] In several instances the missionaries making their recommendations to the government suggested the exact design of the Watson Institute. One missionary pointed out that the students should work part of the day to help reduce the cost of the school;[32] while another suggested focusing on the children of chiefs and councilors as a means of influencing commoners to follow suit and send their children to school.[33] Another missionary emphasized that it was important to isolate the scholars at boarding institutions in order to minimize interference from parents who may make demands for their children's labor or may fear that their children would turn against their customs.[34]

The Watson Institute at Farmerfield therefore contained one blueprint for African uplift before influential seminaries like Lovedale and other schools were established in the 1840s and later decades of the nineteenth century.[35] By 1848, the government had established branches of the Watson Institute at other mission settlements.[36] While Farmerfield continued to provide education to its young inhabitants and neighboring children, the establishment of the Watson Institute at other locales and the creation of seminaries like Lovedale and Healdtown, eventually superseded the earlier efforts at Farmerfield. Instead of drawing students from far-flung places, attracting the children of influential councilors and chiefs, and boarding them, the Farmerfield school now catered to local students.

Daniel Roberts and the young protégés of the Watson Institute lived closest to the makeshift building that eventually became the church.[37] The church grounds stood out as a central feature of the landscape. In fact, when Reverend Thornley Smith drew the only existing sketch of Farmerfield to accompany a laudatory article for the Methodist bulletin, *Papers Relative to the Wesleyan Missions*, he included the church in the foreground; few of the residents and none of the villages were anywhere in sight[38] (see Figure 4.1). The four villages were situated so that the church, a magnificent and large white stone building, fifty feet long and thirty feet wide, served as the departure point from which the different residential areas were arranged[39] (see Figure 4.2). Along with the Assegaibos River that ran through the estate, the church, completed by 1847, provided a crucial boundary mark. The river, the church, and four villages physically defined Farmerfield's landscape as a mission station and an agricultural settlement. Throughout the span of Farmerfield's 124-year history, the river and church remained the two abiding landmarks of the mission.

Early Missionary Acclaim

With the right type of housing dotting its landscape and a local school of industry to boot, Farmerfield was well on the way to representing the new standard of Christianized and civilized Africans that white missionaries wanted to mold. During the first years of the mission's existence, missionaries and visitors to Farmerfield noted the industriousness of the residents. Before admitting them to the mission, Shaw ensured that any potential residents, unlike some at the early Methodist missions, already showed promise of industry by possessing some cattle or by being employed in a particular trade. Shaw wanted to avoid the charges leveled especially at mission settlements in the Cape Colony that they were havens for the idle. He even wanted to move beyond his own pioneering mission strategies when the stations welcomed almost anyone who professed a "nominal" interest in Christianity. The new guiding principle for the Farmerfield mission was a clear commitment to labor and religious discipline.[40] Already in April 1839, according to Shaw's letter to colonel Bell, the twelve men and forty-two women and children who were the first residents at Farmerfield owned 187 cattle and calves as well as 108 sheep and goats.

As Shaw intended, Farmerfield's early progress became a yardstick by which to measure the development of other mission settlements. Describing Farmerfield four years after its establishment, John Centlivres Chase wrote in his guide to the Eastern Cape, "The residents on this place are much more industrious than at the sister institution [Theopolis, an LMS mission about fourteen miles away from Farmerfield] and as a consequence more wealthy."[41] Although Theopolis faced criticism for its supposed shortcomings, the comparison with Farmerfield needs to be contextualized. Indeed the residents at Farmerfield were taking full advantage of the opportunities afforded them. At Theopolis, however, the frequent absence of men for military service, the need to engage in economic activities beyond the mission, the disruption of war and periodic cattle raids, and the out-migration of many residents to the Kat River settlement after 1829 contributed to its uneven development and ultimate impoverishment (see Map 1).[42] With Theopolis so impoverished, any comparison to the newly formed settlement was skewed in favor of Farmerfield. These challenges at Theopolis provide an example of the obstacles that were later in store for Farmerfield's residents. Moreover, certain features of the Theopolis mission were repeated at Farmerfield. For instance, the same rhetoric of African improvement through civilization that the LMS missionaries used to try to change the residents' lifestyles at the Theopolis mission was also found at Farmerfield. It consisted of the same broad categories of changes in clothing, housing, and agriculture.[43]

Agricultural industry was one among several criteria on the civilization grid that missionaries used to judge African Christians and to reconfigure gender roles in African households. Improvements in agriculture went beyond increasing the use of physical inputs like plows, axes, and spades. It also heralded new definitions of African manhood, womanhood, and childhood. Agricultural production at the mission required a redefinition of farming as an occupational category primarily the preserve of men; demanded that women focus on the household; and children focus on school instead of spending their days exclusively on domestic, agricultural, and pastoral chores. This reformation of men's, women's, and children's roles sometimes pitted children against their parents and spouses against each other. At Farmerfield and at other mission settlements, for example, missionaries complained of irregular attendance at school due to parents wanting the children's help with the crops or the home. In the early years of missionary work, African men expressed consternation at playing an active role in agriculture, which was conventionally women's work. It is no surprise, then, that one African chief described the work of the plow in terms of the value of women's work.

The changes expected of Africans also involved improving the farming techniques and the types of implements they used, as well as diversifying the range of crops they grew.[44] To begin with, many missionaries believed that African agricultural techniques were unsophisticated and essentially amounted to scratching the surface.[45] Other missionaries viewed pastoralism as a pretext for laziness, or "a means of subsistence which enabled the people to live in idleness except for the occasional diversions of fighting and raiding."[46] Missionaries complained that men wasted their time in "idleness, revelry and vice."[47] Combined with the criticism of polygamy, "the truly barbarous custom of buying and selling wives," as the missionary Henry Calderwood put it, missionary misperceptions of African agriculture and pastoralism ranked among the most scathing and consistent denunciations of African societies.[48] African men were especially singled out for allowing their women to shoulder the burden of agricultural production.

Missionaries usually cited the institution of polygyny as the great enabler of African male indolence.[49] "One object which the Kaffir has in view on obtaining several wives," the Methodist minister Thornley Smith wrote in his monograph on South Africa, "is that they may work for him whilst he indulges himself in idleness, or in the pleasures of the chase."[50] The woman's lot was one of endless toil, Smith continued:

> To the wife belongs the task of hewing wood and drawing water, digging
> up the ground and grinding corn, erecting the habitation and doing all
> the drudgery of the house; whilst my lord [the African male], during the
> greater portion of the day, has no employment at all.[51]

Smith asserted that however "strong and robust" African women appeared, African men needed to take their proper place in agricultural production so that their women could "attend to the wants of their children and endeavor to promote their happiness and comfort."[52] Smith, who also served as a missionary at Farmerfield while he was stationed in the Albany district, believed the African household, as then constituted, could not really be considered domestic because there were no signs of domesticity in the sparsely furnished houses, in women toiling as beasts of burden, and in children parading around in various states of nudity. African domesticity, to the extent that it existed, was a public and exterior spectacle consisting of "a swarm of little creatures, almost or entirely naked, running about apparently uncared for, in a most neglected and pitiable state,"[53] Smith pronounced. If African men would take their rightful place at the head of the household and supplant African women in agriculture, the domestic circle could be moved into the interior of the home and African women could spend more time taking care of their children and the household.[54]

These calls for the reformation of the African household, then, involved men, women, and children alike and encompassed a range of solutions for the problems of indolence, polygamy, cleanliness, and nudity. Some missionaries considered the role of women as centripetal to the task of civilization. Henry Calderwood believed that a "pious, judicious, educated and good-tempered woman" was the ideal candidate "to create and foster these very amenities which are at once the fruits and means of civilization."[55] In his recommendations for the best way to advance the civilizing mission among Africans, he pointed out that evangelical strategies paid far too little attention to the pivotal role of women. African men and women, for example, were being unequally yoked by Christian men marrying "heathen" spouses. If both spouses practiced a Christianized and a civilized lifestyle, such African households would become "invaluable nurseries for all that is good."[56]

William Shaw and other missionaries wanted to get far away from the disorderly model of African domesticity rife with male indolence, female oppression, and nude children. What was pleasing about Farmerfield to the missionaries and travelers, therefore, was the tangible evidence that men had taken their rightful place as heads of households and, as the primary agricultural producers, had liberated African women from the field. Moreover, the material signs of progress made in agriculture through the use of plows and the larger array of cultivated crops such as wheat, barley, and oats, elicited much comment from visiting missionaries. The residents' housing structures and lifestyles were other markers that drew commendations from visitors and missionaries in the 1840s and 1850s.[57] Shaw was particularly proud of the "substantial and commodious houses . . . dotted about the sides of the hills in convenient places," and the "extensively cultivated lands, with here and there small plots well planted with various kinds of fruit trees [.]"[58] In 1842 George Green, one of the missionaries stationed in the Albany district, informed the Methodist Missionary Society in Great Britain that the houses at Farmerfield "exhibited every appearance of neatness and order, and are quite equal in point of comfort and cleanliness, to the more respectable cottages of the laborer classes in England."[59] Moreover, although by 1847 the residents at Farmerfield had generally adopted European clothing, the missionary Thornley Smith still found it important to draw a stark contrast between the animal skins they used to wear and the European clothes they now regularly wore.[60]

The use of the plow for cultivation, the proliferation of whitewashed cottages, and the adoption of European apparel were visible signs European missionaries cited as evidence of the growth of civilization at Farmerfield. Shaw's grand plans for Farmerfield as well as the early praise heaped upon the settlement raise several key questions about the *vision* of the mission versus the actual experiences of the residents. The missionary acclaim over the settlement suggests that Farmerfield was a relatively independent and thriving African community. In the politically charged climate of the Eastern Cape where whites complained about labor shortages and indolent Africans, how was Shaw able to allay concerns about creating an economically viable African community surrounded by a white one? Moreover, in the aftermath of the war of 1834–35, how was Shaw able to quell potential white settler alarm that such an African community in close proximity would not be a liability as a potential enemy? Finally, how attainable was this model of African agricultural, educational, and industrial prosperity that Shaw fostered at the estate? The answers to these questions can be found by looking at Farmerfield's position as a labor reserve and at the tenants' economic activities.

Creating an African Labor Reserve in the Albany District

From the moment British settlers arrived in the Zuurveld (Albany) in 1820, they complained about labor shortages. As whites decamped from their land allotments and gravitated toward economic opportunities in Cape Town, Grahamstown, and beyond the official colonial borders, complaints about the labor shortage grew vociferous. Great Britain forbid slavery in the new settlement and Africans living beyond the borders of the Colony were not legally permitted in the colony in any large numbers until the promulgation of Ordinance 49 of 1828.[61] Once legal provisions were made for contracting Africans laborers, local officials tried to channel the flow of workers to whites, who then began to gripe about indiscipline and inexperience.[62] In the aftermath of the 1834–35 War of Dispossession, the demand for African workers was met by a growing unease about having to allow individuals into the Colony who much preferred to work for themselves and dishonored labor contracts when they did not work to their benefit. Although Africans were eventually defeated and their economic livelihood undermined in the war, white settlers on the frontier knew that cattle raiding would not cease nor would workers be any more pliable. Moreover, if tensions escalated to the breaking point, as they did again between 1846–47 and 1850–53, no previous defeat would deter the Africans from rising with righteous indignation against their perceived oppressors.

In creating Farmerfield, then, William Shaw had no intention of aggravating white settler concerns about labor shortages and potential enemies in their backyards. Rather, Shaw believed that Farmerfield was a possible solution to both white and African concerns: White complaints about creating a stable working class they could control; and African concerns that they were often beholden to white farmers for residence as well as employment and that they needed adequate access to land in order to maintain basic agricultural subsistence. Shaw hoped that the creation of a "native peasantry" at Farmerfield would represent "a respectable class of colored persons to which the poorest native would soon see that he might easily introduce himself by the exercise of steady industry for a few years in the service of the [white] farmers [.]"[63] Such a plan would be mutually beneficial to the employer and the African laborer, with the one gaining workers and the other supposedly gaining skills, an abode, and a very important lesson in the value of steady employment.

Far from creating a peasantry independent enough to shun working for whites, Shaw had a more dependent relationship in mind. An African applicant would work a few years on a white farm and accumulate enough cattle to gain admittance to Farmerfield. Once established as a peasant, the resident and his family would be expected to provide periodic labor to the surrounding farms. Communities such as Farmerfield would provide whites with "a small but regulated colored community at hand to render efficient help in busy times of sheep shearing, the harvest and the vintage, at which periods, good wages would induce many to work [.]"[64] Shaw believed that good wages were forthcoming and that it was fairly easy for any African to accumulate a few head of cattle by working on local White farms. These beliefs underscored his vision of Africans at Farmerfield living in symbiosis with neighboring whites, each fulfilling their natural role as employee and employer, respectively. Shaw must have shared this blueprint for an African settlement with his missionary colleagues and others, since we have the visiting Quaker missionary James Backhouse repeating, almost verbatim, how much of a beneficial labor arrangement such an agricultural settlement would be to local white settlers.[65] Moreover, one of Shaw's closest colleagues, the Methodist missionary William B. Boyce, stated explicitly in 1838 that Shaw had discussed such a plan with him. Boyce expressed his certainty that with regimes such as Farmerfield, the missionaries "may reasonably expect no small measure of success, and that a religious and industrious peasantry will be raised up, the pride and strength of the colony."[66]

As a blueprint for African social and economic improvement and for teaching Africans their proper place in white society, Farmerfield's design resounded positively with missionaries from all denominations. Farmerfield demonstrated just how much William Shaw and his Methodist colleagues had in common with other missionaries, even those with whom they disagreed about frontier politics. Perhaps the most momentous of such disputes between William Shaw and John Philip escalated into an institutional conflict between the Wesleyans and the LMS. Despite disagreeing with LMS superintendent John Philip about the complicity of local white settlers in fomenting turbulence and violence on the frontier, and conversely, about the nature of African exploitation, Shaw shared with him a fundamental belief about how to promote British notions of industry and capitalism among Africans.[67] The essential proposal was a marriage of Christianity and civilization to create a new Christianized, civilized, consuming African laborer. "The government of a free people can never compel the poorest classes to steady industry, in a country like this where they can exist without it," Shaw wrote to the colonial government in 1839. "Nothing but the introduction of new wants, new tastes and new principles will effect this," Shaw further asserted.[68] Shaw's model for Farmerfield, therefore, was not solely drawn from local experiences in the Cape Colony. Everywhere missionaries went, whether it was to Africa, Asia, or the Caribbean, the plan was to create new consumers, new laborers, new Christians.

As was commonplace at many other mission stations, the British socioeconomic traditions provided a useful prototype for William Shaw to emulate at Farmerfield. The position of the laboring classes in England informed Shaw's ideas about what the mission residents' houses should look like, as well as their proper relationship with their white neighbors whom Shaw stated were the "class of capitalists and masters, while the colored people are generally the class of laborers."[69] Shaw looked beyond the Cape to Britain to explain why his model for Farmerfield was simply a naturalization of the preexisting socioeconomic order he found in the colony. He called upon class relations in England to explain why his model Farmerfield precluded a totally independent African peasantry; or rather, why he always envisioned Africans working for, and often still dependent on, whites. Although Shaw was responding to the circular about ex-slaves mentioned earlier in the chapter, he used the opportunity to peddle his view of a native peasantry to the colonial government:

> This plan [for Farmerfield] is not liable to the objection that it would tend to keep up a distinction in the various classes of society. The objection is often urged vaguely. It cannot be meant that there is to be no distinction betwixt the wealthy and the poorer classes, that the master and the servant, the capitalist and the laborer are to be placed in exactly similar circumstances and that there be no distinction betwixt them. No sound mind can entertain such a theory for a moment. As therefore the European settlers form in this colony the class of capitalists and masters, while the colored people are generally the class of laborers, it follows that there must inevitably be some distinction arising from circumstances wholly independent of color, viz the distinction, which in all civilized countries exists betwixt the wealthy and the poor classes. And in fact, the plan . . . is in principle the very system pursued by many benevolent noblemen and gentlemen on their estates in England where they have

lately discovered that to offer small plots for cultivation, and grass for keeping a cow or two, to the laboring classes at low rent, has the very best effect in stimulating moral and industrious habits as well as in concentrating in convenient places, a number of valuable laborers whose services thus became available to the neighborhood farmers by whom their estates are chiefly rented and occupied.[70]

When examined from Shaw's perspective, the initiative of the Grahamstown congregants was easily superseded and elaborated into a blueprint for proper labor relations between whites and Africans in the colony.

Whatever general fear and unease white settlers may have had about a local African mission, the combination of a labor reserve and a strict mission station populated by the best class of Africans did not then seem so objectionable. Farmerfield's design was greeted with enthusiasm and hope particularly because Shaw was not just an experienced missionary; he was considered among the settlers' most influential advocates. Farmerfield's tenants had a stake in soil, a vested interest in remaining loyal to the Colony during any outbreak of war and in showing some signs of conforming to a Christian lifestyle. Otherwise they risked expulsion from the mission. Most of the residents, having just recovered from the destitution of the war of 1834–35, were grateful for the access to land and the chance of economic recovery, whatever other strings came attached with mission residence. It was an effective method of social control that also guaranteed to whites a certain access to African labor. But what did this plan mean for the Africans who were now subjected to such a regime of social discipline and labor extraction? Perhaps a foray into the lives of some of the settlers, as much as can be gleaned from the existing evidence, will provide some sense of the divergence between Shaw's plans and the lives of the African residents.

William Shaw's Plan Versus the Tenants' Reality: An Economic Mosaic

The voices and desires of Farmerfield's residents are almost inaudible in Shaw's grand scheme for promoting ideal labor relations between whites and Africans. What did such schemes for creating a laboring, agricultural peasantry living in symbiosis with neighboring whites actually mean for the African residents? Population and property censuses provide a glimpse of how closely the mission residents' lives matched the vision of Farmerfield. The early years of the 1840s brought in a steady stream of residents to the mission (See Table 4.1). Within a year of its foundation, for example, the initial population of fifty-four people at Farmerfield had quickly risen to 296. Instead of twelve households, there were now sixty-three; the number of women and children had grown from forty-two to 227. Within four years the population had burgeoned to approximately 320 people,

Table 4.1 **Human and Animal Populations at Farmerfield, 1839–1849**

Year	Population	Cattle	Sheep and Goats	Horses
1839	54	187	108	2
1840	296	935	338	10
1842	320	1,135	220	15
1849	487	1,117	34	19

Source: Cape of Good Hope, *Master and Servant, Addenda to the Documents on the Working Order in Council,* July 21, 1846.

consisting of "74 Hottentots and other colored colonists (including former slaves), and 246 'native foreigners.'"[71] Africans migrating from chiefdoms beyond the borders of the colony constituted the vast majority of Farmerfield's residents since former slaves availed themselves of the opportunity to move to their own mission, Haslope Hills. By 1849, a decade after the settlement was founded, the population was at 487 individuals, the largest number of people found at the mission from its creation in 1838 to its demise in 1962.

The rapid population increases over the first decade of the settlement brought in propertied individuals who owned cattle, goats, horses, sheep, oxen, and wagons. The 187 cattle and calves, 108 sheep and goats, and two mares on the estate in 1839 had now increased to 935 cattle, 106 goats, 232 sheep, and ten horses.[72] Four years later the number of horses had grown to fifteen while the cattle on the estate had increased to 1,135.[73] These increases in property reveal one of the most important advantages of living at the mission. Tenants were allowed to accumulate far more property than if they were living on the premises of white farmers, thus granting them leverage in their decisions to buy, sell, or trade animals. Missionaries were apt to attribute early signs of success and industry at Farmerfield to the triumph of the gospel and civilization rather than to the hard work and industry of the Africans who were now placed in more favorable circumstances for amassing property and securing a modicum of economic self-sufficiency, if not independence.

If the Africans agreed with the missionaries unanimously on any issue, it was certainly that the provision of land at the mission significantly increased their chances for economic advancement and placed them in a better bargaining position vis-à vis any potential employer. Individuals who had come from the ravaged missions beyond the colonial borders certainly got a better deal at Farmerfield than they could secure by working exclusively in Grahamstown or on a local farm. They had more independence, more reliable access to land, and opportunities to produce a surplus for the market. Historian Colin Bundy pointed out long ago that African agricultural producers in a region of the Eastern Cape, when given the opportunity, responded positively and with alacrity to the expanded prospects for autonomy, material progress, and production for the market that mission residence afforded them.[74] While Bundy's case study focuses on the later nineteenth century, he cites Farmerfield as an early example of an African peasant community. Historian Helen Bradford has taken the rise-and-fall thesis to task, however, pointing out how limited the case study was that purported to represent the South African peasantry and challenging the dates and chronology used to support the main argument.[75]

What remains instructive in general in assessing nineteenth-century peasantries in South Africa is capturing the rather diverse and flexible meaning of production associated with them. In the case of Farmerfield and many other mission settlements, the agricultural peasantry envisioned was one that always had to hedge their subsistence by engaging in multipronged economic strategies. Moreover, the peasantries planned in the mission context, like the pioneer mission models, all held the seeds to its own destruction against the backdrop of the rising tide of landlessness in South Africa. In the case of Farmerfield, the best clue is the manner in which a 6,000-acre farm that accommodated a single farmer was now repurposed for almost one hundred Africans household heads. Would Africans—the ones who adopted "European" cultural norms—eventually assume that they, too, should have an individual expanse of 6,000 acres, with tenants perhaps? As landlessness engulfed the Eastern Cape and the rest of South Africa, the more people who sought land access, the more it became evident that missions could never meet the land needs of even the most industrious Africans. Missions may have served as the cradle for many African peasant producers and for a burgeoning elite, but their scope was conceptually limited. Both Christianity and African farmers had to eventually move beyond the missions in order to find the fullest expression of independence. Christianity would get that opportunity. African farming endeavors, however, would continue to be thwarted.

Farmerfield's history as an early peasant settlement diverges from Bundy's chronology of a gradual, fitful embryonic peasantry. If the emergence of a peasantry was generally a "piecemeal and hesitant process at first," as Bundy describes for the 1840s through the 1870s, then Farmerfield was novel in that its creation was a deliberate, decisive, and successful move to create an early peasantry. Farmerfield was already in its heyday when the process of peasantization was just getting underway elsewhere in South Africa. In an interesting turn of events, the only time the male household heads at Farmerfield were all enumerated as "farmers" was during the apartheid era when the Native Affairs Department (hereafter NAD) conducted inquiries to assess whether the anomalous location of the mission violated the host of laws enacted by the segregation and apartheid-era governments in order to restrict African land access and residential proximity to whites.

Another way in which Farmerfield differed from the conventional examples of early African peasant production was that most of the accolades for assiduous productive peasants usually refer to Mfengu, whereas missionaries described a much more heterogeneous mix of people at Farmerfield as industrious. Like other migrant communities, every group at Farmerfield had a story to tell. For some of the Xhosa, Tswana, and Mfengu escaping war, the journey that eventually brought them to Farmerfield was nothing short of a life and death exodus. Former slaves welcomed their hard-won independence and the opportunity to cultivate for themselves. The small cohort of Khoekhoe, with their life chances shrouded in the long history of discrimination, land alienation, and restrictions on their mobility also embraced Farmerfield for what it was: an opportunity to start anew. Missionaries commended all these groups for their collective efforts at Farmerfield without differentiating whether one was more industrious than the other.

With access to land, many of Farmerfield's tenants could now focus on their own agricultural pursuits rather than their employer's. Once settled at the mission, the tenants' economic livelihood developed around a four-pronged strategy: agricultural production for subsistence and the market; pastoralism; self-employment in various trades; and working for local whites as farmhands and servants. A census conducted in 1849, a decade after the mission began, provides the best available overview of how the tenants were faring. By then the population of Farmerfield had burgeoned to 487 people: 101 male household heads, three female household heads, ninety-eight wives, eleven elderly women, and 274 children.[76] There were 1,117 head of cattle on the estate, nineteen horses, and thirty-four goats. The experiences of Titus Dubula, a fifty-five-year-old patriarch, provide a glimpse of African initiative and prosperity as well as a sense of how missionaries defined the "ideal resident."

Titus Dubula was among the first residents who moved to Farmerfield and one of the 101 male household heads listed in the census of 1849. By then he was entering almost four decades of association with Methodist missionaries and missions, ten of them spent at Farmerfield. Dubula and his wife Mary Nomanto met each other in the 1820s at the earliest Methodist mission settlement of Wesleyville, where they were both baptized in 1829. They married in April 1841 at Farmerfield and had one child.[77] At Farmerfield Dubula concentrated his economic energies on the business of transport riding, whereby he carried goods and people for a fee. His only crop for that year was just enough to cover the annual one pound rent, so his main earnings came from his transport business. Dubula and a cohort of approximately six other male household heads owned between forty-six and fifty head of cattle each. He also owned one of only nineteen horses on the estate and had a garden separate from his farmlands. Since only the corn from his agricultural allotment is included in the census, perhaps most of the other crops produced from the garden were used for household consumption. Dubula appears consistently in the contribution lists of church offerings throughout the 1840s and into the 1850s, suggesting an ability to pay.[78] Compared with the other household heads in the census, Dubula was one of the more successful tenants at Farmerfield.

Thomas Papume, like Dubula, was one of the refugees from the missions in the interior destroyed by the war of 1834–35. He too had lived at Farmerfield for ten years. He was forty years old and by 1849 he had married, had six children, and amassed forty-six head of cattle. Furthermore, as a transport rider or carrier, he had little time left for agriculture and thus his only crop that year was an amount of wheat valued at one pound. With this many cattle and his transport business, Papume can also be considered one of the most successful men at Farmerfield.

In March 1848 Thomas Pringle, 1820 settler, poet, and colleague of the famous missionary John Philip, encountered a resident of Farmerfield employed as a carrier or transport rider. Pringle's encounter in the city of Port Elizabeth provides us with an idea of how lucrative this occupation could be and how far off the mission it took these men. The wagon driver and owner was Abram Malgasse, whom Pringle described as a "Bechuana," who "acknowledged Moshesh as his chief but had resided for some years at the Wesleyan Institute called Farmerfield."[79] According to Pringle, Malgasse was involved in a very profitable business and had made a good deal of money conveying goods and people between different cities. Malgasse's earning potential, like that of other carriers like Titus Dubula and Thomas Papume, increased astronomically during the outbreaks of war when travel costs were at a premium. Malgasse, Pringle tells us, usually earned a wartime rate of twenty to twenty-five pounds per load in 1846. War elevated the earning potential because of the danger of traveling and the many demands made on those who had the means of conveying people and goods. Even in peacetime, however, this profession was in general better paid than farm work, with the daily wage scale of one shilling, six pence quoted for local agricultural workers. Malgasse had also made much profit during the war, when he received as much as twenty shillings per hundred weight and had made as much as forty-five pounds sterling for one of his loads.[80] While the sums were far more modest in peace time, it is clear that this occupation was one of the few that could provide Africans with the economic independence they sought without having to contract themselves to whites for meager wage rates.

After he arrived in Grahamstown, Pringle observed that Abram Malgasse was in the company of four or five others who were in the same occupation and who also spoke the same language. It appears that the ox-wagon transport riding business had afforded some Tswana individuals the opportunity to carve out a decent economic niche for themselves. Perhaps this relative independence had allowed Tswana individuals to be the first to move to Farmerfield. Approximately two years after Pringle's encounter with Malgasse, Robert Gray, the bishop of Grahamstown, while on tour to Farmerfield, estimated that there were some twenty to thirty wagons on the estate in 1850.[81] His observation was quite correct since the census of 1849 puts the number of wagons on the estate at thirty. Transport riding, therefore, allowed a significant number of people at Farmerfield to secure a sphere of relative independence and provided the funds with which they could amass cattle and take care of their families. Missionaries made little mention of

Table 4.2 **Occupational Categories of Household Heads
at Farmerfield, 1849**

Category	*No.*	*Gender*
Laborer	55	Male
Carrier	25	Male
Wagon Driver	7	Male
Thatcher	3	Male
Farmer	3	Male
Tailor	2	Male
Schoolmaster	1	Male
Ploughman	1	Male
Mat Maker	1	Male
Wool Washer	1	Male
Carpenter	1	Male
Mason	1	Male
Servant	1	Female
Washerwoman	1	Female
No Occupation	1	Female

Source: Cape of Good Hope, *Master and Servant, Addenda to the Documents on the Working Order in Council,* July 21, 1846.

who did all of the agricultural work while these men worked off the estate; nor did they readily acknowledge that the vision of a peasantry they cultivated was one where Africans shunned subservience to whites and viewed farming as just one among many other economic strategies.

The occupation of carrier or transport rider provided twenty-five male household heads with an independent and frequently profitable means of earning a living (see Table 4.2). Other occupational categories included seven wagon drivers, three farmers, three thatchers, two tailors, and one person in each of the categories of schoolmaster, carpenter, servant, wool washer, ploughman, mat maker, and mason.[82] The carpenter, mason, ploughman, thatcher, and tailors could ply their trades within the local community, yet there was no guarantee of frequent steady work. During the early years of the settlement when people needed to establish homes quickly and get ready for the agricultural season, the ploughman, thatcher, and mason were probably in high demand. Yet as people became more settled, the demand for masonry, carpentry, and thatching services was less steady. With few sheep at Farmerfield, the thirty-year-old Adonis Kasepe who identified himself as a wool washer must have hired himself out to local white farmers. If the tailor and washerwoman catered exclusively to the Farmerfield community, it is likely that they fared well since both the young and old, men and women, were in need of clothing to be made, mended, and washed. Looking at the economic activities of the household heads at Farmerfield suggests that of all the jobs on the mission, the position of schoolmaster was most likely the steadiest job, while transport rider or carrier was the most potentially lucrative.

In a situation where Africans were hardly considered legitimate farmers, it is not surprising that only three of the 101 male household heads at Farmerfield identified themselves as such. These individuals were the least likely to engage in labor for white farmers and rather focused their efforts on agricultural production. In contrast, the vast majority of laborers who combined work for whites with their own farming pursuits did not fit into the occupational category of farming. Consequently, the individuals whose crops were given the highest value on the estate as well as the ones who owned the most cattle were farmers. Take Esau Jonas, for example, a sixty-year-old farmer living at Farmerfield since its inception with his wife and four children. His wheat and barley crops for 1849 were valued at fifteen pounds and he owned fifty-six cattle. Materially he was among the most prosperous men on the estate. His earnings were sufficient to take care of all rent and grazing fees, school costs, church offerings, and other cash expenditures. In addition, his family also had a garden plot that provided some of the food for household consumption.

The second farmer, Jacobus Linka (also rendered as Linker), was exactly thirty years younger than Esau Jonas and had also lived at the estate since 1839. He was married but did not have any children. His wheat and barley were valued at thirteen pounds and he owned twenty cattle. The third farmer, Petrus Jager, was not as successful as his counterparts. He had lived at the mission for eight years but his wheat crop was only valued at one pound and he only owned six cattle. While not all farmers fared well, as a full-time occupational category farming still held tremendous potential for economic stability and prosperity. Along with transport riding, farming afforded opportunities to earn significant amounts of money and both occupations provided the best access to cash of any other occupation on the estate.

By 1849 the most common occupational category at Farmerfield was "laborer," comprising fifty-five of the 101 male heads of household. The overall number of people fitting this description, however, is much larger. Whereas the census figure relates primarily to men listed as heads of household, the older children of some of these household heads also engaged in a variety of services that would class them as laborers, though perhaps more intermittently than the adult men. The term "laborer" encompassed work in the immediate area as well as Grahamstown and its environs. Since many of the residents at Farmerfield had worked intermittently on farms in the Eastern Cape, engaging in periodic farm labor on surrounding farms was no surprising element of their residence at the mission. Seasonal or intermittent farm labor was therefore one of several strategies the residents continued to use once they were settled at Farmerfield when they needed extra money or wanted more cattle, or when other avenues of income were closed.

As laborers in the local agricultural community, Farmerfield tenants worked in all aspects of the production process. They could be employed in planting, harvesting, and transporting the same sorts of crops they grew at Farmerfield, such as wheat, barley, and a host of vegetables and fruits. They also assisted in herding, washing, and shearing sheep. Some individuals in other occupational groups probably worked as laborers before they could secure independent enterprises for themselves or continued to work seasonally. In 1844, for example, we find the carrier Thomas Papume (discussed earlier) engaged in a wage dispute with a local white farmer. The farmer hired Papume to shear sheep and had made arrangements to pay while the work was ongoing. Receiving no wages for the amount of work completed, Papume lodged a complaint with the local authorities and explained why he left "before the sheep were finished." The magistrate advised Papume to settle the matter and return to work.[83] We do not know the outcome of the dispute but by 1849 Papume no longer identified himself as a laborer. He had established himself as a carrier and one of the wealthiest men on the estate.

Working intermittently as a laborer certainly was one way that tenants minimized subsistence risk and provided a quick avenue for cash. Africans periodically entered the local labor market to minimize the threat from episodic crises such as droughts, warfare, or cattle diseases. When these catastrophes struck, for example, you had far more individuals identifying themselves as laborers than at more prosperous times. Some household heads worked only seasonally in the neighborhood to supplement their income, but just about half of the male population worked mainly as laborers. Thus, although Farmerfield was noted for its early prosperity, the mission residents did indeed become the semi-independent peasantry, combining farm labor for whites with their agricultural pursuits that Shaw intended. The population increases during the early years of the settlement created a labor reserve for the local white farmers to draw upon such that by even as early as 1842 approximately one third of the men at Farmerfield worked seasonally on the surrounding farms at a daily wage scale of one shilling, six pence. The number of laborers had jumped to one half the men of Farmerfield by 1849. Notwithstanding the prosperity of some, many households were still recovering from the losses associated with the war between 1846 and 1847.[84]

While most of the male household heads at Farmerfield were self-employed or worked for whites, the same cannot be said of the women at Farmerfield. Whatever economic contributions adult married women made to their households, they did so by remaining at the mission and seldom venturing into employment far beyond the premises. Only three women identified themselves as heads of household while the remainder appeared in the census as wives of the household heads. Missionaries celebrated instances of agricultural productivity at Farmerfield as the triumph of their vision of a peasantry abiding by their proper gender roles. As a vision of an ideal mission, missionaries probably had more control over the process that "induced" and "enabled" "virile men to do women's work" and "adopt alien masculine norms," as Helen Bradford described this process.[85] Close supervision in the early years of the estate suggests that missionaries were able to enforce more strictly the gender roles that had elevated men to the position of farmers, although women did not stop producing food. With so many males working as carriers and laborers, however, the production figures of the census elides female contribution to agriculture and privileges crops cultivated for the market rather than for consumption. The relegation of women to more subsidiary roles in agricultural is a missionary narrative that discounts women's own farming enterprises. The garden plot was seen as women's space, one in which their work did not contravene the new gendered division of labor; while the allotments of arable land were the "official" preserve of men.

Despite officially assuming more auxiliary roles, some women did contribute to the household in paid labor. Lentje Bagot, a household head living at Farmerfield for ten years with her three sons, for example, worked as a washerwoman. As one of the earliest residents, she had established her residency through her husband, Hendrick, who passed away by 1849, leaving her as de facto head of household.[86] Two of her three sons supplemented her income by working as wagon drivers, leaving open the question of who produced the household's food. Lena January, a widowed household head also living at Farmerfield for ten years, worked as a servant in the local area, while her daughter worked in Grahamstown. The third female household head had no "official" occupation. Of the remaining ninety-eight married women, only three worked off the mission as domestic servants.[87] The relative economic stability of Farmerfield households perhaps allowed most married women to shun domestic service. Furthermore, by moving to the mission and accepting the rules for residence, African women had to conform to the requirements of their new roles. The presence of only three off-mission workers among the ninety-eight married women suggests some missionary success in delimiting women to the domestic sphere. In all likelihood, however, it was the initial success of their husbands' income-generating strategies that allowed the wives to remain at the mission, if not exclusively within the household. With the changes missionary ideology demanded of African men, women, and children, men seem to have carved out a modicum of economic independence while women obeyed only some the proscriptions against working primarily in agriculture. The case of children was more difficult to delineate. One of the most important areas of leverage that mission residence provided African households was the disposal of their children's time. When working and living on white farms, the entire family was usually part of the package, with the employer expecting some input of labor from each family member. Once individuals in these situations moved to Farmerfield, they had more control over what their children did from day to day, though the missionaries made it explicit from the outset that children were expected to attend the mission school on the premises. Despite this general rule, parents made personal decisions about the use of their children's time, sometimes pulling them out of school to assist with the crops. Farmerfield residents were not alone in these actions, as other missionaries complained of the same problem. Parents were more likely to do this at periodic intervals since the risk of expulsion for breaking this rule was minimal.

The issue of education took an interesting turn once children reached the age of twelve. Children were assumed to reach a certain level of maturity at this age and from that point it is not entirely clear what the mission rules entailed. The vast majority (seventy-two of seventy-six) of the residents' children above the age of twelve worked off the mission in various domestic arrangements and thus provided an important source of supplemental income to the household. Girls above the age of twelve usually worked as domestic servants while the boys usually worked as wagon drivers or leaders of oxen. Moreover, in contrast to the married women, most young girls above the age of twelve could be found working in domestic service in the vicinity of Farmerfield and Grahamstown.[88] Mission ideology and the expectations of white colonial society removed women from the agricultural sphere, rather pushing them toward domestic servitude as more appropriate "work" for African women. That so many of the young women at Farmerfield were already found in domestic service in the 1840s provides some evidence of the subservient, menial roles that young African girls were being socialized to assume.

An overview of the livelihoods of Farmerfield's tenants paints a complex portrait of economic independence. There is ample evidence that Farmerfield provided opportunities and resources difficult to duplicate elsewhere in the Eastern Cape, the most important being land. That Africans took the initiative to ask the missionary to intervene is certainly testimony to the hardships they faced by seeking employment with whites as the sole means of subsistence. William Shaw was inundated with applicants for every available spot at Farmerfield and when people did move there, many of them experienced the material improvement they had sought. Some residents, like the twenty-five carriers and few farmers, for example, carved out a niche for themselves, earned decent sums of money, and accumulated a significant amount of property in cattle. Other tenants continued to ply their trades as masons, carpenters, and tailors even with the unpredictability of their income. Farmerfield's general story, therefore, is partly about an early African economic independence. When refracted through the lens of gender and generation, however, this independence becomes more qualified. Even with men installed as the official household heads, their wives and children supplemented their activities. Women worked on subsistence crops in their garden lots and maintained the home. Adolescent children worked in the local area to supplement the household income. Families churned butter, cut firewood, and raised chickens to expand their total income. It was a multifaceted economic strategy Farmerfield's tenants used to diversify access to cash, minimize subsistence risk, and avoid toiling for whites.

Even with some evidence of prosperity and industry, the composite portrait of the economic livelihoods of Farmerfield's tenants raises some important questions about the viability of African peasantries. For example, the most prosperous men on the estate were carriers who spent little time on agriculture and earned only a small amount of cash from their crops. That only three household heads identified themselves as bona fide "farmers" also casts some doubt on the missionary's sanguine emphasis on agriculture as a viable and realistic means of African self-sufficiency. Missionaries shone a spotlight on the issue of land as a panacea for African impoverishment in the Eastern Cape. They assured themselves that by meeting the African clamor for land, and combining this with a plan for religious instruction and education, they had a practical formula for African improvement. What the missionaries did not discuss in their blueprint was the crucial distinction Africans themselves made between land usage and access.

What the activities of Farmerfield's tenants reveals is that when provided with land, Africans used it as part of a repertoire of strategies for economic survival instead of looking to agriculture as the sole means of subsistence. They did not limit their economic activities to the missionaries' prediction that they would become a peasantry partly living off the land and providing labor to local whites. By paying rent for their property, the tenants expected that they could use the land however they wanted; the most important feature was that they had the *access* and the choice was theirs. It seems, therefore, that while the missionaries were focused on forging a specific kind of African peasantry, Farmerfield became for the tenants a place for setting down roots and claiming legal access to a plot of land. In a situation where whites were usurping land all around them, it is certainly understandable that Africans would see land *access* and land *usage* from different perspectives. The very land that became Farmerfield, after all, was once part of an African chiefdom—land that whites now claimed exclusively through a government grant. In the roles of employers and missionaries whites, as opposed to African chiefs, became the primary benefactors through whom Africans could access land.

Even from this early period in the nineteenth century, therefore, Africans developed a general sense of injustice about land that went beyond irredentism. It was certainly true that the tenants at Farmerfield were not the same Africans who were cleared from the Zuurveld in the early decades of the nineteenth century. Yet the landlessness that brought Farmerfield tenants to the Eastern Cape in search of opportunities was all bound up in the same broad African experience of colonial dispossession. One chiefdom after another lost its land, sending landless economic refugees all over the Cape Colony. As Africans watched other chiefs, families, and friends lose their land, they had enough reason to believe it would eventually happen to them. Under these circumstances any issue relating to land took on a heightened importance. In his opus *The Making of the English Working Class*, E. P. Thompson provides an apt description of how the process of land alienation in England also elicited a similar sense of injustice and sensitivity about land even for individuals who did not experience it firsthand. Working-class grievances, Thompson points out, were channeled into the generalized sense of loss during the enclosure movement and the industrial revolution. When he wrote that "Land always carries associations of status, security, rights—more profound than the value of its crops," Thompson could also have been describing nineteenth- and twentieth-century South Africa.[89] Colonial encroachment in South Africa made so many rapid inroads on the status, rights, and security of Africans that they too came to view issues of land loss, land access, and land usage through the general lens of exploitation.

Having lost their lands, the people who became tenants at Farmerfield acknowledged the great advantage they gained by living at the mission station. They were willing to compromise with their new missionary overlords by agreeing to live according to certain rules about the type of houses they constructed and clothing they wore, for example. Yet they were unwilling to concede that tenancy meant forfeiture of all choices about what to do with the land. As a result there remained a latent potential for disagreement about land access and actual land usage. For the missionaries land access was synonymous with land usage. They assumed that when they fulfilled the African clamor for land, the Africans would respond by engaging in agriculture as the foundation of their subsistence strategies. When actual land usage fell short of missionary expectations, whites fell back on the usual explanations of African indolence and the need for white supervision, issues that are discussed further in Chapter 6.

Despite the different perceptions Africans and missionaries had of land access versus land usage, limitations on agricultural production at Farmerfield went beyond Africans' assertion of their right to try economic endeavors besides agriculture. Agriculture remained a central part of Farmerfield's economy yet fell short of being the mainstay, partly because it could not realistically sustain everyone. Moreover, while all household heads had access to land to engage in some level of subsistence agriculture, not everyone had the additional resources or the time to maintain production for the market. Those engaged as regular laborers with local white farmers, for example, after spending the better part of the day working for someone else, had little time for their own agricultural pursuits. This is borne out by the low agricultural output of laborers at Farmerfield. The 1849 census shows that approximately twenty of the fifty-five laborers had no crops at all. Of the remaining thirty-five who did have some crops, the value fell between a mere two shillings and three pounds. The highest market value for any of the laborers' crops was five pounds.

Tenants focusing on trades such as carpentry, masonry, or tailoring also cultivated few crops. The seventy-year-old tailor, Petrus Wienand, who had been living at Farmerfield for eight years, only fetched ten shillings for his wheat crop. The thirty-five-year-old mason Robert James, who was among the first tenants at Farmerfield, earned only five shillings for his wheat crop. The crops of the three thatchers and one carpenter fetched a pound each while the mat maker's and ploughman's crop both came in at a little under eight shillings. Compared to all other occupations, the twenty-five carriers and three farmers living at the mission showed the most consistency in their agricultural production and received the most value for their crops on the market. All but one of the carriers had crops at the estate. Three carriers had crops valued up to three shillings; fourteen of them had crops valued between one and three pounds, while another five had crops valued between four and eight pounds. The remaining two had crops valued at nine and ten pounds, respectively. These carriers not only maintained regular production, but also owned the wagons needed to transport their goods to the markets, whereas laborers had to hire a wagon at an additional expense.

In addition to the level of agricultural production, the extent of property ownership provides a useful measure of prosperity and stratification at Farmerfield. Collectively, the twenty-five carriers on the estate owned 474 head of cattle of a total 1,112 head on the estate, while the fifty-five laborers owned 468 head (See Table 4.3). Clearly, the carriers and farmers owned the most property, cementing their position on the estate as the most prosperous, as well as the groups with the most stable agricultural production. The trades of carpentry, tailoring, thatching, and masonry did not increase the likelihood of extensive cattle ownership at Farmerfield. Thus, although these individuals found work that gave them independence and control over the use of their own labor, they were not guaranteed paths to the kind of success that would keep the household heads and their families out of the labor market completely. Two of the three thatchers had no cattle at all, while the third owned only two head. The carpenter, who also had no cattle, supplemented his household by his wife's income from domestic service off the mission (see Table 4.3).

Despite the discouraging picture with regard to agricultural production, the laborers' situation in relation to the accumulation of property for pastoralism was a bit more optimistic. Since they were often paid with cattle, some laborers were able to amass property. By 1849 one thirty-year-old laborer named Goda, for example, had accumulated forty-nine head of cattle; two other successful laborers had amassed twenty-eight head, while another had twenty-three head. The vast majority of laborers, however, owned only between one and sixteen head of cattle.

Looking at actual agricultural production and property ownership certainly qualifies any overly rosy picture of peasant prosperity at Farmerfield. Yet even these measurements do not tell the whole story of the economic challenges Farmerfield's peasants faced. Moreover, the missionaries and the tenants had varying views of what constituted success. Everyone generally agreed that the presence of at least thirty wagons and twenty-five plows on the estate indicated material progress. Still, tenants focused much more on accumulating wealth in cattle, maintaining basic subsistence, and engaging in occupations that gave them control over their labor than missionaries would have liked. The more tenants produced agricultural goods and labor for the market, the closer to Farmerfield's original missionary blueprint they came.

Table 4.3 **Cattle Ownership at Farmerfield, 1849**

Category	Households	Cattle
Laborer	55	468
Carrier	25	474
Wagon Driver	7	46
Thatcher	3	2
Farmer	3	82
Tailor	2	7
Schoolmaster	1	16
Ploughman	1	3
Mat Maker	1	3
Wool Washer	1	1
Carpenter	1	0
Mason	1	5
Servant	1	5
Washerwoman	1	0

Source: Cape of Good Hope, *Master and Servant, Addenda to the Documents on the Working Order in Council,* July 21, 1846.

The composite picture suggests that despite material improvement for some residents, African economic progress at Farmerfield, just as elsewhere in the Cape Colony, had limits. Several other factors undercut Farmerfield's prosperity between the 1840s and the 1870s and prevented the range of their agricultural pursuits from equaling those of their white counterparts. Some of these constraints resulted from the nature of the local market insofar as everyone—both Africans and whites—produced some of the same staple agricultural goods, thereby flooding the market and often depressing prices. Thus, when Farmerfield's tenants brought firewood, butter, eggs, and other agricultural produce to the market in Grahamstown, they faced stiff competition from other Africans, as well as whites. Sometimes when they gathered firewood on or near other neighborhood farms, whites complained about the residents at Farmerfield trespassing in areas beyond the mission.[90] Other restrictions were based on the undercapitalized nature of African agriculture, the lack of diversification in economic activities, and the insufficiency of Africans' land compared to that of whites.

While Colin Bundy and others have emphasized that even white farming enterprises suffered from some of these same characteristics, they also point out that these restraints were more pronounced and consequential for Africans. One only has to look at some of the removal notices of the white settlers posted in the

Graham's Town Journal and the *Cape Frontier Times* to see how they fared in comparison to some of the Farmerfield settlers. For example, there are farms advertised for sale that have the same approximate acreage (6,000) as Farmerfield and yet are owned by only one family. Whereas you might have approximately 1,000 head of cattle and sheep owned by the entire population of Farmerfield, one white family would own hundreds of cattle. The missionaries reinforced some of these disparities through their belief and assertions that Africans required less land to satisfy their needs than did whites. The noted Methodist missionary W. B. Boyce, when discussing a plan similar to the Farmerfield mission, for example, exclaimed that farms between 3,000 and 6,000 acres are "far beyond the wants or means of individuals of this class."[91] Instead, what Boyce and other missionaries had in mind was the plan implemented at Farmerfield, whereby approximately one hundred families were settled on 6,000 acres.

In addition to the problems of a saturated market and undercapitalization, the tenants faced additional challenges over which they had little or no control. Ecological and geographical constraints contributed to underproduction at Farmerfield and informed the tenants' decision to expand their economic activities beyond agriculture to minimize risk. The ecozone of the Albany district in which Farmerfield was situated was prone to drought and locust infestations and as soon as the tenants began settling there between 1840 and 1843, they confronted these obstacles. In the annual report for 1843, the local missionary John Richards wrote: "The last year has been a year of great trial, in temporal matters, to the inhabitants of this place. Their crops failed, in consequence of a long and severe drought; and when the rains fell and partially revived some of the crops, the locusts came and blighted the renewed hopes of the people."[92] By the time Farmerfield's residents were able to regain a measure of prosperity, war broke out in 1846, revealing the mission's geographical vulnerability on the frontier. Despite being the "scene of repeated deadly conflicts" there was no loss of life at Farmerfield and only a few people were injured. With some people huddled in the church for protection and others keeping vigil, however, the tenants were unable to prevent the loss of cattle and other moveable property and could not tend to their lands.[93] The census of 1849 reporting 1,117 head of cattle on the estate reflected some of these losses, down from the 1,300 head reported in 1844.[94]

The 1846–47 War of Dispossession occasioned the first complaint of both temporary and permanent out-migration from Farmerfield and the Albany district in general. Just as the 1834–35 war had dispersed Africans into the Eastern Cape, eventually bringing people to Farmerfield, so too did the 1846–47 war send people scrambling for safety. This time, however, Farmerfield experienced a net loss of residents as individuals sought their fortunes elsewhere. For the first time since they started coming into the colony in the 1820s, local missionaries reported that Sotho-Tswana individuals had made a slow, steady retreat from the Eastern Cape significant enough to affect the distribution of this population group in the

Albany area and at Farmerfield. The numerical decline of this particular group was significant enough that services were no longer conducted or translated in the Sotho-Tswana language.[95] Impoverished tenants at Farmerfield sent their children out to seek work or pulled them out of school temporarily to help them farm.[96] By 1849 the tenants faced another season of crop failure, partly accounting for the low crop values enumerated in the 1849 census used to explore the economic livelihoods of Farmerfield's tenants.

Between 1850 and 1853 another costly War of Dispossession depleted even more of the cattle herds at Farmerfield and disrupted agricultural production and the residents' transport business. While some of the tenants were transporting tea, rice, and other goods to Grahamstown, Africans fighting against the colony attacked nine of their wagons and descended on Farmerfield. By the end of the war, the people—including Titus Dubula, one of the prosperous tenants discussed earlier in this chapter—had lost 250 head of cattle. Dubula and other male residents put up a valiant chase, but were unable to recover the stolen property.[97] For the duration of the war, the men of Farmerfield were called upon to assist in local defense and asked to keep watch.[98] Even when the war subsided in 1853, the tenants had no reprieve; by 1854 they had lost an additional 200 head of cattle to disease and after a succession of dry seasons had only small crop yields for 1855 and 1856, while another drought ensued in 1859.[99] The 1860s and 1870s proved no kinder to the residents and for the first time local missionaries warned in their annual reports that starvation was threatening to break up the settlement.

Although the missionaries remarked on the great forbearance of the residents, the succession of war, drought, and cattle disease undermined their ability to bounce back from each disaster. Between 1840 and 1850 the residents had a relatively prosperous decade despite the interlude of war, locusts, and drought. The following two decades, however, escalated the difficulties tenants faced as the challenges continued almost unabated year after year. The small trickle of individuals who began leaving the estate became a steady stream as people sought succor at other mission settlements and with their families beyond the borders of the colony. The tenants wanted to maintain their access to the mission, yet were unable to adequately feed themselves without seeking work wherever they could. The very same processes of war, dispersal, and starvation that brought people to Farmerfield in the 1840s were now causing a rapid turnover rate at the mission and undermining the agricultural viability of the once-successful peasantry established there. Although the exact numbers are difficult to tabulate, local missionaries expressed alarm about the constant mobility that these crises spawned. As can be expected, it was the younger cohort of tenants and dependents who usually exercised this mobility, each time leaving behind the older, impoverished, and often infirm residents who were less willing or unable to relocate.[100] Though some of the tenants left Farmerfield for other mission settlements, the out-migration still affected morale at the estate and the overall state of the mission. Seen from this broad perspective, it appears that the peasantry of Farmerfield reached its zenith between 1840 and 1850, thereafter experiencing a slow yet constant barrage of disasters that precipitated a subsistence crisis.

As a "selected class" of Africans, the tenants of Farmerfield represented a new phase in Methodist evangelical expansion, and a novel turn in mission enterprise at the Cape in general. Conceptually, Farmerfield embodied the goals of missionary enterprise between the 1790s and 1830s. The mission was created at the end of a phase of pioneer evangelism when missionaries from all denominations complained that Christian evangelism had thus far resulted in "nominalism" at their missions and disregard for missionary work among the wider African populace. Farmerfield thus heralded a new strategy for future missions at the Cape by starting off with what many of the pioneer missions lacked: a population already screened for their commitment to a Christian lifestyle, a pilot industrial school, European marriage customs instead of polygynous unions, and a gendered division of labor that relegated men to agriculture and women to the domestic sphere. As the only African Methodist mission station established within the boundaries of a white community and within the borders of the Cape Colony, Farmerfield also had the distinction of being an early African labor reserve where Africans were expected to provide labor to local whites. The vision of Farmerfield was such an idealistic elaboration of missionary goals, and such a concerted effort to avoid the pitfall of pioneer missions, that the tenants were both burdened and liberated by what was expected of them.

The economic livelihoods of the tenants revealed the problem with this new model of missions. Missionaries supplied the land access necessary to nurture a peasantry and Christianity to provide education and social discipline, and expected that a combination of agriculture and working for whites would maintain African prosperity. Farmerfield's tenants, however, demonstrated that working for whites was hardly a path to economic independence and avoided that kind of labor when they could. In fact, by moving to Farmerfield many of the tenants were trying to get away from contractual labor relations that left them with little arable or grazing land and bound their entire families to the employer. Yet the most sobering part of the mission's design was that land was no panacea for African economic independence and sometimes even the best efforts of the peasants themselves were insufficient to maintain subsistence. Farmerfield's peasants rose between the 1840s and 1850s, when African peasantries barely existed elsewhere in the Cape Colony, and experienced a near catastrophic economic decline when a discernable peasantry was finally beginning to emerge.

In spite of the population losses and near famine conditions between the 1860s and the 1870s, the tenants expected that the final decision to move or stay at Farmerfield remained in their hands. Elsewhere in Albany and other parts of the Cape Colony, everyone was trying to weather some level of subsistence crisis and natural disaster. By the early years of the 1880s the tenants faced a different battle, this time with their missionary overlords, who apprised them that the continual subsistence crisis had precipitated discussions about dissolving the mission. Residents were taken aback that their impending removal would come by administrative fiat and with little personal consultation. The most surprising aspect of this administrative review for the tenants, however, was that their Christian conduct featured prominently in the negative assessments of the mission. In this review Farmerfield's economic and evangelical design came under intense scrutiny, placing the issues of African land access, land usage, and the progress of African Christianity at the forefront of discussions. Chapter 5 examines the religious component of Farmerfield's design in order to shed light on where and how missionary expectations and the residents' Christian lifestyles diverged. Chapter 6 then provides an in-depth exploration of the administrative review precipitated by the tenants' alleged religious and economic shortcomings.

"'Incipient Civilization' and 'Nominal' Christianity?"

The African Christian Experience at Farmerfield, 1838–1884

"All the practices of 'heathenism' are entirely banished from the place [Farmerfield]. It is, in the strictest sense, a truly Christian village."[1]

Between 1838 and 1839, when Africans learned of plans to establish the new Methodist mission settlement of Farmerfield, the general superintendent of Wesleyan Missions in South East Africa, William Shaw, affirmed that the ideal resident would be associated with the Methodist Church and possess property in the form of cattle, sheep, or goats as evidence of hard work and industry. When the official application process began, the original African congregants who had made the request for the mission must have greeted the opportunity with a measure of anticipation, excitement, and relief. They would get to leave Grahamstown and its immediate neighborhood where the life chances of most of the Africans can be best described as eking out a living. Other areas in the Eastern Cape afforded few opportunities for Africans to settle and avoid labor on white farms. The local white community near the few settlements Africans managed to establish, like the Kat River or enclaves in Somerset East, proved inhospitable to the idea of Africans living independently.[2] Yet in the 1830s the Methodist congregants Shaw had earmarked for Farmerfield were not the only ones who welcomed the opportunity to secure access to arable and grazing lands in the Eastern Cape. Other Africans, who had a superficial affiliation to Methodism or no connection at all, also sought residence at Farmerfield. On the 6,000-acre farm that normally served one white farmer, space was limited to approximately one hundred families. The residents Shaw eventually selected molded the Christian community and shaped the African experience of Christianity at Farmerfield in the ensuing decades. The supposed shortcomings of these individuals in turn influenced missionary perceptions and assessments of Christianity at Farmerfield, especially in relation to the prevailing ideals of the civilizing mission.

Shaw encountered few problems identifying Africans who met the property qualification for residence. His missionary colleague, William Boyce, writing about the possibility of establishing agricultural communities for Africans living in the colony, declared that Shaw was "well acquainted with this class of coloured people and is of the opinion that there are in the neighborhood of Graham's Town, in the district of Albany alone, two or three hundred individuals." Boyce added that these individuals would themselves be *ultimately* paying every expense," giving Africans a stake in the land and defraying the initial purchase price of the farm.[3] If Shaw questioned this mode of selecting applicants as a guarantor of the kind of religious community he wanted to create, he did not say. His commitment to selecting "industrious" residents revealed how much he wanted Farmerfield to be a true paragon of successful mission strategy.

The potential residents' commitment to Christianity was far more difficult to ascertain than their accumulation of property through industrious habits. Shaw had to acknowledge that the existence of a pool of industrious, reputable Africans was often independent of their exposure to Christianity. Indeed, there were many individuals so defined who "by industry having acquired property in cattle and money and by long residence in the colony have become aware of the value of the possession of legal rights and security of property," yet remained detached from any formal expressions of Christianity.[4] Despite William Shaw's attempts to create a population composed only of experienced Christians who were already in the Methodist Church, the early residents still encompassed varied associations with mission Christianity. Some had no association at all to Christianity when they first came to the station. This chapter explores the Christian component of Farmerfield's design from 1838 to 1884, when the Methodist Church considered selling the land and terminating the settlement. Vignettes of two of the earliest residents at the mission highlight the diverse paths that brought a heterogeneous mix of people to the Farmerfield mission and underscore how these and other inhabitants were representative of the spectrum of African affiliation with Christianity.

The chapter argues that since Farmerfield was still considered part of a pioneering, evangelizing effort, missionaries assessed their progress based on the lenient yet condescending criteria of "nominal" Christianity and incipient civilization. In this way missionaries left some room to acknowledge that although Farmerfield itself represented a novel turn in missions by trying to earmark experienced African Christians for residence, there was still a latent understanding that the evangelical process required many decades to produce a mature, vital African Christianity. Hence the early missionary acclaim over Farmerfield should be seen from the perspective of how far the Methodists thought they had come since the pioneer days of the 1820s. The chapter posits that between the 1830s and the 1880s, missionaries expected Africans to demonstrate the transition from a pioneer to a more entrenched Christianity. Farmerfield especially was laden with this ambitious task from the outset. By the 1880s missionary optimism and élan had given way to a mixture of disappointment and sometimes exasperation. Methodist missionaries were ready to dissolve the Farmerfield settlement and declare defeat, a development explored in the subsequent chapter. This chapter allows us to substantiate or disavow the missionary claim that Farmerfield was in decline. It provides a lens through which to view what the African residents experienced while their missionary supervisors grew increasingly frustrated with the alleged persistence of "incipient civilization" and "nominal" Christianity at the mission.

Calibrating African Interactions with Mission Christianity

Missionaries, theologians, and historians alike have acknowledged the multiple gradations that existed in African interactions with mission Christianity.[5] Africans responded to the missionary message with a mixture of curiosity, disregard, and at times outright profanity. Missionaries complained that Africans had no fear of their God and persisted in holding individuals such as healers, rain makers, and diviners in great esteem despite theatrical missionary efforts to discredit them. European missionaries created a dichotomized system of believers and nonbelievers that lamented the "heathens" who rejected Christian missionaries outright and celebrated the pious, baptized, European-clothed Africans they counted among their church members. In this Manichean struggle between Christian and "heathen," often captured in metaphors of "light and darkness," "enlightenment and ignorance," "good and evil," and "progress and tradition," missionaries left little space to acknowledge any other association with Christianity as legitimate.[6] While missionaries maintained this dichotomy as their primary description of African relationships with Christianity, the continuum of relationships with Christianity was more complicated than these categories allow. Even at Farmerfield with its blueprint of ideal Christian inhabitants, the dichotomy of Christian/"heathen" revealed little of the residents' actual relationship with Christianity.

By 1839, when tenants began settling at Farmerfield, residents could be divided into four categories based on their association with Christianity. The first group was comprised of those who by the late 1830s had had a long association with Methodist missionaries and had gradually changed their lifestyles to become church members by the time they applied for residence at Farmerfield in 1838. The second group consisted of those who had disavowed "heathenism," and showed a strong interest in Christianity but were not yet baptized. These individuals were being catechized in Christian ways with the intention of future baptism and church membership. These first two groups constituted a cross-section of the best of pioneer Methodist work between 1823 and 1838. Some of those who fit in this category had indeed come from the pioneer missions destroyed in the war of 1834–35. From the outset these two groups comprised the vast majority and the nucleus of the Farmerfield settlement.

In the middle of the scale was the third group of people—"adherents" or "hearers"—who exhibited some interest in going to church services yet made no particular commitment to eventually becoming formal Christians. While individuals who fit this description diverged from Shaw's ideal residents, some of the Africans who met the property qualifications for residence fell into this category. They adopted basic clothing such as pants and shirts or dresses, and had enough interest in Christianity to go to church, without necessarily pledging to become church members. Shaw admitted a few such individuals for residence, already showing the divergence between his vision and reality. Church services on Sunday consisted of even more individuals who fit into this category since some of the local Africans living and working on European farms close to Farmerfield periodically attended church there.

At the very end of the continuum stood a few individuals who represented a small, yet symbolic part of the population of Farmerfield; individuals whose lifestyles in the missionaries' view still exhibited "heathenism" in a public manner. The practices that most consistently fit this description included polygyny and male circumcision rites. Some missionaries condemned these practices as two of the most unrelenting vestiges of "heathenism" hindering the progress of Christianity.[7] While few cases of polygyny appeared at Farmerfield, it is more difficult to tabulate how many people allowed their children to be circumcised since the practice could be done covertly. In 1839 it was a very public case of polygyny rather than the now-clandestine practice of circumcision that sounded a discordant note in Shaw's ideal model of Farmerfield. One of the first challenges William Shaw and his missionary colleagues faced within the early months of the Farmerfield settlement was how to resolve a dilemma over the polygynous marriage of one of the residents.

While in theory Shaw created Farmerfield to demonstrate the best of missionary evangelization, conforming to model Christians was idealistic. The people at the mission sometimes did not fit comfortably into the four-tiered category laid out above since the definitions of "heathenism" and Christianity were flexible for some Africans and usually quite rigid with most missionaries. In their daily lives, Farmerfield's residents worked out how their behavior in and out of church moved them, like pegs, along the continuum of Christianity and "heathenism." Long-term residence at the mission required staying at the far end of the continuum as experienced Christians or catechumens on the verge of church membership. Even though missionaries made some complaints about impiety and backsliding at Farmerfield, their assessments were relatively satisfactory in early decades of the mission. The annual missionary reports of Farmerfield varied from tempered approbations of the mission's progress to more enthusiastic appraisals of the triumph of Christianity and civilization.

Complaints about "nominal" Christianity and incipient civilization proved to be more of a pretext for ending the mission when it came under review, rather than actual reflections of the state of the mission between the 1840s and the 1880s.

Titus Dubula and the Tswana Patriarch

To understand the experiences of the earliest cohort of Farmerfield's settlers, consider the following sketches of two of the mission's first residents: a destitute young Xhosa man in his late twenties who found himself bartering for beads at a mission station after he had lost his cattle; and an elder Tswana patriarch who, along with his three wives and children, lived and worked on a white farm in the Eastern Cape.[8] When and how did these two men end up as part of William Shaw's vision of an ideal Christian mission? How were their changing associations with mission Christianity reflected on the hierarchical continuum of church members, catechumens, adherents, "hearers" and "heathens?"

Sometime in the 1820s misfortune befell Dubula, a Xhosa-speaking man born in the 1790s beyond the borders of the Cape Colony. One of the infamous commandos whites used to recover stolen cattle confiscated his cattle. These commandos, consisting of armed men tracing the tracks or spoors of the stolen animals, proved an important feature of the military defense on the Eastern frontiers of the Cape Colony. They were the main avenues for restitution to which white settlers resorted since the colonial government was relatively powerless in preventing the intractable problem of cattle thefts. White communities near the borders of the Cape Colony complained ad nauseam about these cattle thefts as a constant nuisance and as evidence of lax security on the frontier. By the 1830s and 1840s they tabulated their losses under the title of "Kaffir depredations" in the newly created newspapers, the *Graham's Town Journal* and the *Cape Frontier Times*.[9]

Various individuals, including missionaries, Africans, white settlers, government agents, and travelers to the Cape, identified the operation of these commandos as one of the incendiary factors fueling conflicts between Africans and whites. White settlers cast themselves as unwitting victims and conversely portrayed Africans as inveterate cattle thieves. Meanwhile, missionaries hoped that progress in Christianity would be commensurate with a decrease in the incidence of cattle raids. While the government sanctioned the use of commandos for cattle restitution, in practice the commandos represented a sort of vigilante justice of whites against blacks. There were no guarantees that only the stolen cattle would be seized and communities and individuals who took no part in raids often suffered indiscriminate restitution. Divergent government, settler, missionary, and African opinions about the efficacy and abuses of these systems heightened debates between various parties at the Cape about the most effective way to maintain order on the frontier.[10]

Living close to the Eastern Cape frontier, individuals like Dubula experienced first hand, or at least heard about, these dreaded commandos. We do not know if he was involved in the initial cattle raid that sparked the reprisal. Regardless, soon after the seizure of his property, a now impecunious Dubula went looking to earn beads at the Wesleyville mission, established in 1823 as the first in a chain of stations that stretched several hundred miles beyond the borders of the Cape Colony. Perhaps he got the beads he and other Africans used as currency to trade for cattle and rebuild or increase their herds.[11] As the founder of Wesleyville and the superintendent of Methodist missions, William Shaw was long accustomed to the use of buttons, beads, and brass wire currency that prevailed among Africans beyond the borders of the colony. Those Shaw employed as laborers in the early years at Wesleyville were paid five strings of beads per day.[12] When Dubula came to Farmerfield, therefore, Shaw would not have been surprised by his request for beads. However, although he used these currencies in his interactions with Africans, Shaw bemoaned the interest in "Beads and Trinkets" as opposed to what he thought were more "useful articles" like the clothing, hatchets, and cooking pots available at the mission's store.[13] From the outset of the mission, therefore, transforming African consumption patterns became closely attached to the larger evangelical goal.

Dubula got more than the beads he sought. His sojourn to the Wesleyville mission was the beginning of a lifelong association with the Methodist evangelical mission and his eventual connection with Farmerfield. Sometime after his excursion to the mission, Dubula developed an interest in Christianity and in relocating to the Wesleyville mission. He gained William Shaw's trust and accompanied at least one of Shaw's wagons on trips to Grahamstown. In his journal Shaw proclaims triumphantly that during one of these journeys Dubula underwent a significant spiritual experience that inspired him to take the necessary steps to become a member of the Methodist Church. We do not know the content of Dubula's momentous spiritual awakening, but his epiphany was followed by specific actions that missionaries identified as evidence of his conversion to Christianity. Dubula moved along the continuum from being labeled a "heathen" by the missionaries to becoming one of several catechumens receiving instruction in Christian ways and awaiting baptism.

Dubula was one of four catechumens baptized at Wesleyville on October 11, 1829. He was given the Christian name of Titus and thereafter called Titus Dubula.[14] While William Shaw, the missionary stationed at Wesleyville, rejoiced that four individuals had chosen to become members of the church, he was particularly proud of one person, Chief Kama. Kama was one of only two chiefs who converted to Christianity at the Cape.[15] Shaw was so overjoyed and triumphant about the chief's baptism that he pronounced, "I could scarcely command my feelings so as to finish the service."[16] Dubula's baptism, therefore, was overshadowed by the symbolism of Chief Kama's baptism, which William Shaw deemed "a triumph of the power of the Gospel."[17] With their baptisms, Chief

Kama and Titus Dubula joined the small ranks of African Christians at the pioneer mission. In 1830 Dubula was one of thirty-one church members on a mission with several hundred inhabitants.[18] The Methodist missionaries seemed to place a significant degree of confidence in a hectic four-day itinerant preaching schedule in October 1830, where William Shrewsbury noted that he was "Much assisted by Titus Dubula from Wesleyville."[19] By the outbreak of the War of Dispossession in 1834, Dubula had lived at Wesleyville and Mount Coke, two of the pioneer Methodist missions beyond the borders of the Cape Colony. The war lasted into 1835 and destroyed several mission stations including some in the Methodist chain: Wesleyville, Mount Coke, and Butterworth all succumbed to fire.[20] Scores of Africans, including former mission residents like Dubula, migrated into the Cape Colony and settled on the eastern frontier where they sought to rebuild their lives.[21] Misfortune had struck Titus Dubula again.

As these events unfolded in Dubula's life and brought him into contact with the Methodist missionaries in the 1820s and 1830s, a family tragedy was looming at the Klipheuvel farm, the future site of Farmerfield. An elder, respected Tswana man employed and living on a European farm near Grahamstown learned that the property was going to be sold. Although we do not know his name or precisely when he was told that the farm was going to become the new Methodist mission station of Farmerfield, we can guess that this news must have created some anxiety. After all, the Christian mission station normally did not permit polygyny on their premises and this man had three wives. The Tswana patriarch was perhaps fortunate, however, depending on whether we see the resolution of this dilemma from his family's or the missionaries' perspective. While William Shaw strictly prohibited polygyny at Farmerfield, he was willing to consider a solution other than eviction. The family was permitted to remain at Farmerfield and given a grace period to determine how best to dissolve the polygynous family unit into a nuclear arrangement.

Shaw had at least two reasons for pursuing a compromise. James Cameron, one of Shaw's colleagues stationed in the Albany District, noted in his journal that the Tswana patriarch was no ordinary man. As he was "rather a respectable headman, notwithstanding his polygamy and willing to submit to the regulations of the station, it was not deemed advisable to put him away," Cameron asserted.[22] While Cameron provides some insight into the deference William Shaw was willing to accord this Tswana man, the later actions of the missionaries reveal their opportunism as well. As Chapter 2 has shown, Shaw and other Methodist missionaries engaged in a diplomatic game with African chiefs, councilors, and headmen as long as they believed it would promote their long-term evangelical goals. The benefit of having an influential African headman disavow polygyny or any other practices the missionaries opposed was greater than any point that could be made by publicly and unceremoniously reproving him.

The missionary euphoria over the baptism, conversion, and monogamous marriage of Chief Kama underscored the strategic importance of getting African chiefs and other men of influence to convert. Therefore, while the initial rapprochement between the polygynist patriarch and the Methodist missionaries at Farmerfield undoubtedly challenged Shaw's vision of an ideal mission station, it also provided him with an opportunity to make a symbolic statement. Converting someone whose lifestyle was the antithesis of what he envisioned for Farmerfield was, after all, the very purpose undergirding the evangelical mission to Africa. If this Tswana headman could move from the "heathen" end of the continuum to become a catechumen and eventually a church member, Shaw would have another paragon of the triumph of Christianity over polygyny.

As he was already living at the farm when Shaw purchased it, this Tswana gentleman, his three wives, and his children were perhaps the first residents at the mission station in 1839. Just how long would William Shaw allow the man and his family to remain? After all, he was allowed to stay with the proviso that he accept the rules of the mission—one of which was monogamous marriage. The latent conflict was bound to come to a head. By the early months of 1840 when James Cameron visited the station, the patriarch had made a rapid progression toward expressing a basic interest in Christianity. Moreover, he had selected the youngest of his three wives to marry in a Christian ceremony as a precondition for remaining at the mission and eventually becoming a member of the church. When the two remaining wives learned that their marriage would soon be declared illegitimate by the Christian marriage of their husband, they asked Cameron and the catechists to intervene. It was nothing short of a conundrum for the missionaries and catechists because the most senior wife was determined that the missionaries should provide some sort of redress for the family crisis, or a more equitable criterion for choosing who would become the sole, Christian wife. As the most senior wife and the mother of six children, she believed herself to have a rightful claim.

Whatever the protestations of the senior wife, James Cameron refused to intervene and allowed the patriarch to use his personal discretion to select one of three wives. According to Cameron, the patriarch decided to remain with the youngest wife, because her "better temper and greater attention to his comfort promised him more connubial happiness."[23] Cameron advised everyone involved in the conflict to wait two months before they made any final decisions. By then, the marriage banns had already been proclaimed and the Tswana patriarch seemed determined to proceed with his plans. We do not know the outcome of this turn of events. At least eighteen couples were married at Farmerfield in 1840, but there is no way to determine which couple, if any, was the marriage of the Tswana patriarch.[24] What is certain is that Shaw's deference to the status of patriarch was temporary and that monogamous Christian unions remained a cardinal requirement for mission residence at Farmerfield. Moreover, since the husband did not seem inclined to changing his residence, wanted to become a member of the church, and "had become convinced of his sins with the necessity of his fleeing from the wrath to come," putting away two wives was the only legitimate avenue to becoming one of the ideal African Christians Shaw wanted living at Farmerfield. It is likely, therefore, that the patriarch did indeed marry the younger wife while the others were left to cope with the emotional and material hardships accompanying the dissolution of the polygynous family unit. It was no easy decision for the patriarch, Cameron pointed out. He had only determined to live monogamously after "much consideration and many painful exercises of the mind."[25] Throughout the history of missionary enterprise at the Cape, family tragedies like these repeated themselves as some Africans tried to realign their marriage customs and family structures to comply with mission Christianity.[26]

The trajectories of mission residence for Titus Dubula and the Tswana patriarch highlight just two of the diverse paths that Africans took to the formal expression of Christianity through baptism, conversion, church membership, and the commensurate changes in their lifestyles. From the missionary perspective, the story of the Tswana patriarch highlighted polygyny as an obstacle to Christian mission enterprise even at a mission created to demonstrate the best of pioneer work. Yet there remain additional angles to this vignette, including how quickly Africans complied with mission rules to qualify for residence since few other residential options were available in the Eastern Cape and the tremendous human costs of one person's decision to convert to Christianity. The missionary story of triumph over the "heathenism" that polygyny represented to them was also a family tragedy and an index of African disadvantageous access to land.

With his three wives, the Tswana patriarch presented Farmerfield's missionaries with their most egregious example of "heathenism." Yet he was not alone in declaring and demonstrating his commitment to a Christian lifestyle at the eleventh hour. Other residents also fell short of the ideal yardstick of church membership. Of the forty-eight church members enumerated in 1839, for example, half of these individuals had only become Christians in that same year.[27] That William Shaw even allowed individuals without any official affiliation to Christianity to reside at Farmerfield highlights how few Africans met the original, strict residential qualification that they be members of the Methodist Church. Although the Methodists had created a sphere of influence in the Eastern Cape and attracted Africans to hear the Christian message, most Africans still saw no reason to declare a stance by becoming church members. They could continue as "adherents" or "hearers" indefinitely without enduring the mandatory and restrictive lifestyle changes church members had to make.

With no African missions in the Eastern Cape before the creation of Farmerfield, the access to residential space and agricultural land that attracted Africans to the pioneer missions was irrelevant in Grahamstown. With little leverage over Africans in town, Methodist missionaries noticed that many of the Africans attending church on Sundays remained unmotivated to make a commitment beyond hearing the message. These intermittent encounters certainly made Christianity more familiar to Africans yet won few church members. Outside the confines of the church, the missionary impact was minimal. Africans demonstrated that they held little reverence for or interest in the sort of rigid faith the Methodists and other missionary bodies advocated.

Denominational competition divided potential African members between Methodist, Baptist, Catholic, Anglican, and Congregational (LMS) sects in Grahamstown. Even when Africans shunned official church membership, they were quite savvy about how to use the missionaries to gain other advantages. The presence of so many denominations and the lack of tangible commitment by Africans in the vicinity of Grahamstown impressed upon Methodist missionaries that after concerted evangelical work between 1823 and 1838, progress was relatively slow. A religious revival in Grahamstown between 1837 and 1838, however, gave African evangelism a considerable and necessary boost. Between one hundred and 130 new members swelled the ranks of the Methodist Church in Grahamstown. When making his decision about creating Farmerfield, Shaw was careful to consider what would happen if the Methodist Church did not take advantage of the new interest in Methodism that Africans demonstrated.[28] From the Africans' perspective, the competition made them religious commodities of sorts. The earlier disinterest they had shown stood in sharp contrast to the revival of 1837 and Methodist missionaries certainly wanted to capitalize on it. In this context Africans could and did play one missionary society against the other or at least reminded the Methodists that they had other options.

Farmerfield provided a means for missionaries to separate the curious from the committed and to enforce the cardinal rules of Christian lifestyle such as monogamous marriage. The opportunity to live at Farmerfield, predicated as it was on church membership or a promise of eventual membership, forced Africans to make a clear choice, and removed some of the fleeting leverage they had held in Grahamstown. They had to abide by mission rules and make the necessary arrangements to attend church, expose themselves to the Christian message and teaching, and eventually become church members. If the basic goal of missionaries was to increase the number of church members, then the balance of power shifted significantly in their favor when they operated in the controlled environment of the Farmerfield mission station rather than in the wider society.

Missionaries envisioned their evangelical work as both a social and spiritual experiment. Separate from the wider society, the mission provided a crucible for missionaries to implement their civilizing and evangelical goals. The relatively closed environment of the mission guaranteed a degree of commitment to the package of Christian conversion and a civilized lifestyle that was not forthcoming in Grahamstown. At Farmerfield, mandatory church and school attendance and proscriptions about dress, marriage customs, and architecture supported the civilizing goals. Rules about clothing and housing styles that missionaries could not realistically impose on adherents in Grahamstown, they enforced at the mission. The threat of expulsion guaranteed more conformity at Farmerfield than was the case in Grahamstown. Africans therefore conceded to change their lifestyles enough to qualify for residence. They gave up multiple wives and smoking and alcohol, for example. While these exterior changes are easy enough to recognize, assessing African spiritual commitment is difficult to gauge. Ultimately each convert had a personal relationship with God and was responsible for his own salvation. Indeed this individual outlook had made Methodism a revolutionary force in eighteenth and nineteenth-century England. When applied to the nineteenth-century Cape Colony, this characteristic of Methodism restricted the power and responsibilities missionaries had delegated to themselves as arbiters of African Christianity. At Farmerfield missionaries hoped that the direct link between land access, residence, and church membership, as well as the structure of weekly class meetings, would motivate the people of Farmerfield to discipline themselves accordingly or risk losing it all. Yet the spiritual relationship ultimately lay between each African convert and his conception of God.

Missionaries accepted that some of the conversions effected in this manner entailed a degree of compulsion on their part and undoubtedly opportunism on the Africans' part. If Africans capitalized on the material opportunity and only conformed to the outward aspects of a Christian lifestyle, such a situation encouraged "nominalism," perhaps the most serious danger of all and a frequent criticism that was leveled at many nineteenth-century missions. Yet it was a more manageable approach than hoping for conversions and lifestyle changes through the influence of local Christian churches where European congregants showed little enthusiasm about sharing pews with Africans. The multiracial congregations that had impressed Shaw in the 1820s gradually gave way to racially exclusive ones. The growing social and economic chasm between Africans and whites in the Eastern Cape was reflected in the religious realm and affected the Methodist as well as other denominations.[29] Moreover, though Europeans complained about nudity and inappropriate dress, they were not altogether certain if they wanted to see Africans dress just like them and acquire the same standard of living. A residential African mission removed most of these concerns so that missionaries could focus on how to combat what they interpreted as "nominalism." Even when missionaries acknowledged that they could not monitor the spiritual relationship between Africans and God, this did not stop them from trying. They responded to suspicions of "nominalism" or opportunism at Farmerfield by extending the trial periods of individuals whose allegiance they deemed uncertain, delaying baptismal ceremonies, and lengthening the time allotted for catechism.[30]

With the balance of missionary power more clearly delineated at the mission station than in Grahamstown, Africans quickly made the necessary steps to safeguard their residence at the Farmerfield estate. Personalities like the Tswana patriarch, with no previous interest in a Christian lifestyle for most of his adult life, changed his family structure and marital status. In the first year of the settlement approximately twenty-five individuals got themselves on the church rolls as catechumens and baptismal candidates. By the end of the year, these individuals swelled Farmerfield's church membership to forty-eight, and by 1840 this number had grown to eighty-nine. Compared to the pioneer Methodist missions of the 1820s and early 1830s, therefore, Farmerfield had an auspicious beginning. Often, after a decade in existence, some of these early missions could barely count fifty members on the church rolls even though hundreds of people lived there. Wesleyville, begun in 1823, had only thirty-one registered church members by 1830; and in 1832 all six pioneer missions (Wesleyville, Mount Coke, Butterworth, Morley, Clarkebury, Buntingville) together had a total of 150 church members.[31] From this perspective, Farmerfield made a crucial break with the trends found at pioneer missions. Fourteen adults were baptized in the first year of the settlement, while another twenty-one took this crucial step a year later.[32] Within two years of its creation, Farmerfield already had eighty-nine church members.[33] Though Farmerfield maintained a core of resident church members, missionaries at Farmerfield maintained the practice of allowing non-Christians to apply for residence upon promise of undergoing catechism, baptism, and eventual membership in the church. Individuals filling the vacancies created by death, war, and migration at Farmerfield, therefore, provided a potential source of new converts, as did children who reached adolescence at the estate.

Neither the missionaries assigned to Farmerfield nor its residents provided any substantive evidence with which to explore the spiritual aspects of Christian conversion. Nonetheless, missionaries tried to determine the sincerity of the residents' commitment to Christianity and to evaluate the overall progress of religious work at the mission. In 1840 the local missionary wrote that the work was progressing in "a very cheering aspect." The following year he informed the WMMS in London, "The work of God is delightfully going forward," and that the religious state of the people was "highly gratifying."[34] In 1843 the missionaries informed the WMMS of "constant progress" at Farmerfield and the reports up to 1850 continued in a similarly positive vein. What contributed to such positive reports?

First, the missionaries were pleased with church attendance, the congregations growing so large at times that the chapel could not accommodate everyone. Between 280 and 380 people attended service on Sundays. Second, the congregation "listened with great attention to the word" and became very emotional during the sermons. Third, in its early years, Farmerfield received regular batches of new converts who were put on long periods of trial and eventually baptized. In the first few years of the mission, at least twenty baptisms occurred per year. With no first-hand testimony from the residents, it is difficult to say how they perceived these signposts of religious progress. Certainly there is some truth to the statement that people were attentive, yet there was also ample room for confusion when white missionaries delivered their sermons. Most of the Methodist preachers had an imperfect knowledge of Dutch, yet had to use it in their sermons because their interpreters had an even more imperfect knowledge of English. These sermons went through several distillations, the sermon first delivered in Dutch and then translated to Xhosa and Tswana. It is possible, therefore, that the residents received a diluted message. People had to be attentive to understand what the missionaries were saying.

The effectiveness of the Christian sermons lay with the interpreter who may interpret the words, yet not convey the vigor or passion of the message. When James Cameron delivered a sermon at Farmerfield in April 1839, for example, he declared, "I was pleased with the attention of the people but my Bechuana (Tswana) interpreter was exceedingly lifeless and unenergetic, which operated against the effect of my discourse." At the evening service that same day, Cameron was more pleased with his interpreter who "spoke like one who felt the importance of the truths which were conveyed to them through him."[35] With the morning service conducted in Dutch and the afternoon and evening services conducted in Xhosa and Tswana, each resident could attend the one they understood best. Yet translation was insufficient to address the needs of such a heterogeneous community. The "Colored" residents at Farmerfield, for instance, did not seem too pleased about this arrangement since they eventually requested but were denied their own church.[36] Finally, as was characteristic of the Methodist administrative structure, missionaries rotated to different posts so that throughout its history Farmerfield received an influx of missionaries with variable and often nonexistent linguistic skills in Xhosa, Dutch, and Tswana. Furthermore, no one missionary had a chance to leave a legacy of truly connecting with the tenants for more than a few years before they were circulated to a different post. The early correspondence of Farmerfield's local missionaries identified none of the residents by name and spoke in very impersonal terms about the affairs of the mission. Even if Daniel Roberts in his capacity as supervisor shared any information with the local missionary about Christian allegiance at Farmerfield, none of what he may have said survived in the written records. As the visiting Quaker missionary James Backhouse observed in his tour of missions in and beyond the Cape Colony, "The evils attendant on the frequent removals among the Wesleyans in this country are great, and they are not the only community in South Africa whose work has been impeded by injudicious removals."[37] Within a decade of its creation, the WMMS had assigned at least eight different missionaries to Farmerfield. Although a few of these same missionaries ended up at Farmerfield in subsequent rotations, the mission's relationship with the resident missionaries was fleeting. Far more important were the relationships with class leaders, exhorters, and preachers who conducted their lessons in their local languages and thus had a tremendous amount of influence over the cohort of members they were assigned. Methodism devolved authority to local Africans long before missionaries ever became comfortable with this idea.

In addition to the full congregations on Sundays and the increasing number of catechumens and church members, the missionaries assessed piety and knowledge of Christianity. While they provided no specific details on any one convert, Farmerfield's missionaries wrote of satisfaction with the overall devotion of the people.

"Their experience is sound and scriptural," Farmerfield's missionary asserted in 1841. "Generally they are walking in fear of the Lord and the comfort of the Holy Ghost," he continued, "and those who have not obtained the blessing of pardon are earnestly seeking the Lord. Some have obtained a high state of holiness and are going on to perfection."[38] The following year, the local missionary wrote that the residents' religious experience "exhibits the scriptural marks of genuineness."[39]

Farmerfield's reputation as a Christian settlement thrived on the status of residents like Titus Dubula whose long association with Christianity highlighted the compromises some Africans willingly made. Even if he had only material interests on his initial visit to Wesleyville to obtain beads, Dubula eventually made a choice to become a Christian and live as a Christian for many decades. Although it is impossible to recover his spiritual experience, Dubula's choice to live as a Christian, his long-standing membership in the Methodist Church, and eventual appointment as a headman and class leader at Farmerfield serve as testament to the sincerity of his convictions in lieu of his conversion narrative. For Dubula and other residents, the path to respectability and permanent habitation at Farmerfield rested on one's Christian status. Once residents were church members, leading classes and becoming local preachers and evangelists were the primary avenues for cementing their status in the church. These opportunities for residents to participate in their own salvation and supervise each other complimented the broader Methodist goal of fostering what they termed "native agency."

"Native Agency" and Spiritual Surveillance

The commencement of Farmerfield overlapped with an important development in Methodist evangelism in Southeastern Africa. At a district meeting in 1838, the year when the idea of Farmerfield was also implemented, missionaries discussed the need to expand the use of Africans in their evangelical work for the "promotion of the work of God in this district" (the Albany and Kaffraria districts). The missionaries declared, "The time has now arrived for the employment of converted natives possessing suitable qualifications on a more systematic plan than heretofore as Exhorters, Class Leaders and Local Preachers"[40] (see Figure 5.1). From the 1820s when they began pioneer evangelical work, Methodist missionaries acknowledged the important roles Africans played in getting their own countrymen to listen to Christian messages and teachings. Initially they relied on a handful of converts to influence other Africans to come to church or listen to the missionaries when they itinerated beyond the mission premises.

Formal plans for cultivating "native agency" centered on establishing schools. Schools, William Shaw firmly believed, were "a means of civilizing and evangelizing the Caffre people," and "the only . . . hope of raising up native interpreters, schoolmasters and preachers."[41] The fifteen years between the establishment of the first Methodist mission in 1823 and the creation of Farmerfield in 1838 had allowed for the cultivation of a small yet significant group of Africans who could begin to assume leadership roles on the lower rungs of the Methodist Church hierarchy. With a chain of missions established beyond the borders of the Cape Colony and other successful ventures in Natal and among Tswana chiefdoms, the WMMS lacked adequate personnel to keep pace with both their missionary and educational efforts. The Watson Institute at Farmerfield, named after a benefactor from Leeds, England, served as a crucible for the creation of a cohort of Africans to serve as "subordinate agents in the mission work."[42] These "native agents" were ideal, William Shaw told a committee on aborigines, because they could "live on a lower scale of salaries," and the Wesleyans could maintain "a larger number of schools without very seriously augmenting the expenditure."[43] At Farmerfield the white catechist/schoolmaster earned fifteen pounds per year while the African schoolmaster/interpreter—in this instance a Tswana man named John Roberts—earned eight pounds.[44]

The Methodist administrative infrastructure of class leaders and catechists supported their attempts at secular and spiritual surveillance at Farmerfield and provided a means for implementing plans to create "native agency." Daniel Roberts, head of the Watson educational institution, also served as supervisor of Farmerfield. Since he lived at the mission, he kept a keen eye on its daily affairs. He was the sole white person with whom the residents had daily interaction. The local missionary who lived four miles away in the European village of Salem took responsibility for spiritual supervision of the mission and consulted with Roberts on the general management of the estate. A network of class meetings provided an informal forum for missionaries to interrogate Africans about what they had learned and for Africans to have their questions about Christianity answered. Some of these class leaders later became local preachers, which for a time was the pinnacle of African promotion or agency in the Methodist hierarchy.

Africans fitting the description of "native agent" at Farmerfield were those like Dubula who had migrated from other mission stations in the aftermath of the 1834–35 war and those who had become members of the Methodist Church in Grahamstown in the 1820s and 1830s. More recent converts qualified for these positions, though missionaries preferred those who had more experience. These experienced African Christians were accustomed to the strictures of mission life and in the missionaries' view had weathered the tests of their sincerity. At Farmerfield each class had a local leader whose position was akin to a religious and spiritual prefect. Each leader had the responsibility of talking to each member, answering questions, and acting in an intermediary fashion with the minister.

By 1841, three years after the settlement began, Farmerfield's own residents began appearing in the church records as class leaders. One of the first residents, James January, born in approximately 1799, married his wife Mary in 1840 at Farmerfield and from 1842 appeared for seven years as a class leader in the 1840s and at other periods in the 1860s.[45] By the time a wagon accidentally ran over and killed him in Salem, he was a revered local preacher.[46] The number of class leaders varied from three to seven in the early 1840, but by the 1870s between fourteen and seventeen class leaders from Farmerfield were serving the mission and its local preaching places. Of this number, only one woman, Katarina Minto, appeared regularly from 1841 up to 1877. Two other women, Martha Ncoza and Elizabeth Daniels, joined the ranks of class leadership in the late 1870s.

Once mission educational institutes addressed theological training along with general education, Methodist and other missionary societies could depend on the select group of candidates graduating each year to become a part of the Methodist administrative structure. Before the establishment of Healdtown in 1866, the Watson Institute was the most important supplier of African "native agents" to Methodist evangelism in South Africa.[47] The nascent Methodist native ministry began in 1864 in the Peddie district of the Eastern Cape. The creation of Healdtown in 1867 paved the way for the systematic training of Africans for the Methodist ministry. A centenary celebration of Methodism in 1923 outlined the development of an African native ministry as "one of the great chapters of the Missionary enterprise in Africa. Interpreter, catechist, schoolmaster, local preacher, evangelist, minister—this seems to have been the natural process of development which has given us the Native Ministry."[48]

While the Watson Institute was a pioneer establishment for the Methodists, other missionary societies took the initiative when it came to founding seminaries and ordaining ministers. The Scottish missionaries established the Lovedale theological institute in 1841 and the Presbyterians ordained the first African minister, Tiyo Soga, in 1856. The LMS had a long history of employing "native agents," the most famous of which was Jan Tzatzoe. The LMS, however, lost this important initiative in the 1820s and 1830s. Many of its missionaries (with some exceptions) grew critical of the efficacy of African agents and resentful of the influence on indigenous congregants.[49]

When the Watson Institute was divided in branches and reestablished at other Methodist settlements, the original branch at Farmerfield gave way to a regular school, thereby losing its novelty and pioneer status. The African seminary at Healdtown in many ways eclipsed the work of the Watson Institute. The cultivation of an African Methodist ministry received an important boost in the 1860s, sparked by the revivalist American preacher, William Taylor.[50] One African evangelist, Charles Pamla, traveled with Taylor on some of his tours and played an instrumental role not only in interpreting Taylor's sermon with passion and charisma, but also carrying the revival to a wider sphere.[51] Pamla was later ordained as a Methodist minister and appointed as the first African superintendent of a circuit, an important accomplishment for a denomination that was often uneasy about African aspirations. In the wake of this important revival movement, Africans entered the Healdtown institution in increasing numbers between the 1860s and 1880s. A few of these candidates were born and raised at Farmerfield.

For devout Christian men at Farmerfield, entering the ministry meant leaving the mission permanently. Once trained, those individuals raised at Farmerfield had few opportunities to return to that community since they were then subjected to the Methodist system of rotating ministers to different circuits. Success in the ministry and in education meant leaving Farmerfield. The Lwana family of Farmerfield sent three of their sons to the Methodist ministry, an ambitious move that made history in the annals of Methodism and took them far from the mission. Samuel Ntsiko and Christopher Lubisi, both born at Farmerfield in the nineteenth century, also ended up ministering in circuits far away from their birthplace.[52] As the pinnacle of "native agency," the ministry was reserved for men; women were, at best, considered helpmeets to their husbands. To the extent that missionaries considered women's education and spiritual development an important aspect of their evangelical work, it was in their capacity to become "suitable wives for ministers, evangelists and teachers," that the WMMS and other denominations expended funds and personnel.[53] For African women, the primary avenue for respectability and status in the church was to become class leaders, interpreters, teachers, assistant teachers, and seamstresses. In the late nineteenth century women's payer unions emerged, building upon women's particular spiritual response to Christianity, their crucial role as lay workers and "native agents," and their informal gatherings in class meetings, sewing classes, and prayer groups.[54]

Although African laymen and auxiliaries played important roles at the pioneer missions as well as at Farmerfield throughout the 1830s and 1840s, plans for "native agency" rested partly on the education of the youth. Generational differences between those who converted to Christianity in their late adult years and young people who were exposed to Christianity and education in their childhood or adolescence influenced long-term evangelical goals. Between the 1840s and the years leading up to the review of 1884 missionaries identified certain generational trends in their assessment of Christian evangelism at Farmerfield. On the one hand, they pinned their hopes for the creation of a vital, mature Christianity on the younger generation of Africans reared at the mission from birth or early childhood, and on the young men registered with the Watson Institute. Writing about the young people at Farmerfield in 1843, the local missionary asserted, "In them the results of religious instruction are rendered visible. Their piety is of a much more enlightened and intelligent character than that of their parents, who grew to middle or old age in barbarian ignorance."[55] In 1849, a decade after the mission began, 274 children and 213 adults lived at Farmerfield. As all other missionary societies acknowledged, the young were far more impressionable and more malleable than their elders. On the other hand, many of the elders exhibited a seriousness, sincerity, and commitment in their devotion that was often lacking in the youth. Methodist missionaries tried to balance this characteristic of the young and adult populations at their mission settlements to produce a vital African Christianity.

Yet another concern about children and adults was that many parents did not share the missionaries' view that education was a necessity. When Africans took their children out of school during peak labor periods, missionaries complained. In a chronicle of missionary work between 1823 and 1923, one missionary described the difficulties they encountered:

> For fifty years the work of day schools was hampered by difficulties arising from the fact that boys and girls in primitive African conditions were too useful to be spared by their parents for school attendance. As we all know, boys relieve the household in the dull occupation of herding, and keeping the cattle away from the fields; their help is needed in ploughing and ox-wagon transport expeditions; while girls are indispensable to their mothers in water fetching and wood collecting and weeding.[56]

Another concern was the influence of "heathen" parents over Christian children. Writing disdainfully of a chief's daughter who had been educated in England, one missionary declared that upon returning home nothing awaited her but the "old barbarous surroundings, the kraal, the smeared hut, and the kaross. A few years later she greeted a Wesleyan minister in the purest English," the missionary continued, "but she wore a Kafir blanket, had bead bangles on wrists and ankles, and was the wife of a polygamist."[57]

Boarding schools like the Watson Institute were one solution to isolate children from their parents; yet missionaries acknowledge that the more important problem was cultivating Christianity as a family affair. Since most of Farmerfield's tenants fell into the category of catechumen or church members, these particular problems occurred only intermittently. Even then, practical concerns about labor and subsistence crises forced some parents to remove students from school at Farmerfield. An 1849 census for Farmerfield showed that most children above the age of twelve were sent out to work.[58] Only later in the nineteenth century did African parents become more invested in educating their children. By then the option of becoming a prosperous African farmer grew dimmer as the younger generation of Africans came to grips with the realities of land alienation. Education played a far greater role in determining African life chances in the 1870s and 1880s than in the 1820s and 1830s when Africans had not yet experienced the brunt of destructive wars of dispossession and the expropriation that followed in their wake.

Besides education, missionaries acknowledged that secular matters affected the overall progress of Christianity at Farmerfield as well. Some of the same push factors that had brought African refugees to the Eastern Cape in the 1820s and 1830s—such as war, migration, and impoverishment—also destabilized mission settlements. In the aftermath of the 1834–35 War of Dispossession for example, Methodist missionaries observed that their congregants were "so scattered that it is difficult to collect a congregation and so migratory that they are not found long at one place."[59] The same observation held true in the war of 1846–47 and 1850–53. Parents sent their children in search of work and others left the mission station altogether, seeking residence and employment elsewhere. Already severely impoverished by the end of 1847, more than one hundred people moved out of the Salem and Farmerfield area after the war of 1850–53.

Although war, poverty, and migration impeded continuity in mission work, missionaries also worried about the minutiae of everyday life. At Farmerfield and the missions reestablished after 1835, missionaries noted "pleasing signs of an incipient civilization."[60] No aspect of the residents' lives escaped missionary scrutiny as either a potential indictment or commendation of their piety or departure from the white standards of civilization. The crusade to encourage square houses and have congregants decently clad continued alongside the quest for conversion. At Farmerfield specifically, Methodist missionaries scrutinized the residents' behavior and interaction with each other and with their neighbors to assess the Christian civilizing mission.

Civil Disputes and the "Civilizing Mission"

While accolades on the religious state of the Farmerfield were forthcoming, missionaries expressed more mixed sentiments about the "civilizing" mission they had attached to their evangelical work. In 1840 the resident missionary at Farmerfield declared:

> There is still much to be corrected and for the present borne with. The natural indolence of the people often leads to unpleasant consequences, while pride and indiscretion, the inseparable bane of incipient civilization, sometimes causes litigation and quarrels.[61]

Quarrels between residents, missionaries believed, showed the residents in a poor light. They cited the civil cases at Farmerfield as proof of incipient civilization, with harsher assessments than their views on housing or clothing. Whenever a dispute occurred, the residents of Farmerfield approached one of three headmen to resolve the matter. If this first step failed, manager Daniel Roberts or the assigned local missionary was usually next to intervene. When such interventions did not work, Farmerfield's residents did not hesitate to approach the local magistrate in Salem or Grahamstown. The residents disputed a range of issues, including disposal of inheritance, appropriate wages, and fines for adultery, hardly issues that indicted them as somehow less civilized than their white counterparts.

A few of these disputes involved practices or activities that missionaries singled out as evidence of the persistence of "heathenism" and therefore a low state of civilization on the estate. These infractions, such as bridewealth exchange, demonstrated that Africans did not always share the missionary perception of their practices. Unlike polygyny, bridewealth was easy to conceal. Parties involved in an exchange of cattle could carry on the transaction months before or after the marriage and mask it as a simple sale, loan, or gift of cattle. As a result, bridewealth was one of the prerogatives some residents at Farmerfield were unwilling to relinquish if they could hide it successfully. Success in concealing this practice means that the nature of bridewealth exchange at mission settlements is inaccessible to the historian. Only when parties could not settle disputes among themselves do these transactions come to light, and even then the parties divulged no more information than was necessary to resolve the case.

Sometime in the early 1840s, for example, Willem, a Xhosa man living near Farmerfield, acquired a wife at Farmerfield. He transferred to her father or guardian, Jacob, four animals. Since she was moving off the mission to live with her husband, this transaction was easier to hide from the missionaries, though probably not from Jacob's neighbors. By 1844 the marriage was dissolved. Willem's wife left him and rather than return to her guardian, relocated beyond the borders of the colony. Willem wanted Jacob to return his cattle. We do not know if he asked Jacob first and then was rebuffed. Regardless, Willem recruited the local magistrate, who subsequently sent him to see the manager of Farmerfield, at which time the original bridewealth exchange came to light. In another case, John, a young Mfengu man living at Farmerfield, asked the magistrate to intervene because his father had arranged a marriage for him without his knowledge and had already accepted the bridewealth. Since he did not like the woman his father had chosen, he wanted the cattle returned.[62]

No disciplinary action was taken against Jacob or against John's father even though the practice was forbidden. Perhaps the missionaries had accepted that they could not stamp out bridewealth, since Africans did not share their disdain of the practice. Besides highlighting the important fact that Africans continued practices that could be hidden from direct missionary purview, Willem's and other cases hint at interactions between Farmerfield's residents and Africans who lived in the local area. Although missionaries proclaimed that most of the local Africans had an affiliation with the Methodist Church, they remained concerned about the contact Farmerfield's relatively sheltered residents had with other Africans not professedly Christians. They did not wield the same influence over the local Africans as they did over Africans residing at Farmerfield. Marriage and employment brought nonmission residents into frequent contact with Farmerfield. Local Africans and Farmerfield residents bought or borrowed cattle, horses, wagons, and farming equipment from each other and even entered into clandestine sharecropping arrangements. In 1840, for example, a man named P. Roman lodged a complaint with the magistrate to recover a mare he allegedly purchased from a Farmerfield resident but never received.[63]

Frequent disputes arose between Farmerfield residents and local Africans over labor arrangements, the care of animals, and the hiring of equipment. For instance, the two-year plowing arrangement between residents James January and Jeptha turned sour in 1854 when Jeptha accused January of "fraud" for withholding his pay.[64] In 1858 Lucas, an elderly, blind resident of Farmerfield, complained that the young man he hired to assist him had neglected duties.[65] In instances when they owned cattle above the allowed limit at Farmerfield or when they could not tend the cattle themselves, residents of Farmerfield left such property in the care of Africans in the local area. These arrangements were sometimes in exchange for cash, for part of the herd, or for rendering other services. One such arrangement between Zwartboy, who worked on a local European farm, and one of the residents at Farmerfield fell through in June 1842. When Zwartboy contracted to keep certain cattle for ten months but found he could only do so for three months, he approached the magistrate to ask if he could still receive the amount of money stipulated in the original contract.[66]

In September 1852 Jeptha, who worked on a neighboring European farm, agreed to lend his span of oxen to one of the headmen of Farmerfield, Noah Mozambiker. Mozambiker took so long to pay that Jeptha complained to the magistrate. When Mozambiker finally complied, he remunerated Jeptha for less than he expected.[67] In another case, Josiah Badi hired his wagon to Malgas April. While they had no dispute over the fee, Malgas left the wagon in Grahamstown and made no arrangements with Badi to have it returned to Farmerfield.[68]

Women, customarily at a disadvantage in inheritance matters, often turned to magistrates for assistance to recover their dead husband's property. When her husband died in 1839, for example, the widow Hlebikazi asked the magistrate to assist her in recovering two cows and several calves he had left in charge of a young man who lived in the area.[69] The young man, Makonja, returned the animals within two days of the request. In another case, Kitje approached the magistrate regarding seven cows of her deceased husband, Peter. After Peter's death in September 1839, his brother January claimed that since one of Peter's wives now lived in his household, he had claimed seven animals from his property. When he appeared before the magistrate, January promised to eventually return the cows.[70]

Disputes with whites usually occurred over wages, the length of labor contracts, trespassing, or destruction of property. When two young men from Farmerfield shot a pig belonging to a local settler, J. Dicks, the magistrate imposed a fine of three pounds and ten shillings on their parents to pay for the damages.[71] Similarly, when Thomas Abraham and Willem Africa were found cutting wood on a local white farm, their fathers were notified of the trespass and asked to pay a fine. Although no specific infractions were cited, some of Salem's farmers decided in 1862 that Farmerfield's residents should be categorically disallowed from grazing any of their cattle on Salem lands.[72]

While missionaries expressed grave concerns about litigation Farmerfield's residents brought against each other, most of the cases were resolved with fines and admonitions. Few people received the ultimate threat of expulsion from the mission. In June 1851 when John Pato appeared before the magistrate on charges that he had beaten his wife Anna, and frequently mistreated her, he was fined and warned that he could lose his place at Farmerfield.[73] According to a complaint Anna lodged four months later, John responded to the sentence by refusing to continue the relationship. Despite the threat of expulsion the magistrate's and manager's typical response to women's complaints of being beaten seems to have been to issue warnings. In March 1856, for example, Sanna complained to the magistrate that her husband Jacob had beaten her. She had received some articles of clothing for her children and decided not to share them with her brother-in-law's children. Jacob asked her to divide the clothes, perhaps wanting to share the family's good fortune. Sanna refused and when he beat her, he got away with a mere warning.[74] In another example a woman named Sarah made repeated trips to the magistrate to complain that her husband Kunuck beat her. On January 12, 1860, Kunuck "engaged to treat her well in the future," only to appear again on May 24, 1860, on the same charge. Perhaps in frustration with the ineffective nature of the magistrate's warnings, Sarah threatened Kunuck that she planned to leave him and the children. She did not make good on the promise, however, and landed back in front of the magistrate in July 1860.[75]

Domestic squabbles at Farmerfield and disputes with local white and African neighbors revealed clandestine activities to missionaries that were expressly or implicitly forbidden at Farmerfield. Still, the manager of Farmerfield and the local missionary and magistrate found a way to deal with this behavior through a combination of admonition and restitution. Whatever concerns they aired about "incipient civilization," missionaries ultimately acknowledged in their annual reports that conflicts between residents were typical of any other small community. They shared this opinion with local whites who made no serious complaints about having an African settlement in their proximity. For the local whites, the ultimate assessment of Farmerfield rested on the residents' loyalty during outbreaks of war, and not on the occasional cases of trespassing or wage disputes. Given their familiarity with the surroundings and physical location in an otherwise white community, any subversion from the residents of Farmerfield would have lent the enemy a decisive advantage. This fact was not lost upon whites who counted on levies of men, arms, and ammunition from Farmerfield for assistance during the outbreaks of war from 1846–47 and 1850–53.[76]

Disputes between the residents, and with local Africans, yielded far more mundane and personal concerns about daily interaction than the missionaries' apprehension about loyalty during war. Since Malgas April left his wagon behind in Grahamstown, Josiah Badi may have been hesitant about renting it to him in the future. Likewise, Jeptha may have been reluctant about renting his oxen to Noah Mozambiker again without receiving payment first. The relationships between the residents revealed who could be trusted with rental property or who would pay for services rendered. It revealed the kinds of bonds that developed between tenants and the instances of breach of trust that weakened these relationships. Whatever the nature of the dispute, these individuals had to see each other regularly, whether it was at one of the Sunday services, prayer meetings, weekly class meetings, adult education classes, in the fields, by the river, on one of the roads to the mission, or at the market in Grahamstown. It was in the residents' interest to settle their issues amicably and they seem to have done so in most cases.

Adultery was among the most sensitive of cases that could potentially cause long-term rifts and complications at Farmerfield. In 1862, for example, Pompey Bem and his wife Clara had a falling out over his affair with another woman. Pompey appeared before the magistrate in March 1862 for beating his wife. He was most likely issued a warning since neither a fine nor a threat of expulsion is mentioned. Clara's parents seemed to have been very upset about Pompey's treatment of their daughter and visited the magistrate to see what could be done since Clara had taken ill. Five months later Clara returned to the magistrate to complain that Pompey continued the relationship with another woman, to the detriment of her family. He refused to provide her with food and she told that magistrate that she was at a loss for what to do about the children. Clara continued to seek the magistrate's advice and in September, Pompey agreed to end his relationship with the other woman and reconcile with his wife.[77]

In July 1852 Gudula lodged a complaint with the magistrate that a young man named Jonas was having an affair with his wife, Mechi. Between July and September 1852, Gudula, Mechi, Jonas, and their families made several trips to the magistrate to assess appropriate damages and determine if the marriage could be saved. Ultimately, Gudula and Mechi made a decision to stay together, Jonas was assessed a fine, and Mechi's family agreed to pay an ox. In September, Jonas and his family delivered fifteen shillings, five cows, and one calf to Gudula to settle damages for Mechi, whose family still had not paid the ox. By the end of November, the conflict deteriorated when the families discovered Mechi was pregnant with Jonas's child. The magistrate's final entry on this case stated that Mechi's father or guardian demanded that Jonas pay or he would "have nothing to do with him."[78]

Aside from the bridewealth exchange and the one instance of polygyny discussed at the beginning of this chapter, the sample of civil litigations at Farmerfield provided no evidence that the residents were living in a state of incipient civilization. That residents continued practices they could hide from the missionaries suggests that they did not share the missionaries' opinion that polygyny and bridewealth were "heathen" or uncivilized practices. They had to disavow polygyny because it was not negotiable, but they held on to other practices that could be hidden in private transactions. None other than the architect of Farmerfield, William Shaw, declared proudly in 1850 that Farmerfield was, "in the strictest sense, a truly Christian village," since "all the practices of 'heathenism' are entirely banished from the place."[79] Farmerfield tenants would likely have shared this opinion with him.

As more Africans became familiar with Christianity in the nineteenth century, the label *Christian* became as much an indicator of status and identity as it signified a particular belief. When missionaries merged the civilizing mission of transforming African economic pursuits, land use patterns, architecture, and dress with their evangelical goals, Christianity provided Africans with an arsenal of tools to understand the cultural arm of imperialism and to assimilate features that helped them navigate colonial society. For some Africans this meant using missionaries as liaisons with the colonial government; for others it entailed experimenting with new agricultural implements and crops. For still others it meant adopting a new cosmology and experiencing a novel form of spirituality. These characteristics of the pioneer missions demonstrated to the missionaries that rather than commit to monogamy and church membership, for example, Africans treated Christianity as a resource from which they could selectively appropriate elements they found useful and ignored more rigid specifications. Modeled on the strict idea of Christianity and civilization the missionaries propagated, Farmerfield departed from the experimental phase of Methodist evangelism. At Farmerfield, missionaries focused more on spiritual surveillance and discipline than they did at the early missions. They concentrated less on the rudiments of evangelization such as introducing the concept of the Christian God, or of heaven and hell, and directed their energies at cultivating a mature, vital African Christianity. Rather than allow multiple interpretations of "civilization," they categorically forbade beehive-shaped homes and practices like polygyny. The African Christian experience at Farmerfield highlights how this uncompromising model of mission worked in reality.

The African Christian experience at Farmerfield, to the extent that it is filtered through the lens of missionary accounts, showcases a mission that transcended the shortcomings of pioneer Methodist missions established beyond the borders of the Cape Colony between 1823 and 1830. The high proportion of Christian residents, the rigorous rules of residence, and the presence of a resident manager ensured a degree of conformity with missionary standards of Christianity that was lacking at the pioneer missions. Despite Farmerfield's ambitious model, missionaries complained that "nominal Christianity" and "incipient civilization" still characterized the mission, a charge that reveals far more about missionary perceptions than it does about how Africans experienced or perceived Christianity. Even if the path to the mission began with more material interests in securing access to arable and grazing land, the infusion of religion into daily ritual ensured that residents had an intense exposure to Christianity. If "'heathen' surroundings" engendered "'heathen' habits," and peer pressure in chiefdoms encouraged conformity with African cultural practices, as missionaries argued, then it can also be argued that the mission structure of catechumen classes, weekly class meetings, and prayer and revival meetings promoted a Christian lifestyle at Farmerfield. Peer and missionary pressure and material interests certainly shaped Christian allegiance at Farmerfield, yet it was not an indication of "nominal Christianity" as missionaries were quick to claim. As agents of their own spiritual experiences, Africans ultimately made the choice to convert. It would take a great act of dissimulation to feign sincerity in catechumen classes, during baptism, during class meetings, and in one's daily life as a Christian.

When residents like the Tswana patriarch made the decision to convert and live monogamously under duress, it still represented a choice to convert and live as a Christian—a difficult choice, but a choice nonetheless. Throughout southeastern Africa, individuals faced with similar dilemmas as the Tswana patriarch remained in their polygynous unions. Moreover, by the time Farmerfield was established in the late 1830s, missionaries still complained about their difficulties in getting Africans to accept the total package of Christianity and civilization, an instructive example of how African agency can be inferred from their behavior, in this case a rejection of rigid mission Christianity. At the time when individuals opted to move to Farmerfield therefore, many of their compatriots still shunned missionaries and mission stations, with their strict cultural codes. Farmerfield residents chose to live at the mission with the knowledge of what a Christian lifestyle entailed. Without any available testimony from the converts, only their behavior reveals the agency in their Christian conversion.

Since Farmerfield's residents made the necessary cultural compromises to become a Christian, I contend that their supposed lapses represent instances of disagreement with the missionaries' ideas about Christian and unchristian behavior rather than evidence of insincerity. African Christians who accepted or paid bridewealth, for example, probably never agreed with the missionaries that this practice was immoral and unchristian, just as they continued to view circumcision as the sine qua non of manhood no matter what kind of fines or restrictions missionaries imposed on them. Three decades after William Shaw declared Farmerfield "a truly Christian village," the mission came under review from the Methodist Church. As tenants asserted their cultural, spiritual, and personal autonomy, the church administration confronted wider issues about the place of African missions and domestic churches in their long-term evangelical goals in South Africa.

Placing Farmerfield in the larger context of the Methodist Church required a reexamination of evangelism in a colonial context. The relationship between Christianity and colonialism was never far from the residents' minds. As the locus of an economic, cultural, and spiritual inverse of African society, the mission station presaged many of the changes colonialism wrought on African society and culture. Christianity was presented as part of an economic, cultural, and political system, and Africans had responded to it with the rational expectation that this new religion would address their spiritual and material needs. They had little inkling that the quotidian struggles over the meaning of the cultural practices and the charges of "nominal" Christianity and incipient civilization would lead to a scathing, dangerous review. For the leaders of the Methodist Church, however, all of the moral, cultural, and racial questions remained thorny bureaucratic ones. The next chapter turns to the review of 1884 as part of the larger conversation Methodists wanted to have about Christian evangelization and African missions in nineteenth-century South Africa.

Figure 2.1 Portrait, Reverend William Shaw (1798–1872), Methodist pioneer and founder of the Farmerfield Mission. Courtesy of National Library of South Africa.

Figure 2.2 Portrait, Reverend William Shrewsbury (1785–1866). Courtesy of National Library of South Africa.

Figure 2.3 Two views of the pioneer Wesleyan Methodist Mission, Wesleyville, first built in 1823, destroyed during the 1834–35 War of Dispossession, 1832 and 1842. Note the juxtaposition of traditional circular Xhosa homes with the square dwellings. Courtesy of National Library of South Africa.

Figure 2.4 Reverend William J. Shrewsbury and Hintsa, 1828. Courtesy of National Library of South Africa.

Figure 2.5 Wesleyan Methodist Mission, Butterworth, 1842. Courtesy of National Library of South Africa.

Figure 2.6 The Christian Chief Kama. Reprinted from W. C. Holden, *A Brief History of Methodism*, 1877.

Figure 4.1 The only known sketch of Farmerfield, by Rev. Thornley Smith 1847, published along with a laudatory description of the mission station in *Papers Relative to Wesleyan Missions and to the State of Heathen Countries* 110 (5), New Series, December 1847. Courtesy of National Library of South Africa.

Figure 4.2 Front view of the Farmerfield Church, the only remaining edifice from the nineteenth century, 1998. Photo by Fiona Vernal.

Figure 5.1 Johannes Mahonga, "Kaffir" Minister, with shields and spears as traditional relics juxtaposed to the Bible and an assembled congregation in the background; a triumphal portrait of Christianity over "heathenism" as represented in conventional nineteenth-century evangelical literature. Reprinted from W. C. Holden, *A Brief History of Methodism*, 1877.

Figure 8.1 Welsch and Miriam Budaza, 1998. Photo by Fiona Vernal.

Figure 8.2 Mimosa Park Residents, 1999. Pictured *left to right* are Anderson Budaza, Ivan Budaza, Sylvia Zweni, Robert Mquqo, Ernest Ngqondi, 1999. Photo by Fiona Vernal.

Figure 8.3 Nofelity Gaba, 1999. Photo by Fiona Vernal.

Figure 8.4 Mary Jane Maxegwana, 1998. Photo by Fiona Vernal.

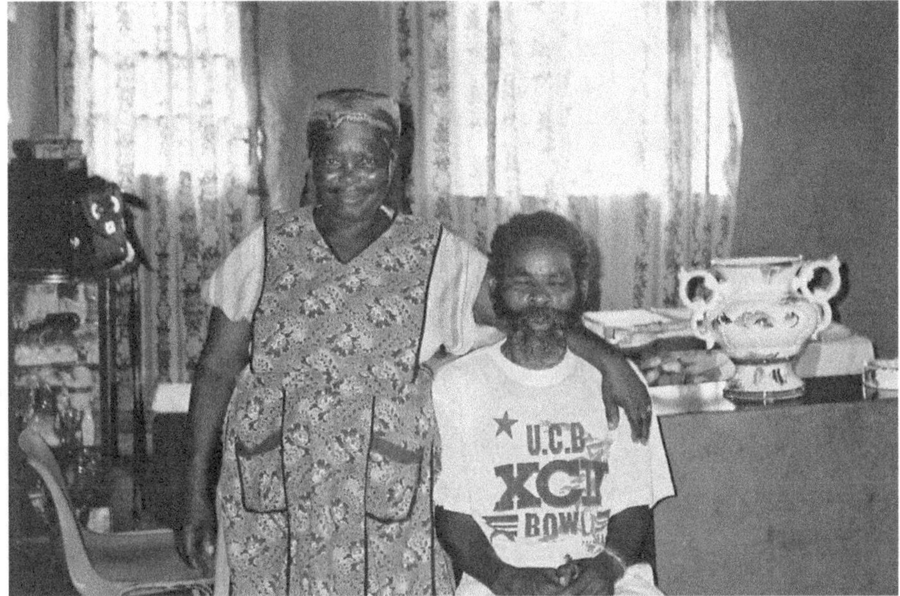

Figure 8.5 Daniel and Florence Matini in their home in Mimosa Park, 1998. Photo by Fiona Vernal.

Figure 8.6 Mongameli Maxegwana, 1998. Photo by Fiona Vernal.

Figure 8.7 Elsie Mzizi, 1998. Photo by Fiona Vernal.

Figure 8.8 Mavis Rasana, 1998. Photo by Fiona Vernal.

Figure 9.1 Daniel and Florence Matini outside their new home at Farmerfield, 2007. Photo by Fiona Vernal.

‖ 6 ‖

The Review of 1884

Farmerfield at a Crossroads

The present enormous expenditure of money, talent, and zeal, wasted on mission stations in Kafirland, I pronounce to be a *perfect failure*. A *savage* is not to be made a Christian of, and civilization . . . must make great advances among them before they can ever understand or appreciate the doctrines of Christianity . . . it is a hopeless case, and a thankless office to endeavor to instill genuine Christianity into the mind of a thorough savage, such as the Kafir.

(John Mitford Bowker, Colonial Diplomatic Agent, 1842).[1]

In 1842 John Mitford Bowker, a former diplomatic agent of the colonial government and descendant of the 1820 settlers, pronounced Christian missionary work a colossal failure and a misguided use of financial resources. Although extreme, Bowker's opinion reflected many of the settlers' perspective and by the mid to late nineteenth century, even missionaries began to express their disappointment about the progress of Christian evangelism. The extreme distrust of missionaries that had punctuated the work of individuals like Johannes Van der Kemp, James Read, and John Philip, as well as the LMS legacy of political advocacy for Africans, still continued to sully the missionary reputation during the 1880s. For those missionary societies that tried to distance themselves from the LMS legacy (the Wesleyans, for example) or entered the missionary field long after the controversy of the early nineteenth century (the Anglicans, for example), the figure of the "political missionary" continued to inform general opinions about Christian evangelism. Long after the controversies of the 1820s and 1830s, missionaries still found themselves on the defensive. Yet by the 1880s, missionary defensiveness had given way to pessimism and disillusionment. The review of Farmerfield in 1884 captures this mood succinctly. The Methodists had founded Farmerfield specifically to address the perceived problems of "nominal" Christianity and "incipient civilization" rampant at their

164

pioneer missions, but considered Farmerfield a failure by the 1880s. The Methodists would no longer showcase Farmerfield as the best of Christian evangelism; instead, they considered the fastest and most diplomatic way to terminate the mission.

This chapter provides an overview of the context, recommendations, and outcome of the 1884 administrative review. While the review hinged on the perceived failure of Farmerfield in the spiritual and economic realms, I argue that this particular moment in Farmerfield's history was symptomatic of the larger missionary enterprise. The first part of the chapter examines the review of 1884 in terms of the prevalent evangelical disappointments of the last half of the nineteenth century and the creation of an independent Conference of the South African Methodist Church in 1883. In this section I assert that the problem of "nominalism" and syncretism the committee denounced at Farmerfield existed at the beginning of pioneer Methodist work and stemmed from the outcome of the missionary's rigid view of Christianity and peremptory treatment of certain African cultural practices as obstacles to evangelization.

The second section of the chapter explores the committee's report and the resolution of the Conference. The committee advised the sale of Farmerfield based on their perception that Africans failed to take advantage of the prime arable and grazing land available to them. Such a recommendation would inevitably transfer Farmerfield to white ownership and leave hundreds of African families landless since few could raise the large sums of money necessary to purchase a 6,000-acre farm. I argue that this recommendation drew on the pervasive belief that Africans were indolent and wasteful instead of addressing the actual socioeconomic disadvantages and hardships that Africans faced in the Eastern Cape. Moreover I show that any independence Africans exhibited in the use and allocation of land was treated as a contravention of white authority over Farmerfield. The final section assesses how the recommendations of the committee as well as the decision of the Conference shaped the Farmerfield community after 1884 and concludes that the remaining tenants emerged from the review as a chastened group who knew fully well that their livelihood depended on the discretion of the Methodist Church of South Africa. The review set the stage for a heightened surveillance of the tenants' Christian lifestyle and land use between 1884 and 1916, when Farmerfield faced another administrative inquiry.

The Methodist Conference of 1883: The Precursor to the Review

In 1883 South Africa officially separated itself from the parent organization of the Methodist Church in England and got its own Conference, a local self-governing body.[2] An independent Methodist Conference in South Africa was on the horizon for some time before the 1880s, so the break with the parent organization was an anticipated and welcomed denouement. In fact, William Shaw, the former general superintendent of Wesleyan Missions in South Africa who had established Farmerfield, had suggested independence for the Methodist Church in South Africa as early as the 1860s.[3] It was conventional for the WMMS to grant independence to colonial circuits as they matured—as their congregations, means of financial support, and local ministries grew. When the independent Conference was finally granted to South Africa, officials of the Methodist Church resolved that it was a step that would "draw more closely together and to consolidate the forces of Methodism . . . by giving more voice in the management of our affairs to influential resident lay men, as well as to ministers."[4] From the South African perspective, then, the need to exercise more autonomy in their fiscal and administrative affairs and to execute decisions without deferring to the parent organization in England made the official 1883 Conference a historic declaration.

The ratification of South Africa's local Conference was preceded by an inquiry into the state of Wesleyan affairs in South Africa. In 1880 the mission committee in England sent the Reverend John Kilner on a year-long investigation into the claim for a separate Conference.[5] Kilner's extensive tour bolstered the local argument that decisions affecting missionary work needed to be made with an understanding of the idiosyncrasies and complexities of South Africa. The parent society was often seen as too paternalistic and high-handed in their interaction with local missionaries and it was inevitable that rifts and misunderstandings would develop. The same situation manifested itself in religious as well as more secular affairs at the Cape. Local government officials at the Cape were often at odds with their imperial counterparts in England, whom they did not believe understood the situation on the ground. It was precisely over matters of financial expenditure, deploying manpower, and mediating relations between Europeans and Africans that both the missionary society and the colonial office in England negotiated and disagreed with their local representatives and counterparts.

From the standpoint of the larger entity in England, the pioneering phase of Methodism in southeastern Africa had taken on its own momentum. By the 1880s the time was opportune for the parent organization to direct its attention away from South Africa, where they had made great strides for Christianity in the preceding sixty years. South Africa's independent Conference afforded the WMMS the opportunity to redirect their manpower and money to other areas seen as a tabula rasa for the next wave of evangelical work, namely Asia and Central and East Africa.

Although many local missionaries believed that one year was insufficient time to survey the situation on the ground, John Kilner's visit facilitated the approval of the South African Conference in London. A constitution drafted in 1880 carefully outlined the extent to which the Methodist Church in South Africa could still call up upon the British Conference for financial grants and for a supply of ministers. The British conference adopted the constitution in 1882 and the first Conference of the Methodist Church of South Africa was held in 1883.[6]

With the logistics of establishing a Conference out of the way, the Methodist Church of South Africa undertook its own investigation into local affairs. It was not unusual that a detailed look into their own missions and churches would follow on the heels of being granted administrative and financial control. Their survey consisted of multiple tasks: assessing the extent and security of church property; reviewing the progress of evangelical work within South Africa; determining where further educational institutions needed to be established; and ascertaining the status of specific mission stations. The Farmerfield mission station came under scrutiny within this context.

The 1884 review, which came one year after South Africa created its own Conference, was an unparalleled administrative examination that threatened to destroy the Farmerfield mission station.[7] Although the 1883 Conference resolved to sell the Farmerfield mission, they wanted to conduct an investigation before they made any final decisions.[8] The investigative committee consisted of various church officials acting in the capacity of administrators and managers of the estate. After considering the original purpose of the mission settlement, the committee concluded that the people of Farmerfield had diverged considerably from William Shaw's model of a prosperous, Christian, peasant community. The committee presented a report to the Conference that recommended the sale and dissolution of the mission community for the first time since its inception in 1838. The future of Farmerfield lay with the Conference. If they followed the committee's recommendations, Farmerfield would be discontinued with little input from the actual residents.

Nineteenth-Century Evangelical Dilemmas and Farmerfield's Fate

By the time of the review in 1884, Farmerfield's residents had faced forty-six years of intermittent droughts, cattle epidemics, war raids, and locust infestations. The tenants' response to these challenges had been varied. Some people endured these problems and remained at the mission. Others left the settlement altogether in search of better opportunities elsewhere at other mission settlements or in town. Many of the people who remained at Farmerfield were teetering on the brink of certain economic disaster by 1884. Far from the prosperous peasants who had brought their surplus agricultural goods to the market in Grahamstown in the early years of the settlement, the tenants at the mission farm, by the 1880s, were now struggling to maintain basic self-sufficiency and to pay rents, taxes, ticket money, school fees, and church offerings. Farmerfield had a boom and bust cycle that challenged even the most industrious person. In some ways this was typical of Farmerfield, not because of the residents' shortcomings but because the climate and topography of the Albany district, as well its location on the edge of a disputed frontier, made it extremely vulnerable. Chapter 4 demonstrated that it was not for lack of trying that Farmerfield's residents faced economic impoverishment. Drought, cattle epidemics, and locust infestations followed the losses sustained during the wars of 1846–47 and 1850–53. This unfortunate succession of disasters undercut economic subsistence at Farmerfield. Long-term residents at Farmerfield got accustomed to this cycle and tried to minimize their risk by supplementing their agricultural endeavors with working in the local area and sometimes by temporary migration to town.

At other mission stations in South Africa and among Africans in general, the late nineteenth century also presented a picture of economic hardship coupled with discriminatory legislation that made it difficult for Africans to own land or compete with their white counterparts. Historian Norman Etherington has argued that in Natal, for example, the first generation of African converts had better opportunities for benefiting from their position as Christians than did their progeny. Even if they had gained the education and acquired the skills necessary to compete with whites, African Christians faced a barrage of colonial legislation that made them second-class citizens.[9] At the Edendale mission in Natal even those who held title deeds to the mission found that they had to struggle for acceptance in colonial society; property ownership was an insufficient guarantor of prosperity when their livelihoods were so closely integrated with the wider colonial society. Blue Book reports leading up to the review of 1884 detailed the economic depression and scarcity of food that Africans throughout the Albany district faced.[10] Legislative and economic pressures made significant inroads on whatever degree of peasant prosperity existed throughout South Africa in the latter part of the nineteenth century and especially in the Eastern Cape.[11] Farmerfield's early prosperity in the 1840s and 1850s and its recovery from two destructive wars had gradually given way to more modest gains in the 1860s. An insidious cycle of poverty, closely linked to frequent bouts of violence and intermittent wars, eroded the quality and security of Africans throughout the Eastern Cape by the 1870s and 1880s.

The gradual impoverishment of Farmerfield's residents provided the church with a powerful leverage against the tenants because tenure was based on paying rent. Church administrators reminded the tenants of their discretionary powers to evict anyone who contravened the rules, yet seldom acted on their threats. Long-term residents, for example, were often granted grace periods to pay arrears; people were given ample warning prior to any summary decisions about eviction being made. The settlement faced a more severe threat of dissolution from poverty rather than any deliberate action of the Methodist Church. Only with the review and the potential closing of the estate did the tenants realize for the first time that an executive decision of the Conference could terminate the mission farm. The threat was very real because the Conference's proposed sale of the estate was exactly what had prompted them to put an investigative committee together.[12] The nature of tenancy thus provided one of the major areas of the committee's investigation and developed into the most contentious issue for the tenants.

While the committee's report mentions the existence of "industrious tenants," the overall assessment of people's land utilization at Farmerfield was negative. According to the committee's report, the questionable character of some of the inhabitants and the lack of active occupation of the land contributed to the economic malaise of the settlement. At Farmerfield, the committee asserted, "Unworthy persons were introduced [and] transfers in [land] were effected with the connivance of the headmen. Rents were allowed to deaccumulate [*sic*] to considerable amounts and the defaulting holder decamped."[13] The committee dated these crucial developments to the departure of Daniel Roberts, the resident supervisor in 1848, and the transfer of the Watson Institute from Farmerfield to other sites. Richard Walker succeeded Roberts in managing the estate, but white supervision of Farmerfield ceased after Walker's death in 1867.[14]

The original design of the mission made room for local residents to assume the positions of headman and councilors in order to facilitate the management of the estate. Whereas at stations like Edendale in Natal the headmanship was more entrenched, at Farmerfield it served as an auxiliary to the functions of the resident manager and the minister stationed in the circuit.[15] The missionary lived a few miles from Farmerfield, whereas at the Methodist chain of stations, he lived on the mission. Logic would hold that a residential missionary wielded more power in the day-to-day affairs of the people than someone who only made intermittent visits during the week and preached mainly on Sundays. As the local missionary John Smith noted of Farmerfield after Walker's death, "It is impossible for the minister at Salem to give all the attention which such an important station demands." Smith's warning that Farmerfield should not be left without residential European supervision generated no proactive response from Methodist authorities.[16] For the Methodists, however, even the residential plan was undercut by the minister's frequent changing of stations. At Farmerfield the long stretches of time without a manager gave de facto power to the auxiliary system of headman and councilors. With no resident manager or any other European personnel supervising the day-to-day affairs of Farmerfield after Walker's death, long-term residents with the most influence acquired more authority at the mission. When land allotments became vacant, the remaining tenants used the land without notifying the resident missionary. Only after tenants were in arrears for several months could the resident missionary truly determine who had left the mission permanently and who had only gone to town to work for temporary stints. Although the Church held final authority over the disposal of land, it was easy for tenants to bend the formal rules. The committee declared, "Men of influence monopolized vacant land for which they paid no rent," and complained that "idleness and criminality more or less prevailed" at Farmerfield.[17]

With Daniel Roberts's departure and Richard Walker's death, older and more prosperous men certainly used their positions as headmen and councilors to take advantage of the power and surveillance vacuum at the mission. The lack of "European supervision" at Farmerfield did not necessarily spawn an automatic increase in "criminality," as the committee asserted. The annual reports of Farmerfield between the 1860s and the 1880s discuss spiritual apathy and economic hardships with little mention of criminal behavior. The available magistrate records of the same time period mostly chronicle complaints about drunkenness, none of which occurred on the Farmerfield premises. In fact, most of the magistrate's cases involving the tenants at Farmerfield had nothing to do with criminal behavior; rather, tenants violated rules for where their cattle could graze or for leading a wagon without the proper supervision of the oxen.[18] Even the civil disputes at Farmerfield revealed few instances of criminal behavior like theft or murder. When applying to the secretary of native affairs for Farmerfield to be exempt from taxation under the provisions of the Native Locations Act, the Methodist missionary emphasized, "The conducts of the residents have been uniformly good and I believe it will be found that the cases in which the people have had to appear in the magistrate's court are very rare indeed."[19]

Along with establishing long-term residency and assuming lay positions in the church, it was in mediating access to land that many of the men at Farmerfield came to occupy powerful positions at the mission. When vacant land became available at Farmerfield, established residents preferred that their adult children rather than new residents gain control of those plots of land. In this way the older men asserted control over the disposal of other land on the estate. They delimited their sons' access to land and took on clients who could farm for, or sharecrop, with them. Residents at Farmerfield entered into various labor and sharecropping arrangements with people on the mission and in the local area. The very lack of supervision that the committee complained about is what reveals how the people of Farmerfield took advantage of weaknesses in Methodist administration and personnel shortages to exercise more agency and control over their day-to-day affairs. These activities definitely fell outside the purview of the established rules, yet hardly warranted the charge of "criminality" leveled at the tenants.

The disapproving tone of the committee's report continued with complaints about how the tenants misused, or did not use, their land allotments. In the committee's view, access to mission lands remained a privilege, not a right, and the residents of Farmerfield flouted the rules without censure. "Not only is there little industry in the settlement on the part of many of the tenants," the report stated, "but some of the tenants make a simple convenience of their holdings."[20] The committee made no attempts to explore why the tenants had long needed and engaged in a variety of strategies besides agriculture to maintain their livelihoods. After forty years of farming and grazing taking place on its same lands, it is likely that the soils of Farmerfield were less fertile, if not exhausted. Moreover, protracted periods of drought made it at times impossible for tenants to plow the land and prepare for the planting season.

Working elsewhere while maintaining a residence at a mission station was a strategy that successive tenants at Farmerfield had used from the 1830s to maximize their access to cash while holding on to a piece of land. Instead of acknowledging this as part of a deliberate strategy to minimize risk, the report decried the tenants' attempts to supplement their agricultural base with wage labor in the towns:

> They leave their families at Farmerfield and proceed to Port Elizabeth, Grahamstown and other places where they earn considerable sums of money. This absenteeism and idleness have smitten the settlement with poverty and demoralization. . . . Enterprising and industrious natives are persecuted and discouraged by their lazy neighbors.[21]

The committee's report glossed over the cause and effects of the poverty and demoralization evident at Farmerfield, misrepresented the nature of Farmerfield's economic decline, and exaggerated the indiscipline at the mission. Indeed the annual reports documented absenteeism and depressed economic conditions, yet indicate in a much more convincing manner that people were forced by dire circumstances to leave the mission to find food and employment. If they could not feed themselves or earn a living, tenants could not remain at the mission for long before they were forced to accept any employment. The committee criticized how much Farmerfield had veered from the idealized peasant hamlet of carefully screened residents, and just how much power had devolved from the Methodist Church to the tenants. At the time of the review in the 1880s, the Methodist Church would no longer cite Farmerfield as an example of the success of Christianity and peasant industry in southeastern Africa.

The gripe about land tenure and land use at Farmerfield was not limited to this particular mission station. The strategy of using the mission station as a base from which one could periodically enter the wage economy was one that was common during the pioneering days of the late eighteenth and early nineteenth centuries. Throughout the entire history of the missionary enterprise in the Cape Colony, land access remained one of the major attractions of the mission station. Access to land enabled Africans of all backgrounds to exert more control over their economic livelihoods and mobility and it was this knowledge that caused conflict between some white settlers and missionaries. As Chapter 1 has shown, access to these mission lands had allowed some Khoekhoe, who felt the brunt of land alienation before other Africans in the interior, to avoid certain peonage on European farms and to prevent their women and children from being drawn into dependent relations with the farmers. Because they were the first to be on the receiving end of the process of land dispossession and colonial subjugation that would be repeated at later stages with other Africans, the Khoekhoe were among the earliest people to have sought the missions for access to land and for refuge. Other Africans followed suit as they too were dispossessed of their land and forced onto the labor market.

For the missionaries, the power to allocate land was one of the grounds on which they were able to compete with African chiefs, even when those same chiefs had initially given the missions permission to settle.[22] In the Albany district, physically removed from chiefly politics, the restrictions on African land access also allowed missionaries to use land access as leverage. In fact, as Chapter 3 has shown, African land access in Albany was limited since few other options existed aside from living in overcrowded locations where subsistence agriculture was virtually impossible. Issues of land allocation, use, and tenure, therefore, shaped the balance of power among missionaries, their potential African converts, white settlers, and the colonial government. Many of the ideas about mission stations as Christian oases and as islands of security from colonial domination and peonage were reinforced during the crucial pioneering period from the 1790s up to the 1840s, when many missionaries, especially those of the LMS, championed the rights of the "Colored" and African populations at the Cape. The missionaries' perceptions about land as a panacea to many of the problems of the African and "Colored" population also took shape during this same period, a time of heightened missionary activity and of unprecedented missionary influence on Cape politics.

From the 1820s through to the 1840s missionaries were able to exert their influence over politics at the Cape and to sway public opinion in a way they had not been able to do before or since.[23] Most missionaries believed that if Africans had land access, along with religious instruction, then industry and civilization would eventually follow. This is the basic principle that lay behind the creation of the Methodist chain of missions and Farmerfield. The tide of land alienation that had accompanied colonial domination in the eighteenth and nineteenth centuries threatened the models of industry and male agricultural production missionaries had envisioned as a crucial part of their agendas. Hence, many missionaries came to view land access, with some advocacy of freehold tenure, as a key part of the solution for the various "Colored" and African populations at the Cape. As Jane Sales so aptly put it, the LMS missionaries in particular "believed firmly, along with most people of the time, that freehold ownership of property was the greatest blessing they could bestow upon the inhabitants of the missionary institutions."[24]

As various missionary societies grew disillusioned and waxed pessimistic about the lofty humanitarian ideals that had buoyed them in the 1820s and the 1830s, the nature of land access at mission settlements reentered public discourse in a controversial way. Even as late entrants to the mission field were embarking on their romantic endeavors, the fundamental question was whether LMS missions had outgrown their original purposes. The tenor of these debates is best represented in an 1872 Select Committee that investigated and reported on LMS missions.[25] At one end of the continuum was a sense that the gains in civil rights and legal equality had now made these earlier missions to the Khoekhoe and former slaves outmoded; another measured axis of the argument was whether the type of tenancy arrangements hampered economic productivity with a potential solution being the devolution to freehold tenure for the "industrious." Finally, more extreme strands of the debates saw the LMS missions as stagnant and retrogressive and therefore outmoded.[26]

While the Methodist Church did not grant freehold tenure to Farmerfield residents and did not undertake any attempts to do so, its mission residents could secure access to land by paying rent at available mission plots. Rent tenancy remained the best arrangement Africans could secure from Methodist missions, this being qualitatively superior to becoming a tenant on white farms. At the mission, land allotments were larger, sharecropping arrangements were not mandatory, and residents had more control over their labor, disposal of their crops, and their families. Many tenants at Farmerfield used these advantages, maximized their access to land, and maintained long-term residence at the mission rather than opting to live on white farms. In addition, expulsion from the mission farm was much less arbitrary than working on white farms. Moreover, mission residents were expected to send their children to school, while on a white farm there was no guarantee that there would be a school in proximity, or that the parents would be the ones to make the decision about their children going to school versus working.[27]

Despite its potential advantages over conventional labor tenancy on white farms, however, mission residency at Farmerfield meant adopting a particular Christian lifestyle. At some missions, the population was differentiated between church members and residents without any formal attachment to Christianity, whereas at Farmerfield missionaries strove to limit the number of "heathen" inhabitants.[28] What the missionaries envisaged for the Farmerfield settlement was the established, inflexible version of mission Christianity they had been unsuccessful in propagating at the pioneer missions. The review of 1884, therefore, is significant for what it reveals about this rigid formulation of Christianity at Farmerfield and for its outlook on general missionary work. It brings into focus some of the major problems that missionary societies at the Cape faced toward the last half of the nineteenth century as they evaluated the outcomes of decades of Christian evangelism.[29] What occasioned Farmerfield's review was particular to the mission farm and what the Methodists saw as its ongoing shortcomings by the 1870s. Yet the kinds of questions the review raised about African Christianity and missionary evangelism were typical of the reflective missionary mood in South Africa and throughout the world.

As historian Andrew Porter has underscored in his lucid evaluation of the British Protestant missionary enterprise, "Feelings of disaffection, disillusionment or merely disappointment with their record contributed substantially to the mid-century decline in support and enthusiasm for the well-established missionary societies."[30] Porter has attributed these declensions to a move away from the "humanitarian dimensions" that had often buttressed missionary work as well as a tendency for missionaries to misconstrue their "ability to exploit to their own advantage the political dimensions of their expansion with indigenous, colonial and imperial authorities."[31] In various outposts of the British Empire from the

Caribbean to South Africa, the weakening of humanitarian fervor in the mid to late nineteenth century brought missions to an important crossroads.[32] In assessing the outcome of humanitarianism, South African historian Tim Keegan has asserted that besides the maintenance of a sliver of nonracialism, "in the end, liberal humanitarianism had turned out to be a shallow, tawdry, deceptive thing."[33] These patterns need not be restricted to the nineteenth century, however; assessments of the shortcomings of the Reformation had led to a new sense of purpose in overseas missions and to the foundation of missionary societies.[34] Even before these developments in the 1790s, the initial efforts of the early Moravian evangelism on the Caribbean island of St. Thomas in the 1730s and 1740s presaged nineteenth-century trends. None other than the Moravians' most famous benefactor Nikolaus Ludwig von Zinzendorf reconsidered evangelical strategy by focusing on "first fruits," and on a more disciplined engagement with Christianity rather than the dividends of mass appeal and conversions. Although all missionaries wished for rigor and spiritual maturity, they also acknowledged that focusing on the small number of stalwarts was an impractical basis for overseas evangelical missions.[35]

Pioneer missionary enterprise throughout Africa, the Caribbean, and the Americas was fraught with doubt and challenges from the outset; yet the imperative call to go forth and preach the gospel to the "heathen" emboldened missionaries to look beyond their initial hardships. Despite the self-pity and self-congratulation evident in the missionaries' own accounts of their difficulties and in the early hagiographical account of their works, an element of romance, if not exoticism, remained.[36] At the Cape and elsewhere, missionaries took pride in the number of books and Bibles printed in the vernacular and in the number of Africans who attended church, registered for school, adopted European clothing and names, and built square houses. Each new mission and missionary society entering the South African field experienced the typical phases of enthusiasm and declension as their earlier counterparts had done. They marveled at the early exciting signs of progress, then worried about why the pace was slow. Any untimely African assertions of spiritual autonomy created anxiety and incorporation of indigenous knowledge systems beyond mere translation was anathema, if not heretical, while the fear of relapse and apostasy loomed constant dread.

Upon arriving in South Africa in the early 1880s, the Anglican missionary Alan Gibson surveyed his surroundings like William Shaw had almost a half century prior. Gibson's was a much more localized view, but an equally eager and romantic one. He mused, "A native deacon playing the harmonium, and conducting service; a congregation of natives, ourselves the only two white people: surely we realized then that we were in the midst of missionary work."[37] Besides the initial problems of vernacular fluency and unfamiliarity with the geography and culture of the places where they were stationed, missionaries grappled with ways of making Christian precepts compatible with existing African beliefs and practices. The missionaries had tried to win over chiefs and influential individuals in

African society to their cause, hoping that commoners would follow their leaders. As shown in Chapter 3, they had challenged any influential individuals, such as rainmakers and diviners, perceived as impediments to the dissemination of Christian beliefs. Another crucial strategy was using access to and distribution of land as tools to woo and reward converts. The missionaries had also attempted to educate the sons, and to a lesser extent the daughters, of chiefs so that common folk would follow suit. The Watson Institute at Farmerfield, and Governor Grey's establishment of Zonnebloem College in Cape Town all supported these attempts with piecemeal results.[38] As early missteps came to light, Farmerfield emerged as a model mission that would correct some of the problems found at pioneer missions.

Between the 1790s and the 1880s, after almost a century of evangelical work, missionary societies claimed success in the number of Africans who now knew of Christianity, attended church, and registered for school. Surveying Anglican missionary work, Alan Gibson noted:

> And so it comes to pass that Christian notions and Christian usages are spreading rapidly even among the "heathen." Men have learnt to work now as well as women; Sunday is often kept as a day of rest even by those outside; and the attribution of power to God by the "heathen" in their talk with us, and to a certain extent in their own thoughts, as when they come to pray for rain, is quite a matter of course.[39]

In 1861 the Methodist missionary William Boyce boasted "[N]o country is *numerically* better furnished with missionaries than Southern [*sic*] Africa."[40] Moreover, in the area that became the Eastern Cape, the Wesleyans had established more missions than any other religious body.[41] Missionaries celebrated the translation of the Bible into vernaculars like Sotho and Xhosa and the government grants they received for African education. The Methodist missionary Samuel Broadbent wrote of his work, "Then they had no book, no writing, nor any knowledge of letters. . . . Now they have books printed in their own language and country; they have schools and writing . . . and are able to instruct others in the same useful arts."[42] Missionaries celebrated new ideas of African manhood, womanhood, and childhood. Whiteside proudly asserted in his history of Methodism in South Africa, "The new man, who can understand the value of trade and the benefits of civilization, is a Christian product."[43] Children's "heathen" development would be arrested by education and boarding schools and, away from the influence of "heathen" communities, would provide a total immersion in a lifestyle befitting a Christian. As these important developments unfolded, Farmerfield's church membership grew and by the 1860s a new generation of African Christians was emerging. Missionaries anticipated that this new cohort of African Christians, born at the mission and raised as Christians, would experience less stigma and disorientation than their parents.[44] Moreover, this new generation would contribute to making Christianity more vital and more mature. Approximately eighty-six such children born and baptized at Farmerfield were reaffirmed as adult church members in 1866.[45]

Despite these important strides in making Christianity familiar, and even in getting some people to convert and creating educational institutions, missionaries remained dissatisfied with the pace of evangelical progress. Reverend Whiteside declared rather gloomily that as much as 60 percent of South Africans fell outside the influence of any church.[46] Speaking from the Methodist perspective reminiscent of William Shaw's early pronouncement of an open mission field, Whiteside stated, "This mass of human beings, degraded by centuries of superstition and war, debased by polygamy and witchcraft, furnishes an unlimited field for evangelistic efforts."[47] As missionaries reflected on and evaluated the progress of missionary work in the latter part of the nineteenth century, they questioned the model of the mission station as an effective evangelical tool.[48] Certainly, it was practical to separate Christians from the temptations of "heathen" society and to provide an alternative, safe residence for those who would be persecuted for their Christian beliefs. Yet the "vast sea of 'heathenism'" missionaries liked to talk about remained. They may have several hundred and even thousands of mission residents, but what about the exponentially larger community that hardly benefited from missionary itineration?[49] "We may not leave them alone," the Methodist Whiteside declared. "As a Christian people we cannot shake off the 'white man's burden' of responsibility."[50]

Missionary introspection entailed far more than the effectiveness of the mission station. Missionary appraisals of evangelical work underscored a discrepancy between the rapid growth in the number of churchgoers and converts on the one hand, and the spiritual apathy and impiety on the other. The annual report of the Wesleyan Missionary Society for 1882 summarized the situation as follows:

> The native churches and missions continue to claim our vigilant care; their numerical growth has been rapid, and out of proportion to their spiritual development. We watch, and we watch, with grave anxiety, the critical processes of transition from a state of pupilage to a state of greater responsibility.[51]

At Farmerfield, missionaries sought reassurance in the mission's historic status as an exclusive community of Christians whose children and grandchildren were reared in a Christian environment from the outset. Yet the committee declared as much dissatisfaction with the progress of Christianity at Farmerfield as they did with the farm's economic viability. Whatever shortcomings missionaries allowed or expected during the pioneering phase of Christian evangelism could no longer be justified or tolerated. If many of Farmerfield's tenants were reared from infancy as Christians and lived at a mission, yet failed to fulfill the missionaries' ideals, then what did this portend for evangelical work?[52]

Despite ample evidence to the contrary, the committee adopted the viewpoint that the Christianity Farmerfield's tenants practiced was, at best, "nominal." Other tenants were cast as simply disingenuous and interested only in gaining access to land without the requisite commitment to a Christian lifestyle. The common periods of declension and revivalism evident in patterns of religious adherence were judged at Farmerfield as the mission's failure to sustain an authentic Christianity. The committee's report echoed the deep skepticism about the sincerity of the tenants' adherence to a Christian lifestyle along with the negative, biased assessments of the problems of land tenure and perceived misuse of land at Farmerfield. The mission's purported failure to fulfill William Shaw's vision of an ideal Christian community was the problem of the missionary enterprise writ large.

Farmerfield's momentous review reflected two long-standing, unresolved questions that resurfaced for the Methodist and other missionary societies in South Africa. Missionaries of all denominations reexamined the relationship between Christian evangelism and the civilizing mission *and* asked what it meant for Africans to make Christianity their own. Missionaries reached no consensus on the ideal relationship between civilizing and Christianizing nor did they always agree on what constituted civilization.[53] As the Methodist missionary W. C. Holden waxed poetically, "Give us Christianity and the efforts of governments and colonists as handmaids and auxiliaries, and we shall thank you. The latter changes the dress, the former new-makes the man." Despite this grand pronouncement, Holden was emphatic that "the business of missionary was not to civilize," yet firmly believed that "all civilizing processes, to be successful must be based upon religious instruction and moral culture."[54] The LMS missionary Henry Calderwood advocated that besides education, Africans also needed "a thorough knowledge of the arts of civilized life. . . . Wants are to be created and the power of supplying these wants imparted[55][.]" Similarly, Holden asserted that missionaries had to "*create the tastes and desires for the conveniences of a civilized life*, to produce that change which shall lead him [the African] to understand and value our [European] improved modes of agriculture and living."[56]

The missionary Callaway, like his predecessors, believed that African women had a central role to play in the civilizing process, asserting "the regeneration of society is in the power of the women, and I believe this is very largely true not only of London, but of Kafir society[.]"[57] Henry Calderwood also imagined a central place for African women. "In the matter of Caffre Christianization and civilization, there is no question of greater importance than that of female influence," he declared. "Who is so likely as a pious, judicious, educated and good-tempered woman to create and foster these very amenities which are at once the fruit and the means of civilization? These must grow up in the family, and gentle female influence is, and ought to be, most potent there," he continued.[58] The Scottish missionary Robert Young also shared Calderwood's views. "Certainly the influence they carry with them, and which after years, *as wives and mothers*, they exercise, is of the most potent kind, far exceeding that of any other."[59]

Despite the varied opinions about the relationship between Christianizing and civilizing, most missionaries acknowledged that their vision of evangelical work could not proceed in a cultural vacuum. Christianity was anchored to particular European ideas of marriage, evil, respectability and work, manhood and womanhood, which contrasted sharply with the social and economic structure of African society. Only among Africans like the Khoekhoe and Mfengu, who were facing serious social dislocation and cultural disintegration, did Christianity make significant headway.[60] In other cases, pioneer missionaries had demonstrated amply that African resistance to and selective appropriation of Christianity were endemic to the evangelical movement in Africa from the outset and was likely to continue. Since they firmly believed that their version of Christianity could not thrive while Africans still believed in witchcraft, participated in inappropriate festivities during circumcision, consumed alcohol, and entered polygynous marital unions, missionaries promoted the adoption of some aspects of European civilization as an essential part of Christian proselytizing. Like Cape slaves had to be made "fit for freedom," and apprenticed before they got their full emancipation in 1838, so too potential converts had to be made fit—had to be civilized—so that Christianity could take root.[61]

Missionaries won some cultural battles with their converts, who came to share some of the missionaries' perceptions of certain customs. Charlotte Maxeke, while asserting that Africans had their own ideas of cleanliness, morality, and purity, also pinpointed bridewealth and polygyny as impediments to women's progress. "Owing, no doubt, to the practice of paying a fixed value for a wife, men considered women and children their inferiors, their property and children," she declared in an article entitled, "The Progress of Native Womanhood in South Africa." Maxeke emphasized, "Not being allowed equal opportunity with men, and being kept down," women's "progress was thus hindered."[62] William Shaw Kama, the son of Chief Kama who was celebrated by the Methodists as a chiefly convert, testified before a commission on native affairs that circumcision and girls' puberty rites (*intonjane*) were traditions that were of no use to him and other Christians. Although he was a Christian and a local evangelist, Kama kept a number of councilors who disagreed with him about polygyny, circumcision, and girls' puberty rights. One such councilor, McLean, in response to Kama's declaration that the nakedness and dancing of the girls during intonjane was "against the laws of decency," openly disagreed, asserting, "We have a right to do as we like with our own." Furthermore he added, "What the piano and violin are to the Englishman the intonjane dances are to us." Another councilor, Magama, when asked if he had anything to add declared, "We say in regard to the statement that Kafir girls are sold for cattle that there was never such a thing, and no one has any right to say that the cattle given at marriage is for the purchase of the girl."[63]

The nature of missionaries' victories at mission stations meant that polygyny was categorically banned on mission premises and that mission residents were usually clothed. As Whiteside noted in his history of the Methodist Church, polygyny was one of the few areas where most missionaries were dogmatic. Allowing chiefs to have multiple wives would have been one way to perhaps win over these influential personalities, yet it was more important to maintain the rule since, "by yielding, a deadly blow should be dealt at Christian purity."[64] At Farmerfield, white residential supervision between 1839 and 1867 ensured that these rules about clothing and marriage were rigidly enforced, one more successfully than the other. Clothing was a new cash outlay the missionaries encouraged while bridewealth exchange was an expense they believed dissipated productive resources.

Mission residents were far more immersed in the outward aspects of European civilization than the surrounding community. As Alan Gibson traveled among the Xhosa in the 1880s, for example, he noted that mission stations still stood as the singular signs of civilization. "Now attention is caught by a few sod enclosures, a few square built houses: natives pass us dressed and we are told that this is a mission station by which we are going," he observed. "Soon the marks of greater refinement and civilization are lost," he continued, "and we are back in the midst of heathenism again."[65] The arsenal of civilization included wearing certain types of clothing, marrying one woman, practicing agriculture with particular farming implements, and building square houses. For Gibson the difference between the mission and the surrounding community was demonstrated by a series of dichotomies: huts with "windows as well as doors," as opposed to "the hurdle which generally closes the aperture that the ordinary hut contains;" "crops of wheat and oats," instead of only "maize and millet;" "bedsteads, tables and seats, in place of mats and the logs which form the ordinary furniture of the Kaffirs home."[66] His colleague Callaway noted that once Africans chose to build their huts in a European fashion, there was no "crouching down to avoid the extremely low limit of the doorway, no straining of the eyes on account of the darkness and pungent smoke, no flutter of disturbed fowls [and], no general sense of dirt and red ochre."[67]

Africans selectively appropriated some aspects of this civilization package, often for reasons that had nothing to do with Christianity. Commenting on this trend, the missionary Callaway declared that the choice was not "between 'heathenism' and a Christian civilization. The greatest danger of all is in a civilized 'heathenism,' where the man remains a 'heathen' but adopts as much or as little of European custom as suits his fancy."[68] Donavan William noted in his examination of missionary endeavors in the Cape, for example, that the early integration of Khoekhoe into Cape colonial society meant that many adopted European clothing without it signifying an allegiance to Christianity. At the pioneer missions among the Xhosa, European clothing took on greater significance as a marker of association with Christianity and its civilizing mission.[69] As Alan Gibson noted in the 1880s when he began his missionary work, "the policy of the past has so identified the English dress with civilization and religion, that it would probably be almost impossible to make any alteration now."[70] Blankets and bodies bedaubed with red ochre remained a constant symbolic marker of "heathenism." Both the custom and the costume contrasted sharply with notions of Christian decorum and fashion. As J. Whiteside rather boasted in his chronicle of Methodism in South Africa, "Conversion created a desire for personal cleanliness, and the red clay . . . [was] cast aside for the products of the looms of Manchester and Whitney."[71] His statement is partly correct; not everyone who adopted such European clothing converted to Christianity. Writing in the first decade of the twentieth century, Maurice Evans, a local politician who served in the Natal legislature on the 1904–06 Native Affairs commission, noted, "Broadly speaking, in past times every native wearing clothes was regarded as a Christian, every unclothed native a heathen. This clear distinction does not now hold good."[72]

The way in which Africans observed the rules of Christian living also demonstrates that missionary victories were qualified. Observing certain rules for Christian living did not necessarily mean that Africans concurred with the missionary perception of traditional customs or costumes. It seems that some individuals continued those practices that could be hidden from immediate public view whereas actions like wearing European clothes or having one wife were difficult to hide. In the 1870s mission residents at Edendale found that one influential and revered headman had contravened the rules about polygyny and had in fact maintained two families.[73] Against their best efforts to outlaw or stigmatize circumcision, beer brewing, and witchcraft beliefs, however, missionaries had in some instances mixed success and in others total failure. At Farmerfield, parents sent their children off the mission to be circumcised or hid the practice on the mission. When discovered they simply paid the fine, suffered the temporary exclusion from church membership, and carried on when the punishment was over. Anglican missionaries observed similar actions at their missions. Even when forbidden, Alan Gibson asserted, circumcision "is practiced all the same in secret in defiance of parental and clerical authority."[74]

Some residents at Farmerfield tried to consume alcohol clandestinely; when caught they promised to abstain, yet there was no certain way to enforce this rule when alcohol could be consumed privately. Other residents consumed alcohol off the mission and ended up in the magistrates' courts for drunkenness. Farmerfield's investigative committee cited these cases as evidence of criminality. But they reflected far more about the missionaries' failure to fully convince even African Christians that temperance was about adhering to the Christian principles of decency and respectability. Denominational variation also fueled these inconsistent patterns in adhering to the missionaries' version of a proper Christian lifestyle. The Methodists, for example, were fastidious about beer brewing and consumption in some instances. The Anglicans, however, prohibited the sale of beer and its use at weddings and beer parties, but allowed women to brew beer for their husbands and for it to be consumed at home.[75]

Practicality and expense also featured prominently in how Africans adopted and maintained certain standards of "European" civilization and even affected which Christian denominations Africans supported.[76] In the 1830s the missionary James Backhouse observed at the Mount Coke mission that those individuals who had purchased clothes did not have the income to maintain this expenditure. When their clothes had worn out, they simply reverted to their previous mode of dressing, to the missionaries' chagrin.[77] With a bit of humor the LMS missionary Calderwood exclaimed that "considerable discouragement is . . . sometimes experienced in the very first step towards civilization," because men often tore the seat of their pants when they tried to sit on the floor in their new "European" attire. In keeping with the idea of creating wants and needs, Calderwood pointed out that once people adopted European attire they would want chests and stools in their homes.[78] Since there were no stools or chairs, however, Africans generally sat on the floor, which made it easy for their clothes to get dirty.

At Farmerfield, house upkeep was expensive. While the residents of Farmerfield observed the rules that only square homes should be constructed on the mission, for example, few were able to afford materials like bricks and stones, which were necessary to make permanent, durable homes. Missionaries proudly hailed the whitewashed, square homes that dotted Farmerfield's landscape as signs of civilization, yet those structures were made of mud and required constant reapplication of mud, cow dung, and lime to keep them from appearing shabby. After a three-year drought between 1876 and 1879, for instance, many of Farmerfield's able-bodied residents sought temporary employment off the mission, leaving their homes, "mean and dilapidated."[79] When he received several young male students at an Anglican mission school, Alan Gibson faced an important decision about the relationship between civilization and Christianity. Showing that indeed no consensus existed on this important question, Gibson decided "as far as possible to keep away civilization, not only for their sake, but also because of expenses." Gibson wanted basic clothing for the boys, but noted that civilization in this case needed to be about the bare essentials. "I do not see that the man is better because he sleeps in a bed, eats meat every day and drinks coffee, and I would willingly add, wear European clothing, though on the last named point we had to make a virtue of necessity."[80] While Gibson was away on a visit to England, one of the young boys wrote a letter that lent a bit of humor to his need for new clothes. The young boy informed Gibson, "I have no trousers, and I have no coat. My trousers are worn out. Still I am not asking, just reporting."[81]

Even when Africans did adopt "European dress," missionaries were not entirely pleased with the outcome. It seems in the missionaries' estimation that many people donned European garb with little thought about fashion. Robert Young declared of one congregation that their European clothing made them appear "grotesque."[82] Alan Gibson thought the European clothes the young students at his mission wore were so unbecoming and unnecessarily cumbersome that he too questioned the automatic link between Christianizing and civilizing.[83] With more amusement than judgment, Holden likened one of his early congregations in Natal to "a small regiment of soldiers" when they came to Church wearing damaged soldier jackets that had been sold for a shilling.[84] Maurice Evans, writing at a later period about Zulus in the first decade of the twentieth century, noted that, "Clothed at best in cheap, ill-fitting ready-made clothes, and often in odds and ends cast off by the white man, their really fine figures are masked and they look like slouching bundles of rags."[85] Concerns about "uppity" Africans, and perhaps too wholeheartedly an attempt to emulate "European" ways, arose more often in settler than in missionary circles. Presenting evidence before a commission on native affairs, W. C. Jeffrey told the commissioners that Mfengus at the Kamastone location adopted European marriage and dress to "a ruinous extent," so much so that they also wanted to ride a buggy to church.[86]

Perhaps one of the most compelling factors that compromised the Christianizing and civilizing enterprise was the African experience of colonialism. Already skeptical of the missionaries' collusion with the colonial governments in the early decades of the nineteenth century, Africans grew increasingly suspicious as the British conquered and incorporated the remaining independent chiefdoms by the late nineteenth century. The African experience of colonialism was marred by duplicity, exemplary violence, political subjugation, economic domination, cultural imperialism, and racism. Missionaries were well aware of their role as mediators, if not harbingers and implicit supporters of these destructive developments. Even when Africans distinguished between individual missionaries versus their white colonial counterparts, the deep suspicion of Christian evangelism remained. Moreover, missionaries fostered aspirations in Africans for inclusion in colonial society that fell on mostly deaf ears and preached doctrines of equality that were violated in innumerable ways. The missionary Godfrey Callaway expressed during the early years of his missionary work that he feared some Africans had seen that "European clothing does not often go hand in hand with loyalty, manliness and courage . . . [and] prayers and hymns are not always associated with the Christian virtues."[87]

In the late nineteenth century Africans tried to break free of the strictures of mission Christianity through independent Christian movements. Missionaries had to incorporate new terminology besides "Christian" and "heathen" to categorize the two important developments that changed the face of Christian evangelism in the Cape Colony as well as in many other parts of Africa. In the last few decades of the nineteenth century Africans initiated a flowering of independence movement within the established mission churches that broke away from European mission control. The Methodist Church was among the earliest denominations affected by the first wave of this schism. African Christians asserted their autonomy by creating their own churches. By the early decades of the twentieth century a different cohort of Africans in South Africa, who usually did not have any previous association with Christianity, took the message of a short-lived yet influential entourage of American missionaries and transformed it into an evangelical movement that combined African traditional religious beliefs with Christianity. Writing of these late nineteenth- and early twentieth-century developments, the theologian Bengt Sundkler provided a useful schema for organizing African relationships to Christianity, in light of these two new challenges to the monopoly that established mission churches tried to exert over Christian evangelization and the Christian message.

To the existing continuum of Christian and "heathen," or believer and nonbeliever, Sundkler added two groups: the "Ethiopians" who broke with the mission churches;[88] and the "Zionists," named eponymously for the abortive American mission from Zion City, Illinois, who selectively appropriated aspects of the Christian message.[89] To Sundkler's four-tiered spectrum, is a fifth generic category of "adherents" that describes yet another nuance in African associations to Christianity. Individuals described as "adherents" did not strictly uphold African tradition or missionary Christianity, nor advocate any particular allegiance to more selective Christian traditions like Ethiopianism or Zionism.[90] Instead of founding their own churches or melding African and Christian religious beliefs in any formal, institutional declaration, these adherents, historian Mahoney asserts, "participated in mission church activities without submitting to missionary authority or the missionaries' narrow conception of proper Christianity."[91] These categories provide a continuum for understanding the range of African associations with Christianity after more than a century of missionary work.

Sundkler taxonomies are useful for exploring African relationships with Christianity in the late nineteenth and twentieth centuries, when Farmerfield faced its first serious threat of dissolution. By then Methodist concerns about "nominal" Christianity and declension in piety at Farmerfield echoed sentiments similar in other missionary circles in the Cape Colony as European missionaries lost control over the dissemination and interpretation of Christianity. The formal schismatic movements in mission Christianity engendered the sort of syncretism missionaries feared. Africans were making Christianity their own; they were taking ownership in a way that often made white missionaries superfluous and that reinforced or embraced some cultural practices missionaries wanted to suppress.

Africans' creation of their own churches and selective appropriation from the package of Christianity and civilization resulted in a variety of Christian traditions aside from mission Christianity. The people were not only "heathen"; they were also "unresponsive" and "indifferent," Godfrey Callaway had noted of the pioneer phase of missionary work.[92] But thereafter, the development of a range of responses to Christianity besides outright rejection or eventual acceptance made it difficult for missionaries to launch a unified assault on the obstacles to Christian evangelism. The battle was no longer simply between Christianity and "heathenism." The missionaries were now confronted with individuals with different levels of exposure to Christianity theology, who had embraced those aspects of

Christian dogma that made sense in their worldviews. These individuals, for example, had made a "convenience" of God by only going to church when they endured a drought and wanted to pray for rain.[93] Chiefs had acknowledged the importance of missions and acted as patrons of religious and educational work, yet failed to take the important step of converting. To make matters worse Africans were institutionalizing these syncretic and supposedly "nominal" variants of Christianity.

African independent movements compounded the sense of crisis felt in missionary circles. Representatives of the Methodist Church had special reasons to think critically about these developments since they were most affected by them. While Farmerfield was no scapegoat, these developments certainly lent an additionally pessimistic bent to the diagnosis of the mission's status. The economic challenges of the tenants compounded by the complaints about piety and morality on the estate provided the investigative committee with two compelling and mutually reinforcing justifications for terminating the settlement. If the generation of Africans born and raised as Christians still practiced a "nominal" or syncretic form of Christianity, perhaps it was time for the Methodist Church to cut its losses and sell the estate. The very real threat that an executive decision could end the mission made the 1884 review, recommendations, and the subsequent decision a watershed period in Farmerfield's history. By the 1880s there were enough individuals scattered throughout different levels of the church administration who were doubtful about maintaining Farmerfield as a mission. But it was a local farmer, two Methodist ministers, and a justice of the peace who provided the crucial information about Farmerfield so that the Conference could make a final decision.

The Conference Decides the Future of Farmerfield

The committee that investigated and reported on the status of the mission estate in 1884 consisted of four key individuals. Reverend John Walton, the chairman of the Grahamstown District, presided over the committee. The other three individuals were Reverend Henry Cotton, the resident minister of the Salem and Farmerfield circuit; Simon Amm, a local farmer; and William Henry Dawson Matthews. Dawson Matthews, whose father William Henry Matthews was the local justice of the peace for Salem and dealt with the civil disputes at Farmerfield, took a keen interest in the mission's affairs in a similar capacity.[94] The composition of the committee certainly affected their stance on the mission station. Of the four, Walton was perhaps the most far removed from the daily affairs at Farmerfield, yet had to keep the general interests and reputation of the Methodist Church in mind.

The Reverend Cotton came in at the end of the committee because he was only stationed at Farmerfield from 1885 and could add little to the proceedings besides the information he could glean from the previous annual reports. His presence on the committee was a formality that added little substance to the committee's report. Even if Cotton had been stationed in the circuit before 1884, he still would have been somewhat removed from the daily affairs of the community. Since Wesleyan ministers changed their stations frequently, it was difficult for any one missionary to really develop a deep understanding of the community. Cotton came in 1885 and left the circuit at the end of 1887, hardly enough time for the tenants' resentment of the recommendations and the new rules of the committee to abate. Cotton's departure from the circuit after only three years, leaving his successor to deal with a disgruntled community, was exactly the sort of discontinuity that made it difficult for the people of Farmerfield to trust that their local missionaries could advocate for their best interests.

Simon Amm and William Henry Dawson Matthews were local to the Salem area and had a long-standing relationship with the Methodist Church. They also came to have a long-standing relationship as in-laws when their children (Simon George Amm and Amy Matthews, respectively) courted then married.[95] As locals they were both very familiar with affairs at the mission estate. Simon's father helped the Church to manage affairs at Farmerfield and Simon inherited this role.[96] As a farmer who undertook agriculture on a commercial scale, Amm was in a good position to assess Farmerfield's agricultural potential. At his farm, Lindale, (see Map 2) Amm reared cattle, raised ostriches for feathers, and cultivated a wide range of crops like wheat, barley, citrus, peas, corn, and pumpkins.[97] From his perspective, perhaps these were the same agricultural pursuits that the people of Farmerfield should have been engaged in if they were indeed the industrious peasant farmers that William Shaw had envisioned. Amm therefore could imagine what would happen at Farmerfield if an English farmer such as he owned the place, instead of impoverished African tenants. Whatever the shortcomings of the local tenants, the Amm family had many opportunities to interact socially with Farmerfield's residents. They attended concerts, anniversary celebrations, and fundraisers, and Simon's mother often wrote about the "excellent tea," or the children being "beautifully and fashionably dressed" and singing "beautifully." Perhaps these social interactions tempered the assessments of the residents.

William Henry Dawson Matthews had been intimately involved in Farmerfield's affairs since his father adjudicated cases there, and took over the role as special justice of the peace for Salem. The senior Matthews had dealt with cases ranging from assault to adultery over the years, and was perhaps in the best position to question the Christian character of the community. Some of the tenants appeared before Matthews for repeat offences, perhaps contributing to the charge of "criminality." Dawson Matthews preserved his father's judicial notebook. It is likely that the Farmerfield cases Dawson Matthews and his father adjudicated made an impression as he deliberated the fate of the farm. With the committee constituted as it was, with people who had both close and loose ties to the mission, it seemed likely that the termination of the estate would be included in the recommendations.

To remedy the decline of the Farmerfield settlement, the committee suggested three possible solutions. In light of the committee's complaints, the first proposal—the sale of the estate—was the most predictable suggestion. "It is certain that in such a case," the report stated, Farmerfield "would fall into the hands of an English farmer, and the native community would at once be dissolved."[98] Farmerfield was indeed "choice" property, and the perception that the African tenants simply made a "convenience of their holdings" did not encourage a decision in the tenants' favor. Since part of the reason, if not the primary reason, why many people had come to the mission station was access to land, the committee did not understand why the land was not being farmed by the occupants. In the Eastern Cape and elsewhere, the African clamor for land was growing. Land appropriation by the state and by white settlers had created land hunger among Africans. From this perspective, the committee suggested that the behavior of the tenants should have reflected their gratitude and dependence on the Methodist Church for access to land. Instead the committee asserted that Farmerfield's tenants were wasteful of the land, their absence of industry proof that they lacked the agricultural expertise to take advantage of their land allotments.

The committee refused to relinquish the vision of industrious African peasants they had in mind and declined to acknowledge that most of the tenants did not have the means to fulfill what was expected of them. By the 1880s, access to land and agriculture were but basic resources that people needed in order to fulfill the external demands placed on them in the form of various taxes and living expenses, such as clothing and school fees. As discussed in Chapter 4, the people of Farmerfield had combined agriculture with off-farm employment to maintain their subsistence and pay their various cash obligations from the beginning of the settlement. As Christians, their cash obligations had grown, since residence at the mission required European dress and the enrollment of children at school. The attempt to build houses in more European styles and to acquire items like plates and utensils, clothes, and coffee and tea only increased the need for cash. That Farmerfield's residents could not undertake commercial farming on any enlarged scale was more a reflection of their meager resources, lack of markets, and the unsubsidized state of African commercial farming than it was an index of their lack of industry or desire to engage in such enterprises.

The second suggestion for ameliorating the existing problems at Farmerfield was the division of the estate into twenty-acre plots for sale to Africans. Such a scheme would allow forty male household heads to obtain land at Farmerfield. The option of selling the land to Africans and thereby cementing the legality of their land ownership was the most surprising proposal of the committee. In fact, it was a far fetched idea and not a course the Methodist Church wanted to pursue or had ever pursued at their missions. In this instance the main issue was the advisability of allowing Church property to become African freehold land. The committee concluded that if they sold to Africans, "no legal restriction whatsoever could provide for difficulties which might arise in the case of troublesome and criminal native proprietors and it is essential that we should retain total control of the settlement if it is to be a native Wesleyan community."[99] Given the existing concerns with rent tenancy at the settlement, the committee thought freehold tenure would exacerbate the problems because the tenants would have total autonomy from the Methodist Church. Granting freehold tenure to Africans was hardly a feasible option at that point in Farmerfield's history. The opportune moments from earlier in the nineteenth century were gone. Although the LMS took steps to grant freehold tenure to their mission residents up to the 1870s, this was not within the Methodist mission tradition in South Africa. The growing trend at the Cape, beyond mission stations, was to undermine African land rights, not buttress them.

It was precisely the long-standing pattern of land alienation and the resulting immiseration of Africans in the Cape Colony that made the representatives of the Methodist Church carefully consider the plans to sell and therefore dissolve the mission. The committee stated that they were hesitant to destroy the mission "in these times when our people are being driven from their lands by the actions of the government."[100] Since the colonial government played an active role in facilitating and supporting the dispossession of African people, the Methodist Church did not want to be implicated in that process. If they took any steps to end the settlement, the church would be following in the footsteps of the government. Thus, although they considered Farmerfield an eyesore, there was just no decent, Christian way to get rid of all the tenants without calling into question the ideas about the innate altruism of the church and notions about the mission as a refuge from the politics of land alienation. In considering this question the Methodist Church suppressed some of their doubts about whether missions were still necessary in late nineteenth-century South Africa.

Since the representatives of the Methodist Church did not want to give Africans freehold tenure any more than they wanted to be complicit in the alienation of land from Africans, only one option remained. After reviewing the history of the mission station, the committee decided that since there was no feasible way they could get rid of it, the next best solution was to reorganize it. The settlement would continue and realistic solutions to the existing problems of criminality and the misuse of land would be explored. The committee supported its decision by highlighting the original blueprint of the mission estate. The factor that served as a saving grace for the tenants in the 1880s was William Shaw's original goal which the tenants had found difficult to accomplish. Since William Shaw had played such a pivotal role in the evangelization process by establishing a Methodist missionary sphere of influence in southeastern Africa, giving Farmerfield another opportunity would perhaps salvage a part of Shaw's vision. After serious consideration, the committee granted the residents of Farmerfield another chance to fulfill the "original design" of the settlement. This was the only solution palatable to the dilemma that Farmerfield presented to the Methodist Conference.[101]

A concrete solution for overhauling the estate included plans for getting rid of all "unworthy occupiers." The land would be divided into forty plots comprising twenty acres each, at an annual rate of eight to ten pounds per year; grazing rights for ten head of cattle would be provided. The committee made it expressly clear that such cattle had to belong to the tenants, this having not always been the practice up to the 1880s. These plans encompassed the second option discussed above, but without freehold tenure. Instead of being sold to African tenants, the land would be rented at a high rate, and most importantly the Methodist Church would retain ultimate ownership of the property. A resident minister, for whom a "cottage and land shall be provided" was also strongly recommended. Up to the 1880s Farmerfield's minister lived in Salem and divided his time between several churches; only in the few years before the review did Farmerfield receive a resident, African minister. By the time these final proposals were publicized in 1885, widespread discontent and anxiety was rampant at Farmerfield.[102]

Reorganizing Farmerfield: The Aftermath of the Review

The investigation and decision of the Conference prompted a general atmosphere of anxiety among the tenants primarily because the people thought their tenure was secure. Although the tenants signed an agreement upon moving to the estate, a part of which was three months' notice of eviction if the rules were broken, it was mostly a formality. The representatives of the Church and Society had a right to enforce the rules of the estate and they often exercised this right with the threat of removal. However, since people were evicted only for the most egregious breaking of rules such as stealing or serious arrears of rent, most of the people felt secure in their settlement on the estate. Farmerfield had a long-standing history and the settlement had never faced an investigation and overhauling of this manner before.

The tenants of Farmerfield spent much of 1885 discussing the terms by which the mission community would be reorganized. They were particularly disgruntled about the insecure nature of land tenure, the prohibitive rate of rent, the small number of cattle allowed, and the reduction of the number of plots to forty. Reporting on the atmosphere at Farmerfield in 1885, the committee stated that they had "experienced considerable difficulty with the present occupiers." Many of the tenants believed in the perpetuity of access to land at Farmerfield and did not realize until then that an executive decision of the Methodist Conference could dissolve the community. "A number of the oldest and most industrious tenants," the *Report* continued:

> strongly held the opinion that the estate was virtually theirs. . . . Several of the older men state that they were assured by the earliest missionaries that so long as they paid the rent and kept the regulations they would be left undisturbed; that they and their families would remain in possession of the land for ever [*sic*].[103]

The committee went to great lengths to disabuse the tenants of this idea and called a meeting to clarify the nature of rent tenancy at the estate and discuss the new rules. During the meeting, Farmerfield's tenants set forth their views vociferously; they tried to renegotiate the rent and the amount of cattle each resident was allowed to graze and undoubtedly wondered who would be most affected by the reduction of the number of plots to forty.

The committee made it clear to the tenants that tenure at Farmerfield was based on paying an annual rent and abiding by the church rules. Moreover, the tenants were told that this type of rent tenancy was characteristic of the settlement since its foundation in 1838, was always subject to the control of the Methodist Church, and would never devolve into permanent occupancy rights. The issue of tenancy was not one that could be altered whatever the objections of the oldest residents. The tenants were not successful in changing the terms of their occupancy or increasing the number of plots. They were, however, successful in getting the committee to increase the number of cattle allowed from ten to fifteen head, and in getting the rent reduced to six pounds. The committee agreed to present these terms to the next annual Conference of the Methodist Church.

The review of 1884 was a momentous occasion in the history of Farmerfield. The mission's purported failure was placed under a lens for the Methodist Church to examine in fine detail and then decide the fate of several hundred people. Farmerfield was conspicuous as a failure in the missionary viewpoint because its design was an overly ambitious evangelical plan based on rigid, limited notions of Christianity and civilization. Farmerfield's design failed to acknowledge the limits of African economic independence in a colonial society that was extremely prejudicial to African aspirations in any guise. The tenants' position at Farmerfield serves as an economic and evangelical microcosm of the experiences of many African Christians throughout South Africa and captures the mood of reflection and reorganization that characterized many missionary societies in the last half of the nineteenth century.

Farmerfield's tenants experienced the review as the first concrete threat to their existence from an executive decision—as opposed to natural disasters like drought or cattle epidemics. The review set the tone for how the affairs of the mission station would be conducted after 1884; there were constant reviews of the position of the mission station; most of the time the tone was pessimistic and the question of discontinuing the mission station was raised. The review set a precedent for how problematic tenants would be handled on the estate. The idea of culling the residents was the solution the representatives of the missionary society fell back on when the tenants at Farmerfield became "troublesome and criminal native proprietors." Enforced removal was used as a threat from the 1880s through to sale of portions of the estate in the 1930s and up to the final coup de grace in 1962. From the time of the review through to the removal of the last families from Farmerfield in 1962, the issue of autonomy and fixity of land rights were the main points on which the tenants of Farmerfield clashed with the representatives of the church. In the shorter expanse of time between 1884 and 1916, the tenants negotiated their position at the estate and tried to fulfill the original design of the settlement. By 1916, the Methodist Church decided that if an industrious, Christian peasantry was not forthcoming with the changes they had made since 1884, then perhaps what Farmerfield needed was a white overseer, further changes in the number of tenants, and stricter rules. This next phase of overhauling the mission estate is the subject of Chapter 7.

PART THREE

Revamping the Mission

Reincarnations of Farmerfield, 1884–1962

Attempts to rehabilitate William Shaw's vision of Farmerfield resulted in three reincarnations of the mission between 1884 and 1962, each one more embattled than its predecessor. In the first phase from 1884 to 1916, the Methodist Church enforced the new plans for Farmerfield, expelling tenants they deemed "unworthy" and redrawing the map to reflect the new assignments of land. During this time, local missionaries and representatives of the Methodist Church continued to voice disappointment in the mission, albeit in a somewhat guarded fashion. While paying some deference to palliative measures for revitalizing the mission, the Methodist Church believed it still had not sufficiently curbed the tenants' autonomy. Reports between 1884 and 1916 decried lapses into "heathenism" evident at the estate and the persistence of "nominal" Christianity. The disillusionment voiced in the review of 1884 resurfaced, resulting in calls for white residential supervision in 1916.

The second reconstruction of Farmerfield commenced in 1916 with plans for finding a suitable white supervisor and amending the rules of the estate. The tenants interpreted these decisions as further attempts to erode their rights and by 1920 were locked in a battle over the management of the estate. The white overseer resigned, however, prompting the church to sell a portion of Farmerfield and reduce its population. By this time a new generation of residents who had few kinship ties, if any, to the earlier residents, had established themselves at the mission. Nonetheless, they faced the same persistent economic pressures and criticism of their Christian faith and lifestyles. The third and final reorganization of Farmerfield lasted from 1930 to 1962. By the 1930s the Methodist Church had resolved to let the mission die a natural death. Shaw's vision of Farmerfield could not be realized; all hopes of a renascent Farmerfield faded. In the 1940s the Methodist management of the mission capped the population, allowing no new tenants. They pursued this policy until 1962 when the apartheid government of South Africa stepped in to do what the Methodist Church had been unwilling to attempt: raze the community and remove an African settlement amid a white community that was an anomaly in South Africa's apartheid landscape.

What can the history of Farmerfield, now an impoverished labor reserve dependent on subsistence farming and remittances from family members, contribute to our understanding of late nineteenth-century evangelism and African communities in South Africa? A brief pamphlet on Farmerfield summarized that after the Methodist Church reduced its population and sold off portions of the estate, the rest of the population was removed in 1962. This essay asserts that the underlying historical import of Farmerfield lay primarily in its early phase as a model of pioneer Christianity. The story could end there. Indeed by the late nineteenth century, Farmerfield and other pioneer missions had long passed their heyday. No longer heralded as a signpost of epic, romantic victories against "heathenism," Farmerfield's local missionaries now wrote terse, laconic reports that contained few of the positive assessments from the 1830s and 1840s. Yet the twentieth-century history of Farmerfield remains as essential as the early romantic tale. It is important that historians do not commit the same act of elision evident in official mission records. Many official mission historical accounts dismissed mission stations that reflected poorly on the parent churches or missionary organizations. While the reasons for this are obvious—no one wanted to advertise or showcase "failure"—it means the histories of the populations who remain at these missions become obscured. Whereas a steady stream of visitors publicized Farmerfield's success, only insiders of the Methodist Church foretold of its economic stagnation. The story of stillborn, stagnant or thwarted peasantries remains as important as the tales missionaries liked to tell about the "rise" of thriving African peasantries.

Addressing the obscured history involves more than simply adding Farmerfield to the existing narrative. As Cherryl Walker has noted in the context of land reform, it is important to assess what happened to the land and to people after land expropriation to understand how these lost histories impact the feasibility of South Africa's land restitution agenda.[1] In the context of Farmerfield as a contemporary mission, it is crucial to understand that however short its residents fell of William Shaw's vision, and in spite of the scripts the Methodist Church used to assess their "failure," Farmerfield still represented something crucial for its remaining families: a degree of autonomy and relatively unencumbered access to land in a region where most Africans worked as laborers on local Eastern Cape farms. Africans maintained an ideological commitment to farming even though it could not meet all of their subsistence needs and protected their land access even if they did not have the resources to develop their land holdings. The meanings Africans attached to land remained consequential for the economic horizons they envisioned for themselves. While many abandoned farming for full-time employment in town, South Africa's economy had long moved on from the era when whites complained about African labor shortages to an era of unprecedented unemployment and immiseration. The meanings Africans attached to land are thus consequential for understanding why some individuals held on to multipronged economic strategies to hedge against a bleak financial landscape.

The dead zone in official mission history privileges the pioneer era and the romantic story of epic battles against bridewealth, circumcision, and war-like "natives." But what happens after the epic battles, once Africans become Christians and challenge missionaries to make good on their assertions of racial liberalism and to deal with racial discrimination in their own church? This era of mission history found cautionary tales in the rise of separatist Christian movements among Africans. Yet Farmerfield's tenants chose another path. They asserted their spiritual independence and the right to determine for themselves whether they were good Christians or not. This decision reaffirmed the importance of the legacy of missions. Farmerfield was not alone in this. Long after Farmerfield and other pioneer missions had passed their heyday, latecomers to South Africa as a mission field continued to establish missions with the same gusto and romance associated with pioneer missions. Moreover, the conquest of the remaining independent African polities and the emergence of an African urban population opened up new opportunity to evangelize, if not establish, residential missions for Africans.

Reorganizing Farmerfield, 1884–1916

The Methodist Church of South Africa implemented the administrative reorganization of Farmerfield at the cost of undercutting the tenants' security and raising new fears about their future at the estate. Despite assurances that Farmerfield would be spared from dissolution, the tenants emerged from the process both indignant and chastened. The few concessions they gained on rent and grazing rights did not mitigate the injustice they felt. Moreover, the committee had not altered its general perception of Farmerfield as a place "smitten with poverty and demoralization" and beset by "idleness and criminality." The negative and condescending outlook on the mission overshadowed any measure of altruism or philanthropy evident in the decision to retain it. For the next three years after the review of 1884, it is likely the tenants felt besieged as they tried to understand the intentions of the Methodist Church. The white committee assigned to manage Farmerfield and implement its reorganization served eviction notices to those tenants pinpointed as most troublesome and "unworthy." Expulsions reached a crescendo between 1884 and 1887. In the six months between December 1884 and June 1885, for example, the number of church members had fallen from approximately 156 to 121. The following year witnessed a further decline to ninety-nine members and by the end of 1887 that figure had plunged to seventy-two.[2] The individuals most susceptible to expulsion were those accused of violations like drunkenness, those who had left the estate in search of work without giving formal notice, and anyone who was not a registered church member.

As a group, local leaders and preachers were perhaps among those most immune from these evictions. These individuals were selected for their knowledge of Christianity and exemplary behavior at the mission. They led class meetings, collected ticket monies and church offerings, and served as local councilors or headmen. In their quarterly meetings they faced scrutiny on all aspects of their lives and suffered immediate censure for any misdeeds. It is not surprising therefore to find many of the same individuals still leading classes in the late 1880s and 1890s after the mass expulsions had transpired. These local leaders and preachers had also established long-term residence at the estate. Benjamin France and Samuel Masilo, for example, moved to the mission in the 1850s, raised their families at Farmerfield, and died there. Both were baptized as adults, France in 1854 and Masilo in 1857.[3] Both France and Masilo led small classes in the 1860s and gained influence at the mission, eventually advancing to the rank of local preachers. In the years leading up to the review of 1884, Samuel Masilo's class grew so rapidly that he eventually had to divide the members into three separate groups.[4] France and Masilo represented a wave of tenants who had taken over vacancies at Farmerfield in the 1850s and 1860s. This wave of tenants had trickled into Farmerfield as the earliest inhabitants grew older and eventually passed. Of the 104 household heads enumerated in the census of 1849, almost half (forty-nine) were already in their thirties; another forty-five individuals were aged forty and older; only ten individuals were in their twenties.[5]

Even if most of the original tenants had remained at Farmerfield by the time of the 1884 review, the youngest cohort among them would already be in their fifties and the remainder would be in their sixties and seventies. Death, war, and migration allowed men like Masilo and France to secure residence, raise their families, and gain influence at Farmerfield. France and his wife, Sarah, reared eight children at Farmerfield, a generation of children born at a mission and raised as Christians from birth.[6] The eldest son, Abraham, who was born at Farmerfield in 1857, had married and started his own family at Farmerfield by 1880. Benjamin France died at Farmerfield in 1909 and was remembered as one of the "oldest and most capable local preachers."[7]

By the end of 1887 the last of the evictees left Farmerfield. The European management committee lamented the congregation's decline but accepted this as a necessary step for amelioration.[8] The remaining tenants resumed their normal lives under intense surveillance and with new neighbors. The management screened new applicants to fill vacancies at Farmerfield, perhaps the most significant steps taken to steer Farmerfield in the new direction it wanted. By 1888 missionaries reported that a small religious revival took place at Farmerfield. Despite these early signs of recovery, the missionaries and management of Farmerfield suffused favorable assessments of Farmerfield with unenthusiastic, skeptical sentiments. As early as 1890, for example, the missionaries reported,

"Much earnest and conscientious work is being done with pleasing results; but native customs and beer drinking are prevalent and prove a serious hindrance to the spread of truth."[9] By 1894 the reports of Farmerfield spoke of spiritual apathy. The people, the missionary asserted, did not "manifest that interest in the welfare of the church and its institutions which we would like to see."

While the Methodist Church was keen to promote "native agency" in principle, the supervision of African class leaders and local preachers proved insufficient to curb spiritual inertia or curtail the "vast amount of 'heathenism'" at the mission.[10] We have no testimony from Farmerfield's residents to explore their perceptions of the situation. Some of the residents' behavior suggests, however, that they did not necessarily share the missionary disdain of alcohol, or the belief that circumcising their sons represented a lapse into "heathenism." Local missionaries made it clear in their reports that white supervision of Africans was the key to maintaining control of Farmerfield. Notwithstanding the importance they attached to "native agency," by creating a small group of African ministers and a network of local preachers and class leaders, European missionaries were not ready to relinquish control. For example, when Gana Kakaza, one of the probational ministers stationed at Farmerfield in 1880 questioned what he believed was an unfair hierarchy based on race, the Methodist Church quickly reprimanded him. During his trial period as a minister in 1884, Kakaza asked why Africans who had passed their probationary period were placed under the authority of whites who were still on trial. He also questioned why retired ministers still supervised the ministry when their retirement technically implied they were disqualified for the full work of the ministry.[11] As a result of these inquiries, Kakaza lost the endorsement of white Methodists in the Grahamstown District necessary to become a full minister at that time.

The European management of Farmerfield remained equally displeased with secular affairs at the mission. They continued to complain that the tenants' children were frequently absent from school during the plowing and reaping seasons, a long-standing source of conflict at Farmerfield. Although school enrollment fell between fifty-four and fifty-five students in 1893, average attendance was only thirty-seven. In the last quarter of the year, only twenty-eight pupils attended school on average.[12] These numbers showed little improvement in 1894 and by 1895 the Farmerfield school failed its government inspection, losing part of its financial grant due to irregular attendance.[13] Facing several dry seasons between 1890 and 1895, the tenants could hardly maintain basic subsistence, let alone subsidize the school. The very dry year of 1895 got increasingly worse as locusts and cattle diseases descended on portions of the Eastern Cape, destroying crops and cattle in their wake.[14] As they had done on countless other occasions when they faced hardships, the residents of Farmerfield left the mission in search of work—some permanently. So significant was the population dispersal that the local management no longer needed the services of one of the evangelists and let him go.[15] Before the tenants could recover from the severe compromise of their subsistence base, rinderpest carried off some of their cattle.[16]

Farmerfield's tenants faced the same economic woes as other Africans in the Albany District. Throughout the entire area food was scarce, seed was expensive, and local work was unavailable. Parents pulled their children out of school because they could not afford school fees; people left the district in search of work.[17] Since Farmerfield residents had just emerged from a serious threat of mass expulsion, their inability to pay school fees, rent, and other expenses at the mission placed them in jeopardy of losing their place of residence. The protracted drought between 1892 and 1896 saw further removals from the mission and from the Albany area altogether. These migrations reached a peak with the outbreak of the South African War in 1899. Despite the hundreds of miles separating Albany from the theaters of the war between 1899 and 1902, Africans still faced pressures to support the war effort. By 1902 the military had not only scoured the area for men but had also commandeered their horses. Thousands of Africans left the Albany area in connection with the war, creating a temporary labor shortage.[18] Since local farmers needed help with their harvest, those remaining in Albany had a chance to earn cash or a few head of cattle. Individuals headed to the diamond mines of Kimberley, the gold mines of Johannesburg, and the harbors of Port Elizabeth seeking economic relief.

Tenants wanted to guard their position at Farmerfield because their prospects were significantly worse if they left the mission and remained in the Albany area. As an agricultural district, Albany had little to offer Africans seeking refuge from drought, locust, and cattle epidemics. Almost six decades after Africans filtered into the area, Albany had few opportunities for economic advancement and no residential options aside from white farms or overcrowded African locations. As the civil commissioner pointed out in his report on the Albany district in 1899, "This division does not lend itself to the improvement of the native, who can never become more than a servant or a tenant at the pleasure of a landlord." He continued to say that other than the African locations on the outskirts of Grahamstown, "there is no place where the native can make himself a permanent home, consequently there is little room for improvement."[19] Dispossessed of land and too impoverished to purchase any, Africans sought employment on white farms and entered into sharecropping arrangements as the only avenue for pursuing an agricultural lifestyle. By the latter part of the nineteenth century, even these opportunities were curtailed as some white farmers dispensed with the conventional crops and began experimenting with ostrich farming.[20] Too poor to attempt this experiment, some of Farmerfield's residents allowed Simon George Amm, whose father sat on the committee of 1884, to hire their lands for ostrich farming. Amm, who had a farm near Farmerfield, paid tenants in cash and in kind to use their lands. By 1899 he had sixty-six ostriches at Farmerfield.[21]

While local white farmers like Simon Amm diversified their agricultural endeavors, Farmerfield tenants continued to rely on the same staple crops of maize and vegetables. How would Farmerfield fare in the twentieth century? If plagued by the same problems of drought and locusts, the tenants' economic prospects in the twentieth century promised to be no different than the preceding century. Land tenure remained in the hands of the church and surveillance undercut their autonomy. Elsewhere in the Cape Colony, Natal, Orange Free State, and Transvaal, Africans faced similar struggles over land and autonomy. The last half of the nineteenth century had witnessed the final war of dispossession to subjugate the African population and bring them under colonial control. In the economic realm the mineral revolution of the 1860s and 1880s guaranteed a permanent British interest in the region and presaged a political showdown between the English and Afrikaner sectors of the white population. When this fallout came to a head in the South African War, Africans saw a chance to secure a position in the emerging political economy. In the aftermath of the war Africans sent a deputation to England to secure a position in the new entity of South Africa. The African delegation returned disillusioned. Peace between whites in South Africa came at the cost of African political marginalization. The Natives Land Act of 1913 dealt a further blow to Africans' aspirations by allotting a mere 7 percent of the land for African occupation and reserving the majority for white use and occupation. The Land Act gave legislative reality to the process of African dispossession, which had escalated in the nineteenth century, and reached its zenith in the twentieth century. Outside of the reserves, African access to land was filtered through de facto white ownership. Africans occupied white-owned land as tenants and farm laborers.[22]

As historian William Beinart noted in his survey of twentieth-century South Africa, "Markets, empire, industry, capital, railways and political union in 1910 were the motors of change."[23] The Albany District of which Farmerfield was a part remained relatively peripheral in these developments; African dispossession already a fait accompli by the mid-nineteenth century. The physical center of gravity of the mineral revolution may have been far from Albany but its impact was no less consequential. Farmerfield tenants' perception of economic opportunity and of the church as part of a paternal political network became even more heightened during this era. The mineral revolution skimmed Albany of some of its denizens; both black and white sought better opportunities in the emerging port and mining areas, as well as opportunities for farming.[24] Although the twentieth century proved no kinder to the tenants of Farmerfield in the economic realm, they held on to their positions at the mission. One of the most important concessions they gained was a suspension of the two-pound rental increase proposed in 1884. Only in 1920 did the rent hike finally become effective. The management committee remained vigilant of the tenants' activities and continued to enforce evictions for breach of the rules. As a result, Farmerfield always had a handful of new tenants.

Between 1884 and 1916, most of the problems noted at Farmerfield fell within the domestic realm. Several cases of premarital sexual relations and adultery came before the local missionary and the African councilors. After a short absence from the mission, for example, Diamond Tukulu returned in November 1907 to find his wife pregnant by another tenant, Thomas Maqanda. Maqanda admitted before the council that he had made several advances on Mrs. Tukulu. Diamond Tukulu demanded five oxen as an appropriate fine and asked Maqanda to take the child. The parties settled on two oxen and undisclosed sums as compensation, that Mrs. Tukulu would keep the child for the first nine months, and Thomas Maqanda would forfeit his position at the mission. Later Tukulu decided he wanted a divorce.[25] Cases of adultery cast a similar moral stain as did the instances of premarital sex that came to light. Several young and unmarried women became pregnant, violating the implicit mission rules about premarital sex. The mission frowned upon such behavior and prohibited illegitimate children on the estate. In keeping with these rules, Joseph Malakane received written notice in July 1907 that four children in his household (three grandchildren and one great-grandchild) were illegitimate and had to leave the mission within one month.[26] By 1914 a steep fine of six pounds, the equivalent of one year's rent, was imposed on individuals who violated this rule so that the mission would not be used as a "dumping ground for illegitimate children."[27]

Throughout the Grahamstown district, which incorporated Farmerfield, and several other local circuits, missionaries reported a "growing laxity" toward "old native customs." Bridewealth exchange, beer brewing and drinking, and circumcision were noted among the most difficult practices to banish.[28] All of these activities were comparatively easy to hide. The sense of urgency evident in missionary concerns about "heathenism" did not necessarily come from any qualiitative increase in activities they labeled as such—except for circumcision. As noted in the preceding chapter, the Methodists and other missionary bodies believed that after many decades of pioneer work, certain practices should have been dying out; yet by the 1870s, from their perspective recidivism was all around them.[29] At all levels of administration, from the Conference to the district and circuit meetings, the Methodist Church echoed its disapproval of these activities. Beer brewing and circumcision were banned through written legislation but even as late as 1912 the church was unwilling to go that far on the issue of bridewealth. They advised African parents to be vigilant in this regard, but would not officially "sanction any legislation" on the practice. *Lobola*, or bridewealth, lent a certain legitimacy to marriage and family that even African Christians still desired.[30] Missionaries knew they could not abolish it altogether through legislation.

At Farmerfield, alcohol brewing and consumption, bridewealth exchange, and circumcision were prohibited. In practice, however, a more suitable term would be "discouraged" because none of the sanctions against these practices involved outright expulsion from the mission. The church was far more deferential to some African cultural practices than they were to moral lapses surrounding sex. For example, the church temporarily suspended two tenants from membership for exchanging bridewealth in July 1905.[31] Elizabeth Chaki, the mother involved, agreed to return the cattle. Joseph Bam, the teacher who had made the payment, was restored to his position and eventually became a local preacher. The marriage proceeded as planned in July 1905.[32] One local preacher found guilty of drinking in 1916 faced a six-month suspension from his position.[33] Although the church forbid circumcision, willing parents as well as young men wanting to be circumcised against their parents' wishes seemed to have found a clever way to continue the practice. Some parents pleaded ignorance, asserting their children were circumcised against their wishes. Or, sometimes the young circumcised boys refused to divulge the name of the persons involved in the circumcision. It was a difficult battle to win when tenants denied knowledge of the event.

With these loopholes, more and more tenants circumcised their male children, so much so that the local preachers noted its increasing prevalence at the mission.[34] In July 1906, the quarterly meeting of class leaders and local preachers drew up a more specific set of punitive measures to counteract circumcision. A few days later, none of the tenants voted against the rules, but it is likely they were reluctant to assert public support of circumcision at a meeting held to discuss how best to prevent it. To combat the practice, the tenants voted to levy a fine of two pounds and ten shillings on any young man circumcised. They also agreed to impose a similar fine and a year's suspension from church membership on the parents only if they consented to the act. Likewise, another fine would be imposed if the young man refused to disclose who carried out the ceremony. With no threat of expulsion written in the rules, the management left wide berth for the tenants to continue the practice. In effect, if parents wanted to circumcise their children, they had to be prepared to pay fines totaling seven pounds and ten shillings.[35] Approximately a year after this meeting, five tenants were fined the same sums of two pounds and ten shillings, most likely for violating the rules on circumcision.[36]

When the tenants assembled in January 1916 to pay their rents and discuss matters relating to the mission, the local missionary impressed upon them that the outlook on the estate was unfavorable. Both church and school attendance were lax, non-Christians still lived at the mission, people cohabited, and children were born out of wedlock. Moreover, circumcision was on the rise.[37] In the three decades since the review of 1884, the various whites assigned to Farmerfield's management committee had maintained a guarded, provisional assessment of the estate. By 1916 the recommendation for sale to Europeans, first suggested in 1884, was once again tabled and vetoed as a potential solution to the Farmerfield problem. Instead the committee recommended reform in the guise of a resident white overseer.[38]

In 1915 Farmerfield was divided into fifty-three plots of land, roughly equivalent to the number of household heads. Its tenants worked a total of 682 acres of land. As they searched for a suitable candidate for overseer, the management committee continued to make small changes to overhaul the estate. As people were expelled for infractions of mission rules, the division of land was reorganized. Two residents, Gilbert Malgas and John Damon, were evicted for the alleged theft of fowls and oranges, respectively. George Sam left the mission for employment in Port Elizabeth and lost his plot for nonpayment of arrears.[39] Absentee tenants Christina France and Jacob Makoni were given notice that they had to live at the mission or forfeit their land allotments. The most severe, public case of discipline during this period, however, concerned the principal of the Farmerfield School, Nathaniel Magobiyane. Magobiyane committed adultery with a widow at Farmerfield and was dismissed from both his positions as principal and class leader, and suspended from the church membership for one year. Magobiyane's behavior had far-reaching consequences in addition to the damage to his marriage and his career. He had to forfeit the house, land, and grazing rights provided with the position.[40] The Magobiyane family disappears from the Farmerfield record after 1919, since the loss of their privileges at Farmerfield forced them to relocate.

In several other cases, residents entered into sharecropping arrangements with each other, thereby creating vacancies. Simon Maxegwana voluntarily vacated his plot of land to farm with his brother, Charles. Unable to pay his debt, Albert Daniels agreed to forfeit his plot to another tenant and sharecrop with him in exchange for debt relief.[41] The committee filled the vacancies by accepting applications from nonresidents and sometimes by extending the plots of existing tenants. One such new tenant was Hendrick Jantjes, whom the committee granted a small piece of land in January 1919 to build a house. Jantjes had secured a spot in Farmerfield many years before but asked to delay his residence until he had retired. Jantjes paid another tenant, Phaus Norongo, three goats to build the house for him. With all these changes, Farmerfield received several new residents, but the total number of holdings was reduced from fifty-three to forty-one within a year.[42]

The early months of 1918 showed every prospect of a good agricultural season, something of a rarity for the tenants of Farmerfield. They faced a decent likelihood of paying off their arrears in rent and thus receiving a favorable report from the missionaries for a change. Tenants gave generously to missionary work. Three tenants, for example, Ben Budaza, Jane Malakane, and Simon Maxegwana, contributed five pounds each for missionary work, one pound more than their yearly rent.[43] Before their economic fortunes could be fully realized, however, the influenza pandemic of 1918 crippled the estate. By October 1918 almost every family was afflicted. Aside from a few people who resisted, the population of approximately 400 men, women, and children managed to be inoculated in time to prevent mass fatalities. Most of these people were vaccinated in their homes as they were already too ill to leave.[44] Nevertheless, influenza killed fourteen people and dashed their economic recovery. By 1919 the tenants faced another drought and many fell behind by more than a year's rent.[45] In that same year, the management committee asserted that the rules of the mission were "more honored in the breach than in their observance." They launched a search for an overseer and made plans to devise stricter rules.[46] In this way the committee set the stage for an acrimonious confrontation with the tenants reminiscent of the review of 1884.

The management committee of Farmerfield made it known in the local area that they were seeking an overseer, and posted an advertisement in the magazine *The Methodist Churchman*. They received several applications for the position. Upon visiting the mission, one candidate declined the offer, but the committee had several candidates from which to choose. They settled on William Shepstone-Jeffrey, a former stock inspector in the Department of Agriculture. Shepstone-Jeffrey informed the committee that as his parents and in-laws both came from the Grahamstown area, he was interested in the position.[47] While the search for an overseer had taken almost the entire year, the committee revised the rules and announced the changes to the tenants in February 1919. The amendments focused mostly on issues of animal and human trespassing, asking tenants to erect proper fences, sties, and byres for their animals. The most substantive changes dictated, first, that expulsion from the mission for any breach of the rules would be immediate and without compensation, and second, that signature of the new rules was compulsory. To "clear out the undesirables" and "improve the class of tenants" the committee also instituted the rent hike of six pounds that was initially suggested in 1884. None other than one of the most powerful persons in the Methodist Church, the secretary of the South African Conference, James Robb, warned the tenants that breaking the rule could result in the permanent dissolution of the mission.[48]

The local management committee announced the impending changes to the tenants in February 1919. By April the tenants made their protest in writing to the committee:

> There are certain points which we like to bring before the Synod Committee. (1) The fifteen head of cattle which we find we cannot come out with that number [sic]. (2) The point of an overseer; we got our overseer— the local committee which are dealing with us faithfully. (3) The raising of the rent; we have got lots of other things to be paid. All these facts we kindly beg the committee to consider them.[49]

Little came of these protests and the standoff continued throughout the rest of 1919. The local committee focused on the routine administrative matters at the estate and continued their search for an overseer. Everything about the year 1920 seemed a novelty to the tenants. A new overseer, stricter rules, and a rental increase impressed upon them a sense of crisis. As the earlier cohort of tenants had done in 1884, Farmerfield's residents in 1920 interpreted the committees' actions as a violation of their rights and a threat to their future. When the local management reasserted the claim of the Methodist Church to the land, the tenants responded with a measure of confusion and alarm. Writing on the tenants' behalf, the resident evangelist informed the chairman of the Grahamstown District, "There is this thing also which we have found as a new expression from our fathers when speaking to us here at Farmerfield—in that they now say we think that the land is ours. We do not know what that expression means."[50]

To compound matters, the current generation of tenants was unused to residential white supervision. The last supervisor had died in 1867 and despite warnings from the local missionary then assigned to Farmerfield, was never replaced. The local missionary had counseled then that Farmerfield's blueprint called for a resident white supervisor. Moreover, by the 1880s, Salem, the white community adjacent to Farmerfield and included in the duties of the local missionary, had grown so large as to occupy much of the missionary's time. Farmerfield needed a resident white authority that represented the Methodist Church or the tenants would gain a level of autonomy never envisioned for them. Institutional positions in the Methodist infrastructure such as class leader and local preacher accorded the tenants some power, but it was the intention that tenants exercise such power under white supervision. Since the minister lived in Salem and spent his time preaching and administering at several locations, it was difficult for him to keep watch over Farmerfield. Moreover, the habit of rotating missionaries to different circuits of the entire Methodist Church in South Africa meant that no one missionary was very familiar with Farmerfield. Herbert Allen came to the circuit in 1915 and was assigned specifically to Farmerfield only in 1918 and 1919. The extent of his familiarity with Farmerfield was perhaps to hear an annual report or two read at annual meetings or synods.

Reverend Allen had nothing favorable to say about Farmerfield and the fallout escalated as soon as the tenants were asked to ratify the changes by signing. After announcing the new rules, the tenants refused to sign, but Allen gave them an opportunity to reconsider. After several visits the tenants remained recalcitrant. "I have been twice to Farmerfield," Allen wrote to the chairman in February. "They are still inclined to be stiff-necked and probably a few will leave rather than sign the agreements, but I fancy from the tone of the last 'indaba' [meeting] the majority will fall into line. One or two have tried to lead the meeting into rebellion."[51] A month later in March, little had changed. Members of the committee reported to the synod that the tenants were "insolent and defiant."[52]

The tenants tell their side of the story in a letter drafted to John Mitchell Watkinson, the chairman of the Grahamstown District. This is one of the few instances in Farmerfield's history when the tenants' voices are not filtered by the missionary and it is worthwhile to quote them fully:

> At the last rent day held at Farmerfield on the 31st day of Dec 1919 the Synod Committee brought us tenants certain Rules and Regulations to sign. We find it impossible to sign them. We refuse to do so. The Synod Committee impressed on us to do so. We wouldn't do it. After refusing to sign the committee gave us two weeks to think over the matter. After two weeks were expired the committee came to listen how far did we think our reply was; we thought it over and found it impossible. Under all circumstances we can't sign them. We got a month's notice to quit the Farmerfield mission station. We got only one week more left to leave the

estate therefore . . . [We] write a letter to ask you as chairs of the Synod, why does the Synod deal so hard with us as we are your church for many, many years and was obedient all these many years. At last Synod, to treat us like this. Dear Sir, we as your church we find ourselves pressed to write to you, Sir, such a letter. As we belong to you as a church, we kindly beg chairman to be so kind and bring this matter before the Conference. Why does the Synod and Conference treat us in such a serious way as it seems that we are not your church? Dear Sir, kindly reply soon as you can as our time is very short. If you like, we can send you a copy of these rules.[53]

Despite Allen's visits to persuade the tenants to sign, they remained adamant in their refusal. Alerting chairman John Mitchell Watkinson of the tenants' impending letter, he pointed out that fear was motivating the tenants to take such a position. "Their revolt is not so much against the appointment of an overseer, or the alteration of any rule, as far as I can see," Allen wrote to Mitchell a few days before the letter arrived. "They simply fear to sign."[54]

The tenants presented a united and brave front to the local governing committee and the chairman of the Grahamstown District. The standoff reached a crescendo between January and March of 1920. The chairman of the district wrote a strongly worded response to the tenants:

If the refusal of the Natives to sign the agreement is simply a refusal to submit to authority, then the committee has only one course open—that is to send away those who are not willing to live according to the rules. You will see that it is the proper thing for the committee to make the rules for the natives and not for the natives to make the rules for the committee.[55]

Although the tenants ignored all verbal and written warnings for several months following the chairman's warning, the impasse continued. Perhaps frustrated with the stalemate and having exhausted all their options, one by one the tenants started to capitulate. By July 1920, half of them had signed the new rules and the others followed suit in the ensuing months. By the beginning of 1921 the committee reported it was satisfied with their handling of the conflict and the matter was settled. Unfortunately, the overseer was released from his contract after only eight-and-a-half months in the position. The conflict over the rules could not have made a good impression on the overseer and the delay in constructing his residence at Farmerfield compounded matters. The tenants were delighted to see him depart, as they had never wanted an overseer at the mission. Perhaps this was a victory for both the tenants and the church. The overseer "had little influence with these people and did nothing for them," Farmerfield's newest missionary, John Saunders, informed the chairman when he took over for Herbert Allen in 1920.

As in the review of 1884, victory for the tenants had come in the form of continued residence at the mission. Since the committee complained of the same sorts of problems after the tenants signed the rules, however, it seems their capitulation was inconsequential. In all respects the tenants had no reason to suspect that their victory was tenuous. The confrontation was a jockey for power—an assertion of the tenants' autonomy versus the Methodist Church's authority. This point was not lost on either party involved in the conflict. In a letter to the chairman, local missionary Herbert Allen had indicated that the tenants did not abhor the rules so much as their symbolism. "They did not mind it [the rule] evidently when they were not compelled to sign," Allen asserted, "but they were clever enough to see that if they sign we have the whip-hand of them in any case of discipline."[56] In a situation where literacy acquired ever greater meaning for Africans' life prospects, the power of written contracts was salient to the tenants.

The tenants had misread their victory and miscalculated the actual threat they faced. Although the committee had exhibited forbearance in handling the conflict and had expressed relief when the tenants finally signed, the reputation of the mission had declined irreparably in their view. The committee was exasperated and the majority of those who had to deal with the administration of Farmerfield expressed disdain for the mission. Farmerfield had lost its identity as a Christian mission station and was now regarded no differently from the other areas where Africans lived. "The general opinion is that Farmerfield had simply degenerated into a location, but a location which is privileged because it is regarded as a mission station!" Herbert Allen had informed the chairman of the Grahamstown District during the crisis over the rules.[57] The tenants could not have predicted or planned for the next intervention of the church.

What should have been relatively tranquil years between 1921 and 1924 resulted in the sale of portions of the estate and the most significant reduction of the population since 1884. The tenants had not factored in their chronic inability to maintain their subsistence base as their ultimate weakness. The perceived insolence of the tenants was heightened by their inability to pay rent. The committee suggested that if the tenants could not farm properly, the least they could do was provide their services to local whites—an imposition the current tenants, unlike their nineteenth-century counterparts, tried to avoid. Although the local committee acknowledged the presence of some good farmers at the mission, ultimately they believed the land was being spoiled and wasted. The tenants had no inkling of what was in store for them after they signed the rules.

Economic disaster awaited the tenants in the early years of the 1920s. A drought blighted the 1920 season, the tenants becoming so desperate that they sold some of their cattle for food. In 1921 cattle disease carried off 126 of the 399 cattle on the estate. Tenants were unable to make the necessary repairs to their fences, homes, and cattle byres as stipulated in the rules. The local committee reduced rents and gave advice about combating the afflictions of the cattle. Although the local committee was sympathetic, the tenants' economic hardship was a reminder that Farmerfield tenants were in constant arrears. Because of drought, bad seasons, low yields, and extreme fluctuations had become the norm. By 1923 the forty-five families living at the mission had fallen into extreme debt. Whereas in earlier periods most debts had fallen between five and seven pounds, tenants now owed between eight and twenty-one pounds. Dissatisfied with the financial returns of the mission, which the white administrators asserted were "inadequate for a property of such value," Farmerfield faced a partial dissolution. The annual Grahamstown Synod of 1923 decided that selling Farmerfield was the best solution and agreed to make such a proposition to the Conference, the highest Methodist authority. Representatives of the Grahamstown Synod presented a plan to sell three quarters of Farmerfield and reserve "such portion as will be provided for the aged tenants presently residing there." The Conference ratified the synod's resolution, changing Farmerfield's fate forever.

Old tenants, those who had made a concerted effort at farming, those who were current with their expenses at the mission, and those who had observed the rules were the most likely to remain.[58] Conversely, individuals most vulnerable to expulsion fell in the following categories: those without a long history at the mission; young women who had children out of wedlock; tenants who had fallen into arrears and had no collateral such as cattle to pay; and residents still on trial for church membership. In addition, many of the landholders at Farmerfield had adult dependents living with them without formal consent. By these criteria, a few tenants had to watch their adult children and grandchildren leave the mission in 1924. Others awaited notice about whether space was available for them on the small portion of the mission now reserved for Farmerfield.

The 1923 decision to sell Farmerfield had its critics, just like a similar resolution had in 1883. In the 1880s the Methodist Church expressed concern that such a step would make them complicit in the alienation of African lands at a time when Africans already faced tremendous hardships. They were not ready for such a step and spared Farmerfield as a result. By 1923, the pressure on African land had escalated and land alienation was given an unprecedented formality and legality in the Natives Land Act of 1913. Yet the Methodist Church showed none of the same concern; the saving grace of the church would not halt the sale of Farmerfield. The Synod argued that since funds from the sale would be diverted to African education, Africans in general would still benefit, if not the specific residents of Farmerfield. The Synod's position reflected a change in missionary approaches to African social improvement. Whereas the mission station was heralded in the nineteenth century as a crucial site for changing African societies, the disillusionment over "nominal" Christianity and independent expressions of African Christianity had led missionary societies to change their focus by the late nineteenth century. Education, which had always been included in the plans for social change, was given a new direction and a new focus. Missionaries channeled a lot of resources and manpower into meeting the growing African demand for education from the 1880s onward and hoped that the cultivation of "native agency" would receive a more lasting boost in this fashion.

John Saunders, Herbert Allen's successor as Farmerfield's local missionary, questioned the justification for the sale of Farmerfield. While discussions on the potential sale were underway in 1922, Saunders expressed his belief that "compared with other mission stations the character of the people is not worse." Moreover, he asserted, "To call the place a sink of iniquity is in exaggeration."[59] Saunders was not alone in looking at Farmerfield from a less partial perspective. Methodists in the neighboring village of Salem held varying opinions of the mission. Despite being its immediate neighbor, the white community in Salem was unaffected by issues pinpointed as problems at Farmerfield. Adultery, illegitimate children, occasional cases of circumcision, and alcohol consumption—all underscored as conduct unbecoming of a Christian community—had little bearing on the white community in Salem. While the Methodists in Salem requested the separation of the two communities from the same circuit on administrative and financial grounds, most thought that selling the mission was an extreme solution. When one of the eighteen board members suggested a vote on the sale of Farmerfield in 1920, no one seconded the motion.[60] The few communities that constituted the Salem and Farmerfield circuit maintained their opposition to sale in 1921 and 1922, pointing out that "such sale would be detrimental to the native work within the Salem and Farmerfield circuit."[61]

Despite the support for Farmerfield, the annual reports of the mission reinforced the decision of 1923. Each successor to the position of local minister in the Salem and Farmerfield circuit faced a litany of documents chronicling the problems at Farmerfield. Moreover, these ministers served three to four years in a circuit before they were transferred again, hardly enough time to familiarize themselves with their new positions, fulfill their duties to other congregants, and deal with a mission labeled as problematic. The duties of the local minister had become so far-flung that even the residents of Farmerfield complained they wanted to have him at the mission for an entire Sunday instead of only an afternoon.[62] With so many responsibilities upon transferring to the circuit, few ministers would welcome the conflict that arose from managing the Farmerfield mission. Even if missionaries like John Saunders were sympathetic, once problems arose, they were on the frontlines of the frequent traveling and the flurry of correspondence. "The management of this estate is a source of anxiety," John Saunders's successor to the position of local missionary, F. J. Rhead Marsh, complained in 1923. The tenants showed no reverence for the rules that had been such a source of conflict just a few years earlier. "Even some of the oldest residents ignore them or treat them as a joke," Rhead Marsh further exclaimed.[63]

Rhead Marsh spent an unusually long post of seven years in the Salem and Farmerfield circuit preparing the mission for sale. During his tenure, he dealt with tenants in a summary fashion, advocating in various committee meetings and in his correspondence with representatives of the Methodist Church that sale of the entire estate would be best. "A valuable asset to the church remains unrealized," Rhead Marsh concluded in his annual report of 1923. His assessment of 1924 began with the sour note, "Reporting on Farmerfield is neither easy nor pleasant and further experience convinces one of the unwisdom of carrying on or muddling through as at the present." Although he acknowledged the presence of some good farmers at the mission, on the whole he asserted that the tenants' reluctance to work for whites in the area contributed to their poverty and inability to maintain regular rent payments. During his tenure, Farmerfield experienced its most significant alteration since its inception. Rhead Marsh implemented the Conference's decision to sell portions of the estate through summary dismissals, keeping "only the best of the farming people." Just three years after he assumed his position, the number of families living at the mission dropped from forty-five to eighteen.[64]

All the tenants were put on notice that only a few people would remain and that space was limited for even some of the tenants considered worthy. By 1925 Rhead Marsh had met with the remaining tenants to allocate their new plots, reminding them that houses should be built in an orderly fashion to form streets. The tenants thus spent much of 1925 and 1926 rebuilding houses, whitewashing them with limestone, fashioning new streets, constructing cattle byres, branding their animals, and fencing their lands. It was an expense few could afford, but Rhead Marsh exacted these changes as the price for getting one of the few prized spots at the mission. Compliance with the rules had never been as high as during this period. Tenants watched as the remainder of the estate was resurveyed and reappraised, and potential buyers came to inspect their former lands. Each tenant was allowed eighteen head of large stock such as cattle and twenty head of smaller stock like donkeys, pigs, and goats. The new allotments were much reduced from their former sizes. Whereas a full plot measured approximately twenty acres before, tenants now received between ten and sixteen acres; ten of the seventeen new allotments fell between ten and twelve acres (see Table 7.1).

While the proposition to sell Farmerfield proved a relatively straightforward matter, executing the sale involved more difficulty than the Grahamstown Synod anticipated. In 1925 the property was surveyed and advertised for sale. Two African members of the church, one a minister, the other a layman, saw this as an opportunity for Africans to acquire freehold tenure of Farmerfield through purchase. With such a purpose in mind, Reverend Benjamin Rwairwai and M. D. Foley proposed in June 1926 that a consortium of 150 Africans purchase individual lots at Farmerfield for sixty pounds each. They would make a down payment and submit an application fee amounting to thirty pounds and pay the remainder in ten pound installments for three years. Ownership would pass to Africans, and to prevent complications, Methodist affiliation would be compulsory for eligibility. For the first time, someone put forth a vision of Farmerfield based on African freehold tenure, which, like Shaw's nineteenth-century vision, was anomalous for

Table 7.1 **Farmerfield Tenant Allotments: 1925 and 1926**

No.	Plot Holder	Acres
1	Alex Budaza	12
2	Thomas Mzizi	11.5
3	William Mpati	11.5
4	John Madinda	12.75
5	Wellington Zatu	8.75
6	Timothy and Harry Mquqo	20
7	Alfred Dassie; William Kadi	16.33
8	James Gaba	11.33
9	Philip Hewana	11.33
10	John Malakane	11.33
11	Stephen May	11.33
12	August May	9.5
13	Philip Nthlali	14
14	Charles Maxegwana	14
15	Simon Maxegwana	14
16	January Rooi	14.66
17	Fannie Kopo	11
18	Clifford Budaza	11.33

Source: CL, MS 15 880, Report of the Farmerfield Estate, 1925 and 1926.

its time. Just when Africans faced losing legal opportunities to own land in most of South Africa, Rwairwai and Foley saw a way for them to secure legal title to land at Farmerfield. They deferred to Reverend Rhead Marsh, who, along with a local management committee, was responsible for Farmerfield.[65]

In many ways the dream of African freehold tenure at Farmerfield was still-born. White ownership of Farmerfield was preferable and was always one of the suggestions discussed whenever the topic of reform or sale had arisen. Rather than veto Foley and Rwairwai's plan outright, or discourage them altogether, however, Reverend Rhead Marsh handled the matter in a roundabout fashion. He discussed the plan with Foley, altered the number of projected plot holders to one hundred, changed the installment plan so that all monies would be paid upon occupation, and added the proviso that if other offers came while he considered selling to Africans, he would have to entertain them. Besides these specifications, Foley had all indications that his plan was worth pursuing. Rhead Marsh asked him to submit the names of one hundred applicants, which would then be forwarded through the various channels of administration from the local committee to the district synod and finally the Conference.[66]

Even without the copious correspondence available to confirm the assertion, the history of Farmerfield up to the 1920s suggests that the Methodist Church would treat the possibility of African ownership of the mission cautiously. In every confrontation the representatives of the Methodist Church administering the estate had impressed upon the tenants that the Church retained control of the property and that their land rights—though long-standing—remained violable. Moreover, with an emphasis on realizing the sort of revenue that was never forthcoming from the existing tenants, it was also improbable that Rhead Marsh and the local committee would accept a proposal for any installment plan; just as it was unlikely that most Africans could find the sixty pounds due upon occupation and for outright purchase. Rhead Marsh informed the chairman, J. M. Watkinson, of the plan.

As chairman of the district since 1915, Watkinson was well aware of the problems of Farmerfield. Though he considered the proposal to sell to Africans, he thought the move unwise. "If anything miscarried, we should get all the knocks," Watkinson wrote to Rhead Marsh in September 1926. By "miscarriage," Watkinson had several scenarios in mind. First, the possibility of settling too many people on the mission. Second, Watkinson warned, "We must be careful not to introduce a situation which may culminate in another Bull Hoek [sic]."[67] The police had attempted to disperse a millenarian gathering of some 3,000 at Bulhoek, led by Enoch Mgijima, an African Methodist who had broken away and formed his own church and community. The standoff ended in the death of almost 200 people when Mgijima's adherents ran toward the police.[68] Watkinson was not alone in projecting his fears onto Farmerfield. Elsewhere in South Africa and the rest of Africa, both religious and secular authorities reacted with apprehension and dismay at the growth of African separatist and millenarian movements.[69] "Native agency," especially in the Methodist Church, was running amok.

Watkinson's final reason for discouraging sale to Africans hinged on the government policies of segregation and land alienation. "Suppose government introduces some sort of segregation legislation and declares that neighborhood a European neighborhood and tries to clear them all out! Hell!" he declared. Rhead Marsh concurred. Despite his hesitation to ultimately sell the property to Africans, Watkinson advised Rhead Marsh to allow the proposal to proceed through all the administrative channels "rather than for you and me to force an issue on our own now."[70] These were two skilled Methodist Church officials cognizant of public perception. They could not thwart Foley's plan outright and so they allowed him to submit his list of one hundred buyers in January 1927. Based solely on the names of former and current tenants, only seven of the one hundred names submitted appeared to have had a link to Farmerfield. In the meantime, Rhead Marsh entertained other offers for leasing and selling the estate, all of which fell through. After visiting Farmerfield, F. P. Long withdrew a lease/ purchase order because of insufficient water and the expense of clearing the land of certain bushes.[71] Another offer was invalidated since it was for the portion that the Church wanted to retain. By October 1927, African freehold tenure was the only proposal still open. Fearing that the "natives will feel aggrieved if anything is done and their offer has not been considered," the highest Methodist authority, Theophilus Curnick, advised Rhead Marsh to think about the plan. On November 24, 1927, the representatives of the church convened a meeting with Foley and Rwairwai to decide on their proposal. Curnick, the president of the Conference, J. M. Watkinson, the chairman of the Grahamstown district, and Simon George Amm, who sat on the local committee, missed the meeting. If the church wanted to put on a good public face, absenting themselves from the meeting was a misstep. In their correspondence with Rhead Marsh, Curnick and Watkinson seemed disinclined to ratify the move. Notwithstanding their support for Farmerfield, Simon Amm, whose family had the closest association with the mission, demurred on African ownership. Two days before the meeting, Amm informed the committee that he believed it would be "better to sell the property to Europeans rather than natives, as I have a very poor opinion of natives without European supervision."[72] Only the two Africans who had made the proposal voted for it. Foley's and Rwairwai's dream of African freehold tenure at Farmerfield died at this meeting.

Foley and Rwairwai undoubtedly left the meeting disappointed, not even one vote forthcoming from the whites on the committee. At the Conference convened a few months after the committee's meeting, Rhead Marsh sought to have the entire estate sold and the remaining families resettled elsewhere.[73] Foley, Rwairwai, and other Africans voiced their opposition, stating that they had not voted on such an issue in their own meetings and opposed the resettlement of Farmerfield's tenants. The Conference agreed with the Africans' right to vote on the matter, gave them a chance to eventually do so, but reaffirmed the earlier decision to sell three quarters of the estate, leaving the remainder for the existing tenants. Rhead Marsh gained permission to put three-quarters of the estate up for public sale.[74] Rhead Marsh and Watkinson viewed African opposition to the sale of Farmerfield with alarm. "If we do not watch out now and they catch the Conference in the right mood they may take the whole thing out of our hands," Watkinson warned Rhead Marsh, advising him to "SELL! SELL as soon and as best we can."[75] This Rhead Marsh had every intention of doing. Foley and Rwairwai continued to assert their opposition, even writing to the new president of the Conference, Reverend Flint, that the auction should be postponed until the question was reconsidered. The result was a flurry of correspondence that delayed, rather than prevented, the auction. Whatever Africans decided, the matter was out of their hands.[76] "I am afraid it seems," Reverend Rwairwai wrote in a disappointing tone to Reverend Rhead Marsh, "we, as native members of this committee, are after a wild goose chase."[77] Indeed, they were.

The committee faced further problems in trying to sell the estate, especially with the worldwide economic depression of the 1930s. Reverend Rhead Marsh had ended his seven-year tenure without completing the sale of Farmerfield. Another syndicate of Africans tried to purchase Farmerfield, but they too were unsuccessful.[78] Only in 1935 was two-thirds of the estate finally sold for 5,000 pounds, and the interests of the proceeds disbursed for educational stipends and maintenance of church property at Fort Hare.[79] By then, Farmerfield had received its third successor to the post of local minister since Rhead Marsh's tenure had expired in 1929. Harry Weavers, Rhead Marsh's immediate successor, praised Marsh's administration of the mission. Weavers delivered a relatively favorable report in 1930, almost reminiscent of the nineteenth-century views of the mission:

> Thanks to the excellent work of my predecessor, Farmerfield is now a peaceful and happy colony. Several tenants are proving themselves to be energetic and successful farmers. One or two plots are well worth seeing: the splendid crops of wheat in a few cases gladden one's eyes.[80]

As with most of his white missionary colleagues, however, Weavers could not refrain from adding a proviso to any positive assessment of Farmerfield. "The dignity and joy of labor still need to be emphasized to other plot holders," he appended to his praise of the wheat fields.[81]

A century after Farmerfield had begun, the mission stood as but a shadow of the Methodist missionary vision and African request for land that had given birth to it. Thoughts of a prosperous agricultural community and African freehold tenure were unrealized. Tenants had come and gone, with the land now reduced to two-thirds of its former size. The formerly magnificent church of white stone now stood in disrepair, in some ways embodying the story of the mission's fortunes and misfortunes. The estate had maintained its identity as an African Christian mission amid a white community, but this identity no longer made it special. Although thoughts of prosperous African communities still abounded in missionary circles, Farmerfield was no longer showcased as a specific example of what could be achieved if Africans adopted the package of Christianity and civilization. The Farmerfield of 1938 now shared a common history with other African communities in South Africa. The Church proved no different from many of the white landlords who controlled the fate of their African tenants' access to land. Farmerfield's residents had experienced the administrative reviews, disputes over rents, and sale of portions of the estate as encroachments on their rights. With subsistence and residence tied into the package of church membership, they found their behavior as Christians, their ability to pay rent, and their agricultural pursuits, all closely scrutinized. Even with the "energetic farmers," by the late 1930s, the grandest design for Farmerfield was to allow the mission to become a reserve of aged Africans raising their grandchildren, while their adult children sought educational and employment opportunities elsewhere. By capping the population, the Methodist Church hoped the mission would die a natural death. The apartheid government that gained ascendancy after 1948 provided the Methodist Church with a final solution to its problems at Farmerfield. The next chapter of the book explores the denouement of Farmerfield's destruction in 1962.

‖ 8 ‖

Becoming a "Black Spot"

The Removal of 1962

"We should not create a Black Island in an [sic] European area."
—Reverend F. J. Rhead Marsh, *Minister of the Salem
and Farmerfield Circuit, 1926.*[1]

"Suppose Government introduces some sort of segregation legislation and declares that neighborhood a European neighborhood and
tries to clear them all out! Hell!"
—Reverend John Mitchell Watkinson, *Chairman of
the Grahamstown District, 1926.*[2]

In the late 1950s, the eighteen black families occupying Farmerfield heard rumors that the government had declared their community a "black spot" in a white area. By the time the government removed Farmerfield's residents in 1962, approximately 350 such black spots existed.[3] Farmerfield's location amid a white community was its primary distinguishing characteristic in the 1830s when the mission was first established. This geographical feature then represented an important departure from the other Methodist missions established in the 1820s and 1830s and had proven advantageous on several occasions. For example, Farmerfield's position had spared it from the worst ravages of the nineteenth-century wars of dispossession. In their military confrontations with the Cape Colony, insurgent Africans had extended the theater of war to include pioneer Methodist and other missions, which they set ablaze and looted in retaliation. In these wars, local whites had welcomed the loyalty and assistance forthcoming from their African neighbors at Farmerfield.

Between the 1870s and the 1930s, as Africans came under increasing surveillance from the government, Farmerfield's location also proved beneficial. Throughout this period, Farmerfield remained at the margins of legislative attempts to restrict African ownership of land, limit African settlement in urban areas, and circumscribe African tenancy and land ownership in areas demarcated for whites.

In each case, Farmerfield's supervising missionaries had succeeded in exempting the estate from most of the restrictive and discriminatory legislation.[4] The position of the mission as a "black spot" was not lost upon its administrators, however, as highlighted by Reverends Rhead Marsh and Watkinson's statements above. In the 1920s, as the government implemented its segregation agenda, Reverend Watkinson entertained the possibility that the government could declare Farmerfield for exclusive white occupation. "Hell!" was his prediction of the outcome.

During the segregation era, administrative restructuring of the mission impinged more on the tenants' future than government policies, though the Methodist Church kept abreast of government legislation that sought out "black spots" in white areas.[5] By the 1950s, however, Farmerfield's geography brought the mission within the direct purview of the government. Afrikaner political ascendancy, cemented when the National Party (NP) emerged victorious in the 1948 election, heralded an unprecedented period of social engineering whereby each racial group was allotted and restricted to "group areas." The declaration of Farmerfield as an exclusive neighborhood was no longer a supposition. As a "black spot" in a white area, Farmerfield's anomalous geography, which had given it a distinctive history, now became the basis for its residents' expulsion.[6]

This chapter explores the final phase of Farmerfield's history from 1938 up to 1962, when the government resettled the people in Mimosa Park. The chapter asserts that government surveillance of the mission turned the Methodist Church, once resigned to letting the mission die a natural death, into reluctant advocates for the African tenants. When faced with internal administrative problems they translated as impudence from their tenants, the church was willing to reprimand Africans and expel them from Farmerfield. However, I argue that once the tenants faced threats from the government, the church invoked its role of protector and intervened on the residents' behalf. During this period Farmerfield underwent another critical generational change as the residents of the early twentieth century died, passing their tenancy rights to their adult children. It is this generation of residents whose experiences and testimony provide the evidence for the last part of the chapter.

Several generations removed from the first nineteenth-century inhabitants, the testimonies of this last cohort of tenants at Farmerfield nonetheless invoke a connection to Farmerfield that transcends the generational differences. The chapter also engages an observation sociologist Cherryl Walker made in her incisive examination of land reform in contemporary South Africa: the analytical dead zone between the era of dispossession and land reclamation, when rural landscapes and livelihoods underwent significant changes. The steady pace of urbanization has generated a growing gulf between an older generation dependent on, or theoretically committed to farming, and a new generation for which an agrarian lifestyle is often unrealistic. From multiple vantage points as a citizen, academic, activist, and land claims commissioner, Walker asked a crucial question about what happened to the land and the people in the intervening years, about a land reform discourse in which a return to the land is not necessarily a return to farming and about land reform in relation to the government's larger social and economic reform agenda. The restitution of Farmerfield's lands, the return of some its former residents, and the new challenges of postapartheid Farmerfield provide one answer to Walker's important lines of inquiry.[7]

Like their predecessors, the last group of tenants found in the mission a certain sort of economic refuge that was unique in the Albany district. My informal discussions and interviews with the remaining residents revealed that this notion of "economic refuge" did not necessarily involve farming as the sole option, though its sine qua non was land access for a putative future where perhaps money would be sufficient to invest in cattle. Yet the security of their land access up to the 1950s rested on a strict adherence to Christian social norms, including continued attempts to curb circumcision and lobola—struggles that, while epic in nineteenth-century mission discourse, appeared immaterial by 1999. Residence at Farmerfield automatically entailed an ongoing struggle for cultural autonomy, more theatrical than epic. Residents showed public deference to church rules and continued their cultural practices clandestinely. Upon finding themselves free of Christian prohibitions when the government removed them from Farmerfield, however, the tenants longed for the quiet community they had left behind and realized that cultural freedom under apartheid came with its own burdens.

Prelude to the Removal: The Tenants between the 1930s and the 1950s

Between 1935 and 1950, ten of Farmerfield's tenants passed away. Had these deaths occurred in any other time period, they would probably have been reported by the families to the local minister. Since the population of Farmerfield was restricted to about twenty-two families with no intention of increasing the population, however, the deaths took on an added significance. The Methodist Church was waiting for the mission to die a natural death. In practice, this meant when the male plot holder died, the church would "allow the eldest son to come and live on the farm to care for his widowed mother. When she dies the son has to find other pastures. No new squatters are allowed."[8] The tenants' interpretations became evident in their behavior. These ten deaths raised the crucial issue of whether tenancy rights would automatically pass to the adult children of the deceased tenants and if so, how long those children would be allowed to stay at Farmerfield. "The deaths were never reported to the superintendent but each year when the list of tenants was called the representatives of each family gave the father's name whether dead or alive, and unless he was known to the superintendent, his absence would go unnoticed," the native commissioner of Grahamstown discovered in 1952.[9] Fearing the loss of their status as tenants at Farmerfield, and thus their residency rights, some of the families of the deceased lessees left the deaths unreported and assumed responsibility for the land. In this way, the following transfers in land transpired (see Table 8.1):

The native commissioner was perhaps only partially correct in his assessment. Perhaps some tenants continued to use their fathers' names on rent day; yet given the church's close administrative, almost obsessive surveillance of Farmerfield, it seems unlikely that the supervising ministers remained unaware of all of these deaths on the estate. Even with the policy of no new squatters, the local minister still received applications for vacancies and had to decide whether to allow outsiders to fill the spots or choose tenants from the existing resident pool. It seems more likely that the ministers delayed reporting the death of tenants because of the paperwork involved in transferring land access to another family member. Beginning in 1938 the Methodist Church had to ask the government for permission to lease residential rights to the tenants and to claim exemption from legislation about squatters. The addition of any new lessee, even a family member already residing at the mission, required an annual application. The intervention of the government only heightened the surveillance of the Church as discrepancies had to be explained. These renewal applications proved a cumbersome administrative task for Farmerfield's supervising ministers and an implicit challenge to the church's authority over the disposal of the land.[10]

Table 8.1 **Land Transfers, 1935–1950**

Deceased Lessee	*Year*	*New Household Head*
Timothy Mquqo	1935	Son, Alfred Mquqo
James Gaba	1937	Widow Gaba; Son Harrison Gaba
August May	1941	Son, Edward May
John Madinda	1941	Son, Isaac Madinda
Fannie Kopo	1943	Widow, Sarah Kopo
William Rasana	1944	Widow, Sarah Rasana
Thomas Mzizi	1946	Son, Frank Mzizi
Wellington Zatu	1946	Son, Chalmers Zatu
Simon Maxegwana	1949	Widow, Lizzie Maxegwana
Alex Budaza	1950	Son, Welsch Budaza

Source: SAB NTS 2598 102/305, "Farmerfield Mission Lands: Albany District," December 3, 1952.

Upon assuming his duties as Farmerfield's supervisor in the late 1930s, for example, Reverend George H. P. Jacques complained to the magistrate of Grahamstown that the need to renew the tenants' exemptions "imposes a constant condition of uncertainty on the Church with regard to these tenants and equally so on the security of the tenure of the land by the tenants themselves." Having challenged the security of the tenants throughout the 1920s and the 1930s, church representatives now questioned government regulations that had a similar impact. "I should be glad if you would put this disability before the Native Affairs Department with a view to . . . having this exemption put on a more equitable basis," Jacques asked the magistrate.[11] The Methodist Church could easily have used the new restrictive laws applying to Africans to justify the sale and resettlement of Farmerfield's population. Instead, the Methodist Church found itself in the role of a paternal protector, keeping the tenants in line with the rules of the church while mediating on their behalf with the government and filling out applications every year.[12] Some of the missionaries even exceeded the ordinary degree of respect in official correspondence. Reverend Owen R. Thompson, for example, wrote to the native commissioner in 1939 to explain that any mistakes in the number of tenants reported at the estate could be accounted for because compliance with the new laws was akin to "teething troubling attendant on new-born policies. . . . Meanwhile we crave your sympathy and indulgence."[13]

Despite earlier missionary claims that Farmerfield's tenants did not take full advantage of Farmerfield's agricultural capabilities, Africans continued to seek out the mission because it became increasingly difficult for them to obtain independent access to land in white communities without attaching themselves as labor tenants to white-owned farms. Engaging in dissimulation over who was registered as the official lessee versus who actually farmed the land demonstrated how far the tenants were willing to go to keep the government at bay. A century after Africans settled at Farmerfield, mission residence remained one indicator of the relative disabilities they still faced in securing access to land. Under the instrumental Natives Land Act of 1913, approximately 7 percent of the landmass of South Africa was "scheduled" for African occupation.

Solomon Plaatje, who traveled about the Orange Free State region of the country detailing the impact of the 1913 legislation, proclaimed, "Awakening on Friday morning, June 20, 1913, the South African Native found himself, not actually a slave, but a pariah in the land of his birth."[14] Only in 1936 did the government address the inadequacy of such "scheduled" land and additional areas termed "released land" were made available for African occupation in the Native Trust and Land Act of 1936. Together, these lands amounted to approximately 13 percent of the total landmass of South Africa. These instrumental land acts, inter alia, limited the extension of freehold tenure to Africans by prohibiting them from purchasing land outside of the "scheduled" and "released areas," undermined sharecropping arrangements between Africans and white farmers, and delimited areas for occupation according to race.[15] Even with the addition of land in 1936, overcrowding was rife in the reserves. By the late 1930s, legislative attempts to restrict the mobility of Africans in urban areas, limit African purchase of land, and monitor white leasing arrangements with Africans compounded the experience of land dispossession and poverty. Indeed, as Plaatje and the rich historiography of the Highveld has shown, Africans were progressively becoming pariahs in their own country as segregation, then apartheid policies, caught up with the remaining pockets of African land access and sharecropping.[16]

Whereas in the 1830s Africans could retreat to the few remaining independent chiefdoms, this last resort was no longer available as an option in the 1930s. Similar stories unfolded elsewhere across the South African landscape as more invasive government policies thwarted African farming.[17] Given how early the Albany district came to represent trends in nineteenth-century colonial dispossession, African autonomy at Farmerfield still provided opportunities difficult to obtain in the Eastern Cape. At mission stations throughout South Africa, Africans clung to their land claims, even if it meant battling for cultural autonomy from the rigidity of mission Christianity. In dealing with the church, the tenants' poverty placed them in the most precarious position since defaulting on rent often meant expulsion. Yet the church's demands for rent fell within the contractual terms of the leasing arrangements the tenants signed when they moved to the mission. The Methodist Church was overbearing, but it was not capricious. When confronting the government, however, the tenants knew it was primarily their race that determined their fate. Race became the sole criterion that increasingly subjected the tenants to arbitrary laws over which they had little or no control. Throughout the rest of the country, African farmers with more acreage, more oxen, and more family labor than Farmerfield's residents still had their ambitions foiled by white farmers and the white government that penalized their endeavors and rendered sharecropping illegal.

With an ever wider scope of legislation undermining their efforts at maintaining land access, the tenants' reluctance to report deaths and vacancies becomes more understandable. In this way, for example, Frank Mzizi, Harrison Gaba, Isaac Madinda, Chalmers Zatu, Alfred Mquqo, Welsch Budaza (see Figure 8.1), James Hewana, and Edward May all inherited their fathers' occupancy rights at Farmerfield and assumed the position of household head between 1935 and the early 1950s. Contrary to the magistrate's assertions, the supervising ministers had to have been aware of most of these transfers. They kept detailed records of the number of adults, children, and property on the estate, made notations of individuals who were absent on rent days, and also indicated on occasion when tenants were old and infirm. The supervisors even contravened their own rules about letting the mission die a natural death by introducing a few new tenants in the 1940s when spots became vacant. Perhaps this small conspiracy represented both administrative expedience as well as a measure of protection for the existing tenants.

By the 1940s, most of the tenants living at Farmerfield had few blood ties with the mission's nineteenth-century inhabitants. This answers one of the questions about what happened to people in the intervening years between dispossession and restitution: voluntary migrations, death, and expulsions had opened up Farmerfield to new groups of people with diluted ties to this specific land. Still, even if the nineteenth-century ties were weak, many of the tenants' fathers and grandfathers had moved to the mission at the turn of the century. Families like the Zatus, Mquqos, and Budazas had ties going as far back as the first decade of the twentieth century. No matter how difficult it was to maintain a life of subsistence farming, land access remained a crucial part of Africans' survival strategies. Notions of birthright and irredentist claims combined with economic deprivation made land access an emotive issue throughout the twentieth century. In spite of the government's choice to focus on post-1913 dispossessions, colonial and segregation era policies had long set the stage for romanticized, and sometimes millenarian, expectations about land. Despite the years separating each successive generation of tenants from the nineteenth to the twentieth century, Farmerfield's identity as an agricultural Christian community had bound all who had lived there to a common vision and a collective experience.

Like their nineteenth-century counterparts, Farmerfield's twentieth-century inhabitants found it difficult to meet all of their needs through agriculture alone and many combined mission residence with employment in cities like Grahamstown, Port Elizabeth, and King Williams Town, and further afield in Cape Town and Johannesburg. In addition, it became increasingly difficult for existing plot holders to pass their tenancy rights on to more than one heir. The tenants found that once their children reached adulthood and wanted to marry, there was no land available to make provisions for all of them. Several adult men could not remain in the same household and subsist on the same plot of land with their parents. It was common therefore for tenancy rights to pass to one or two adult males; other adult men had to find alternate ways to make a living. Given the limited land at Farmerfield, this was one of the major motivations for male migration. Women's exit from Farmerfield took similar paths with employment and to a lesser extent, educational opportunities, spurring women to leave. But whereas men often moved to Farmerfield with their wives upon marriage, young women at Farmerfield usually married off the estate. By the late nineteenth century, the problems with Shaw's vision of an agricultural peasantry living had become even more pronounced. Since only one or two adult men could gain access to their parents' allotments, and few other economic avenues were available to the children as they reached maturity, leaving Farmerfield was an eventuality that many who grew up there had to face.

Of all the tenants living at Farmerfield in the 1930s and 1940s, Fanati Kopo had the closest link to the nineteenth-century tenants. His parents, Eliza and William Kopo, had moved to Farmerfield in the early 1860s and were baptized as adults in 1864 and 1867, respectively. Fanati was born in 1878, the seventh of eight children the Kopos would bear and raise in Farmerfield.[18] He married another Farmerfield resident, Sarah Daniels, in August 1907 and they remained at Farmerfield and eventually bore nine children between 1907 and 1930. Fanati was just a child when Farmerfield underwent its first administrative overhaul in 1883 and his family was among those who had survived this initial period of expulsions. Even as early as 1915, Fanati was one of few tenants with such deep roots at Farmerfield.

Children born at Farmerfield had, in their adulthood, sought wives, jobs, and other opportunities off the mission. Taking the place of those born at Farmerfield were new tenants seeking access to land, education for their children, and attracted by the total package of school, church, and residence that the mission offered. A few such new residents moved to Farmerfield in the early decades of the twentieth century. Alex Budaza, his younger brother Clifford, and a few other siblings, for example, had moved to Farmerfield in 1900. Three other tenants, James Gaba, January Rooi, and Wellington Zatu, had moved to the mission between 1905 and 1906. Timothy Mquqo had relocated to the mission in 1910. Charles Maxegwana and his brother Simon moved to the mission in 1913. All other household heads at Farmerfield had moved there between 1915 and 1930.

The children and grandchildren of these families—the Budazas, Maxegwanas, Zatus, and Gabas, for example—provide a glimpse of life at Farmerfield from the late 1930s up to the removal in 1962 (see Figures 8.2 and 8.3). Their experiences after removal and during restitution help to paint a mosaic that provides a partial answer to the question of what happened to the land and the people on the eve of removal and during their near forty-year exile from Farmerfield. Their stories touch on themes clearly delineated in the historiography of twentieth-century South Africa, including the ways that African families attempting to maintain land access had to supplement their incomes with off-farm employment; the critical role of women in maintaining the domestic functions of the household while also farming; the persistence of the authority of patriarchs over their adult children; and the delegation of women's land access rights to the adult males in their lives. These glimpses also captured something about the value of quotidian life for Farmerfield's residents.

The wider landscape of dispossession in South Africa made people from far and wide experiment with Farmerfield and try to hold on to claims there even as they sought opportunities elsewhere. Most of the interviewees expressed gratitude for the ability to lead an ordinary life at Farmerfield that harkened back to the havens missionaries from the previous century envisioned their mission stations to be. The decision to remain at Farmerfield was based on conscious, deliberate choices about a certain quality of life and a certain protection that came from having the Methodist Church as arbiter against a landscape in which first segregation, then apartheid-era, policies made their economic options more ambiguous and indeterminate than when natural disasters sometimes visited the region.

When the farm they were living on was taken over by whites, one member of the Budaza family recounted, the family had relocated to Farmerfield in 1900. Like other tenants before them they took the requisite steps to become members of the church and established themselves as one of the families involved in the land claims with the longest history at Farmerfield.[19] It was fortunate that so many members of the Budaza family found accommodation at Farmerfield, but land was not available for all of the men when they wanted to establish their own homesteads. Alex and Clifford established their homes and started their own families there. Alex's older brother Hantjie, however, eventually left Farmerfield to work on another farm. Since women only gained access to land through male family members or husbands, they often left Farmerfield in search of employment. Unless they married a man already living at Farmerfield, women commonly did not spend their entire lives at the mission. Alex's sisters Toggy and Nonatyolo, for instance, left Farmerfield and started their own families in Grahamstown.[20] Alex and his brother Clifford set up their homes at Farmerfield and endured the invasive administrative overhaul of the mission in the 1920s and 1930s. Clifford almost lost his position as a tenant when portions of the estate were sold and left room for only about twenty-five families to subsist adequately on the remaining land. Unable to find alternative residence, Clifford sought a job in Grahamstown to help pay his rental arrears and awaited a vacant plot at Farmerfield.[21] Upon his death in 1950, Alex's residency rights passed to his children.

Between Alex and his brother Clifford, the Budazas had raised and educated fifteen children at Farmerfield. To underscore how central Farmerfield was in all aspects of his life, Buyisile Ivan Budaza, one of Alex's sons, shared his very curt life history with me. "I was born at Farmerfield in 1930. I was brought up at Farmerfield and I was at school at Farmerfield until we were grown-ups."[22] Like other young boys growing up at Farmerfield, Buyisile divided his time between attending school and helping his parents in the fields. Though the work could be arduous and time consuming, young men accepted it as part of their duties and even took great pride in performing their tasks. Tamsana Bangushe, for example, proudly recalled that during his youth he had become a popular leader of oxen at Farmerfield. While plowing the fields limited his and other young boys' playtime, he said he especially enjoyed leading the ox-wagon for special occasions like wedding parties. "In every wedding that was taking place, I was called on to lead the span of oxen . . . from the church to the bride's place," he recounted with enthusiasm.[23] For leisure, young boys would take their dogs along to hunt wild game and comb the forests in search of honey or prickly pears.[24]

Young women had a host of different tasks based on their gender. Mary Jane Maxegwana (see Figure 8.4), whose grandparents had moved to Farmerfield in 1915, stated she had to rise very early in the morning to make coffee and clean before going to school. "After school we rush home," she stated, "if there's washing to wash, I wash it. And after that go to fetch water from the river . . . sometimes if there's no wood, I go to the forest to collect some wood . . . during the weekend . . . I clean . . . we were using something what is called cow dung."[25] Even with all the chores required of young women, being married brought even more burdensome workloads. It was customary for a young married couple to live with their in-laws before establishing their own homesteads, increasing the number of adults who expected services from the young bride. "I had to wake up first and go to bed last; I had to work right through the day—cleaning the house, looking after the garden, hoeing mealie lands and reaping the crops," Nonyameko Mpati recounted.[26] Sylvia Zweni (see Figure 8.2) was particularly evocative in her description of her duties as a married woman, a *makoti*. "Like any married woman," she began, "when I arrived here at this homestead I have my husband. I have the relatives . . . I have to wake up early and make coffee for my father in law as well as my husband. I have to give them [all the men in the household] water to wash."[27] For Miriam Budaza (see Figure 8.3), performing her daily duties became more difficult with small children. "I have to carry a bundle [of wood] on my head; on my back the baby."[28]

Sylvia Zweni pointed out that in-laws relished the status and privilege they gained once a new *makoti* entered the household. Even when supper was prepared, Zweni mused, her in-laws would not dish for themselves under any circumstances. For instance, she said, after returning from the forest her in-laws would never say, "Shame, she's collecting wood. [Rather] they will wait for you so you can dish for them while they're sitting."[29] Despite detailing the heavy workload they had to endure, most of the women accepted that this was part of their role as *amakoti* and looked forward to the day when they could also sit while a younger woman dished for them. Florence Matini also pointed out that *a makoti's* life only partly entailed hard work. Their in-laws provided a level of protection for the marriage itself, serving as arbiters in conflict and ensuring that a man treated his wife well.[30] Most young men saw it as their duty to take care of their parents and obtaining a wife was essential for this purpose. Although both he and his wife were employed in Durban when single, Daniel Matini moved to Farmerfield upon getting married (see Figure 8.5). "My aim was that when I get married, my wife should stay with my parents so that the homestead should have somebody to look after it."[31]

When young men did not marry, wages played an even larger role in securing the necessary services for their parents. With his father deceased, Mongameli Maxegwana (see Figure 8.6) stated that his mother did not mind him being far away at the mines because his income was able to support the household. When their own children got older, women tried to lessen their workloads by delegating chores to them. Sylvia Zweni and Florence Matini noted important generational differences and perhaps some change in women's workloads. Although she acknowledged the legitimate claims on her as *a makoti*, Zweni hoped that when her daughters got married things would be different for them. The hardship was a "rite of passage" for her, yet at the same time she exclaimed, "It is not my wish that any child of mine should have the difficult times like I did have."[32] The hope that their children would have a different experience was a somewhat realistic one. Many new married couples now established their own homesteads independent of their in-laws—sometimes in other towns. While this would certainly lessen some of the work of married women, for other women the escape from working in their own homes meant more toil in the context of working as domestics in white households.[33]

Like their predecessors, the residents in the 1930s combined wage work with some agriculture and pastoralism. They reared cattle and grew crops such as potatoes, cabbage, maize, sweet potatoes, peas, beans, tomatoes, and pumpkins. In hard times people would sell their animals but as one resident, Mongameli Maxegwana, reminded me, "Selling was not the idea, but we would sell whenever there was a need."[34] Nofelity Gaba (see Figure 8.3) and his brother Mongezi both took turns working in Grahamstown and looking after the cattle at Farmerfield. In Grahamstown, they took whatever opportunities came their way—working at a wholesale shop, a pottery factory, and for the municipality. When Gaba got married in 1961, he now had the female labor to take over farming, including weeding, hoeing, and harvesting at Farmerfield. With his wife farming, Gaba now worked steadily in town. For some young men and women growing up at Farmerfield, an agricultural lifestyle proved too limiting in terms of its economic potential and its contribution to their social lives. The adventure of the mines beckoned a few men while many women left Farmerfield to seek wage employment. Grahamstown and Port Elizabeth were the two most common destinations while a daring few sought out Cape Town and Johannesburg. Curiosity, adventure, and the prospects of earning money spurred Mongameli Maxegwana and some of his friends from a neighboring farm to leave home and travel hundreds of miles to work in the diamond mines.

Employment, education, and marriage most frequently spurred women to leave Farmerfield. As in the nineteenth century, when women did find wage employment, domestic service was the main sector where opportunities were available.[35] Although a few fortunate women were able to pursue careers in teaching and nursing, for many others, the options were few once they left school. Without a higher education, domestic service was almost a certainty for many black women in twentieth-century South Africa, as Jacklyn Cock has amply demonstrated.[36] "There was no choice except to go to work; that's all," Murphy Mquqo stated bluntly in her interview.[37] Any education beyond grade seven brought young people to Port Elizabeth and Grahamstown where economic hardships often tempted many to seek work because education was costly and their families still needed financial support.[38] These were also the main urban areas where women sought work as domestic servants since all of the surrounding farms could choose female workers from among the families already employed and living at these farms. It was mainly marriage to Farmerfield men, or care of elderly or ill parents, that kept women who were born and raised at the mission there into their adulthood.

Although many adults left their parents at Farmerfield to seek wage work as primary or supplemental income, they did not forget the important position of Farmerfield as a refuge from landlessness. In the 1930s and 1940s few such enclaves of Africans amid a white community existed. Murphy Mquqo recounted that her father sought a place at Farmerfield because the number of cattle he could own was severely restricted at the farm where he worked. The owner of the farm told her father, "There can't be two farmers on one farm."[39] The Gaba family was attracted to Farmerfield for similar reasons. "At Farmerfield in those days . . . people could have a lot of livestock, as much as he wished . . . and my father liked this place."[40] This characteristic of Farmerfield was not lost upon other Africans who worked on neighboring white farms. Many of these families had moved from farm to farm, sometimes relocating an average of four or five times. Cecil Manona's research on the migration of farm workers to Graham-stown reinforces the testimony of Farmerfield's residents and tenants from neighboring farms. Low wages, poor working conditions, inadequate rations, the death of a family member, the death of the owner, or the sale of the farm were among the variety of reasons spurring African tenants to leave white farms.[41]

Africans living in the vicinity of Farmerfield highlighted important distinctions between lifestyles at the mission compared to the local farms. Elsie Luzipho Mzizi (see Figure 8.7), who grew up on a neighboring farm called Spring Farm and eventually married a Farmerfield man, provided a particularly succinct perspective on how Africans at the local farms viewed Farmerfield:

> There was a big difference between Spring Farm and Farmerfield. At Spring Farm most of the people were red blanketed; they were illiterate. There was no church and there was no school. At Farmerfield it was a place where people were Christianized and schooled. It was not a place that was under the white people . . . [they] were independent. They could plow and they could have livestock. Besides that, Farmerfield was a very quiet place.[42]

Despite the visit of the local minister, residence at Farmerfield involved a certain independence that was not forthcoming on the white-owned farms Mzizi described. Violet Nqqondi added that the educational opportunity available at Farmerfield was the prime motivation for her parents moving there in the 1930s.[43] Whereas school was mandatory at Farmerfield, education on the local farm was a measure of "the goodwill of the farmer, not a right."[44]

On the local farms, everyone—adults and children alike—could be called out to labor. On many occasions, adolescents at Farmerfield were also pulled from school to assist their parents; unlike the local farms, however, the decision remained in the hands of the parents. Living at a white-owned farm meant losing some parental authority over the ultimate disposal of children's time. Although farmers used boys more commonly than girls, Mzizi stated that if the farmer wanted to pull girls out of school to work, "Our parents could not say, 'No.'"[45] Such interruption led to cumulative deficits in children's education; moreover, retention sometimes led to disinterest and high dropout rates.[46] On other occasions, when young men left the farms without seeking the express permission of the farmer, they would not be allowed to return and possibly jeopardized their parents' tenancy.[47] Disadvantages like these made vacancies at Farmerfield prized opportunities to secure a measure of autonomy. Whenever residents envisioned what an alternative life as a labor tenant was like, the sea of white farms around them was a constant reminder of Farmerfield's benefits.

Africans on neighboring farms could also turn to Farmerfield for some of the food they needed. "Since they were their own farmers, we used to ask of each of [them] the things we need," Jayile Saki of a neighboring farm stated.[48] For many of its older residents, Farmerfield's tranquility provided a much needed relief from the hustle and bustle of life in the city. After spending a lifetime working on the railways, her husband Alfred had settled into a peaceful retirement at Farmerfield, Nonyameko Mpati stated.[49]

Concerts, weddings, and sporting events like rugby, soccer, and netball provided leisurely activities for spectators or participants while it also gave the people of Farmerfield a chance to mingle freely with individuals from the surrounding farms and the neighborhood of Salem a few kilometers away.[50] Adults in particular looked forward to the church quarterly meetings when they could see their friends who sometimes lived up to twenty-five miles (forty kilometers) away. On these occasions, Farmerfield residents and their visiting friends would have a festive weekend filled with church and other social activities. Since children and adults from the local neighborhood also attended church and school with the tenants, Farmerfield was a part of this wider social world. These interactions led to long-term friendships and sometimes marriages. They also gave those Africans working on neighboring white farms opportunities to look out for potential vacancies at Farmerfield.

For some of my informants, questions about Farmerfield evoked memories of growing up in a place where Christianity still had a major impact on their lifestyle. The Christian character of Farmerfield lent a certain degree of strictness to the residents' lifestyles that resurfaced as one of the most enduring features of the mission. "You couldn't make beer; you couldn't do traditional customs; anything that was against Christianity then was prohibited at Farmerfield," Buyisile Budaza reminisced.[51] "Fighting and drinking and all those things; the place was not for that," Michael Madinda pointed out when explaining how Farmerfield was different from other farms in the area.[52] All of the interviewees recalled Farmerfield's Christian structure with pride, yet made it clear that they did not share the church's opinions on the morality of certain practices, particularly in venerating their ancestors and performing the circumcision ceremony as crucial rite of passage for manhood. Missionary interdictions on circumcision found no legitimacy among Farmerfield's residents and many cited the Bible as an authority for their own views. "That is the way it had been done; even the Bible states that," Miriam Budaza asserted in her interview. For Budaza and others, the prohibition of the practice seemed even more illogical when they took into account that, "Even the white people are doing this ritual; they are doing it in the hospital!"[53]

For a young man, circumcision was a question of when and not if. As Nelson Mandela underscored in his autobiography, Xhosa manhood was "achieved through one means only: circumcision. In my tradition," he continued:

> [A]n uncircumcised male cannot be heir to his father's wealth, cannot marry or officiate in tribal rituals. An uncircumcised Xhosa man is contradiction in terms for he is not considered a man at all, but a boy. For the Xhosa people, circumcision represents the formal incorporation of males into society. It is not just a surgical procedure but a lengthy and elaborate ritual in preparation for manhood.[54]

The ethnic heterogeneity that had characterized Farmerfield at the outset had changed drastically by the late nineteenth century. Migration had created an increasingly homogenous community so that by the 1930s and 1940s, the vast majority of people living at the mission were Xhosa. The May family were the only remaining Sothos and Rasanas were the sole "Colored" family (Figure 8.8). For most of the Xhosa young men growing up at Farmerfield, therefore, circumcision was a certainty they planned for. "We left school and we tilled the fields until I became a man. I became circumcised,"[55] Buyisile Budaza asserted.

In the late nineteenth century Farmerfield's missionaries had acknowledged that Africans would practice circumcision despite the threat of steep fines and suspension from the church. In the twentieth century Farmerfield's residents found ways to avoid the prohibitions. According to one former resident, Setchaba May, certain rituals were done clandestinely. "Some things were done but they were never given exact names . . . things were never mentioned because of the fear of retribution."[56] Ceremonies venerating ancestors were fairly easy to conceal, with families conducting the slaughter of animals at night.[57] In contrast, the surgical procedure accompanying circumcision, the construction of dwelling huts, and the bedaubing of young men and their long seclusion period required a more elaborate strategy. Employment or visiting relatives could easily explain young men's absences but everyone in the community knew what was happening. Some people thought of hiding huts among the cornfields. "They tried to make some lodges right in their mealie lands so that they cannot be seen by the authorities of the church," Setchaba explained in his interview.

In most cases, however, young men and their families sought places on neighboring farms to perform the ritual. Mtozami and Tamsana Bangushe, for example, avoided the complications of hiding at Farmerfield by performing their ceremonies off the mission. Michael Madinda, however, having spent much of his time in Grahamstown, was not familiar enough with any of the surrounding farms to have his ceremonies performed there. He opted for Farmerfield while his brother chose

Grahamstown. Conducting the ceremonies at neighboring farms held one major advantage: the family and community could still participate and support the young men by bringing them food. It was during one of her trips to take food to the young men that Miriam Siwisa first met her future husband Welsch Budaza.[58] By the time Farmerfield was declared a "black spot," Miriam Budaza proudly noted that she and Welsch were the only young married couple that had established their own homestead there; others still remained with their in-laws. Welsch and Miriam Budaza were one of eighteen families who began considering their options as rumors swirled that the government had now designated Farmerfield a "black spot."

Becoming a "Black Spot"

"Black spot" is one of the apartheid era's panoply of terms signifying the demarcation of land according to race. Yet from its creation in 1838, Farmerfield had borne the anomalous characteristic of being a community of Africans surrounded by a sea of white farmers without depending on them for land access. Even when they battled with missionaries over what it meant to be Christian and what qualified as farming, successive generations of Africans had seen Farmerfield as a unique opportunity to secure access to land. The infamous Natives Land Act of 1913 combined with the colonial policies of the nineteenth and preceding centuries resulted in the widespread alienation of land from Africans. This process was given even more legislative strength in 1950 with apartheid legislation such as the Population Registration Act and the Group Areas Act. These acts, among others, further entrenched African dispossession and reinforced the goal of territorial segregation based on race.[59]

From the 1920s the Methodist Church became increasingly aware of the potential politicization of Farmerfield's geography. The mission's various administrators used terms like "black island" and "black spot" to describe the mission, already demonstrating that Farmerfield's location in a white area was an implicit challenge to the increasingly segregationist policies in the country. As the government expanded its authority over where Africans could live, the Methodist Church expressed some concerns about the future of the tenants, but stopped short of raising any principled objections to the policy of segregation. The Methodist Church itself had long established the principle of segregation both in their evangelical work as well as in their formal administrative apparatus. At the administrative level, local meetings, synods, and conferences were all separated into "European" and "Native" sections. The initial concept of "missions" was predicated on the idea that African Christianity needed to be incubated before it could thrive in the wider "heathen" society. When African Christians advocated for more autonomy and challenged segregation within the church, the Methodist Church balked at these signs of independence.[60]

As the Methodist Church wrestled with issues of authority and power at Farmerfield, the South African government confronted its own administrative dilemmas. African urbanization, agitation for political representation, the growth of a vocal, educated elite, and widespread resistance to white domination all created a sense of urgency among whites in dealing with what the government called the "Native question," or the "Native problem." The result was an increasing number of commissions of inquiry and legislation aimed at addressing various issues such as African urbanization, labor migration, and economic development in African reserves.[61] As historian Saul Dubow aptly stated, "The political turbulence of the 1920s ensured that segregation talk came to impinge more and more directly on the political agenda."[62]

The creation of the NAD in 1910 had already expressed the reality of separate administration of Africans. The Native Administration Act of 1927 gave a measure of uniformity to the more ad hoc approaches. Not only would Africans have their own "reserves," they would have their own government, their own laws, their own courts—in short, giving an even more "statutory underpinning to the cultural dimension of segregation."[63] Through this act, historian William Beinart asserted, "Segregationist politicians sought to 'retribalize' African society in order to defuse national political organization."[64] Even though Farmerfield had long left formal chiefly politics behind, places like it would be zoned according to race and their residents relocated according to their ethnic status. A particular part of the act, section five, empowered the South African government to move people where they deemed appropriate, laying the legal lattice for the forcible removal of people.[65]

After winning the 1948 elections, the Afrikaner-dominated government intensified its efforts to remove Africans still residing in mostly white areas. To accomplish these goals the government used a spate of laws (like the Natives Land Act of 1913, the Urban Areas Act of 1923, and the Native Administration Act of 1927) enacted in the first four decades of the twentieth century as well as amended or passed additional legislation in order to accomplish its goals of territorial segregation.[66] The aim of "black spots" legislation was to restrict African freehold tenure and land access in areas falling outside of the "scheduled" and "released" lands delimited for blacks. Usually these "black spots" were areas where blacks held freehold tenure before the 1913 Natives Land Act—areas that were later demarcated for white occupation. Other types of tenure arrangements, like the rent tenancy established at Farmerfield since 1838, were also found in these "black spots." In some instances Africans held certificates of occupation or other claims to long- term occupancy of the land. In the case of Farmerfield, the residents held no title to the land, but had claims to long-term residence since its purchase in 1838 as a mission station for Africans. From Farmerfield's foundation in 1838 to the removal of its last residents in 1962, successive tenants had paid rent to obtain residential plots, arable fields, and grazing rights. At no point in its 124-year history did the tenure devolve from rent tenancy to freehold. The Methodist Church had gone to great lengths to remind the tenants of this important fact in its administrative reviews between 1884 and the 1930s and had successfully blocked attempts by Africans to purchase Farmerfield from the church. Even if Africans had been able to secure freehold tenure at Farmerfield, the mission would still have been labeled a "black spot."

Rumors started circulating at Farmerfield as early as 1958 that the government would remove the people because the settlement was a "black spot." "It used to be said you'll be leaving Farmerfield and then after some time it gets quiet. And it continues again and then it was kept quiet," Buyisile Budaza, one of the last cohorts of tenants, explained in an interview.[67] These rumors represented the final phase of intense government scrutiny of the mission through the NAD. Despite the acknowledgment in the NAD correspondence that "these families have resided on the farm for over a hundred years" each round of inquiries provided fodder stressing Farmerfield's anomaly as a black community surrounded by whites.[68] Throughout the 1950s the government solicited minutiae concerning the tenants, from their official African and English names and how many goats and cattle they possessed to the depths of their historical connections to the mission. The various local and national officials connected to the NAD asked questions about whether residents were born at Farmerfield and if not, when they first moved there. Government authorities wanted further data on the tenants' marital status, employment, household size, rental rates, and acreage farmed at the mission. The results reveal that most of the families farmed approximately four acres of land and owned between six and ten head of cattle and a few goats.[69]

The NAD collated the information to monitor who was a legal "squatter"—a rather oxymoronic category but one that now made sense according to apartheid logic. The government declared that the tenants legally did not belong at Farmerfield but would be given a legal exemption through the Methodist Church. The NAD also assigned each resident a N. I. N. (Native Identification Number) and solicited information on everyone's ethnic identity. When it was discovered that the majority of the residents consisted of Mfengu and Xhosa with one Sotho family, government officials made further inquiries into the specific Xhosa lineages represented at the mission. Other than one family who noted "Ndlambe" as their lineage, most of the residents noted "Ngqika" as their affiliation.[70]

Each round of probing justified the next steps the NAD took. How, after all, would they have discovered the tenants' conspiracy to hide the deaths, and thus vacancies, at the estate? In a rather amusing exchange, the NAD officials also acted as if they had discovered a major travesty when they realized—from their inquiries—that the "native" school in Salem, close to Farmerfield, was "only 100 yards from the European schools." The Eastern Cape commissioner recommended the closing of the Salem school and for the "native" children from the eighteen surrounding farms to go to the Farmerfield school since the pupils "could just as easily walk the extra distance to Farmerfield."[71] The Farmerfield school accommodated 158 students. Throughout the correspondence in the late 1950s, as the

NAD officials came to understand Farmerfield's anomalous location and learned more details about its tenants, the Eastern Cape native commissioner in particular challenged any attempts to clarify or justify the status of the farm. "The farm in question can hardly be described as land 'held for the purpose of religious instruction.' In fact the farm is merely a squatting ground."[72] In spite of the school catering to Farmerfield's tenants and children from eighteen local farms, the commissioner noted in his "opinion," the phrase "active educational and religious instruction," that described mission institutions was only applicable at boarding schools like Lovedale or Healdtown.[73]

The NAD also tried to discern whether the tenants at Farmerfield had poor relations with any of their neighbors. A local farmer's association reported back, however, that a meeting of local farmers had "absolutely no complaints against Natives at Farmerfield," so that route proved immaterial for impugning the character of the farms' tenants. Before the fateful decision to finally remove the tenants, the NAD also suggested repurposing the farm as a tuberculosis sanatorium. As late as November 1958, these plans were still in the "embryo stage."[74] The random plans for a sanatorium, the glut of correspondence over the status of the farm and its tenants proved confusing for all involved, not least the Methodist Church and Farmerfield's residents. The ultimate authority lay with the apartheid government, which was still trying to combine segregation-era legislation with its own measures to define the exact position of the farm. But the farm was also the private property of the Methodist Church, which had some influence on what would happen to the land and the people. The tenants also had important decisions to consider, their deliberations made more tense by the NAD's decision that anyone who had moved to the farm after 1936 had no residency rights. Among those affected were Barney Matini with his wife and six children; Daniel Matini, then old enough to work; Barney Bangushe with his wife and seven children; and widow Gertrude Kungwayo and her five children. Although the NAD granted these particular tenants temporary relief until they could find alternate accommodation, everyone was rather skittish by this point.[75] After the government decided to remove the tenants, the land went on the market as private farm. By the time the tenants heard firm news of the removal, the disposal of the land, whether as a government sanatorium or as a private farm, hardly mattered anymore. It would come to matter in reclaiming the land four decades later, but in those difficult months leading up to the removal, the question each family pondered was whether they should act preemptively and seek alternate accommodations or wait to see if the Methodist Church and the apartheid government would help them relocate.

In consulting state laws to decide Farmerfield's fate, the NAD pursued several key questions. Did Farmerfield deserve consideration as a mission? If so, the supervising missionaries could ask for particular exemptions, which the Methodist Church made on behalf of Farmerfield. The church was unwilling, however, to take on the expense of paying a fee for the "squatters" as rents were nominal and produced no income to defray the costs they were asked to pay after 1957.

Did its tenants have permission to be in the area given they were five miles from the urban border of Salem?[76] Farmerfield had never been considered an urban area at any time in its history. Yet this law became applicable now in the 1930s as the government sought one pretext after another to deal with black tenants living so close to whites. Did the residents have permission to lease the land since it fell out of the scope of territory Africans were allowed access to after 1913? All of the information the NAD collected led to uncertainty and indecisiveness as regional commissioners received recommendations from their superiors who were still seeking legal grounds within the apartheid legislative framework to evict tenants they considered no more than squatters. The tenants' perseverance throughout the uncertainty demonstrated how few options were left as the apartheid government closed in on the few remaining pockets of black land access in white areas. The ethnographic data collected was the final nail in the coffin. The tenants would be removed to the Ciskei, one of two ethnic homelands demarcated for the Xhosa.

As rumor gave way to reality, distress settled in and people wondered where they would go. The community held discussions among themselves and with the representatives of the Methodist Church. Neither the families nor the church could do anything to prevent the government from proceeding with the forced removal. Alfred Mpati and Walter Siwisa, in their positions as respected leaders at Farmerfield, explored alternate places to settle, injecting a sham sense of community participation into a decision over which they had little control.[77] The government left it up to the community leaders to convince the rest of the people to go along with the decision. The community had no avenues to express their resentment and desperation to the government. Mpati and Siwisa, like other Africans in positions of leadership, received the brunt of the criticism as they tried to get the tenants to accept the removal as a fait accompli and to at least participate in it by visiting the suggested resettlement site.

The people's anguish was compounded by a sense that the community leaders colluded with the government. As he detailed the brewing conflict over the removal, Solomon Mzizi, a member of one of the remaining eighteen families, emphasized how the government tried to manufacture consent through the community's leaders. "There's a hidden story about those who did not want to go. The church leaders are also the community leaders. The government through the church leaders . . . divided the people."[78] Miriam Budaza echoed the same sentiments when she described how the community reacted to the impending removal. "There were the headmen, the people who came to survey the place [Mimosa Park] . . . Others were sad; others were leaving for they couldn't do anything. They had to leave. Others didn't want to leave. They were divided."[79] As in many other instances throughout South Africa confronting removal, the decision split the community at a time when they could ill afford to face such discord. Moreover, with no avenues to voice their dissent to the government, their own community members absorbed the frustration, if not wrath, of the community.[80]

In an attempt to make the removal more appealing, Farmerfield's supervising minister D. J. Crankshaw reminded the people that they would no longer be under the jurisdiction of the Methodist Church. "The way that Crankshaw approached those people was traditional," Napthali Mbozanani, the current preacher at Farmerfield, related. Hoping that the lack of Christian proscriptions would be enticing, Crankshaw reminded them that at the new settlement they could follow their "traditional ways."[81] The people were given several choices, some say as far away as Cape Town. After visiting three places, the community leaders decided on Mimosa Park, which offered 633,6325 hectares of land ten kilometers (six miles) outside of King Williams Town.[82] A few individuals opted to go to Grahamstown rather than relocate, including the Rasana and Mzizi families as well as most members of the Madinda family.[83] In 1962 the government packed the eighteen remaining families onto trucks with their household belongings and moved them to Mimosa Park. The eighteen families of Farmerfield, surrounded by a sea of white farms, were among approximately 614,000 people who were forced to move between 1960 and 1983 because they lived in places labeled as "black spots."[84]

In the years leading up to the removal, the mood at Farmerfield was uneasy. It had begun with the rumors of removal, then the certainty. Most people had accepted that they could do little about the situation and some were proactive in leaving so they could exert some control over the decision. Those who awaited the arrival of the government trucks remained perturbed. Was there an actual date for the removal? Would they be compensated? Different dates were mentioned for the removal to begin, dates as early as 1961. In December 1960 government representatives visited the estate to assess home values and determine compensation rates. There is no record, however, of any compensation paid to Farmerfield's tenants. In this tense atmosphere the tenants were also told that the government would transport only thirteen horses and seventy-seven head of cattle and were left to decide amongst themselves whose cattle would be included and who had to sell their cattle or bear the expense of their transport. After the cattle was removed, officials warned the community that "any day now there would be trucks coming for us."[85]

The Removal

No one at Farmerfield could forget the day the government trucks came to transport them and their belongings to the government relocation site at Mimosa Park on February 9, 1962. The sound of tires on the unpaved gravel and dirt road leading to Farmerfield betrayed the presence of the incoming trucks—which people called lorries—to the residents long before they arrived at the first house. After several years of bickering amongst themselves about possible relocation sites, the community had accepted its fate; they had even prepared carefully for the trip. They had alerted family members far and wide—some working nearby in

Grahamstown, others as far afield as the diamond mines. A few weeks before, the young men at Farmerfield had begun the initial stages of the move. They had driven the cattle some twenty-two miles (fourteen kilometers) on foot to Grahamstown. Navigating the first six miles (nine kilometers) was easy as they only had to pass neighboring farms. Thereafter, the journey was a treacherous game of dodging traffic on the main highway and the men spent countless, frustrating hours trying to corral the enervated, thirsty cattle. Once in Grahamstown, they boarded the train and accompanied the animals to King Williams Town, then continuing on foot to Mimosa Park.[86] Man and beast were languid by the time the journey was over.

Solomon Mzizi, whose family along with the Rasanas (see Figure 8.8), had opted to leave Farmerfield in 1958 rather than wait for the ignominious moment of removal, remembered the men in Grahamstown. "I watched their stock being loaded on the train. I can still hear the bellowing of the cattle as if they, too, were protesting."[87] During that painful day, the residents of Farmerfield undertook a heart-wrenching event that was repeated in countless other places throughout South Africa between the 1960s and 1980s. In other provinces, the number of people removed was larger than the community at Farmerfield, and the removals sometimes resulted in violent confrontations. Yet, the overall sense of injustice and the indignity of the removal was a common thread binding communities in a common South African tragedy.[88]

Although the residents of Farmerfield had been forewarned about the move and had begun the initial stages of preparation, they could not prepare for the rush of emotion they would experience as the trucks approached. Wailing and screaming pierced the landscape and residents lamented as they tried to expedite the dismantling of their houses. Former residents of Farmerfield testified that despite the prior notice, the move was still haphazard and impersonal, with the truck drivers showing no particular interest in facilitating the move for the people or giving them sufficient time to get their belongings together. People were ordered to fill the trucks with as many belongings as they could and as quickly as possible. "It was hard work, I can tell you," Buyisile Budaza stated as he recalled the day the trucks came. No one was particularly satisfied with the time allotted for each household to load its belongings. "What was happening then, we had to take down the house and put the belongings and everything just in front of the homestead while the truck is busy loading somebody else."[89] Many people had to wait until the very day of the removal to break their houses down to salvage as much of the building material as possible; they would have been exposed to the elements had they broken down their houses before that day.

Once the lorries passed the residences near "Middelplaas" (Middle place), the area closest to the church that had always served as the center of the mission, they moved on to Elisuthu (the place of the Sothos), the area closest to the Assegaibos River that ran through the Farmerfield estate, and then "Emakhobokeni" (the place of slaves). Only the names grafted onto Farmerfield's landscape recalled an era when Africans of all different ethnic backgrounds, speaking multiple languages, lived in one community. Farmerfield had left this multiethnic history behind to become a Xhosa enclave, but its location still challenged apartheid principles. With the enactment of the Bantu Authorities Act in 1951 and the Promotion of Bantu Self-Government Act in 1959, the apartheid government laid the groundwork for the creation of ethnically based homelands, or "Bantustans," where Africans, stripped of their South African citizenship, were relocated according to ethnic criteria. Under these grand apartheid schemes, the inhabitants of Farmerfield, which had evolved into a predominantly Xhosa community, were now going to be resettled in the Ciskei, one of their supposed ethnic homelands.

Sylvia Zweni, who had moved to Farmerfield only in 1960 when she got married, attested to the sorrow that overcame the residents as the trucks approached. "You know the place called Elisuthu, when you get just down there by the river," Zweni motioned with her hand during her interview, "We could hear people crying from the church."[90] Another resident, Florence Matini, stated that on the day of the removal, "There was bitterness, cries around. Some of them were crying and one who was exceptionally crying was [Ida] Budaza, the wife of Clifford Budaza."[91] Describing the procession of trucks, Petrus Zatu exclaimed that it was like "a sad wedding. All the mamas were crying, really crying," he added.[92] To make matters worse, because of the hills and valleys that characterized the landscape, people could see the lands and homes they were leaving behind. Some areas would come into view, then disappear for a few hundred meters and then reappear. Farmerfield may have been a shadow of its nineteenth-century legacy, but for these eighteen families, it still conjured a specific space, place, and idea. Residents bid farewell to the places where they skinned their knees, stubbed their toes, where a wagon overturned, and wayward cattle were corralled; to the paths that led to local farms where they visited friends, the shortcuts they took to fetch wood and water. They left behind spaces that held sacred memories—the first foundation stones for a house, the school, and the church that was the center of community activities, the burial sites of their predecessors and their loved ones. Farmerfield's former tenants could only take with them a few belongings and their memories and visions of what their community was like.

Sylvia Zweni had a particularly difficult time that day because her young daughter was ill and had to sit at the back of the truck and endure the arduous eighty-mile (130 kilometer) trip to Mimosa Park. Other people had a difficult time because they were elderly and were being uprooted from a settled situation into one that was not only unfamiliar, but challenging to their health and their livelihood. The vulnerability of their elders proved an indelible memory as people found themselves planning or attending one funeral after another. "Our old people died one by one," Mbulelo Mquqo noted in his interview.[93] Many of the other former residents interviewed also made references to older people succumbing to ill health during the first few years they were living at Mimosa Park. Undoubtedly, the former residents became more susceptible to opportunistic infections because they had to endure the cold, rainy season without proper shelter when they first got to Mimosa Park. Many ran short of food while they waited to reap their initial crops, aggravating their difficulties. Even healthy individuals in their thirties and forties when they moved to Mimosa Park attributed their current ill health to the early difficulties of settling down. "The place remained wet for almost two years and that had damaged our health," Nonyameko Mpati asserted in her interview. Mbulelo Mquqo was the most emphatic of the interviewees when explaining the deleterious effects of the relocation on his health. "When I still was at Farmerfield, I was a very strong man with no problems about my health. But when I came down to Mimosa then my life, my being, my health got ruined."[94]

The most consistent image of Mimosa Park that surfaced in the interviews was of a forest. The first thing that came to mind when she saw Mimosa Park was "bush veld," Nonyameko Mpati stated. Similarly, Mbulelo Mquqo, who had left his job in Grahamstown for a short while to assist with the removal, described this scene when the trucks arrived at Mimosa Park: "It was just a mere forest." The government had done nothing to accommodate them and the community did not have the financial means to obtain building materials before the move. "There were only bushes around here," Buyisile Budaza recalled of his first impression of Mimosa Park.[95] Mongameli Maxegwana, who was working at a diamond mine when he got news of the removal, also thought of a forest when he finally made it to Mimosa Park. "It was no man's land, a forest; no houses were seen," he stated. Mongameli's cousin, Mary Jane Maxegwana, who was living in Grahamstown by the time the people were removed, went to Farmerfield to assist on the day of the removal. When the trucks arrived at Mimosa, she declared, "There were thorn bushes and everything! There was not even a site where you can say that this is my place." The trucks that transported them to Mimosa Park, according to Maxegwana, were "tipping lorries." That the trucks could expeditiously unload the residents' belongings and leave them to fend for themselves only reinforced their sense of injustice and despair. No specific plots of land were demarcated for the eighteen families. "They off load your things and your furniture and they just dump you saying that this is your property."[96]

Daniel Matini, currently the assistant headman at Mimosa Park, became particularly irate when he remembered the injustice of the removal. "We were just like slaves when we arrived here," he asserted. "There was no place that was prepared for us and there was no promise that anybody was going to build up or construct something like a house; and you had to sort for yourself and as you know that the first thing is the stomach . . . they were starving very much."[97] There was no road and no allotments demarcated.[98] The tenant could not imagine worse circumstances. For a removal that was discussed and debated, and where tenants chose the relocation site, the fact that Mimosa Park seemed the best of all given options spoke volumes.

Torrential rains made the physical removal and resettling much worse. Men scurried to establish makeshift accommodations and women did their best to create temporary spaces so they could cook, feed everyone, and calm the fears of the young children. Suddenly, every mundane decision from where to sleep, dress, cook, urinate, defecate, bathe, and hang nappies, took on epic proportions. The relocation and the rather stark condition of Mimosa Park introduced a level of personal indignity that incensed everyone. Rain delayed the construction of living quarters and destroyed many of the people's belongings. Settling in was very difficult, Sylvia Zweni explained. "It was hard, you see. It was so long that even the furniture we brought around here in those days got destroyed by the weather."[99] Mbulelo Mquqo also recalled, "We kept our belongings under bushes and some were damaged. And then we managed to take our iron sheets and make some tents out of them."[100] Even under the best of weather conditions, living in makeshift tents would have been uncomfortable. The wet weather exacerbated a bad situation and lengthened the time people took to establish new homes.

The residents of Farmerfield arrived in Mimosa Park with meager resources. They participated in the theater of removals performed throughout South Africa with bureaucratic ease, despite moral condemnation and protest. Like their counterparts throughout the country, their main possessions were their fields, crops, livestock, and homes. They had to go to Mimosa Park with the minimal of building materials they could salvage from their houses and no crops. None of the planning that had gone into the removal had considered what would happen to the people dumped on the veld. To make matters worse, the cattle started dying. The long trek to Grahamstown and again to Mimosa Park had weakened the cattle. "They were thirsty; they were hungry . . . so they died," Petrus Zatu declared emphatically. Moreover, once the cattle made it to Mimosa Park, they could not thrive on the type of grass available. All of the former residents interviewed stated that they had some problems with their cattle. Even those that survived the initial trip died in the ensuing years. "Most of our cattle died when we arrived here," Mbulelo Mquqo stated sadly during his interview. "Most of them died and we couldn't replace them. As you can see that the mealie lands, nobody is touching the mealie lands because there are no cattle to drag the plows," he continued.[101]

Nofelity Gaba was particularly aggrieved about the outcome for his family. Knowing the risk the cattle faced from the transfer to Mimosa Park, he and his brother Mongezi sold most of their animals and went to Mimosa with just ten head of cattle; they had planned to restock. Even after attempting to rebuild his herd through local purchases, the new cattle still adjusted poorly. "We had a big problem, most especially myself because I was just buying and sending them [cattle] over," Gaba sighed. "In Farmerfield I can assure you, goats and cattle are good, and in Mimosa they die like flies. Not a one [survives]!" Gaba exclaimed as he recalled his many losses at Mimosa Park.[102] Other people sold their cattle in Grahamstown before they came to Mimosa Park to hedge against total loss but quickly found their cash reserves depleted and faced the same problem of how to plow without sufficient cattle.[103]

Although the quality of arable land at Mimosa was excellent, Daniel Matini pointed out, the grazing land was unsuitable for the cattle and most of the animals fared poorly. The only alternative to ox-drawn plows were tractors, a very expensive option few people could afford in the 1960s or in the late 1990s when I interviewed them. "The reason why I don't till my fields is because I don't earn enough money to feed myself and my family as well as to get a tractor to till for me," Matini explained.[104] Almost everyone at Mimosa Park experienced the same hardship. Even when production had stagnated at Farmerfield throughout the 1930s, 1940s, and 1950s, most people noted that their families' wages provided for their basic subsistence needs; even beyond the basics, wages were also sufficient for periodically reinvesting in cattle. During the most difficult economic times at Farmerfield, cattle herds proved a reliable investment, provided milk, and could be sold quickly if an emergency cash need arose. Mimosa Park exhausted all of these conventional coping strategies with few safety nets. Cash remittances from family went into acquiring building materials to address the immediate housing crisis; cattle restocking also proved unwise in the short run.

By almost any measure, Mimosa Park was a poor choice, in the tenants' recollection. Housing construction proceeded in a piecemeal fashion as cash-strapped residents added one room, then had to wait months or years to begin another to accommodate their families' needs. The government waited five years to begin road construction, and farming languished. Resentment and the sense of personal indignity lingered. Msewu May's sentiments captured the general views of the tenants: everything about Farmerfield seemed qualitatively and quantitatively better than Mimosa Park:

> We had bigger lands at Farmerfield. The river was running there. Pools were never dried up. There was nothing scarce at Farmerfield and even the livestock was excellent. When we were at Farmerfield, we never knew that you could take something and sell to somebody. You know that you could just give to somebody. Like if there are pumpkins, you just give pumpkins . . . you don't sell at Farmerfield. There's no water here. We are starving here. The schools are very far from us.[105]

Msewu May was not alone in detailing Farmerfield's advantages, both in absolute terms and in relation to Mimosa Park. The difficulties of settling in at Mimosa Park certainly influenced many people to reflect on Farmerfield with nostalgia. When asked about what they liked or remembered best about Farmerfield, interviewees recounted far more than romantic reminiscences, however. Farmerfield's former residents invoked a particular moral and economic universe that involved a specific set of rights and obligations tenants owed each other as members of a community, as neighbors, and as congregants of the Methodist Church. They also spared no reproach about how the church had failed them in their penultimate years at the mission.

Although Farmerfield's former tenants understood and accepted that the Methodist Church could do little to stave off the "black spot" removals policy of the apartheid government, they chafed at how church representatives had cunningly cloaked the removal in the garb of "tradition." After generations of staunchly enforcing strict rules on the customary practices of circumcision and *lobola*, the church now coaxed their congregation to accept resettlement because they could practice the very traditions the church thought unbecoming of African Christians. What the tenants remained uncertain about were the origins of what they considered an opportunistic and craven strategy, if not a duplicitous one. For some, responsibility clearly rested with the current minister, D. J. Crankshaw; for others, it was the larger church administration of which Crankshaw simply happened to be spokesman. One interviewee pointed out that minister Crankshaw was furious about the decision.

Notwithstanding some ambiguity about the position of the church in the oral histories as well as the church's own records, what was unanimous among the tenants was a sense that this moment represented a low point in the Methodist Church's handling of Farmerfield's affairs. The subsequent inaction of the church confirmed their views that the Methodist Church had taken the easy way out by blaming the government and by not making any attempts to facilitate the resettlement or even provide assistance with building another church. When faced with further discord among the ranks of tenants, interviewees also concurred that the church delegated the ultimate responsibility for this decision to "traditional authorities." Farmerfield's elders bore the responsibility for convincing the people to go to Mimosa Park. Furthermore, by not making any plans or inquiries into building even a rudimentary church at Mimosa Park, the tenants announced that the church had "thrown them away."[106] Such sentiments, expressed during a visit in 1981, prompted a search through the church's records for what exactly had been promised.[107] As late as June 1981, nineteen years after the removal, a letter from the circuit steward in Uitenhage clarified, to what appeared to be his relief, that although the church had assured Farmerfield's tenants they would receive comparable land, "No church building had been promised."[108]

Even without any formal church premises, Christianity remained central in the former tenants' conception of community, but the actions and inaction of the Methodist Church and the absolute deprivation of Mimosa Park sparked an important reevaluation of their lives. Without church supervision, Farmerfield's former tenants reassessed the meaning of Christianity as an expression of faith and as a lifestyle, and reconsidered the meaning of community. In the process, they became more certain of who they were in the context of both the grand nineteenth-century visions of Farmerfield and the disillusionment and disappoint of the twentieth century. Farmerfield's white supervisors in the twentieth century may not have had anything salutary to say about the tenants' religious commitment. In their assessment, however, those ministers overlooked how Christianity informed the tenants' notions of community and shaped their moral universe in a far more enduring way than was evident if they only looked at the metrics of church attendance or fidelity to traditional customs. The African Christianity William Shaw cultivated at Farmerfield bonded its tenants to certain ideals notwithstanding their challenges to rigid church rules and restrictions on their tenancy rights. Of the more than thirty missionaries posted to Farmerfield throughout its storied history, only Shaw had nurtured grand ambitions for the mission. The peasantry ideal may have been thwarted, but his enduring vision of Farmerfield as "a truly Christian village," was evident as Farmerfield's tenants—now without a church—summoned ideals of community and morality based on their identity as Christians. In the context of Mimosa Park, Farmerfield's former tenants now demonstrated more clearly how strong those bonds remained and how much it still informed their contemporary notions of community.

Despite their disappointments with the church, tenants also reconsidered the secular benefits the church provided aside from access to land. The Methodist Church had provided a measure of security and discipline they now found difficult to recreate or enforce at Mimosa Park. While the community had been able to ensure conformity to basic moral sanctions at Farmerfield, "security" had come largely through the restrictions the Methodist Church placed on residency and their vigilance about squatting. The perennial advice from outgoing white ministers to their successors at Farmerfield was, "You have to watch for squatters." [109] Farmerfield thus remained a closed community because the church closely scrutinized the residents. Notwithstanding the restrictions on their ability to settle their children and family members at Farmerfield at will, most of the interviewees acknowledged that the cumulative effect of church supervision was to keep the boundaries of the community clear. Mimosa Park, however, became a more open community. After the initial eighteen Farmerfield families had settled there in 1962, people from the local area slowly started filtering into the community. With no real authority to deter them, new families joined the core of Farmerfield's former tenants and found them to be both reluctant hosts and guarded sympathizers.

The Christian legacy of Farmerfield veered sharply from the open community that emerged at Mimosa Park as new residents arrived. Rather than generic complaints about "spiritual apathy" or "lapses into 'heathenism'" that had characterized missionary complaints about Farmerfield, the tenants engaged in frank and specific critiques of how commonplace alcohol, smoking, and stealing had become at Mimosa Park. Where the church and school were once intricately interwoven in people's lifestyles and daily activities, Mimosa Park had neither accommodations for school nor church services; and now some of the Farmerfield people were drinking and smoking like the new residents. The addition of new people to the core of Farmerfield's resettled tenants created sharp divisions between the two groups of residents and brought both the idealized images of Farmerfield into sharp relief.

Within this context the Christian tradition of Farmerfield served as a moral critique of Mimosa Park. As Nofelity Gaba pointed out, "There's always a problem between those ex-Farmerfield people and those ex-farmers around here. And you see both think they are better than each other. There's always a conflict."[110] Anderson Budaza dichotomized the fault line as one between "red-blanketed," unchristianized people and the Christian tenants from Farmerfield. Mongameli Maxegwana (see Figure 8.6) concurred. "At Farmerfield, nobody was a thief, but here all the time you have to watch your belongings," Maxegwana complained.[111] Even Miriam Budaza, who more than any of the other interviewees emphasized that she has found a sense of community with the local people settled at Mimosa Park, acknowledged that the moral landscape and sense of security was drastically different from that of Farmerfield:

> If you look at the mealie lands, those are the things we don't admire. When we came here we had out mealie lands properly fenced using wire . . . At night we don't know what happens to the fence. When we wake up the fence is not there; these people come around and steal the fence . . . That had never happened at Farmerfield.[112]

Summarizing this crux of the conflict, Maxegwana said of the new tenants, "They said they were born here and we are foreigners."[113] In considering the boundaries locals were now drawing, most of Farmerfield's former tenants agreed yet defended their rights at Mimosa Park.

All of my formal and informal interviews with former Farmerfield tenants took place against the backdrop of a land reclamation suit they filed, the subject of the final chapter. After almost a year of visiting with Farmerfield's former tenants, most of the interviewees pushed me beyond this initial foray into the early years at Mimosa Park. My interviewees urged me to move beyond a focus on the relative merits of the settled community at Farmerfield compared to the "virtual forest" of Mimosa Park. The government had dumped them in a desolate landscape with no accommodations and no plans for social services or amenities; the church as an abiding symbol, a source of refuge and a benefactor, had abandoned them. Any relocation site with these shortcomings would be a poor choice. That everyone recalled the 1960s with despair, however, was only one part of the story.

The multiple and nuanced meanings people attached to land in apartheid's dumping grounds were also crucial parts of the narrative, perhaps even more so with land reform on the agenda. With locals trickling into Mimosa Park and apartheid dispossessions continuing apace, Farmerfield's former tenants now sought ways to assert the legitimacy of their occupation. People from the local area believed that because they were indigenous to the area they had more valid land claims than the Farmerfield residents. They too had suffered forced removals and racial discrimination had generated similar hardships for them. Whatever their particular economic or employment situation, finding residential space was paramount for Africans as influx control laws restricted residence in major urban enclaves. This vein of the conflict highlighted how apartheid-era removals had intensified land struggles between Africans so that even a "no-man's-land" like Mimosa became prized, contested territory. People from the local area believed that their own experience of land shortage should take precedence over that of new settlers. Even as they lambasted the apartheid government, therefore, Farmerfield's former tenants now had to defend as valid, claims on land allotments made to them through unjust removal policies. What happened to the land and people, Cherryl Walker asked? Land maintained its ability to provoke powerful and conflicting, irredentist claims; apartheid dispossessions rend African communities in new ways after resettlement, and set the stage for problematic fault lines in the land reform agenda.

Amid growing tensions, Farmerfield's former tenants acknowledged that both they and the locals were all victims of the apartheid government. Despite a genuine legal claim on Mimosa Park, they were indeed "foreigners." The solution most of the Farmerfield people agreed on, but could not enforce, was for everyone to "live in a Christian manner." Rather than a call to faith or denomination per se, this represented a more generic wish for the cohesion and mutual respect evident at Farmerfield. Residents from both groups crossed paths, developed common interests, and built friendships. Others remained aloof and viewed each other with suspicion. With neither side able to impose its will or its vision, relationships developed in a piecemeal, individual fashion. By the 1990s, with the option to leave Mimosa Park for Farmerfield now official, the mission's formers tenants also found little consensus among themselves. The youth and young married couples dumped at Mimosa Park were now the elders. Many of their own children had now grown up, had ventured far afield for education, employment, and marriage, and had mixed feelings about Mimosa Park and no particular attachment to Farmerfield.

Tasked with deliberating a momentous return to Farmerfield and with staking legal claims that would impact the next generation's access to land, the elders steered the interviews toward a deeper understanding of Mimosa Park's and Farmerfield's symbolism. In considering a return to Farmerfield, the designation of Mimosa Park as a "poor choice" and the memory of a past injustice informed people's sentiments about their potential return, yet proved wholly insufficient bases for such an important decision. The removal from Farmerfield and resettlement at Mimosa Park were now cautionary tales that raised crucial new questions about land reform. Would elders suffer a precipitous decline in their health? Would they have to forfeit the land claims at Mimosa to return to Farmerfield? Would their children have legitimate claims to the land at Farmerfield if they chose not to settle there? Would they be financially compensated for their houses at Mimosa Park? Could some family members maintain their homes at Mimosa Park, while others resettled at Farmerfield? At the time of the initial interviews, none of the answers to these questions were certain as the court awaited a response from the two white farmers who owned Farmerfield.

As the former tenants weighed their options and sought answers, the two white farmers who now owned the Farmerfield property also pondered how land reform would affect them. For the first time, the property resembled its pre-1838 status as the sole property of white farmers with more acreage, easier capitalization, and access to credit and markets than any of Farmerfield's previous tenants. This is by no means a simple story. Historian Colin Bundy has called for "more rounded histories of white landowners" in the early twentieth century as the 1913 Natives Land Act caught up with black farmers and tenants.[114] We can no more cast the histories of white farmers in broad, facile narratives than historians did with white missionaries in the past. Engaging white farming history through oral accounts or with the anthropological lens the Comaroffs employed in their groundbreaking exploration of non-Conformist missionaries in southern Africa is outside the scope of this book. Still, Bundy's observations are also part of the answer to Cherryl Walker's query about the land. Farmerfield's lands reverted to exclusive white ownership, which by the 1990s meant that their owners were among the thousands of white farmers impacted by the market-driven land reform agenda of the postapartheid government implemented on the principles of willing buyer, willing seller, and fair market compensation.

Whatever the outcome of the court case, all of the former tenants had to reassess their lives at Mimosa Park and decide how they would participate in the land reclamation process, and ultimately, if they were going back to Farmerfield. The contours of conflict among residents at Mimosa Park impacted the land claims process that unfolded in the 1990s. At Mimosa Park, people forged new relationships with locals against the backdrop of new tensions about who was an outsider, who was local, and who was foreign-born. In this formerly barren, poorly conceived resettlement zone, residents engaged in new conflicts over the meaning of legal claims versus local claims and beyond the broad parameters of race and ethnicity that had originally brought Farmerfield tenants there. Many yearned for Farmerfield as a tranquil place where Africans could be autonomous, practice agriculture and pastoralism, where neighbors respected each other's property, where they could draw the boundaries of who belonged to and could live in the community, and where the church acted as a form of cultural and spiritual mooring. Many welcomed the opportunity to attend church services even without formal church accommodations rather than travel far distances into King Williams Town to worship. Farmerfield's former tenants brought all of these moral, spiritual, and economic visions to bear on their experiences at Mimosa Park. For some residents, it had taken a long time but they had finally settled in; for others, Mimosa was still exile. Miriam Budaza had proudly declared that she and her husband Welsch were the only young couple to have established a household independent of their in-laws by the time of removal in 1962. More than forty years later, she and her husband were now among the elders confronted with questions of resettlement on completely different terms and feeling ambivalent about the process.

‖ 9 ‖

Reclaiming and Resettling Farmerfield

In 1990 Solomon Mzizi and Patrick Hewana, whose families were included among the last group of tenants at Farmerfield, began exploring the possibility of land restitution for the eighteen families removed in 1962. The Mzizi family had left voluntarily in 1958 to resettle in Grahamstown rather than await removal, while some members of the Hewana family had opted for Mimosa Park.[1] Inspired by the changing political landscape of South Africa in the 1990s, Mzizi, Hewana, and other people sharing Farmerfield's heritage began serious discussions about the possibility of resettlement. The removal of the ban on African political organizations like the African National Congress (ANC) and Pan African Congress (PAC), and the release of Nelson Mandela after twenty-seven years of imprisonment, signaled to people throughout the country that political negotiations would soon transform South Africa.[2] While the political aspiration of seeing South Africa finally ruled by blacks was coming to fruition in the near future, many people focused on the more immediate concern of land restitution.

To say that the transition to ANC rule awakened new hopes and aspirations would be an understatement. Africans coupled their vision of political freedom with high expectations of social and economic transformation. To be effective, political freedom also had to address apartheid-era legislation underpinning black poverty and landlessness. Even during the apartheid era, dispossessed communities had continued protesting the illegitimacy of resettlement. Africans who had been forcibly removed from their lands, those living in overcrowded homelands, and labor tenants who endured poverty and exploitation on white-owned farms all looked to the government for redress. The newly elected ANC government acknowledged from the outset that land reform in the guise of restitution, redistribution, and compensation was central to the process of the socioeconomic development millions of South Africans anticipated after the historic elections in 1994. Old and new NGOs, lawyers, and community representatives took center stage in a new drama where expectations ran high, economic and political mandates were ambitious, and the bureaucracy was initially slow. Communities awaited news and white farmers held out for just compensation.

Since 1994, land reform has been a veritable cottage industry for academia and the media.[3] From shack dwellers living on the outskirts of or near major urban centers and women in rural areas, to farm workers concerned about the security of tenure and individuals expecting to return to particular communities from which they were forcibly removed, the land reform process has had to address diverse forms of landlessness and poverty. Scholars, journalists, community organizations, NGOs, think tanks, and a host of other organizations have acknowledged that the land reform debate has shifted in the eighteen years since the ANC came to power.[4] Most of the analyses share the consensus that the negotiated settlement leading to the first elections and to ANC political ascendancy occurred in the context of significant compromise about maintaining the sanctity of private property. These compromises, with the goal of maintaining political and economic stability, constrained what the government could actually accomplish, especially in terms of redistribution. In the nascent stages of legislating and adjudicating claims while navigating its role as the first postapartheid administration, the ANC government faced significant obstacles with the slow pace of restitution. What the government described as "institutional restructuring, policy formulation and legislative reform" appeared to claimants and the landless and their advocates to be incompetence and ineffectiveness.[5] Balancing the expectations of its constituencies and the fears of those who especially found fodder as they looked north to Zimbabwe's expropriation of white farms and to attacks on local white farmers, created a thorny political landscape.[6] Moreover, notwithstanding the emotive power of land, for millions of landless people, the solution may not necessarily be found in a return to land.

Farmerfield's reclamation captures some of the crucial issues shaping the land reform process in contemporary South Africa. Farmerfield reveals that land restitution is far more than the postscript that bookends the narrative of loss and restoration. Armed with the belief that an African government could redress the legacies of colonial and apartheid-era land dispossession and impoverishment, many communities are finding, as academics predicted, that legislative overtures are insufficient in redressing the tremendous losses people sustained in the last century. The ANC government recognized during the initial phase of implementation that restitution without development would sap the reform process of its ability to truly empower people. Still, it was slow in delivering the housing, infrastructure, and economic aid people desperately needed to make the "success" stories indicative of more than courtroom victories. The case of Farmerfield highlights how, throughout postapartheid South Africa, Africans confronted the bittersweet realities of a painful and slow process of socioeconomic transformation.

The Restitution of Land Rights Act provided one of the major legislative backbones of land reclamation in contemporary South Africa. Promulgated as Act No. 22 of 1994, the Land Rights Act aimed:

> To provide for the restitution of rights in land to persons or communities
> dispossessed of such rights after June 19, 1913, as a result of past ra-
> cially discriminatory laws or practices, to establish a Commission for the
> Restitution of Land Rights, and a Land Claims Court, and to provide for
> matters connected therewith.[7]

Through a commission that receives and facilitates claims and a Land Claims
Court, claimants whose lands were expropriated were given the legal means for
redress. Eighty-one years and several generations had passed since the infamous
1913 Land Act. Applicants had to file their claim between May 1, 1995, and May
1, 1998. The Land Claims Courts could take up to five years to confirm and settle
all claims and ten years to enforce court orders. From the outset, these official
guidelines hardly satisfied demands for and expectations of speedy restitution.
Constitutional clauses on compensation at market value further undermined and
constrained what the commission and Land Claims Court could do on its own. As
individuals used the new administrative apparatus created to address land claims,
new problems became apparent.[8]

Assessing the progress of the restitution process in 1999, for example, the Department of Land Affairs (hereafter, DLA) acknowledged among other difficulties,
"the protracted nature of the adjudicative process, the complexity of the investigative process, limited financial resources and intra-and inter-community disputes . . . which can delay the finalization of claims for years."[9] By moving for more
administrative settlements and using the court to negotiate the more contentious
claims, the various provincial and regional offices handling restitution cases
cleared a significant bureaucratic bottleneck. By the end of March 2007, the government had made significant strides toward addressing the backlog of restitution claims associated with the 1913 Natives Land Act. Of the total 79,696 claims
lodged, 74,417 had been settled—representing an astonishing 93.38 percent.[10]
This figure represented a reorienting of settling claims through administrative
rather than judicial means and using the court for problematic claims where the
parties needed legal intervention. By 2010, the new figure was 75,844.[11] While
government reports do contextualize the official numbers, the statistics often
mask the more complicated meanings of settled claims.[12] Only in disaggregating
the numbers, as Ruth Hall has duly noted, can the provincial and local perspectives, the role of cash compensation compared to land restoration, and the distinction between urban and rural claims be understood. Moreover, counting
claims can be a misleading metric for gauging the progress of land reform, especially when individual households were sometimes counted as one claim, rather
than the group claim they more accurately represented.[13]

Despite these impressive figures, the DLA acknowledged that in terms of its
overall goal of transferring 30 percent of white-owned agricultural land by 2014
(now revised upwards to perhaps 2025), it was sorely laggard, having only
transferred 4.3 percent.[14] The department recognized that it needed to ensure a

smoother collaboration between and integration of the central, provincial, and municipal arms of the government to "scale-up the pace of delivery and maximize the developmental impacts of land reform."[15] The plight of farm workers, especially the alarming rates of farm evictions, the empowerment of women, and the integration of development projects within the larger framework of the wider economic development objectives of the country all featured prominently as areas that still needed significant attention.

Despite the difficulties of the restitution process, the 1994 act provided an important tool for the National Land Committee (NLC), a nongovernmental consortium of organizations dedicated to assisting people with issues of land reclamation, land use, resource allocation, and development.[16] Even before the promulgation of the Restitution of Land Rights Act in 1994, communities that were forcibly removed from their lands, many assisted by the NLC and its affiliates, were already exploring various avenues for reclamation. Demonstrations as well as appeals to the courts, the government, and to various churches featured among the strategies different communities employed.[17] A group of Mfengu who had been removed from the Tsitsikamma area in the Eastern Cape had already taken the initiative and had won their restitution claim.[18] Solomon Mzizi, Patrick Hewana, and others, motivated by the Tsitsikamma victory, sought a similar outcome for Farmerfield. They approached local Methodist clergy for advice and assistance since Farmerfield was a Methodist mission when it was declared a "black spot." With no tangible results forthcoming from the church, they enlisted the help of a local legal aid organization and an NGO: the Legal Resource Center and the Border Rural Committee.

Like thousands of other claims, impoverished and underprivileged communities sought assistance from local legal centers and NGOs to reclaim their land. Anyone criticizing the initial slow pace of land reform in general and restitution in particular needs to place the critique against the backdrop of the bureaucratic organization and paperwork required to get the infrastructure of the DLA operational and to substantiate claims. To submit Farmerfield's claim required a dizzying spate of research through the various relevant government legislation that authorized the dispossession and resettlement—including the 1913 Natives Land Act, the Development Trust and Land Act of 1936, the Promotion of Bantu Self-Government Act of 1959; and the specific provisions of the Restitution of Land Rights Act of 1994 that framed the right to return to Farmerfield. All of these laws revealed the variety of "tenure" arrangements that encompassed places like Farmerfield. Whether the tenants owned the land or paid rent, research substantiating the land claim acknowledged that the key characteristic of the areas the government zoned as "black spots" was their location in a white area.

The DLA had to verify that Farmerfield satisfied the provisions of the restitution guidelines. After this initial verification, researchers then had to obtain information from the state archives in Cape Town, Pretoria, and Port Elizabeth from the files of the Department of Bantu Administration and Development to supplement data available from the Methodist Archives at the Cory Library in Grahamstown. Finally, researchers had to collect a labyrinth of legal documents such as deeds, certified copies of powers of attorney, and identity documents.[19] Most of the claimants could have never filed a land claim without the indefatigable research of local legal aid organizations. The overall progress in researching, verifying, and settling claims was thus closely related to staffing capacity of the government bureaucracy aided by a host of NGOs.[20]

Through these circuitous avenues, Solomon Mzizi and Patrick Hewana, as community liaisons, assisted with the collection and collation of information and formally lodged Farmerfield's reclamation case in court on February 15, 1996.[21] In relation to some other claims, Farmerfield was easy since most of the potential claimants still resided at Mimosa Park and those who lived in other locales because of employment could be easily contacted through their family members. Official public notice to all relevant parties appeared in the government gazette a few weeks later on March 8.[22] By December 1997, a local newspaper reported "a very significant victory," when the Land Claims Court ordered the restitution of Farmerfield's land. In the context of the Eastern Cape, the Farmerfield decision was noted as "the first for a province where the court has given back lost land rights to claimants who were not only dispossessed but forcibly removed from serviced and viable agricultural land to a barren stretch of veld with no services."[23] Farmerfield was also a first in terms of gauging how "expropriation" of the land, now owned by white farmers, would take place as a legal and financial transaction.

By the time of the land claim, Farmerfield was divided into two portions, both owned by white farmers. John Michael Mullins owned a large portion comprising 506,9020 hectares, while Lawrence Raymond Riddin held the remaining 252,5899 hectares. By 1999 the government had appropriated Mullins's property for the Farmerfield land settlement and compensated him. Expropriation of the Riddin farm raised issues of water access and whether the government would set the rate of compensation for the land before the official expropriation. In the language of the court, the issues rested on whether the court had the "necessary jurisdiction . . . to determine the question of just and equitable compensation payable to a landowner in respect of land to be expropriated for purposes of restoration prior to, at the same time, or as in the proceedings relating to, the issuing of an order to expropriate the said land."[24] The court finally adjudicated on November 23, 1998, almost a year after the original decision, finding that the court could not "determine compensation" before the land was taken. With no clarification on the amount of compensation, however, the Farmerfield Trust Committee could only communicate further delays to the people waiting for news at Mimosa Park.

While the "willing buyer, willing seller" clause calmed some fears about a whole scale government grab of white-owned land, it also contributed to significant delays in restitution cases. Even in Farmerfield's case where the concern was not an adversarial stance of the white land owners, the negotiations showed that even among the most cooperative of whites involved in the land reform process, fair, equitable compensation was a major sticking point. But exactly what that land value was in relation to the contemporary land market and in relation to the state subsidies white farmers received as well as their own investments in and improvements to the land was a difficult formula on which to reach a consensus. Like Farmerfield's owners, other white farmers agreeing to be "expropriated" without knowing how compensation would be determined were nervous about what they would get in the end. Most analysts have pointed out that whites involved in the restitution process in the early phases have been able to obtain exorbitant compensation from the government; in addition, the attempts to empower individual Africans or communities to compete on the open market to purchase land has been slow since whites still have the competitive advantage. Even when the government has stepped in to change the stakes on the land market, they also have not been able to meet their goals. Even as South Africa moves away from appeasing the international community—for example, the likes of the World Bank, which endorsed the "willing buyer, willing seller" principle—the alarmist views of the international community still appear prominently in global media coverage of land reform. Much of this coverage still uses Zimbabwe as a worst-case scenario for South Africa. Even when these accounts feature some positive assessments, they still often succumb to facile statements and shallow reporting. Take Marian L. Tupy's 2006 *Washington Times* article, for example, which concluded that "having a perpetually aggrieved population may be in the African National Congress' interest. That way, the ANC can use the landownership issue in the elections and divert public attention from the government's failure to fulfill many promises made during the last go-round."[25]

At the center of such legal claims was the issue of who had a right to reclaim the land. Only those people who were physically removed in 1962 became legitimate claimants in the 1990s. Anyone taking the initiative and finding alternate residences beyond Mimosa Park before the trucks actually came had forfeited a right to Farmerfield. In this context, Patrick Hewana pointed out in his interview, it is even more important to follow "the correct channels for reclamation."[26] For example, since the Mzizis left in 1958, they were not legally eligible to return. The handful of families who voluntarily left Farmerfield in the late 1950s and up to the removal in 1962 mostly settled in Grahamstown where their other family members were established. Few desire to resume their lives at Farmerfield, so their ineligibility has not created too many difficulties. Finding some concordance of interest and agreement was manageable since only eighteen families were involved in the original removal, which resulted in fifty-six claimants in 1996. This was hardly the case in some larger-scale removals involving claimants from different religious or ethnic backgrounds.

For removals that included several hundred or thousands of people settling, the issue of legitimacy created new conflicts that bedeviled the restitution process, delaying the adjudication of claims as well as postsettlement developments.

In the Tsitsikamma case that originally inspired Solomon Mzizi and Patrick Hewana, for example, the "community" claims involved a complicated division and conflict between the "Fingo/Mfengu" claimants and the neighboring Clarkson Moravian mission residents whom the apartheid government designated a "Colored" community. Under apartheid, both communities faced different trajectories as the government dispossessed the "Fingo/Mfengu" individuals in 1977 and left the "Colored" mission residents to occupy the land. These separate historical paths now played a crucial role in the 1990s in delineating the claims both groups made to the land with the government, the Moravian Church, NGOs, lawyers, and fragmented communities engaged in complicated negotiations to balance historical claims and contemporary land needs.[27]

Farmerfield's representatives avoided this conflict by presenting a united ethnic front. Since the Xhosa comprised the overwhelming majority of individuals at the mission in the twentieth century, the land claimants faced none of the sorts of conflicts evident in the Tsitsikamma claim. Farmerfield also stood apart from other land claims in the burden of proof they had to share. As residents of a mission station, Farmerfield's settlers proved easier to trace than people at other types of settlements who relied on oral evidence to support their claims. Methodist Church records facilitated the claim Farmerfield's residents made against the government to secure land in the possession of Riddin and Mullins. In other instance of land reclamation, the lands claim court became the arena for people to restage debates over irredentist claims to land on multiple grounds. At Farmerfield, the language of religious commonality and official residence at the mission legitimated the former tenants' land claim.

Going Back to Farmerfield?

For some of Farmerfield's formers residents, regardless of how many years they have lived at Mimosa Park, the history of their settlement there remains tinged with the painful, visceral memories of removal and being dumped in a virtual forest during heavy rains. In revisiting some of the case studies associated with the Surplus People's Project, Cherryl Walker and Deborah James have noted how emblematic memories of removals many decades ago have become in the reclamation process. Claimants invoked these memories to recreate narratives of dispossession that legitimized and cemented their calls for restitution.[28] In their interviews, Farmerfield's former residents pointed out that it took them two, five, or even more years to reestablish themselves. For others, the four decades since their removal were irrelevant and they conjured popular metaphors of biblical exodus and exile that other claimants throughout the country used to describe their removal.[29] Even after forty years, Mimosa Park will never feel like home for some. "To me, I'm not settled even today," Murphy Mquqo declared solemnly in 1999.[30]

By the time I conducted the first interviews in 1999, the changing political landscape of South Africa had made the possibility of returning to Farmerfield a realistic hope, not simply a lament about a past injustice. Almost four decades after they were removed, many of the former residents remained nostalgic about Farmerfield. "I wish that I can move now," Mbulelo Mquqo also asserted during his interview. Similarly, Mongameli Maxegwana declared that he was "so glad when I heard that we are going back."[31] When asked about how she felt about going back to Farmerfield, Florence Matini's eyes lit up. "Don't even ask me! I'm here—even if they can say today," she replied excitedly.[32] In their initial enthusiasm, Farmerfield claimants shared the same exuberance of the thousands of other claimants—the kind of jubilation that the government tried to capture in photographs they include in their annual reports and other publications. Initial excitement was just a phase, however. Unlike the original removals, people now had time to perform a cost-benefit analysis of resettlement, weigh all of their options, and make individual decisions to suit their needs.

Although many people wanted to go back, the Farmerfield Trust Committee tasked with facilitating the claims and canvassing the community members about their needs and concerns found no consensus on a mass removal to Farmerfield. The passage of almost forty years generated new concerns and multiple fears about resettling. Interviewees pinpointed a number of issues, some of them based on generational differences: the vulnerabilities of ill-health and old age; the economic and social appeal of urban centers like Cape Town, Johannesburg, Port Elizabeth, Grahamstown, and King Williams Town as alternative residences; practical concerns about hardships because of poor access to clinics and hospitals; the feasibility of farming both in the current economic landscape where either oxen or tractors are crucial for tilling the soil; the economic challenges single women may face as farmers; finding local employment; the dire economic prospects for young people who are neither interested in subsistence nor commercial farming; the emotional estrangement of most of the younger generation from Farmerfield; poor roads, housing, transportation, and amenities; and the availability of schools. All of these pragmatic concerns dampened the enthusiasm of the former tenants and influenced their deliberations about what reclamation would mean for them individually and as part of a family and a community.

When asked about going back, Mary Jane Maxegwana, currently living in a township outside of Grahamstown, repeated the question to me with raised brows, laughed, then asserted strongly that her days at Farmerfield were long gone. "No, I don't want to go back; uh uh, because those days we used to have some oxen to plow our fields. They are going to be given fields there. Who is going to plow for me? There's no more oxen. You must hire oxen now, which costs money."[33] As an unmarried woman, she said she fiercely guarded the economic independence she had secured since leaving Farmerfield and getting a job at a local supermarket in Grahamstown. Unlike her unmarried cousin Mongameli, who is pleased about the prospects of returning, resuming an agricultural lifestyle at Farmerfield without the availability of male labor made reclamation an unattractive option for Mary Jane.

The Maxegwana cousins cautioned me against reading too much into their different stances on resettlement. Their positions reflected the opportunity costs of resettlement, and how secure they felt in their current accommodations. With neither spouses nor pensions to supplement their incomes, relocation could be risky. Affection for, and allegiance to, Farmerfield need not be expressed in resettlement, they both suggested. Moreover, the ambivalence about Farmerfield was commonplace long before there was ever talk of their eviction to Mimosa Park. Even within one family, as educational and employment opportunities siphoned off young residents, people held mixed feelings about Farmerfield as a space, as a place, and as an idea, as well as about where Farmerfield fit into their future strategies to secure housing and land access. Some people left Farmerfield and never looked back, relinquishing their land claims with no romantic flourish. Others, like Mongameli, left Farmerfield for years, working far and wide—as far as the diamond mines—assuming they would resettle eventually.

Most people who moved to Mimosa Park in their late twenties and thirties now felt they were too old to resume the lives they had at Farmerfield or risk any new ventures. Getting transportation to King Williams Town ten kilometers nearby was enough of an expense, much less the whole-scale removal of a family, cattle, and one's belongings all the way to Farmerfield. Miriam Budaza was adamant about not resettling for pragmatic reasons and also elaborated on the importance of maintaining her current social networks, even in death:

> [A]t my age, it won't be easy to start a new life because once I get to Farmerfield I have to start from scratch. I'm old. I can't go back. I can't be young. . . . To me, it's better to die here because most of the people around Mimosa know me a lot; and if I do happen to go back to Farmerfield and I die there, the people at Farmerfield [from the local farms and Salem area] would say we don't know her very much; she's from Mimosa.[34]

Similarly, Nonyameko Mpati stated somberly in her interview, "I've got an apathy to go back because of old age and ill-health."[35] Most of the interviewees also explained that the difficulty of watching their elders die at Mimosa Park as they struggled to resettle gave them reason to pause now that they were also elders. Even with the assurances of government houses and amenities like water and electricity, resettlement seemed too taxing a prospect in old age. While many people feel too old to return, a younger generation of individuals who either moved to Mimosa Park when they were small children or who were born at Mimosa Park feel disconnected from Farmerfield altogether. Moreover, young people in general are hesitant about cleaving to rural areas like Farmerfield with few employment prospects. Explaining her children's perspective on the return to Farmerfield, Miriam Budaza pointed out, "Three daughters are married in the surrounding area and four sons are working in Cape Town. Now they don't want to hear anything about going back to Farmerfield. They don't want to hear because they don't know it."[36]

The contrast between Mimosa Park as an open locality free of any Christian regulations and Farmerfield as a strict Christian community is perhaps one of the major reasons why so many people are so keen to return and so apt to resume the life they left behind almost forty years ago. As Miriam Budaza explained:

> It is the incoming of foreigners that make other people to be hesitant of staying here. These people are coming with the ideas and ideology—ideas like having rituals, brewing beer, beast killing or cattle killing or things like that; things that were not done at Farmerfield. So these people would love to go back to Farmerfield and be Christians as they were before; that's why others are forcing [sic] to go back to Farmerfield. They want to remain as they were when Farmerfield existed.[37]

Almost all of the Farmerfield people expressed discontent with community relations at Mimosa Park. "Those people are very notorious," Mongameli Maxegwana declared as he described how their crops and fences were stolen.

Anderson Budaza was particularly vocal about the acrimonious relationship between people from Farmerfield and others who joined them at Mimosa Park. "This place was allocated to us," Budaza began, "but as we used to say to them, 'Okay, you can come in.' Now they are so many that they want to overtake us and they want to have power and they want to give rules and regulations here." Reflecting on Farmerfield's relationships with their surrounding farms, Anderson Budaza further declared:

> You know when we were at Farmerfield the people from the surrounding farms were very docile. We didn't see them as foreigners. We stayed with harmony and peace. But now when we get here to Mimosa, there's a lot of misunderstanding. There's a lot of conflict between us, the Christian- ized and the people that are unchristianized. Those people that don't attend church, they call the people that attend church *amaqoboka*, meaning Christians. Those that are Christianized call them *amaqaba* [unchristianized].[38]

When I attended church services at Mimosa Park, many of the Farmerfield people were noticeably absent. Some people expressed relief that moral policing was now done by their peers, not by any local, white Methodist minister. Among their own peers and elders were local preachers who stated plainly that even the Farmerfield people were far from the ideal Christians, but emphasized that it was primarily the contact between Christians and non-Christians that was the corrupting influence.

The changing character of the Farmerfield people made Mary Jane Maxegwana question the rosy picture painted of the return to Farmerfield. "I don't know whether they are still going to like it; but I don't think they are going to stay the way we used to stay there before . . . they are changed now," she stated. "They are not the way they used to be in Farmerfield because they are mixed now with different kinds of people . . . Farmerfield was a very quiet place. Now they are involved in most of the things that they didn't used to do such as drinking. Yo! They drink a lot now. Yo! and fighting!"[39] Most of the interviewees, however, remained assured that the actual return to Farmerfield, the distance from Mimosa Park, and the serene atmosphere of the rural Salem and Farmerfield areas would encourage their peers to conform to the sort of disciplined life they once led.

Many of the people who moved to Mimosa Park in their adulthood were now pensioners whose children shared few of their memories of Farmerfield and little of the enthusiasm about going back. For the elders, uprooting themselves once again and facing the prospects of living alone held too many possibilities of financial hardship, if not disaster. An undercurrent of fear about forfeiting land and their homes at Mimosa Park without finalizing their claim to Farmerfield also provoked concerns about the security of their legal claims. Nofelity Gaba, for example, spoke at length regarding his concerns about getting compensated for his large house at Mimosa Park if he goes back to Farmerfield. "You see I am still in doubt . . . I couldn't say that I am going back to Farmerfield or not because the first thing that I have in my mind, I've just completed building that huge house as you have seen." Gaba showed me around his home and explained that it had taken him several years to build it; it was finally the right size and in excellent repair. Even if he put the house up for sale, it would not be a straightforward issue of getting back the money he invested in the house. "Even if I want to sell it, nobody is going to pay me cash," he states. Rather, "somebody will pay me a certain amount and then I'll be going up and down asking for the remainder of the money which is also going to cause me quite a lot of trouble going back and forth to go and demand my money." Although, as he made it clear, "My heart is in Farmerfield," leaving Mimosa Park was a complicated decision. It's hard to justify it overnight. I have to think . . . before I can decide."[40] Far more than romantic memories and land were at stake.

Land claims at Farmerfield and discussions about the pragmatism of resettlement also centered on irredentist claims to land. Unlike the claims at Tsitsikamma that centered on distinct notions of ethnic and racial identities, these claims involved multiple discourses on birthright, rather opaque "nativist" claims about being local to the region, amid the legal claims based on past history of dispossession. Just as the people of Mimosa Park who had joined the eighteen families of Farmerfield invoked their birthright to cement the legitimacy of their settlement, so too did Farmerfield's former tenants assert their claims to the mission as their birthplace.[41] Yet neither the claim to birthright nor even the problems with the influx of new residents at Mimosa Park compelled everyone to consider resettling at Farmerfield. Another area of concern was not so much forfeiting existing rights to Mimosa Park, but a final forfeiture of land and the potential end to family legacies by not going back to Farmerfield at all.

Nonyameko Mpati lived at Mimosa Park from 1962 until 1990. Eventually, concerns about her health and standard of living made her seek better accommodation nearer King Williams Town. "I am worried about the issue of going back. I did not want that the name of Mpati stop at Farmerfield."[42] Though she will not return, she would like to maintain her legal claim. Nonyameko and others facing this dilemma are considering sending one or more of their children to represent them at Farmerfield, though few young people are interested. By not returning to Farmerfield, Patrick Hewana pointed out, "People who are staying at Mimosa are doing so at their own risk as they don't have title to the land [there]."[43]

In addition to insecure tenure at Mimosa Park, a general unease also tinged everyone's deliberations about the meaning of going back or not going back to Farmerfield. This unease was grounded in what happened to those families who left Farmerfield preemptively in the 1950s to avoid the government's unceremonious removal. Many of these families had good reason, based on what the government had done in other cases of eviction, to believe that the resettlement may not be orderly no matter how well they coordinated and planned. They were correct; the result, however, was that the tactical decision to move on their own terms voided all subsequent restitution claims. Whatever the final decision about Farmerfield, former tenants still at Mimosa Park had to consider all the serious ramifications of their decisions.

Despite the poignant, wonderful memories of Farmerfield that land reclamation evoked, the initial euphoria about the legal claim gave way to the realities of another uprooting and raised legitimate concerns about the security of land tenure. In the heady days of the immediate postapartheid era, no one understood exactly how land reform would unfold beyond the formal legal process. People placed tremendous faith in the "government" and sometimes misread the land reform landscape when they took newspaper reports about early cases like Tsitsikamma as models of success. Newspaper accounts sometimes missed the contested notions of "community," conflicting claims, class, and other kinds of divisions that reappeared in the reclamation process. The word "community" glossed over other group and individual needs such as that of women, Africans, tenants excluded from the official reclamation process, or people rerouted to pursue their claims on their own. In short, the land reform process left millions of landless people with no clear guidelines for how to constitute themselves to advocate for their needs.[44] While local NGOs working with claimants were aware of these challenges and the DLA bureaucracy also acknowledged these obstacles, misperceptions among dispossessed and landless peoples still led to high expectations of the government.

At Farmerfield, a decade passed after Patrick Hewana and Solomon Mzizi began their initial inquiries in 1990, gathered the necessary information, and filed the legal paperwork. By the time Farmerfield's claim was settled, the DLA (renamed the Department of Rural Development and Land Reform in 2009) had acknowledged that restitution without infrastructure and economic development would do little to radically alter people's lives. No one wanted to return to the land with inadequate housing, few amenities, and no economic development plans in place. Mbulelo Mquqo stated that the people were waiting for the government to compensate them for their property at Mimosa or provide housing for them at Farmerfield, which still stood bare of any edifices besides the church and school in 2001. He was hopeful that the property appraisals conducted at Mimosa Park would result in tangible resettlement assistance unlike the case in 1962. As the months dragged on with no concrete plans, those who were initially hesitant became even more exasperated. The only certainty and consensus in the community was that no one would set foot on Farmerfield for permanent reoccupation until the housing project was completed.

Resettling Farmerfield

Farmerfield's claimants eagerly awaited meaningful information on which to base sound decisions about housing and development against the backdrop of rather complicated bureaucratic developments in postapartheid South Africa. The ANC government attempted to synchronize its overarching national goals while granting the provincial and local governments the resources and autonomy to pursue their objectives within the larger framework. With everyone from the World Bank, the United States Agency for International Development (hereafter USAID), the United Nations (UN), think tanks, NGOs, and new citizens weighing in on the blueprint for South Africa's economic development, however, coordinating all the data, ideas, and debates posed a new challenge in itself. Even with the indefatigable efforts of Patrick Hewana and Solomon Mzizi in Grahamstown, the new government bureaucracy, the new acronyms, the new lexicon, still seemed impenetrable to Farmerfield's claimants and sapped people's political optimism.

Government officials, departments, municipalities, and politicians all struggled with a dizzying array of projects, plans, programs, proposals, and postulations. Constituencies and target audiences watched, understood, and engaged these developments in fragmented ways. Everyone's learning curve was steep. Academics argued that in addition to the economic and other divisions within the communities filing claims, certain claimants had the resources and networks to mobilize assistance. Almost two decades into land reform, the mercurial politics and daunting economic landscape remained. No matter what milestones the ANC government accomplished, their development and land reform objectives seemed like a moving target and international and local and criticism persisted. Throughout the country, some claims moved to the "post-settlement" phase in a reasonable time, some with spectacular ceremonies marking the legal victories. Others languished in limbo between compensation and resettlement. In other instances, some of the rural claimants soon reported that, with insufficient post-settlement support, agricultural production was low or nonexistent and many farms were reported in "distress."[45] Farmerfield revealed several angles to this phase of the land reform story. Revisiting the meaning of its geographic location in the Eastern Cape provides some clues to the contemporary challenges the restituted community now faced.

Of South Africa's nine provinces, the Eastern Cape with 6.5 million residents is home to 13 percent of the total population of 48.5 million people.[46] While 86 percent of the provincial population is African, 7.5 percent is "Colored," and 5 percent is white, with Indians accounting for less than 1 percent of the population. Only 2.9 percent of the province's population works in the agricultural sector. Despite this small percentage, a 2009 report aimed at advising provincial policy makers asserted that this sector remained a "vital" part of the local economy because of the preponderance of Africans as a part of the province's population and given the primacy of subsistence farming and farm employment in sustaining African households. Disaggregating the data at the municipal and household levels demonstrated how crucial farming employment and food production was in supporting the livelihoods and subsistence of most African households throughout the region. At the household level, the majority of the Africans in the Eastern Cape relied on agriculture (providing more than 50 percent of household incomes or supplying the main food source), but significant portions of this population represented low-skilled workers. With the government's renewed economic agenda focusing on supporting the farming sector and meeting broad goals aimed at poverty alleviation, this detailed report provides an important lens into the challenges rural areas in the Eastern Cape like Farmerfield faced.[47]

Even with a small part of its overall economy dedicated to agriculture, the dependence of so many African families on farming incomes and subsistence places the return to land in a different perspective and presents the provincial and national governments with crucial questions about how they envision the agrarian economy in relation to the rest of the economy. Analysts may observe that many people want to move to the urban areas and that the younger generation is disenchanted with farming. However, with unemployment hovering between 20 and 30 percent or higher in the Eastern Cape and with the housing shortages in the urban areas, the aspirations of some people to return to the land seems no less feasible than the desire to move to town and find employment. Stark rural lives have their counterparts in urban desolation. Encouraging rural residents to relocate to town to take their place as part of a vast urban underclass is a dead-end solution. Debates that pit an African and a white farming sector against each other also provide little guidance on how to move forward. The traditional white farming sector, whose profitability and viability was predicated partly on government subsidies, the exploitation of African labor, and the insecurity of farm tenants can hardly be the current litmus test for whether an African agrarian sector can now be developed to boost both subsistence and commercial agricultural production. Similarly, using the state of farming endeavors in the former bantustans now reorganized as parts of different provinces and municipalities also provides little in terms of a way forward. Here, the reform of communal land tenure and the provision of more equitable terms on which women access land are crucial.

As Farmerfield moved from the status of settled legal suit into the resettlement phase, questions about access to clean water and electricity delayed housing construction. Figuring out which municipality would be responsible for Farmerfield affairs, as well as establishing a water account and electric meters all prolonged resettlement. These delays meant that initial euphoria about reclaiming land gave way to frustration with the government about the slow pace of development. Adrienne Carlisle, writing in *Dispatch*, headlined a June 6, 2000, article on Farmerfield as: "56 families stranded as land deal stalls." The article noted that "Bureaucratic inertia has stalled a major land expropriation deal near here [Grahamstown] for almost 18 months."[48] At Mimosa Park, a few people waiting on news about the houses stated that they understood how daunting a task it was for the new government to try to address apartheid's wrongs. With much amusement, Mongameli Maxegwana stated in his interview, "The only thing that gives us hope is the fact that they have mentioned to us that whenever you are dealing with government matters, they don't take a short time; they could take a while."[49] For him, a "while" could be a year or two, a few years, or even a decade. However long it took, however, he was determined to be there.

The *Mail & Guardian* reported on January 28, 2006, "A 56 household community of Farmerfield that was removed in 1962 and dumped at Mimosa near King Williams Town has been restored to their original land." Copying verbatim from the report of the Department of Land Affairs, the article continued, "This restoration marked the construction of 56 houses. The Farmerfield community was a victim of the consolidation of the Ciskei homeland as well as the whitening of rural South Africa, when they were forcibly removed from their ancestral land near Grahamstown to Mimosa near East London." By relying solely on the DLA's report, this kind of journalism elided what it took to get through certain stages of the reclamation and resettlement process. The newspaper report missed, for example, the many years since inklings of restitution first stirred in 1990, how the claim was filed in 1996, and how only a part of it was adjudicated in 1998 as the land owner refused the initial offers for part of the land. It skipped the deliberations at Mimosa Park about who would or would not resettle and how the paperwork on Farmerfield listed different claimants for the housing project than those noted in the legal paperwork at the land claims office. In addition, it omitted how local NGOs partnered with USAID to file for a housing project in August 2000 and, finally, it neglected the frustration with the delays and the challenges once people began resettling.[50]

Former tenants like Mongameli Maxegwana, with a stalwart commitment to Farmerfield, may have had the patience of the biblical Job in awaiting the construction of houses. When the houses were finished, he was among those who opted to stay in Mimosa Park. Unlike the unsurprising choice of most of the members of the Budaza families to remain in Mimosa Park, for example, Maxegwana's decision was somewhat more unpredictable as he was one of the ones certain of his return. Many of the Budazas, notwithstanding their poignant memories of Farmerfield and worries about the mixed and perhaps lax community at Mimosa Park, were ambivalent at best. The senior members of the Budaza family, upwards in age of seventy, eighty, and ninety, made pragmatic decisions. Miriam Budaza had put it best when she said, "the government keeps on promising this year they are going to move; next year they are going to move; and the years pass and I'm growing older and older."[51] As Hall has noted in her analysis of the land reform in South Africa, understanding the meaning of restitution meant probing beyond the decisions of the Land Claims Court.[52] Farmerfield was one demonstration that legal restoration had little effect on who would actually resettle and the potential success of resettlement.

Unlike Miriam Budaza, Mongameli Maxegwana's reasoning for remaining at Mimosa Park had less to do with age than with wider anxieties about economic livelihoods at Farmerfield. "I'm concerned," he had noted. "We were promised that when we get back to Farmerfield there will be development and training like brick making and brick laying . . . we will be taught how to look after the chickens . . . look after pigs."[53] That was in 1999. By 2007, the list of "projects" that community members believed had been mentioned in relation to Farmerfield included a potential ostrich farm. None of these were forthcoming in 2004 as families made their return to Farmerfield. Maxegwana was not among them then. Thus, in Farmerfield's case and in hundreds of others, some of the individuals most nostalgic and excited about their claims refused to go back. Others returned but later decamped.[54] At Tsitsikamma, for example, historian Crystal Jannecke has noted that many people who eventually settled, "had not participated in the resolution of the mission land claim."[55]

The result in Tsitsikamma's contested claim was "a silence . . . regarding the empty spaces that became filled with people who were neither descendants of the Clarkson mission residents, not connected in any way to the returning . . . community." [56] While the housing project at Tsitsikamma made way for homeless and landless peoples with no specific historical connection to the place, at Farmerfield, residential rules were strictly enforced, allowing no "outsiders" to settle. At last count in 2007, more than a third of the houses (approximately twenty-three) remained empty.[57] In addition to high vacancy rates, Farmerfield also shares the problem of post-settlement support. The lack or slow pace of economic development and agricultural production in resettled communities presents a daunting challenge to returnees. Given these enormous hurdles, and the common assertion of the relative advantages of claimants who fell under the category of "black spots," it is perhaps worthwhile to consider what this privilege meant in general and in the context of Farmerfield.

Certainly in the wider context of landlessness throughout South Africa in general and the Eastern Cape in particular, Farmerfield's tenants were privileged. As mission residents with church authorities arbitrating on their behalf, the assertion of privilege also holds. Finally, as claimants with educated members among their ranks who could leverage their knowledge and networks to facilitate their claim, Farmerfield's former tenants were also at an advantage. In absolute terms, compared to the millions of rural landless people and farm tenants leading tenuous existences and experiencing poor standards of living, Farmerfield's current owners are also privileged. But this notion of privilege is hardly a static one. In the same way that scholars have pushed for an understanding of the changes in the land and in the role of agrarian production in relation to the larger economy in the decades since removal, the same analysis also needs to be brought to bear on the people. What happened to the people in the intervening years? What does privilege mean almost two decades into the postapartheid era?

Like the work of historians Charles Van Onselen, Timothy Keegan, and others have amply shown, even the most ambitious, resourceful, and creative of African farmers could not outmaneuver the apartheid state. Proletarianization came early to the Eastern Cape and thwarted African farmers before it caught up to others on the Highveld. The result was that the generation who came of age at Farmerfield before the removal knew that cash incomes had to supplement any farming endeavors. Many of Farmerfield's young adults received a decent education and any ambition for a higher education already required them to leave the mission farm throughout the 1940s and the 1950s. Those who left the farm for educational purposes often abandoned farming. Of those who parted ways with farming for employment opportunities, few returned to it. The result was an ongoing disengagement, sometimes disenchantment, with agriculture as a part of their future. In many instances, farming skills atrophied and as many elders died at Mimosa, they took their corpus of farming knowledge with them.

Those who resettled in Mimosa Park—and managed to survive—suffered significant setbacks to the many years of hard work that had sustained them at Farmerfield. Many were forced to sell their cattle because of the restrictions on how many the government would transport and for fear of losing them. With no oxen, they could not plough. Those who assumed the expense or tried to restock found it took decades for them to recover economically, if they ever recovered at all. The tractors that had given other farmers privilege were always an expensive proposition for most residents at Mimosa Park. In 1999 the land at Mimosa Park lay fallow; few head of cattle were in sight and the majority of interviewees expressed the same concern about not having cattle to plough or being thwarted in their efforts by the high rates of theft. While they had farmed intermittently, the official land lay fallow for many seasons and most of the cultivation took place in their garden plots. In the aggregate, then, the privilege of former "black spots" tenants was a tempered one. Certainly, the mission provided education, and those who were able to own land, or otherwise secure favorable terms of tenancy, formed the backbone of an African economic elite. Most mission residents fared much better than the masses of landless people stuck on farms with terrible labor conditions or in homeland backwaters farming on marginal land. However, it had been extremely difficult for members of that elite to consistently consolidate the gains of their relatively privileged status and to leverage that status throughout the apartheid era to maintain their standard of living. What they maintained was a network of legal aid and NGO links that could be deployed to facilitate their claim. But even this network, in Farmerfield's case, was restricted in what it could accomplish beyond legal restitution.

Farmerfield's privilege begins and ends with land access. Other restituted "black spots" reveal slightly different paths. At Doornkop, a community with similar restricted settlement rules, Deborah James has noted, "Most of those who were entitled to claim did not want to come, while those who wanted to come were not entitled."[58] At Cremin, the divisions that had centered on an African landlord/tenant relationship produced a restituted community where only those with registered land rights participated in the official reclamation process and the accompanying celebrations.[59] The divergences can be accounted for in the variety of land tenancy arrangements included in the net of "black spot" removals: from rent tenancy with the Methodist Church at Farmerfield with strict rules against sharecropping and subletting land to nonmission residents, to African freehold tenure at Cremin and Doornkop where landowners engaged in tenancy relationships with other Africans who did not own the land.

In both the Cremin and Doornkop cases, the gains and privileges before the removals were more evident in the reclamation and resettlement process than at Farmerfield. Walker thus attributes the relative success of post-settlement Cremin to the "social cohesion" of the community and to "effective leadership," and a degree of "material self-sufficiency." These attributes in the reclamation and resettlement process were now central to reproducing inequalities within the broader community of former African landlords and tenants. Overcrowding at Cremin had prevented farming on the scale now envisioned by the exclusive group of people who reclaimed the land.[60] At Doornkop, however, conflicts over leadership, authority, and what the post-settlement community's residential and economic landscape should look like undermined the more vaunted aims of their particular restitution. The farm, until 2001, was thus "scantily populated. . . . [and] little used for agriculture."[61] Doornkop, in its post-restitution phase, shone a spotlight on the relationships between the divided claimants, community members, NGOs, and a government hampered by the pressing need to undo generations of poverty and inequality.

Nothing But the Land

At Farmerfield, returnees expressed gratitude for government-constructed houses, electricity, and boreholes that provided pumped water to their homes. Black South Africans' access to these resources, especially in the rural areas, had been sketchy at best and represented yet another marker of differential living standards under apartheid. The postapartheid government's plans for social and economic reforms as outlined in the reconstruction and development program (RDP) included plans to address these historical inequities. Once considered amenities, running water and electricity feature prominently in the quality of life improvements the government is attempting to implement. Although the government has moved away from welfare-oriented political platform to one focused on growth and economic development as represented by GEAR—Growth, Employment and Redistribution—it touts the original welfare agenda in another guise.[62] South Africa has pegged its quality of life and economic development goals to those milestones delineated in the UN's Millennium Development Goals (MDG) program aimed at expanding access to basic necessities, promoting economic developments, combating the scourges of malaria and HIV, and improving maternal health, child mortality, and access to education.[63]

Resettlement bore too many disturbing similarities to their experience at Mimosa Park. The element of victimization under the apartheid government has been replaced by misinformation or misunderstanding about what the "government" should do or promised to do for them. Most of the resettlers were pensioners who now claimed they were suffering like their elders did in the early years at Mimosa Park. A common refrain in the interview with the indomitable Florence Matini, who could not wait to return to Farmerfield when I first interviewed her in 1999, was the difficulty of life at Farmerfield. "Kunzima apha!" she repeated over and over again. "It is difficult here." She, her husband Daniel, and other family members relocated in 2005, and like their neighbors, found it challenging to maintain an adequate supply of food beyond the vegetables they cultivated in their gardens; the younger adults could find no jobs, either nearby, or in town. Interviews with the three generations of the Zweni family revealed similar sentiments using exactly the same Xhosa adjective to describe their lives at Farmerfield: "Kunzima eFarmerfield."[64]

Listening to his wife's interview, Daniel Matini kept shaking his head and agreed with her about the conflicting emotional currents associated with the return to Farmerfield. On the one hand, they expressed fear and disappointment about the starkly altered economic conditions resettlers faced. On the other hand, they celebrated and expressed joy at finally relocating to the land. Florence Matini was more dramatic on this count. She is happy to live out the rest of her life and die at Farmerfield in spite of the subsistence crisis because she "can't do otherwise." She made it clear that the only solution of returning to Mimosa Park was not feasible so she was prepared to accept the limitations of Farmerfield. "You can't go back again," she stated. Like all the other residents who had planned a return to Farmerfield, the Matinis hedged most of their subsistence planning on farming. The community now had access to a tractor, purchased with incomes earned from leasing the first portion of Farmerfield's land that was returned to the tenants. They tried to raise funds by renting out the tractor locally, but the tractor broke down, and languished at the mechanic's place as they sought funds to make the repairs. They then had to move the tractor to the property of Colin Steyn, Farmerfield's former principal. While some cultivation beyond the garden plots was underway on a visit in 2007, the tractor was nowhere in sight.

With these unanticipated delays to large-scale farming, returnees now had to compensate for shortfalls by purchasing food. Moreover, they had not budgeted for the water and electricity bills. With a third of the homes unoccupied, the collection of small sums from the fifty-six households to defray the expenses of the water pump now fell on those who had a predictable pension income. Rather than the pattern of young adults in their twenties and thirties supplementing the farming and pensions of their elders, the contemporary pattern at Farmerfield had developed into a disturbing, untenable direction. Young adults now looked to pensioners as the only reliable source of income coming into their households. The Matinis' combined pensions provide approximately R1700 to their household. Any travel to Grahamstown, whether to seek a job, to purchase food, or to visit a clinic sets them back R60 for a return trip and more if they have bulk groceries. The family tries to save as much money as possible by cultivating staple and vegetable crops in their gardens as they await the fate of the tractor, but their own sustenance needs as well as their grandchildren's, leave them financially insecure each month.

Among many of those who have resettled at Farmerfield, their nostalgia and enthusiasm proved to be no match for the new economic challenges. Mention the word "ostrich," for instance, and Sylvia Zweni, ordinarily an exuberant, expressive personality, waxes even more passionate. My second interview with her involved three generations of Farmerfield women: her daughter, Patricia, and her mother, Mina. During the interview Sylvia and Patricia rose to demonstrate how their excitement about potential ostrich farming had prompted them to cut down trees and shrubs to prepare the land to enclose the ostriches. They had not gone as far as to consider the actual market for ostrich meat, feathers, hides, and decorative eggs but the idea alone was encouraging. Ostrich farming, after all, had been around in the Eastern Cape since the 1860s so it certainly was not a farfetched idea. The economic potential had justified the hard labor, and both mother and daughter made light of how their bodies were swaying rhythmically as they hewed bushes and trees like they had never done before. With no long-legged, small-headed dolt of a bird in sight month after month, however, their hard work was all for naught. Mother and daughter were incensed but amused in their retelling.

Even with two pensions to cover their expenses, the Zwenis stated that life was still difficult for them. Despite Mina being qualified for and receiving her own house at Farmerfield, she was too old to care for herself completely. It also made little economic sense for her to maintain the expenses of her own house when she could move in with her long-widowed daughter, Sylvia. With Patricia's help, Zweni grows cabbages, pumpkins, beetroot, spinach, and potatoes to supplement the flour, beans, and fish they buy in town. Meat is a luxury. To save on electricity, they use paraffin when they can afford it and wood fires as often as they are able. They unplug the refrigerator and restrict the expensive travel to town. Patricia Zweni has applied for many jobs, but year after year found nothing. After securing nothing temporary even during the annual Grahamstown Festival when thousands of people descend upon the town, she became very discouraged about her future prospects.

At Farmerfield, stark economic conditions proved worrisome in terms of the pauperization and disillusionment of people who were already poor. While most fretted about their daily needs, the concerns about the long-term revitalization of Farmerfield contributed the most to the disquieting mood of the resettled community. With no economic development projects on the horizon for Farmerfield, no jobs, and unemployment hovering nationally at almost 25 percent, according to the 2009/2010 *South African Yearbook*, interviewees revealed that their larger concerns centered on the future of Farmerfield.[65] With the Eastern Cape historically experiencing higher unemployment rates than the national average, attracting young people to settle and raise their families in a rural outpost like Farmerfield presents a significant challenge. Farmerfield will not grow much beyond the fifty-six households if the women and men in their thirties and forties see no future there. With a vacancy rate already approaching one third and residency rules that restrict "outsiders," this new iteration of Farmerfield seems the most troubled of all its previous configurations. This presents somewhat of a paradox as this is also the era of the most secure tenure rights that any of the residents have ever experienced. If Farmerfield cannot attract a younger generation to commit to living in, farming, and developing the community, it will remain stagnant.

The trajectory of Sylvia Zweni's household at Farmerfield provides an important angle for understanding the long-term projections for this rural community. She and her family subsist on two pensions. These, combined with their farming on garden plots, maintain their basic needs. Her mother is elderly and so how much longer the household will have two "old pay," as the returnees called it, is of some concern. According to Sylvia Zweni, the disengagement of the "youth" with Farmerfield begins early and is not solely limited to young adults like her daughter Patricia, who faced difficulty finding a job. Her grandchildren, for example, barely wanted to spend the weekends at Farmerfield. She found it amusing that after the first day, they get bored and want to leave the farm. They have nowhere to go and nothing to do and—with no critical mass of children on the estate—few friends. Most of the children who attend school at Farmerfield from the surrounding farms are not available on the weekends. So her grandchildren opt to go back to town. This experience of Farmerfield does little to cultivate affection for or allegiance to the place.

While Sylvia Zweni would like to keep all of her grandchildren at Farmerfield under her watchful eye, higher education opportunities have to be sought in town. She worries all the time about one of her grandsons, staying with relatives in town so that he can attend school. The family cares for him, she assures me, but they are also a big family with their own food and money shortages. "We don't know how he's living . . . if he is going to bed without food." Whether it was her grandchildren or her own children, Zweni grew uneasy about what their experiences will mean for Farmerfield. While her daughter has relocated to Farmerfield, Zweni also worries about what will happen when she does find a job. Transportation will then be the problem. She would probably have to live closer to town and only visit Farmerfield on the weekends as commuting was impractical. If Patricia stays at Farmerfield without any opportunities to earn an income, the frustration and privation will exact a difficult economic and emotional toll, as her daughter was already describing her situation as "hopeless."

Both instances—moving away from Farmerfield for a job or leaving permanently because there was no job—were problematic. While it created despair for her daughter, it had led to criminal activity for her male counterparts at Farmerfield, who robbed the only store at the farm and drove away the owner. Perhaps they robbed him because he was an "outsider," Sylvia Zweni surmised. They took all of the food and the money. While everyone was upset that they would have to now buy small items a few kilometers away and much larger items in town, they also understood the desperation of young men with no money, no food, and no job. Either way, Zweni noted, the common trend among the youth was moving toward a certain alienation from the Farmerfield of memory. While she and Florence Matini can juxtapose both the good and bad times at Farmerfield, the younger generation automatically associates the place with economic hardship and isolation. The returnees are thus left with unanswered questions about how to cultivate loyalty and interest in enhancing and developing Farmerfield among their children and grandchildren when the economic realities hardly permit such an endeavor.

With the terrible roads receiving no improvement, transportation to Grahamstown being expensive, and the clinic located far away, returnees were left with little to reflect on positively. Sylvia Zweni, with a great sense of humor, noted that their return to Farmerfield was so anticlimactic that they did not hold any celebrations. The only solace was the church. While most of the men interviewed in 1999 referred to a general disappointment in not being able to build a church, most of the women pegged their specific concerns to their yearning for the kind of cohesion and social life the church provided. They held church in makeshift accommodations and carried on with their meetings and classes in their homes until they made more formal arrangements. Now in 2007, the women again expressed how much they sought the forms of sociability the church provided. Sunday services, prayer meetings, and Bible studies during the week provided a break from the drudge of work. The church was where they found solace; it helped them put their worries aside for a time, the Zweni women noted.

Whatever has happened, I indicated rather equivocally during the interviews, the houses were now completed and their land tenure was secured. Everyone was grateful that the land was theirs, tenure was vested in the community, and no one person had the right to alienate their land. They were also grateful that resettlement had not resulted in the makeshift accommodations they had to construct at Mimosa Park, or the type of informal settlements mushrooming near many urban centers. Still, the Matinis and the Zwenis spoke emphatically about their disappointments. Daniel Matini, for example, immediately broke from Xhosa into English at the mention of the houses. He was particularly aggrieved about the "foolish and silly" manner in which the houses were constructed (see Figure 9.1). He rose from his seat to demonstrate and having been huddled during the interview, he showed me why we were all so cold. The house was not plastered and the rain soaked the walls. Most of the residents could not raise the funds to pay for the cement and other materials they needed to plaster the walls. Sylvia and Patricia Zweni noted that they sometimes had to fetch wood up to three times per day to keep the house warm. There was nothing to do, the Zwenis and Matinis noted, except hope that it would not rain too hard, try to stockpile wood and paraffin to help with heating, and use a lot of blankets.[66]

In addition to the shoddy construction, the workers contracted to do the project left all the additional work of demarcating the house and setting up garden plots to the residents. Undoubtedly, no one would disagree with the description of the houses as "starter houses," the term the USAID-funded organization, Cooperative Housing Foundation, used to describe the Farmerfield housing project it had teamed up with ECARP to complete.[67] They perhaps would be more troubled by the pride taken in the government via the DLA announcement that, "This is the first restitution rural housing project in the Eastern Cape that has been developed through an integrated approach."[68] In addition to the state of their houses, residents also complained about the poor state of the roads, which flood and create huge puddles on some segments. The taxis refuse to navigate those puddles and potholes and thus off-load passengers several kilometers from their houses. Trips to Grahamstown had to be planned carefully, especially in light of the exorbitant R60 return fare. If it started to rain, Patricia Zweni noted, you planned to sleep in Grahamstown for the night. After several unfortunate trips like these, the residents, at the suggestion of Petrus Zatu who had gone to prepare the land for farming ahead of the resettlement, arranged for one of their white neighbors to do bulk shopping for everyone. Even then, it was best planned before the rains or the poor roads would delay the deliveries.[69]

Wandering around Farmerfield to assess the housing project in August 2007, I had caught sight of Petrus Zatu attempting to corral many head of cattle. He gave me a tour of the farming areas of Farmerfield and showed me that people had begun to farm but that it was proceeding slowly. The tractor needed diesel and oil. At least people were restocking cattle, I had noted. Without possession of my recording equipment, I could not capture his response to my observation but it amounted to the universal version of "Ha!" These cattle belonged to his employer. With no income and minimal farming on his allotment at Farmerfield, he had sought employment at one of the local white farms and he was herding their cattle, not his. He too talked of suffering. He would not be able to do a formal interview with me, he mentioned, as he spent most of his time on his employer's farm and not at his new residence at Farmerfield.

In lieu of any government assistance, everyone acknowledged that Farmerfield needed to return to food self-sufficiency. In appraising the state of farming at Farmerfield, Solomon Mzizi, who had helped to file the original claim, called for an honest assessment of the younger generation's farming skills. "They haven't been exposed," he declared, which was a serious disadvantage in post-settlement areas. Mzizi acknowledged that part of what was needed in reestablished communities like Farmerfield was a concerted effort by the government to send agricultural extension agents out to teach farming rather than assuming that it was an innate form of knowledge that would trickle down from one generation to the next.[70] The government concurs, as evident in its reorientation of the Department of Land Affairs, to focus on rural development as well as land reform. While the idea of teaching Africans to farm raises all sorts of colonial ghosts, it does not change the "distress" status of restituted farms. With the tide of dispossession and urbanization between the 1960s and 1980s, farming skills have atrophied or are nonexistent. Teaching farming as a form of knowledge should be no less within the purview of the government than creating an educated, informed citizenry.

The cohesion, material resources, and leadership that Cherryl Walker noted are the hallmarks of the moderate success the former "black spot" of Cremin has experienced since resettlement are sorely lacking at Farmerfield. The resettled community is cohesive in its current form—it was quiet, people helped each other, attended church, and engaged in each other's family milestones; they collaborated to pay their water and electricity bills; the youth may have robbed the store, but only out of desperation. But this cohesion is perhaps a return of the poorest of the former tenants. Those who have alternate residences in towns or in townships refuse to come back. Like other cases of resettlement, here it is the poorest people who relocate, with whatever level of privilege these individuals may initially have had as part of a land claim made almost moot in the resettlement phase—especially when landless people or squatters move to the land because other claimants have not done so. At Farmerfield and then at Mimosa Park, the most educated and well off left those communities with no intention of returning, even if they had placed their names on the official land claim. The cohesion at Farmerfield is thus a mask of the inequality that drove the poorest people back to the farm.

Farmerfield's returnees placed tremendous faith in each other, but little in the Trust Committee that represented their interest. While the older generation praised Solomon Mzizi and Patrick Hewana for the instrumental role they played in the restitution process, before 1990 they had continued electing their own leaders to deal with their internal affairs. This leadership structure was effective at Farmerfield, with leaders representing and advocating the tenants' general concerns to the local minister and the church. With the Methodist Church no longer responsible or vested in the interests of Farmerfield's former tenants and with no formal church at Mimosa Park, this leadership structure had little avenue to seek redress on any issue. Moreover, as more and more outsiders moved into Mimosa Park, the authority of these leaders became titular. They could not prevent squatters, nor could they protect their cattle and crops from theft or more serious crimes. While the former tenants rallied together during the restitution process, selecting a headman had become a mere formality.

Whereas the first Trust Committee could at least assert a substantial victory by facilitating the land claim, by 2007 a newly elected, younger Trust Committee was a sore disappointment, with absolutely no accountability and nothing to show in terms of advocacy for the resettled community. The young and savvy were elected and charged with moving ahead with plans to address the post-settlement malaise, but they accomplished nothing. In addition to forcing Solomon Mzizi out on the grounds that his family had no legitimate claim to Farmerfield since they had left the mission farm in 1958, monies collected from leasing Farmerfield have not been accounted for. Patricia and Sylvia Zweni noted of the committee, "They say Mbali [Solomon Mzizi] doesn't have a house here but they've got houses here and their houses are empty. He was honest and now that's why he is no longer wanted on the committee because he accounted for things with receipts."[71] No one wanted to account for what happened to the funds. Furthermore, the Trust Committee refused to visit Farmerfield or to turn over the records, engaged in dissimulation when residents tried to contact them, and used their influence when the conflict resulted in an attempt to oust them from their position. By late 2007, the election of a new committee was at a standstill. Many of those eligible to elect a new committee never resettled at Farmerfield, some still living at Mimosa Park and others settling in different urban areas, leaving the existing tenants unclear about how to effect their ouster. It is certain that an NGO or other legal aid organization will have to get involved. The machinations of the Trust Committee became one of many grievances they had to put aside in order to get on with the business of living. In the meantime, most residents were focused on engaging each other's resources to keep the water and electricity on in the community and to pursue each household's individual needs with their pensions and cultivation.

The poverty of post-settlement Farmerfield can be stultifying. No one I interviewed in 1999, 2001, or 2007 used this specific adjective to describe the challenges they faced. Yet the general impression the interviewees left was one suggesting that while the material experience of poverty under apartheid and in the postapartheid eras may have been similar, the context of their poverty mattered. Under apartheid, the government loomed large as a behemoth, eroding tenants' rights and finally removing them with little concern for their fates once they were dumped at Mimosa Park. The church acted as their arbiter with the government while demanding a proper degree of deference to its own authority and conformity to clearly delineated cultural norms. The Methodist Church authorities ultimately failed them, but their faith sustained them in concrete ways. Farmerfield's residents expressed despair at the delay in government assistance with economic development. They grew bewildered with government bureaucracy and frustrated with local politicians who only showed up when it was expedient and then promised too much. They were resigned to the difficulties of life. The current government was many things—slow, incompetent, bureaucratic—but they had accomplished what mattered most, which was to return the land. Farmerfield's residents thus viewed the postapartheid government and era in a different light— one that bore no relation to any notion of efficiency in government service delivery, nor one that was based on any misplaced romanticism about Farmerfield and justice. The returnees managed to express hope, occasionally tempered with optimism—the hope that they would get the land back and the optimism that they would eventually return when they finally won their legal suit.

One day, shortly before my interviews, an official from the welfare department appeared at Farmerfield with no notice. Residents are never quite sure what to expect; the local politician who represents them has no car and so rarely visits. No one has said anything in years about any plans to assist Farmerfield. In her ever-amusing tone, Sylvia Zweni noted that the representative communicated how the government was looking into the high unemployment rate and the need for assistance at Farmerfield. With the speed of an auctioneer, she rattled off what the government official promised the unemployed: "ten kilograms of rice; five kilograms each of mealie meal, flour, samp, and beans; two liters of fish; one hundred tea bags; soup; sunlight soap; peanut butter and milk powder."[72] Days went by, then weeks and months, and still nothing had come to fruition.

Amid the disappointment, the returnees are quick to point out two important points: they do attempt to help themselves and they are keenly aware of the value of the land. Rather than commit to absolute resignation, Petrus Zatu had sought and gained employment as a farm worker to supplement his own endeavors. Seeing the challenges after the closing of the only shop on the farm, he had reached out to his local white neighbor in order to save the residents high transportation costs. They pool their resources to keep the water pump going and they work hard to maintain a basic self-sufficiency. Patricia Zweni says she will continue to look for work and decipher how to change the leadership of the Trust Committee. Everyone pushes their children to do well in local school and will make whatever sacrifices they need in order to send them on to secondary and higher education, if they can. Their experience with the government suggests that self-sufficiency is the best plan for everyone. If or when the officials from the welfare office or any other government department show up, they will treat their promises in the same way they approach anything else, with hope and perhaps a little optimism.

Conclusion

In the 1830s amid war, insecurity, and population upheavals in the Eastern Cape, hundreds of African men and women could be found donning their best apparel to attend Methodist church services in Grahamstown. They prayed and attended class meetings; they sent their children to Sunday school. Missionaries catechized them in the basics of Christian theology and the particularities of Wesleyan Methodism. Some asked to be baptized and took on new baptismal names they then used as needed. For some African congregants this engagement with missionaries and Christianity was sufficient and they returned to their residences in the overcrowded "native" locations demarcated for Africans on the outskirts of Grahamstown and continued attending church services in town. For others, especially those accustomed to living at the pioneer mission stations, life in Grahamstown eking out an existence and only raising a few vegetables proved frustrating and they turned to missionaries to help them craft a better life. In doing so, they engaged the missionaries' goals of cultivating an African peasantry and a vital African Christianity.

WMMS missionary William Shaw, bent on securing the Eastern Cape as a Methodist sphere of influence and staving off denominational competition, purchased the Farmerfield farm. Although establishing an African mission among a white community veered sharply from his original plans of planting missions among African chiefdoms, he feared losing the allegiance of the growing number of Africans taking refuge in the Cape Colony. Notwithstanding their affiliation with the Methodist Church in Grahamstown, Africans who lacked adequate access to land in town sought assistance from any denomination willing to address their economic needs. Although these congregants symbolized significant gains in Methodist evangelism, they also represented disparate groups of Africans in the throes of confusing social, economic, and political changes.

Missionaries presented themselves as patrons who could assist Africans by offering access to land, new economic opportunities, new lifestyles, and new systems of knowledge. Africans neither accepted the total package of Christianity and "civilization" that missionaries yoked together nor made any solid commitments to any particular denomination. Instead, they assessed which missionaries could assist them with land access, then made the necessary adjustments. Africans' status as prospective Christian souls gave them a leverage incommensurate with their vulnerable political and economic position. These congregants wanted to gain access to land and work in the colonial economy without necessarily having to attach themselves and their families to white employers. The Farmerfield mission station afforded them this opportunity. Christian evangelization, white colonial encroachment, and the resulting violent confrontations and dispersion of people provide the backdrop for the creation of this community. These historical developments brought successive generations of Africans to Farmerfield in search of access to the religious message, to grazing and arable land, and to new places to settle.

The landscape of Farmerfield thus provides a window through which to view how warfare, evangelization, land shortages, and other developments influenced when and where people chose to migrate in the Eastern Cape. I have argued that Farmerfield served as a microcosm of the processes of Christian evangelization and African social and economic improvement in nineteenth- and twentieth-century South Africa. The most powerful evocation of this reform agenda, expressed in the intersection of abolitionist and missionary discourses, resulted in the creation of Christian peasant communities such as Farmerfield. Moreover, the history of Farmerfield linked the dispossessions of the colonial era with the social engineering and forced removal policies of the apartheid government. Residents of Farmerfield in its newest iteration participate in fresh discourses of social and economic improvement framed best by South Africa's postapartheid development agenda, the land reclamation process of the 1990s and the United Nations' Millennium Development Goals.

Throughout its storied history, Farmerfield operated on two interactive, yet distinct planes: first, as a missionary vision of ideal African Christians, fulfilling their roles as a laboring agricultural peasantry; second, as a community of Africans asserting their own notions of Christian piety and socioeconomic independence. Farmerfield demonstrates how mission stations developed as key institutions and loci of power where African residents and white missionaries negotiated a host of issues including land access, the meaning of civilization and authority, and Africans' roles as laborers, consumers, and Christians. I contend that when African and white visions converged in this encounter, Farmerfield emerged as an early Christianized African peasantry, representing a break with the previous era of pioneer evangelism and "nominal" Christianity and epitomizing proper labor relations between whites and Africans. Missionaries placed this model of Farmerfield at the successful end of the evangelical continuum.

Yet this was only one view of Farmerfield, most characteristic of the early decades of the settlement. Dissonance between Africans' experiences and the missionary blueprint yielded another, more critical missionary perception of Farmerfield as a mission relapsing into "incipient civilization" and "nominal" Christianity at the far end of the evangelical spectrum. I argue that although the missionaries reverted to this negative assessment to threaten the residents with expulsion in 1884, the power of the more positive vision of Farmerfield, as well as missionary paternalism, provided the next generation of residents with a second chance to retain access to land and shape their own lives as African Christians. Missionaries, reluctant to become complicit in the process of land alienation, waited for the mission to die a natural death. Farmerfield took on the characteristics of an African reserve where the most economically active members of the community migrated to larger urban centers, leaving behind farmers, the old, the infirm, women, and children. As the residents grew old and died, missionaries capped the population, sold off portions of the estate and waited for a natural demise. It took the power of the apartheid state to deal the final coup de grace in 1962 when Farmerfield and other "black spots" succumbed to the power of state to socially and physically engineer population boundaries according to race and ethnicity.

The behavior and actions of Farmerfield residents highlight the strategies of resistance and survival the mission provided ex-slaves, war refugees, and Christian converts. The often insuperable challenges Farmerfield and her successive generations of residents faced perhaps made survival the most cardinal act of resistance. Once they made the choice to flee hostilities and find safety in the Eastern Cape, the Methodist congregants who founded Farmerfield acted as agents in their own history within the confines of Christianity, the Methodist Church, the colonial government, the apartheid state, and the postapartheid state. Seeking out Farmerfield, setting down roots, and eventually reclaiming the land were thus important indices of African agency and resistance. With full cognizance that African agency occurs within a particular context of domination or coercion, I assert that Farmerfield residents shaped their own lives in myriad ways. The mission as a space, and Christianity as a faith, outfitted them with important material and spiritual tools to navigate the colonial world. They used their privileged position as African Christians—still a rarity in the 1830s—as leverage to secure land. As congregants of the Methodist Church they took the initiative and asked missionaries to make good on their pledge to help Africans. With no plan to establish a Methodist African mission in the Cape Colony, and serious misgivings, William Shaw changed his vision of missions and his evangelical strategies because of his African congregants' request.

Africans at Farmerfield conformed to the requirements of mission residence and Methodist church membership in specific ways. They attended church, sent their children to school, donned clothing considered to be "European," paid their dues, and made offerings in church services. This type of evidence at Farmerfield supports the assertion that missionaries acted as agents of cultural imperialism. They attempted to colonize Africans' consciousness at the level of the heart and mind, and at the level of day-to-day activities. When Farmerfield residents adopted square houses, came to be clad in clothes only whites used to wear, and converted to Christianity, missionaries declared a victory. Africans were moving along a cultural spectrum that held "European" models of civilizations as the norm. To say, however, that the missionary version of victory always comes at the expense of Africans and to say these activities are instances in the colonization of African consciousness is perhaps to award too much power to the figure of the missionary. For Africans to conform to what the missionary termed the "civilizing mission," they had to be discerning, selective, flexible, and creative. Under duress, they examined their cultural traditions and reconsidered fundamental ways of thinking about manhood, about farming, about education. Some chose to engage and experiment with Christianity in specific ways and tried to blend their old and new ways of life in a manner that got them expelled. To change, conform, compromise and experiment with new forms of being and novel forms of spirituality required great courage. This key element of Africans' adoption of Christianity often gets lost in literature discussing just how much Christian evangelism promoted cultural imperialism. Africans can and did dismantle the Christian message from the messenger and dissociated its lifestyle from its particular European cultural moorings when necessary. In doing so, many found value, solace, material resources and an instructive code of conduct to help them adjust to a rapidly changing world.

Once they made the conscious choice to live within the confines of the mission, resistance to missionary dominance or the assertion of cultural autonomy took forms other than open defiance at Farmerfield. For most residents the goal of maintaining tenancy was of cardinal importance and they were willing to compromise, change, conform, and engage in dissimulation to keep it. If maintaining fidelity to cultural traditions is taken as one form of resistance, it took place in a clandestine manner. People exchanged bridewealth secretly by masking the transfer of cattle as other types of transactions. Parents sent their children to be circumcised off the mission, outside of missionary purview, and when discovered, paid the fines the church imposed. When they could, twentieth-century inhabitants even built the huts—where initiates remain in seclusion—amid their cornfields. They consumed alcohol in the privacy of their homes, made ritual sacrifices in a solemn but not public manner, and used euphemisms to mask their practices. In this way, the nineteenth- and twentieth-century residents of Farmerfield safeguarded their long-term interests at the mission and protected those areas of cultural and personal autonomy they considered most important.

With restitution and resettlement, Farmerfield has come full circle. The common economic thread in the 1800s, 1900s, and now in the 2000s is the elusive dream of a self-sufficient African peasantry. In the 1800s missionaries nurtured this dream in the context of a conflict-ridden war zone as Africans struggled to make sense of and negotiate the rapid economic, political, and social change to their ways of life. Yoked to missionaries' evangelical aspirations, this vision of Farmerfield was an ambitious one that provided Africans some autonomy, land access, and self-reliance, if not the economic independence they wanted. Throughout the twentieth century until the eve of removal in 1962, the ever smaller remnants available to the residents still provided some advantages against the wider landscape of Eastern Cape landlessness. Even as a characteristic South African reserve, dependent on a combination of farming and remittances from young people, Farmerfield was a beacon for those who held on to the hope of autonomy. Those with an ideological commitment to land abandoned their tenuous, immobile existence on white farms in exchange for the patronage of the Methodist Church and a chance for land access for Farmerfield. A century after it was founded and long beyond its heyday, Farmerfield still represented an opportunity for some families. Even when they had to struggle for cultural autonomy in the context of the Christian missions' long-standing assault on some African cultural practices, Africans from all over the Eastern Cape capitalized on vacancies at Farmerfield because dealing with the church prohibitions was inordinately preferable to servitude on white farms.

With their removal to Mimosa Park, Farmerfield's former residents were all cognizant and vocal about the different context in which they expressed their Christian faith. The missionary omnipresence was historical context, not their current reality. People ascribed the identity of "Christian" without any requisite attendance to the conventional requirements of Methodist Church membership. They practiced their faith without fundamentalism and asserted their cultural autonomy with impunity—a flexibility that allowed the core of former residents settled at Farmerfield to routinely identify themselves as a Christian community and a Christian people in the conventional way they used any other adjective.

Farmerfield residents used Christianity at Mimosa Park as part of generic moral discourse to criticize the theft and violence associated with "newcomers" and "outsiders" who started to move to there as they too faced land pressures. Their Christian status helped them to maintain a sense of who they were as former Farmerfield residents, even when they could not prevent "outsiders" from claiming land access at Mimosa Park. Beyond the use of Christianity as a moral critique and as a way to delineate a particular sense of community, the core of people who were committed to Christianity remained so. Free from the watchful eyes of missionaries, the faith, if not the behavior, of Farmerfield's residents had changed little. Although church attendance was not as high as the years at Farmerfield and although some people consumed alcohol and did not hide their ritual killing of cattle and circumcision practices, the residents affirm that their Christian values remained undiluted.

Like all churches, the new one erected at Mimosa Park had its share of long-winded preachers to endure as well as its inspirational ones—the kind that made people want to go to services in the morning and evening. There was a different mood on Sunday as people prepared for the day of worship. People also looked forward to the sociability the church provides and the heartfelt renditions from Xhosa hymnody. Sunday is also often the only day they got to dress up. One elderly devout preacher, Nofelity Gaba, proudly took his shoes off on the way to and from church to save them for the special occasion. Women happily donned the red, black, and white uniforms that African women wear in the Methodist Church.

Bibles remain prized possessions. During the interviews, several people requested that I take photos of them in this special regalia. On certain Sundays when I tried to conduct interviews, I had to wait until some people return from service—others asked why I had not joined them in church. Some people attended the routine Sunday services and no more; others studied the Bible in groups and held prayer meetings. No one felt the need to judge each other's faith, leaving it to each congregant and his conscience.

More than a century-and-a-half since he founded Farmerfield, what would William Shaw say of this faith without fundamentalism and fidelity to Xhosa cultural traditions that now define the resettled community? With his wide gaze, he would have likely pointed out that the current vitality of Christianity is now said to rest in the global South. Africans have indeed cultivated a vital, mature engagement with Christianity that is commanding global attention anew. Most Africans had to leave the missions and subvert mission authority to do so, but at Farmerfield, Shaw would have probably argued that the model and legacy of the mission provided a crucible for an enduring African Christianity long before the majority of Africans ever pledged fidelity to Christianity and long after the romance of missions and the actual land was gone. He would almost certainly be proud that the majority of Africans associated with the mainline churches in South Africa are still of the Methodist persuasion and point to the crucial foundation he had laid in making the Eastern Cape a cradle of Methodism.

In postapartheid South Africa, the memory of Farmerfield as a Christian place and space, as well as the meticulous documentation of the Methodist Church, informed a new discourse on justice and restitution. It is likely that Shaw would have contributed his distinct views on this issue were he still alive today. With a keen sense of how denominational politics had emboldened Africans in the 1820s and 1830s, he would certainly highlight how the legacy of missions and various tenure agreements now provided a certain strata of Africans with the leverage, knowledge, skills, and network to employ the land reform machinery in far more effective ways than their landless counterparts. As a pragmatic observer with a keen sense of mercurial politics, he would agree with the need to tread lightly in upending the private property rights of white landowners, while acknowledging the need for restitution on more equitable means. He would also surely argue that the self-sufficient peasantries he and other missionaries envisioned, but never made a full commitment to because of their racial and cultural myopia, perhaps needed revisiting. He would recast the urban areas of South Africa as a renewed site for Methodist proselytization. He would beckon the Methodist Church to step forward again in its patronage role to assist the community. He would also acknowledge what is now commonplace: the vernacularization of Christianity would have to accommodate local African traditions and customs and Africans would continue to be the linchpin in their key roles as lay preachers, evangelists, and ministers.

In this ongoing "long conversation," Africans at Farmerfield would likely respond that, notwithstanding the Methodist legacy that brought them to this juncture, it was no longer within Shaw's purview to decide their futures. They will succeed or fail on their own merits and the white stone Methodist Church building will stand as witness to the new iteration of Farmerfield. Yet a crucial question remains. What role, if any, will the Methodist Church of South Africa play in reconstituting Farmerfield as a viable agricultural community in contemporary South Africa?

African men and women are farming, the new children join the local school making a great din with their arrival and departure, and cattle roam the estate while chickens and dogs wander lazily around their yards. The return to the land is a return to a place conceived of as a Christian space with deep roots and a proud heritage of perseverance. Farmerfield's legacy as an agricultural settlement is far more tenuous, however. Although water access has been secured, the main road to Farmerfield off the highway is still the poorly constructed dirt path that makes the transportation of crops to markets difficult and secludes the estate even from tourists. The same concerns about access to tractors and markets that tenants worried about in the 1950s remain critical obstacles to moving the residents toward the goal of economic independence. Instead of turning their attention to the Methodist Church, the residents now focus their energies on the government and a host of NGOs that participated in bringing the new settlement to fruition. The older residents rely on their pensions and subsistence farming, but their children and grandchildren, now in their thirties, forties, and fifties are hesitant to hedge their own futures on a return to Farmerfield given the economic uncertainties. These generations, however, still guard their access to land even without an ideological commitment to till the soil.

The postapartheid iteration of Farmerfield is rife with all the problems scholars and critics have noted of the land reform process in South Africa, from the slow pace of service delivery to the emergence of an opaque, inefficient bureaucracy. As the government contemplates changing its "willing buyer, willing seller" market approach to land reform and attempts a broader land reform vision that can address rural development, Farmerfield has moved on to the post-settlement phase. From the broadest angle, the restituted community is engaged in a new experiment based on engaging postapartheid citizenship and asserting their rights in a concrete, meaningful way. The "notion" of government has shifted from the oppressive, racist behemoth of the apartheid era to the laggard post-apartheid bureaucracy many have experienced as inept, slow, and often inaccessible. The government's goals of integration and delegation work at cross purposes, creating inexplicable delays. Moreover the government's perspective on their development goals at Farmerfield and other resettled communities diverges from many communities' views. Based on the metrics of the UN's MDG program and its own development agenda, the bureaucracy has successfully provided housing, clean and potable running water, and electricity to the resettlers, and there the matter will have to rest. By the standards of the MDG program, this is a ringing success. The tenants' goalpost has moved, however, and they see electricity and running water as bare necessities they had been denied because of apartheid policies, not because their country was underdeveloped. This perspective places an even greater burden on the postapartheid government now headed toward its fifth election cycle and facing remobilized masses disappointed in the slow pace of economic development and redistribution, and rather unsympathetic about realpolitiks.

Despite these challenges, residents at this new iteration of Farmerfield remain assured that the return to the land is a victory in itself. Notwithstanding the shortcomings of agricultural production, land tenure is an important right in a community that formerly depended on a church bureaucracy to maintain their land access. With legal tenure, residents trust their own stewardship, despite having relied on Methodist bureaucratic traditions and recordkeeping to prove their legal right to tenure. Beyond their concerns about farming, the new residents are conscious of the value of what they do possess: Christianity without fundamentalism and guaranteed legal access to land in a country where the landlessness associated with post-1913 dispossession privileged certain claimants to land while excluding a wider swath of people who are landless. As the realities of what the government cannot do settles in, the Farmerfield community looks inward to confront the immediate challenge of how to survive economically. They attempt to cultivate forms of cooperation, self-reliance, leadership, and allegiance to Farmerfield among the younger generation to ensure the longevity of the farm as a Christian space and a viable economic community.

ABBREVIATIONS

AHR	American Historical Review
AIC	African Independent Churches/African Initiated Churches
ANC	African National Congress
AFRA	The Association for Rural Advancement
BK	British Kaffraria
BRC	The Border Rural Committee
CAR	Cape Archives Repository
CJAS	Canadian Journal of African Historical Studies
CL	Cory Library
CO	Colonial Office
DLA	Department of Land Affairs (after 2009, Department of Rural Development and Land Reform)
DRC	Dutch Reformed Church
ECARP	Eastern Cape Agricultural Research Project
ECLC	East Cape Land Committee
FRRP	Farmworkers Research and Resource Project
GAMS	Glasgow African Missionary Society
GEAR	Growth, Employment and Redistribution
GMS	Glasgow Missionary Society
GTJ	*Graham's Town Journal*
IJAHS	International Journal of African Historical Studies
JAH	Journal of African History
JSAS	Journal of Southern African Studies
LCC	Land Claims Court
LMS	London Missionary Society
MDG	Millennium Development Goals
NAD	Native Affairs Department
NGO	Non-Governmental Organization
OFSRUC	Orange Free State Rural Committee
PAC	Pan African Congress
RCC	Records of the Cape Colony
RDP	Reconstruction and Development

SAHJ	South African Historical Journal
SAIRR	South African Institute of Race Relations
SAL	South African Library
SCLC	The Southern Cape Land Committee
SPP	Surplus People Project
TRAC	Transvaal Rural Action Committee
TRALSO	Transkei Land Service Organization
UN	United Nations
WMS/WMMS	Wesleyan Missionary Society; Wesleyan Methodist Missionary Society
USAID	United States Agency for International Development
VOC	Vereenigde Oost Indische Compagnie, or Dutch East India Company

NOTES

Prologue

1. Alan Paton, *Cry the Beloved Country* (New York: Scribner, 1948).

2. Sam Wineburg, *Historical Thinking and Other Unnatural Acts: Charting the Future of Teaching the Past* (Philadelphia: Temple University Press, 2001); David Lowenthal, *The Past is a Foreign Country* (Cambridge: Cambridge University Press, 1985).

3. S. D. Goitein, *A Mediterranean Society* 5 vols, (Berkeley: University of California Press, 1988), 5:502.

Introduction

1. Landeg White, *Magomero, Portrait of an African Village* (Cambridge: Cambridge University, 1987); Howard Temperley, *The British Anti-slavery Expedition to the River Niger, 1841–1842* (New Haven: Yale University Press, 1991); Lamin Sanneh, *Abolitionists Abroad: American Blacks and the Making of Modern West Africa* (Cambridge: Harvard University Press, 1999); Andrew Ross, *John Philip: Missions, Race and Politics in South Africa* (Aberdeen: Aberdeen University Press, 1986).

2. Andrew Porter, *Religion versus Empire? British Protestant Missionaries and Overseas Expansion, 1700–1914*, (Manchester: Manchester University Press, 2004), 43, 89–90.

3. Eric Hobsbawm, *Age of Revolution, 1789–1848* (New York: New American Library, 1962).

4. William Wilberforce, *An Appeal to the Religion, Justice and Humanity of the Inhabitants of the British Empire on Behalf of the Negro Slaves in the West Indies* (London: J. Hatchard and Sons, 1823), 137; Terence Ranger, "The Local and the Global in Southern African Religious History," in *Conversion to Christianity*, ed., Robert W. Hefner (Berkeley: University of California Press, 1993), 66.

5. Susan Thorne, "The Conversion of Englishmen and the Conversion of the World Inseparable," in *Tensions of Empire: Colonial Cultures in a Bourgeois World*, eds., Frederick Cooper and Ann Laura Stoler (Berkeley: University of California Press, 1997), 238; Michael Ledger-Lomas, "Mass Markets: Religion," in *Cambridge History of the Book in Britain: 1830–1914*, ed., David McKitterick (Cambridge: Cambridge University Press, 2008), 325.

6. Robin Horton, *Patterns of Thought in Africa and the West* (Cambridge: Cambridge University Press, 1993); "African Traditional Thought and Western Science," *Africa* 37 (1967): 50–71; "African Conversion," *Africa: Journal of the International African Institute* 41 (1971): 85–10; "On the Rationality of Conversion," Part 1, *Africa: Journal of the International African Institute* 45 (3) (1975): 219–235; "On the Rationality of Conversion," Part 2, *Africa* 45 (4) (1975): 373–399; Lamin Sanneh, *West African Christianity: The Religious Impact* (Maryknoll, NY: Orbis Books, 1983); *Translating the Message: The Missionary Impact on Culture* (Maryknoll, NY: Orbis Books, 1989); *Encountering the West: Christianity and the Global Impact on the Global Cultural Process: The African Dimension* (Maryknoll, NY: Orbis Books, 1993; *Abolitionists Abroad*.

7. Richard Elphick, "Africans and the Christian Campaign in Southern Africa," in *The Frontier in History, North America and Southern Africa Compared*, Howard Lamar and Leonard Thompson, eds., (New Haven: Yale University Press, 1981), 270–308; "Writing Religion into History," in *Missions and Christianity in South African History*, eds., Henry Bredekamp and Robert Ross (Johannesburg: Witwatersrand University Press, 1995), 11–26; Terence Ranger and Isaria, Kimambo, eds., *The Historical Study of African Religion* (London: Heinemann Educational, 1972); Terence Ranger, *Peasant Consciousness and Guerilla War in Zimbabwe* (London: James Currey, 1985); "Religion, Development, and African Christian Identity," in Karen Holst-Petersen, ed., *Religion, Development and African Identity* (Uppsala: Scandinavian Institute of African Studies, 1987), 29–57; "Religious Movements and Politics in Sub-Saharan Africa, *African Studies Review* 29 (2):1–69; "The Local and the Global in Southern African Religious History," 65–98.

8. For examples of early works on Christianity in Africa that explore inter alia the issues of missionary complicity in colonialism, the link between African nationalism and the missionary enterprise, and the creation of new elites, see: Jacob Ajayi, *Christian Missions in Nigeria, 1841–1891, The Making of a New Elite*, (London: Longmans, 1965); Emmanuel Ayandele, *The Missionary Impact on Modern Nigeria, 1842–1914: A Political and Social Analysis* (New York: Humanities Press, 1966); Norman Etherington, "Mission Station Melting Pots as a Factor in the Rise of South African Black Nationalism," *IJAS* 9 (4) (1976): 592–605; Thomas Beidelman, *Colonial Evangelism: A Socio-Historical Study of an East African Mission at the Grassroots* (Bloomington, IN: Indiana University Press, 1982).

9. Norman Etherington, "Missionaries and the Intellectual History of Africa: A Historical Survey," *Itinerario* (7) (1983): 116–143; and "Recent Trends in the Historiography of Christianity in Southern Africa," *JSAS* 22 (2) (1996): 201–219; Elizabeth Elbourne, "Concerning Missionaries: The Case of Van der Kemp," *JSAS* 17 (1) (1991): 153–164.

10. John and Jean Comaroff, *Of Revelation and Revolution: Christianity and Consciousness in South Africa*, vol. 1 (Chicago: University of Chicago Press, 1991); and *Of Revelation and Revolution: Dialectics of Modernity on a South African Frontier*, vol. 2 (Chicago: University of Chicago Press, 1997); Paul Landau, *The Realm of the Word: Language, Gender and Christianity in a Southern African Kingdom* (Portsmouth, NH: Heinemann, 1995); Bredekamp and Ross, *Missions and Christianity in South African History*; Richard Elphick and Rodney Davenport, eds., *Christianity in South Africa: A Political, Social, and Cultural History* (Claremont, South Africa: David Philip, 1997); Elizabeth

Elbourne, *Blood Ground: Colonialism, Missions and the Contest for Christianity in the Cape Colony and Britain 1799–1853* (Montreal: McGill-Queens University Press, 2002).

11. Natasha Erlank, "Gender and Christianity Among Africans Attached to Scottish Mission Stations in Xhosaland in the Nineteenth Century," (Ph.D. diss., University of Cambridge, 1998); See David Livingstone, *Missionary Travels and Research in Africa* (London: Murray, 1857); Bridglal Pachai, ed., *Livingstone: Man of Africa* (London: Longman, 1973); Andrew Ross, *John Philip: Missions, Race and Politics in South Africa* (Aberdeen: Aberdeen University Press, 1986); Ido Enklaar, *Life and Work of Dr. J. Th. Van der Kemp, 1747–1811: Missionary Pioneer and Protagonist of Racial Equality in South Africa* (Cape Town and Rodderdam, 1988); William Freund, "The Career of Johannes Theodorus van der Kemp and his Role in the History of South Africa," *Tijdschrift voor Geschiedenis* 86 (3): 376–390; Jeff Guy, *The Heretic: A Study in the Life of John William Colenso*, (Johannesburg: Ravan Press, 1983). For the less well known controversial figure of David Clement Scott, see Andrew Ross, "The Origins and Development of the Church of Scotland Mission, Blantyre, Nyasaland, 1875–1926," (Ph.D. diss., University of Edinburgh, 1968) and Kenneth Ross, "Vernacular Translation in Christian Mission: The Case of David Clement Scott and the Blantyre Mission, 1888–1898," *Missionalia* 21 (1) (1993): 5–18.

12. Susan Thorne, *Congregational Missions and the Making of an Imperial Culture in Nineteenth-Century England* (Stanford: Stanford University Press, 1999), 1–9.

13. Henry Mayhew, *London Labor and the London Poor* (London: Penguin Books, 1985), 468–469.

14. Michael Ledger-Lomas, "Glimpses of the Great Conflict: English Congregationalists and the European Crisis of Faith, 1840–1875," *Journal of British Studies* 46 (4) (October 2007), 828–829.

15. J. D. Y. Peel, *Religious Encounter and the Making of the Yoruba* (Bloomington, IN: Indiana University Press, 2000); Elbourne, *Blood Ground*; Paul Landau, *Popular Politics in the History of South Africa, 1400–1948* (New York: Cambridge University Press, 2010).

16. Derek Peterson and Jean Allman, "Introduction: New Directions in the History of Missions in Africa," *The Journal of Religious History* 23 (1) (February 1999), 1.

17. Patrick Harries, *Butterflies and Barbarians: Swiss Missionaries and Systems of Knowledge in South East Africa* (Oxford: James Currey, 2007); Alan Kirkaldy, *Capturing the Soul: The VhaVenda and the Missionaries, 1870–1900* (Pretoria: Protea Book House, 2005).

18. Sanneh, *Translating the Message* and *Encountering the West*. For an interesting snapshot of the translation of the scriptures into the vernacular and the wider application of the notion of vernacular to include not just language, but also culture, see: Ross, "Vernacular Translation in Christian Mission," 5–18. David Livingstone, *Missionary Travels and Research in Africa* (London: Murray, 1857); Pachai, *Livingstone: Man of Africa*.

19. Richard Elphick, "Writing Religion into History," in Bredekamp and Ross, *Missions and Christianity in South African History*, 20.

20. Herbert Chimundu, "Early Missionaries and the Ethnolinguistic Factor during the Invention of Tribalism in Zimbabwe," *JAH* 33 (1992): 87–109; Terence Ranger,

"Missionaries, Migrants and the Manyika: The Invention of Ethnicity in Zimbabwe," in *The Creation of Tribalism in Southern Africa*, Leroy Vail, ed., Berkeley: University of California Press, 1989 (Berkeley and Los Angeles: University of California Press, 1989), 118–150; Rajend Mesthrie, "Words Across Worlds: Aspects of Language Contact and Language Learning: Contact and Language Learning in the Eastern Cape, 1800–1850," *African Studies* 57 (1) (1998): 5–26.

21. Landau, *Popular Politics*, 2.

22. Robert Edgar, *New Religious Movements*, in *Missions and Empire*, Norman Etherington, ed. (Oxford: Oxford University Press, 2005): 216–237.

23. Elbourne, *Blood Ground*, 175; Mesthrie, *Words Across Worlds*, 8.

24. White, *Magomero*, 13.

25. Landau, *The Realm of the World*.

26. Other examples of polities like the Ngwato kingdom where the ruler or king converted to Christianity include: Buganda, Merina (Madagascar), and the Kongo State.

27. Deborah Gaitskell, "'Praying and Preaching': The Distinctive Spirituality of African Women's Church Organizations," and Norman Etherington, "Gender Issues in South-East African Missions," in Bredekamp and Ross, *Missions and Christianity in South African History*, 135–152 and 211–232; Deborah Gaitskell, "Power in Prayer and Service: Women's Christian Organizations," in Elphick and Davenport, *Christianity in South Africa*, 253–267; Erlank, "Gender and Christianity Among Africans Attached to Scottish Mission Stations in Xhosaland in the Nineteenth Century," 1998; "Gendered Reactions to Social Dislocation and Missionary Activity in Xhosaland, 1836–1847," *African Studies*, 59 (2) (2000): 205–227; "'Raising up the Degraded Daughters of Africa:' The Provision of Education for Xhosa Women in the Mid-Nineteenth Century," *SAHJ* 43(2000): 24–38; Elizabeth Prevost, "Assessing Women, Gender, and Empire in Britain's Nineteenth-Century Protestant Missionary Movement," *History Compass* 7 (3) (2009): 765–799.

28. Levine, *A Living Man from Africa: Jan Tzatzoe, Xhosa Chief and Missionary, and the Making of Nineteenth-Century South Africa* (New Haven: Yale University Press, 2010), 5.

29. Wallace George Mills, "The Role of African Clergy in the Reorientation of Xhosa society to the Plural Society in the Cape Colony, 1850–1915," (Ph.D. diss., University of California, Los Angeles, 1975); Donavan Williams, *Umfundisi: A Biography of Tiyo Soga, 1829–1871* (Lovedale: Lovedale Press, 1978); Levine, *A Living Man from Africa*; Catherine Higgs, *The Ghost of Equality: The Public Lives of D. D. T. Jabavu of South Africa, 1885–1959* (Athens, OH: Ohio University Press, 1997); Terence Ranger *Are We Not Also Men? The Samkange Family and African Politics in Zimbabwe, 1920–1964* (London: James Currey, 1995).

30. Donavan Williams, ed., *The Journal and Selected Writings of the Reverend Tiyo Soga* (Cape Town: A. A. Balkema, 1983). *Umfundisi: A Biography of Tiyo Soga, 1829–1871* (Lovedale: Lovedale Press, 1978).

31. Comaroffs, *Of Revelation and Revolution*, 1: 251.

32. Beidelman, *Colonial Evangelism*, 6.

33. J. B. Peires, "Nxele, Ntsikana and the Origins of the Xhosa Religious Reaction," *JAH* 20 (1979): 51–62; *The Dead Will Arise: Nongqawuse and the Great Xhosa Cattle Killing Movement of 1856–57* (Johannesburg: Ravan Press, 1989); David Chidester, *Savage*

Systems: Colonial and Comparative Religion in Southern Africa (Charlottesville: University Press of Virginia, 1996); Peel, *Religious Encounters.*

34. Steven Shapin, *A Social History of Truth: Civility and Science in Seventeenth-Century England* (Chicago: University of Chicago Press, 1994), xxvii.

35. Hebrews 11:1.

36. For an historiographical treatment of frontiers in South Africa, including the Eastern Cape frontier, see: Martin Legassick, "The Frontier Tradition in South African Historiography," in Shula Marks and Anthony Atmore, eds., *Economy and Society in Pre-Industrial South Africa* (London: Longman, 1980), 44–79; for a comparative perspective on the frontier, see Howard Lamar and Leonard Thompson, eds., *The Frontier in History: North America and Southern Africa Compared,* (New Haven: Yale University Press, 1981); for early historiographical treatments of the Eastern Cape and the Xhosa and Khoekhoe experience of colonial encroachment, as well as issues such as education, and the role of missionaries, see: John S. Galbraith, *Reluctant Empire: British Policy on the South African Frontier, 1834–1854* (Berkeley: University of California Press, 1963); Christopher Saunders and Robin Derricourt, eds., *Beyond the Cape Frontier* (London: Longman, 1974); Herman Giliomee, "The Eastern Frontier, 1770–1812" in *The Shaping of South African Society, 1652–1840,* eds. Richard Elphick and Hermann Giliomee (Middletown, CT: Wesleyan University Press, 1979), 421–471; John Milton, *The Edges of War: A History of Frontier Wars, 1702–1878* (Cape Town: Juta, 1983); Susan Newton-King, *Masters and Servants in the Cape Eastern Frontier* (Cambridge: Cambridge University Press, 1999); Ben Maclennan, *A Proper Degree of Terror: John Graham and the Cape's Eastern Frontier* (Braamfontein, South Africa: Ravan Press, 1986).

37. J. B. Peires, *House of Phalo: A History of the Xhosa in the Days of Their Independence* (Berkeley: University of California Press, 1982); Noël Mostert, *Frontiers: The Epic of South Africa's Creation and the Tragedy of the Xhosa People* (New York: Knopf, 1992). Les Switzer, *Power and Resistance in an African Society: The Ciskei Xhosa and the Making of South Africa* (Madison: University of Wisconsin Press, 1993); Timothy Stapleton, *Maqoma: Xhosa Resistance to Colonial Advance, 1798–1873* (Johannesburg: J. Ball, 1994).

38. Basil Le Cordeur, *The Politics of Eastern Cape Separatism, 1820–1854.* Cape Town: Oxford University Press, 1981; Galbraith, *Reluctant Empire: British Policy on the South African Frontier.*

39. Alan Lester, *Imperial Network: Creating Identities in Nineteenth-Century South Africa and Britain* (London: Routledge, 2001); Clifton Crais, *White Supremacy and Black Resistance in the Eastern Cape: The Making of the Colonial Order, 1770–1865* (Johannesburg: Witwatersrand University Press, 1992); Tim Keegan, *Colonial South Africa and the Origins of the Racial Order* (Charlottesville: University Press of Virginia, 1996); Richard Price, *Making Empire: Colonial Encounters and the Creation of Imperial Rule in Nineteenth-Century Africa* (Cambridge: Cambridge University Press, 2008).

40. Lester, *Imperial Networks,* 4.

41. Norman Etherington, "Review of Alan Lester, *Imperial Networks,*" *International Historical Review* 24 (3) (2002), 647.

42. Clifton Crais, *The Politics of Evil: Magic, State Power, and the Political Imagination in South Africa* (Cambridge: Cambridge University Press, 2002).

43. For the making of the slave holding elite at the Cape, its models of inheritance distinct from the British one, and its implications for the maintenance of wealth across generations, see the insightful article, Wayne Dooling, "The Making of a Colonial Elite: Property, Family and Landed Stability in the Cape Colony, c. 1750–1834," *JSAS* 31, (1) (March, 2005): 147–162.

44. Elbourne, *Blood Ground*; Robert Ross, *Status and Respectability in the Cape Colony, 1750–1870: A Tragedy of Manners* (Cambridge: Cambridge University Press, 1999).

45. Price, *Making Empire*, 84.

46. Andrew Porter, "Introduction," in *Religion versus Empire? British Protestant Missionaries and Overseas Expansion, 1700–1914*, ed., Andrew Porter (Manchester: Manchester University Press, 2004), 5–6.

Chapter 1

1. Mary Kingsley, *Travels in West Africa* (1897; reprint, London: Dent/Everyman, 1993), 12.

2. Thorne, "The Conversion of Englishmen," 238.

3. Kingsley, *Travels in West Africa*, 12.

4. D. W. Bebbington, *Evangelicalism in Modern Britain: A History from the 1730s to the 1980s* (London: Unwin Wyman, 1989); Roger Martin, *Evangelicals United: Ecumenical Stirrings in Pre-Victorian Britain, 1795–1830* (Metuchen, NJ: Scarecrow Press, 1983); Boyd Hilton, *The Age of Atonement: The Influence of Evangelicalism on Social and Economic Thought, 1795–1865* (Oxford: Clarendon Press, 1988); and G. M. Ditchfield, *The Evangelical Revival* (London: UCL Press, 1998).

5. Jackson Spielvogel, *Western Civilization*, 2nd ed., 2 vols. (New York: West Publishing, 1994), 2:626; E. P. Thompson, *The Making of the English Working Class* (New York: Vintage Books, 1966), 26.

6. Thompson, *The Making of the English Working Class*, 34–35; George Findlay and W. W. Holdsworth, *The History of the Wesleyan Methodist Missionary Society*, 5 vols. (London: Epworth Press, 1921), 1:28–29.

7. Ursula Henriques, *Religious Toleration in England, 1787–1833* (Toronto: University of Toronto Press, 1961).

8. Colin Graham Botha, *The French Refugees at the Cape*, 3rd ed. (Cape Town: C. Struik, 1970); Jon Butler, *The Huguenots in America: A Refugee People in a New World Society* (Cambridge: Harvard University Press, 1983).

9. Henriques, *Religious Toleration in England, 1787–1833*, 1–17.

10. Bernhard Krüger, *The Pear Tree Blossoms: A History of the Moravian Mission Stations in South Africa* (Genadendal, South Africa: Moravian Book Depot, 1966).

11. James Haskins, *The Methodists* (New York: Hippocrene Books, 1992), 32, 39.

12. Deryck W. Lovegrove, *Established Church, Sectarian People: Itinerancy and the Transformation of English Dissent* (Cambridge: Cambridge University Press, 1988), 23–25.

13. Gordon Rupp, *Religion in England, 1688–1791* (Oxford: Clarendon Press, 1986), 390.

14. Philip Cliff, *The Rise and Development of the Sunday School Movement in England, 1780–1980* (Nutfield, England: National Christian Education Council, 1986).

15. Thompson, *The Making of the English Working Class*, 40; Rupp, *Religion in England*, 448–449.

16. Holy Bible, King James Version, Romans 3:23.

17. Thompson, *The Making of the English Working Class*, 363, 383.

18. Thompson, *The Making of the English Working Class*, 350–400.

19. Thompson, *The Making of the English Working Class*, 355.

20. Rupp, *Religion in England*, 449.

21. Bernard Semmel, *The Methodist Revolution* (New York: Basic Books, 1973), 20; Donald Lewis, *Lighten their Darkness: The Evangelical Mission to Working-Class London, 1828–1860* (New York: Greenwood Press, 1986), 77–78; Thompson, *The Making of the English Working Class*, 351, 352.

22. Lovegrove, *Established Church, Sectarian People*, 14, 16, 23, 27; Michael Watts, *The Dissenters: The Expansion of Evangelical Nonconformity*, vol. 2 (Oxford: Oxford University Press, 1995), 27–29.

23. Thompson, *The Making of the English Working Class*, 351.

24. Findlay and Holdsworth, *The History of the Wesleyan Methodist Missionary Society*, 1: 57–61.

25. Bernard Semmel, *The Methodist Revolution*, 20; Elizabeth Elbourne, "'To Colonize the Mind:' Evangelical Missionaries in Britain and the Eastern Cape, 1790–1837," (Ph.D. diss., Oxford University, 1992), 41; Lewis, *Lighten their Darkness*; Ian Bradley, *The Call to Seriousness* (London: Jonathan Cape, 1976).

26. Thomas Walter Laquer, *Religion and Respectability: Sunday Schools and Working Class Culture: 1780–1850* (New Haven: Yale University Press, 1976); Cliff, *The Rise and Development of the Sunday School Movement in England, 1780–1980*.

27. Lovegrove, *Established Church, Sectarian People*, 14; W.R. Ward, *Religion and Society in England, 1790–1850* (London: Batsford, 1972), 8.

28. Rupp, *Religion in England*, 289–322.

29. Jean and John L. Comaroff, "Home-Made Hegemony: Modernity, Domesticity and Colonialism in South Africa," in *African Encounters with Domesticity*, ed. Karen Tranberg Hansen (New Brunswick, NJ: Rutgers University Press, 1992), 40; on missionary efforts on the local front in London see Lewis, *Lighten their Darkness*.

30. Lewis, *Lighten their Darkness*, 50, 63–71.

31. Andrew F. Walls, *The Missionary Movement in Christian History: Studies in the Transmission of Faith* (Maryknoll, NY: Orbis Books, 1996), 79.

32. Jon F. Sensbach, *Rebecca's Revival: Creating Black Christianity in the Atlantic World* (Cambridge: Harvard University Press, 2005); Emilia Viotta Da Costa, *Crown of Glory, Tears of Blood: The Demerara Slave Rebellion of 1823* (New York: Oxford University Press, 1994).

33. Mary Turner, *Slaves and Missionaries: The Disintegration of Jamaican Slave Society, 1787–1834* (Urbana: University of Illinois Press, 1982), 65; Sensbach, *Rebecca's Revival*, 51, 56, 57.

34. Jon Butler, *Awash in a Sea of Faith: Christianizing the American People* (Cambridge: Harvard University Press, 1990), 134.

35. Herbert Klein, *The Middle Passage: Comparative Studies in the Atlantic Slave Trade* (Princeton: Princeton University Press, 1978).

36. John Thornton, *Africa and Africans in the Making of the Atlantic World: 1400–1680*, 2nd ed. (Cambridge: Cambridge University Press, 1998).

37. Philip Curtin, *The Atlantic Slave Trade: A Census* (Madison: The University of Wisconsin Press, 1969), 269; Phillip Curtin gives a figure of just under ten million for the

number of slaves imported between 1451 and 1870, which is a reduction of previous estimates. The number has again increased, but there seems to be a general consensus that at least approximately ten million slaves were imported to the Americas and Europe as part of the Atlantic slave trade.

38. Linda Colley, *Britons: Forging the Nation, 1707–1837* (New Haven: Yale University Press, 1992), 353; David Brion Davis, *Slavery and Human Progress* (New York: Oxford University Press, 1984) 117, 125; Hilton, *The Age of Atonement*, 209.

39. Roger Antsey, *The Atlantic Slave Trade and Abolition, 1760–1810* (London: Macmillan, 1975); James Walvin, *England, Slaves and Freedom, 1776–1838* (Jackson, Miss, 1986); Colley, *Britons*, 353–355.

40. Andrew Porter, "Religion, Missionary Enthusiasm, and Empire," in *The Oxford History of the British Empire: The Nineteenth Century*, ed. Andrew Porter 5 vols. (Oxford: Oxford University Press, 1999), 3:244.

41. Andrew F. Walls, *The Missionary Movement in Christian History*, 106; Porter, "Religion, Missionary Enthusiasm, and Empire," 235; Sanneh, *West African Christianity: The Religious Impact*, 61.

42. Rupp, *Religion in England*, 522; Andrew Porter, "Trusteeship, Anti-Slavery and Humanitarianism" in *The Oxford History of the British Empire: The Nineteenth Century*, ed. Andrew Porter, 5 vols. (Oxford: Oxford University Press, 1999), 3:202.

43. Hilton, *The Age of Atonement*, 209, emphasis in original.

44. Rupp, *Religion in England*, 523; Porter, "Trusteeship, Anti-Slavery and Humanitarianism," 202.

45. Roger Antsey, *The Atlantic Slave Trade and British Abolition, 1760–1810*; David Brion Davis, *The Problem of Slavery in the Age of Revolution, 1770–1823* (Ithaca, NY: Cornell University Press, 1975); Robin Blackburn, *The Overthrow of Colonial Slavery*, 1776–1848 (London: Verso, 1988).

46. Christopher Fyfe, *A History of Sierra Leone* (Oxford: Oxford University Press, 1962); J. Peterson, *Province of Freedom: A History of Sierra Leone, 1787–1870* (London: Faber, 1969).

47. C. A. Bayly, *Imperial Meridian: The British Empire and the World, 1780–1830* (Essex: Longman, 1989), 141.

48. Sanneh, *Abolitionists Abroad*, 65.

49. Walls, *The Missionary Movement in Christian History*, 102.

50. Sanneh, *West African Christianity*, 53.

51. Sanneh, *West African Christianity*, 68.

52. Walter L. Williams, *Black Americans and the Evangelization of Africa, 1877–1900* (Madison: University of Wisconsin Press, 1982); Bela Vassady, Jr., "The Role of the Black West Indian Missionary in West Africa, 1840–1890," (Ph.D. diss., Temple University, 1972).

53. Sanneh, *West African Christianity*, 64.

54. Walls, *The Missionary Movement in Missionary History*, 104.

55. Francis Jennings, *The Invasion of America: Indians, Colonialism and the Cant of Conquest* (Chapel Hill: University of North Carolina Press, 1975); James Axtell, *The European and the Indian, Essays in the Ethnohistory of Colonial America* (Oxford: Oxford University Press, 1981).

56. Mary Turner, *Slaves and Missionaries*; Emilia Viotti Da Costa, *Crowns of Glory*; and Robert Shell, *Children of Bondage: A Social History of the Slave Society at the Cape of

Good Hope, 1652–1838 (Hanover, NH: University Press of New England, 1994); Catherine Hall, *Civilising Subjects: Metropole and Colony in the Imperial Imagination, 1830–1867* (Chicago: University of Chicago Press, 2002); Jon F. Sensbach, *Rebecca's Revival: Creating Black Christianity in the Atlantic World* (Cambridge: Harvard University Press, 2005).

57. Dutch rule lasted from 1652 to 1795. The British took over the Cape from 1795 to 1803 and resumed control in 1806 after a brief interregnum under Batavian rule from 1803–1806.

58. Robert Ross, "The Cape of Good Hope and the World Economy, 1652–1835" in Elphick and Giliomee, *The Shaping of South African Society*, 243; Bayly, *Imperial Meridian*, 105.

59. Ross, "The Cape of Good Hope and the World Economy," 244.

60. "Report from the Landdrost and Hemraaden of Swellendam to Governor Plettenberg, and Council," March 17, 1775, and "Report from the Landdrost and Hemraaden of Stellenbosch to Governor Plettenberg and Council," January 30, 1775, in Donald Moodie, *The Record, or a series of official papers relative to the condition and treatment of the native tribes of South Africa*, 5 vols. (Cape Town: A. A. Balkema, 1960), 3:46–47.

61. Moodie, *The Record*: "Extract Letter from the Landdrost of Stellenbosch to Governor Van Plettenberg and Council," 3:94 and "Evidence relative to Trade with the Kafirs," 3:73; P. J. Van der Merwe, *The Migrant Farmer in the History of the Cape Colony*, trans. Roger Beck (Athens: Ohio University Press, 1995), 106–127; and Leonard Guelke, "Freehold Farmers and Frontier Settlers, 1657–1780," in Elphick and Giliomee, *The Shaping of South African Society*, 66–108.

62. James Armstrong, "The Slaves, 1652–1834," in Elphick and Giliomee, *The Shaping of South African Society*, 109–183; Shell, *Children of Bondage*, 41.

63. Leonard Guelke, "Freehold Farmers and Frontier Settlers," 67.

64. Van der Merwe, *The Migrant Farmer in the History of the Cape Colony*, 34, 106, 120–125.

65. In the last few years the use of the terms Khoikhoi and Khoisan have been replaced by Khoekhoe and Khoesan. I am grateful to the article by V. C. Malherbe and citations therein for clarifications of this change in orthography, "Testing the 'Burgher Right' to the Land: Khoesan, Colonist and Government in the Eastern Cape after Ordinance 50 of 1828," *SAHJ* 40 (May 1999): 1–20.

66. Richard Elphick, *Kraal and Castle, KhoiKhoi and the Founding of White South Africa* (New Haven: Yale University Press, 1977), 23; for the changing economic boundaries, see xxii, 4, 30, 39–42.

67. There is some debate over all the terms used to refer to the indigenous people of the Cape Colony. The Khoekhoe use of the term "San" to designate hunter-gatherers is sometimes problematic because it is a name the Khoekhoe imposed on the San. "Bushman," the term Europeans invariably used to refer to hunter-gatherers, is self-explanatory regarding its negative connotation, yet there is some movement among academics as well as among the people themselves toward keeping that appellation.

68. Elphick, *Kraal and Castle*, xv.

69. See, for example, the interchange between Richard Elphick and Anna Boeseken, "The Meaning, Origin and Use of the Term Khoi San and Khoesan," *CABO*: Historical

Society of Cape Town, 1(1) (August 1972): 5–10; *CABO* 2(2) (January 1974): 2–9; and *CABO* 2(3) (November 1975): 12–18. See also Elphick, *Kraal and Castle*, xv; Richard B. Lee, *The !Kung San: Men, women, and work in a foraging society* (Cambridge: Cambridge University Press, 1979); Edwin Wilmsen, *Land Filled With Flies* (Chicago: University of Chicago Press, 1989); and Robert Gordon, *The Bushman Myth: The Making of a Namibian Underclass* (Boulder, CO: Westview Press, 1992).

70. Richard Elphick and V. C. Malherbe, "The Khoesan to 1828" in Elphick and Giliomee, *The Shaping of South African Society*, 4.

71. On the origins and use of the term Fingo versus Mfengu, see Alan Webster, "Land Expropriation and Labor Extraction under Cape Colonial Rule: The War of 1835 and the Emancipation of the Fingo," (M.A. thesis, Rhodes University, 1991).

72. On the Mfengu, see Richard Moyer, "A History of the Mfengu of the Eastern Cape," (Ph.D. diss., University of London, 1976); Alan Webster, "Land Expropriation and Labor Extraction under Cape Colonial Rule"; Alan Webster, "Unmasking the Fingo: The War of 1835 Revisited," in *The Mfecane Aftermath: Reconstructive Debates in Southern African History*, ed. Carolyn Hamilton (Johannesburg: Witwatersrand University Press, 1995), 241–276; and Timothy Stapleton, "The Expansion of a Pseudo Ethnicity on the Eastern Cape: Reconsidering the Fingo Exodus of 1865," *IJAHS* 29 (2): 233–250.

73. Stapleton, "The Expansion of Pseudo Ethnicity in the Eastern Cape," 233; See also Richard Moyer, "The Mfengu, Self-Defense and the Cape Frontier Wars," in *Beyond the Cape Frontier: Studies in the History of the Transkei and the Ciskei*, eds. Christopher Saunders and Robin Derricourt (London: Longman, 1974), 101–126.

74. Martin Legassick, *The Sotho-Tswana People before 1800* (New York: Praeger Publishers, 1969), 86–125; Martin Legassick, "The Northern Frontier to C. 1840: The Rise and Decline of the Griqua People" in Elphick and Giliomee, *The Shaping of South African Society*, 358–420.

75. Elphick, *Kraal and Castle*, 68 164, 170–174.

76. Leonard Guelke and Robert Shell, "Landscape of Conquest: Frontier, Water Alienation and Khoikhoi Strategies of Survival, 1652–1780," *JSAS* 18 (4) (1992): 803–824.

77. Elphick and Malherbe, "The Khoesan to 1828," 28.

78. See Jon Butler's discussion of the "spiritual holocaust" among slaves in America in *Awash in a Sea of Faith* and Al Raboteau's discussion of the "death of the Gods" of the slaves in *Slave Religion* (Oxford: Oxford University Press, 1980).

79. "Extract of Resolution in Council," November 14, 1780, and "Instructions for the Commandant of the Eastern Country," in Moodie, *The Record* 3: 99–101; "Extract Letter from the Landdrost of Stellenbosch to Governor Van Plettenberg and Council," in Moodie, *The Record*, 3: 93, 94.

80. John Gerstner, "A Christian Monopoly: The Reformed Church and Colonial Society under Dutch Rule," in Elphick and Davenport, *Christianity in South Africa*.

81. Andre du Toit, "No Chosen People: The Myth of the Calvinist Origins of Afrikaner Nationalism and Racial Ideology," *AHR* 88 (4) (October 1983): 920–953; and Leonard Thompson, *Political Mythology of Apartheid* (New Haven: Yale University Press, 1985); Jonathan Gerstner, *The Thousand Generation Covenant: Dutch Reformed Covenant Theology and Group Identity in Colonial South Africa* (Leiden: E. J. Brill, 1991).

82. For example a commando in 1781 listed the number of men as being, "92 Christians and 40 Hottentots," Moodie, *The Record*, 3:111; and an extract from the criminal convictions before the Court of Justice on October 22, 1772, stated that Willem, a slave, and Fuyk, a "Hottentot" were "convicted of conspiring to murder and rob the Christians (the white people) [*sic*] and endeavoring to persuade several other slaves and Hottentots to join them," in Moodie, *The Record* 3: 106; at the outbreak of the second frontier war in 1793 the Moravian missionaries stationed at Genadendal noted: "The Kaffirs are said to be amongst the Christians deep inside the colony near Graaff-Reinet and brutally murdering anything belonging to the Christians," Bredekamp, H. C. and H. E. F. Plüddemann, eds, *Genadendal Diaries: Diaries of the Herrnhut Missionaries, H. Marsveld, D. Schwinn and J.C. Kühnel*, 2 vols., trans. A. B. L. Flegg (Bellville: University of the Western Cape Institute for Historical Research, 1992–1999), July 7, 1793, 1:113.

83. Gerstner, "A Christian Monopoly," 16.

84. Shell, *Children of Bondage*, 330–370; Gerstner, "A Christian Monopoly," 24–25.

85. Gerstner, "A Christian Monopoly," 27, 28.

86. The Glasgow Missionary Society (GMS) eventually split and became the Glasgow African Missionary Society (GAMS).

87. The most thorough treatment of the rebellion is found in Susan Newton-King, *Masters and Servants on the Cape Eastern Frontier* (Cambridge: Cambridge University Press, 1999).

88. After 1827, the Cape Corps became the Cape Mounted Riflemen.

89. Bredekamp and Plüddemann, *Genadendal Diaries*, December 24, 1:58.

90. Bredekamp and Plüddemann, *Genadendal Diaries*, December 24, 1792, 1:73.

91. Bredekamp and Plüddemann, *Genadendal Diaries*, March 14, 1793, 1:80.

92. Bredekamp and Plüddemann, *Genadendal Diaries*, January 1, 1795, 2:1. One wonders how the Boers convinced the workers, who may have little to no knowledge of Christianity, to fear the Christian Devil.

93. Leonard Thompson, *A History of South Africa*, 58; Le Cordeur and Saunders, *Kitchingman Papers: Missionary Letters and Journals, 1817–1848 from the Brenthurst Collection, Johannesburg* (Johannesburg: Brenthurst, 1976), 12.

94. Elbourne, "Concerning Missionaries," 158; Le Cordeur and Saunders, *Kitchingman Papers*, 12.

95. Bredekamp and Plüddemann, *Genadendal Diaries*, April 18, 1973, 1:91; Viljoen, "Moravian Missionaries, Khoisan Labor and the Overberg Colonists" in Bredekamp and Ross, *Missions and Christianity in South African History*, 52.

96. The missionaries commented on some mission residents who left the mission to work on a farm because of hunger: "They get wine four times a day. . . . Among such people our folk are (working)." Bredekamp and Plüddemann, *Genadendal Diaries*, December 8, 1793, 1:162.

97. Viljoen, "Moravian Missionaries, Khoisan Labor and the Overberg Colonists," 53–54.

98. Viljoen, "Moravian Missionaries, Khoisan Labor and the Overberg Colonists," 50.

99. Bredekamp and Plüddemann, *Genadendal Diaries*, February 2, 1795, 2:21.

100. Krüger, *The Pear Tree Blossoms*, 63; Elbourne, "Concerning Missionaries," 159–160.

101. Bredekamp and Plüddemann, *Genadendal Diaries*, March 25, 1793, 1: 81.

102. Wells, "The Scandal of Rev James Read and the Taming of the London Missionary Society by 1820," *SAHJ* 42 (May 2000): 136–160; for an early account of these hearings, see Doug Stuart, "'The Wicked Christians' and the 'Children of the Mist:' Missionary and Khoi Interactions at the Cape in the Early Nineteenth Century," University of London, Institute of Commonwealth Studies, *Societies of Southern Africa in the 19th and 20th Centuries: Collected Seminar Papers* 18 (1992).

103. On the particular contours of slavery in Africa, see Paul Lovejoy, *Transformations in Slavery* (Cambridge: Cambridge University Press, 1983); Suzanne Miers and Igor Kopytoff, eds., *Slavery in Africa* (Madison, WI: University of Wisconsin Press, 1977); Suzanne Miers and Richard Roberts, *The End of Slavery in Africa* (Madison, WI: University of Wisconsin Press, 1988); Thornton, *Africa and Africans in the Making of the Atlantic World, 1400–1680*; On slavery in South Africa, see Shell, *Children of Bondage*; Nigel Worden, *Slavery in Dutch South Africa* (Cambridge: Cambridge University Press, 1985); and Nigel Worden and Clifton Crais, eds., *Breaking the Chains: Slavery and Its Legacy in Nineteenth-Century Cape Colony* (Johannesburg: Witwatersrand University Press, 1994).

104. John Philip, *Researches in South Africa: Illustrating the Civil, Moral, and Religious Condition of Native Tribes.* 2 vols (1828; reprint, New York: Negro Universities Press, 1969).

105. C. W. Hutton, ed. *The Autobiography of the Late Sir Andries Stockenström*, 2 vols (1887; reprint, Cape Town: C. Struik, 1964), 1:358.

106. A. Stockenström to Colonel Bell, December 13, 1828 in Hutton, *Autobiography of the Late Sir Andries Stockenström*, 1:352; Ordinance 50 was so called in *The Autobiography of Sir Andries Stockenström* 1:353.

107. Hutton, *Autobiography of the Late Sir Andries Stockenström*, 1:354.

Chapter 2

1. Elphick and Davenport, *Christianity in South Africa*, 3.

2. On the 1820 settlers, see Isobel Edwards, *The 1820 Settlers: A Study in British Colonial Policy* (London: Longmans and Green, 1934); Guy Butler, *The 1820 Settlers: An Illustrated Commentary* (Cape Town: Human and Rousseau, 1974); and Lynne Bryer with Keith Hunt, *1820 Settlers* (Cape Town: Don Nelson, 1984).

3. Celia Sadler, comp., *Never a Young Man: Extracts from the Letters and Journals of the Rev. William Shaw* (Cape Town: HAUM 1967), 29.

4. Ben Maclennan, *A Proper Degree of Terror*.

5. William Shaw, *The Story of My Mission in South-eastern Africa* (London: Hamilton, 1860), 315.

6. D. W. Hammond-Tooke, ed., *Journal of William Shaw* (Cape Town: A.A. Balkema, 1972), 53, 43.

7. John Centlivres Chase, *The Cape of Good Hope and the Eastern Province of Algoa Bay* (1843; reprint, Cape Town: C. Struik, 1967); Robert Godlonton, *Sketches of the Eastern Districts of the Cape of Good Hope* (Grahamstown: Office of the Graham's Town Journal, 1842).

8. Shaw, *The Story of My Mission*, 315.

9. Shaw, *Story of My Mission*, 122; Henry Calderwood, *Caffres and Caffre Missions* (London: Nisbet, 1858), 17–22.

10. William Shaw, *A Defence of Wesleyan Missionaries in Southern Africa comprising Copies of a Correspondence with the Reverend John Philip D.D.* (London: J. Mason, 1839).

11. Price, *Making Empire*, 78.

12. Price, *Making Empire*, 113.

13. Shaw, *Story of My Mission*, 324.

14. Similarly, the LMS missionary Henry Calderwood declared in *Caffres and Caffre Missions*, "Their religious ideas if such an expression is applicable to them at all, are so dark and feeble, and indefinite, that it may truly be said we have religious ideas to create in their minds and not simply to correct wrong ones," 203.

15. "Testimony of William Shaw before the House of Commons," August 7, 1835, in, *Report of the Select Committee on Aborigines Select Committee on Aboriginal Tribes*," Great Britain, House of Commons, 1836–1837.

16. Peires, *House of Phalo*, 5, for the direct quote; for Xhosa internal politics, 46–63.

17. Alberti, *Alberti's Account of the Xhosa in 1807*, trans. W. Fehr (Cape Town: A. A. Balkema, 1968), 54; John Maclean, ed., *Compendium of Kafir Laws and Customs* (Reverend H. H. Dugmore's Papers) (Mount Coke, South Africa: Wesleyan Mission Press, 1858), 25–27.

18. Alberti, *Alberti's Account of the Xhosa in 1807*, 68; William Clifford Holden, *The Past and Future of the Kaffir Races* (1866; reprint, Cape Town: C. Struik, 1963), 225; and Peires, *House of Phalo*, 27–44.

19. Ludwig, *Alberti's Account of the Xhosa in 1807*, 53; Stephen Kay, *Travels and Researches in Caffraria: Describing the Character, Customs, and Moral Condition of the Tribes Inhabiting that portion of Southern Africa* (London: John Mason, 1833), 83; and Holden, *The Past and Future of the Kaffir Races*, 223–225.

20. Alberti, *Alberti's Account of the Xhosa in 1807*, 53–54, 56.

21. Holden, *The Past and Future of the Kaffir Races*, 185; and Maclean, *Compendium of Kafir Laws and Customs*, 103.

22. Maclean, *Compendium of Kafir laws and Customs*, 98–100.

23. John S. Mbiti, *African Religions and Philosophy* (Oxford: Heinemann, 1990), 81–84; W. D. Hammond-Tooke, "The Symbolic Structure of Cape-Nguni Cosmology," in *Religion and Social Change in Southern Africa*, Michael Whisson and Martin West, eds., (Cape Town: David Philip, 1975), 17–18.

24. Peires, *House of Phalo*, 64–65.

25. Janet Hodgson, *The God of the Xhosa: A Study of the Origins and Development of the Traditional Concepts of the Supreme Being* (Cape Town: Oxford University Press, 1982), 41; and Peires, *House of Phalo*, 65.

26. Hodgson, *God of the Xhosa*, 6–11; and Peires, *House of Phalo*, 65, 67, 68.

27. Shaw, *Story of My Mission*, 346.

28. Steedman, *Wanderings and Adventures in the Interior of Southern Africa*, 2 vols. (London: Longman, 1835), 1:36.

29. Shaw, *Story of My Mission*, 333–336, 470–475.

30. Shaw, *Story of My Mission*, 335.

31. Shaw, *Story of My Mission*, 478–483, 485.

32. Hildegarde Fast, ed., *The Journal and Selected Letters of Rev. William J., Shrewsbury, 1826–1835* (Johannesburg: Witwatersrand University Press, 1994), 55–57.

33. Fast, ed., *Journal and Selected Letters*, 57, emphasis in original.

34. Alberti, *Alberti's Account of the Xhosa in 1807*, 97.

35. Donavan Williams, "The Missionaries on the Eastern Frontier of the Cape Colony, 1799–1853" (Ph.D. diss., University of Witswatersrand, 1959), 72–83, 149–157; and Alan Gibson, *Eight Years in Kaffraria, 1882–1890* (1891; reprint, New York: Negro Universities Press, 1969), 167.

36. N. K. Hurt, "Wesleyan Missionaries on the Eastern Frontier of the Cape Colony, 1820–1840 with special reference to the Kaffir War of 1834–1835," (MA thesis, University of London, 1957), 38.

37. CL, MS 15 1188, Anonymous Manuscript, (n. d.).

38. "Testimony of William Shaw," *Select Committee on Aborigines*, August 7, 1835.

39. Although William Shrewsbury, when considering the place of witchcraft in Xhosa society, mused that there was "rational ground . . . to suppose it is probable, if not to believe it as fact, that God judicially punishes this ignorant people for their willful and habitual practice of theft, lying, covetousness and lasciviousness—the prevailing sins of the country—by occasionally permitting Satan to exercise, by means of wicked men, greater power in inflicting or causing evil than he ordinarily is allowed to exercise in regions where the name of Christ is known, while that great Adversary also is permitted to tyrannize in the minds of the people and keep them in bondage and fear." Fast, *Journal and Selected Letters*, 36.

40. Samuel Young, *A Missionary Narrative of the Triumphs of Grace as Seen in the Conversion of Kafirs, Hottentots, Fingoes and other Natives of South Africa* (New York: G. Lande and P.P. Stanford, 1843), 25.

41. Young, *A Missionary Narrative of the Triumphs of Grace*, 75–76.

42. Williams, "The Missionaries on the Eastern Frontier," 67, 68.

43. Shaw, *Story of My Mission*, 464.

44. Shaw, *Story of My Mission*, 466.

45. Fast, *Journal and Selected Letters*, 108.

46. Shaw, *Story of My Mission*, 462–466; Young, *A Missionary Narrative of the Triumphs of Grace*, 75–76, 143; Fast, *Journal and Selected Letters*, 65, 66; "Testimony of William Shaw," *Select Committee on Aborigines*, August 7, 1835.

47. Joseph Whiteside, *History of the Wesleyan Methodist Church of South Africa* (London: Elliot Stock, 1906), 170.

48. SAL, "Report of the Wesleyan Missionary Society for the Albany and Kaffraria District for the Year ending 1853."

49. Kay, *Travels and Researches in Caffraria*, 62.

50. Holden, *Past and Future of the Kaffir Races*, 225.

51. Peter Hinchliff, ed., *Journal of John Ayliff* (Cape Town: A. A. Balkema, 1971), 30.

52. Holden, *Past and Future of the Kaffir Races*, 203, 207–208.

53. "Testimony of Stephen Kay before the House of Commons," *Select Committee on Aboriginal Tribes*, March 21, 1837.

54. Robert Young, *African Wastes Reclaimed: Illustrated in the Story of the Lovedale Mission* (London: J. M. Dent, 1902), 31.

55. Philip Mayer, *Townsmen or Tribesmen: Conservatism and the Process of Urbanization in a South African City* (Cape Town: Oxford University Press, 1961); B.A. Pauw, "Universalism and Particularism in the Beliefs of Xhosa-Speaking Christians" and Archie

Mafeje, "Religion, Class and Ideology in South Africa" both in Whisson and West, *Religion and Social Change in Southern Africa*, 153–163 and 164–184; B. A. Pauw, *Christianity and Xhosa Tradition: Belief and Ritual among Xhosa-Speaking Christians* (Cape Town: Oxford University Press, 1975).

56. Upon settling at the Cape as a military colonist, Gustav Steinbert referred to the Xhosa in the 1850s as "wild red Kaffirs," J. F. Schwar And R. W. Jardine, eds., and transl. *The Letters and Journal of Gustav Steinbert*, 2 vols. (Port Elizabeth: University of Port Elizabeth, 1975), 1:119.

57. David Chidester, *Religions of South Africa* (London: Routledge, 1992), 41.

58. As the Anglican missionary Alan Gibson noted in the 1880s, there was a general feeling that "the man gained to Christianity is lost to the tribe—a sentiment which has evoked against Christianity all the force of patriotism," *Eight Years in Kaffraria*, 167. Clarify the sentence—it seems as if the focus is on missionaries' perceptions of African culture rather than African subversion by adhering to Christianity.

59. For an interesting perspective from one of these magistrates in the later nineteenth century, see "Individualism amongst the Africans," in Godfrey Callaway, *South Africa from within, made Known in the Letters of a Magistrate* (London: SPCK, 1930), 117–120.

60. A German military colonist described "heaps" of Xhosa who had succumbed to hunger and "emaciated pictures of misery" who managed to "drag themselves to our settlement." Alfred von Mauntz, "Reminiscences of British Kaffraria," in Shwar and Jardine, *The Letters and Journal of Gustav Steinbart*, appendix, 200.

61. "Testimony of William Shaw," *Select Committee on Aborigines*, August 21, 1835.

62. "Testimony of William Shaw," *Select Committee on Aborigines*, August 7, 1835.

63. Young, *A Missionary Narrative of the Triumphs of Grace*, 75.

64. Shaw, *Story of My Mission*, 381; and Young, *A Missionary Narrative of the Triumphs of Grace*, 47.

65. Fast, *Journal and Selected Letters*, 72, 155.

66. Young, *A Missionary Narrative of the Triumphs of Grace*, 46.

67. Shaw, *Story of My Mission*, 419–420.

68. Hildegarde Fast, "In at One Ear and Out at the Other: African Response to the Wesleyan Message in Xhosaland, 1825–1835," *Journal of Religion in Africa* (23) (2) (1993), 147; and Williams, "The Missionaries on the Eastern Frontier," 64, 66–75.

69. Horton Davies, *Great South African Christians*, (Oxford: Oxford University Press, 1951), 101; See also Landau, *The Realm of the Word*.

70. See the interesting story of a future chief, Mtshazi, who was educated in England and converted to Christianity. He then faced excommunication from the Church for choosing to marry several wives and leading a traditional lifestyle; see Godfrey Callaway, *Sketches of Kafir Life* (1905; reprint, New York: Negro Universities Press, 1969), 61–72.

71. James Backhouse, *A Narrative of a Visit to Mauritius and South Africa* (London: Hamilton, Adams, 1844), 266.

72. Fast, ed., *Journal and Selected Letters*, 40; See Calderwood, *Caffres and Caffre Missions* for a similar anecdote in which a chief, acknowledging how missionaries usurped chiefly power, purportedly observed that, "When my people become Christians, they cease to be my people," 210–211.

73. CAR, BK 90, "John Maclean to Edward Clay, October 4, 1850," emphasis mine.

74. Gibson, *Eight Years in Kaffraria*, 168.

75. William Clifford Holden, *British Rule in South Africa illustrated in the Story of Kama and his Tribe and the War in Zululand* (1879; reprint, Pretoria: State Library, 1969).

76. Peires, *House of Phalo*, 131.

77. Landau, *Popular Politics in the History of South Africa*, 149.

78. Janet Hodgson, *Princess Emma* (Craighall, South Africa: Ad. Donker, 1987), 55.

79. Stapleton, *Maqoma: Xhosa Resistance to Colonial Advance*, 199, 201; for the high death rates of children from the Caribbean visiting or living in Europe, see Sensbach, *Rebecca's Revival*, 183.

80. Samuel Young, *A Missionary Narrative of the Triumphs of Grace*, 123–129; Barnabas Shaw, *Memorials of South Africa* (London: J. Mason, 1841), 201–204.

81. Fast, *Journal and Selected Letters*, 42. Some of these personalities include Lieutenant Colonel Somerset, who was commanding the troops on the eastern frontier, Donald Moodie, and the chiefs Phato, Mqhai, Kama, Quasana, Kobe, Nqeno, Umpethlo, and Abana.

82. See Landeg White, *Magomero: Portrait of an African Village* for a good example of this in Nyasaland (Malawi).

83. Fast, *Journal and Selected Letters*, 34; "Testimony of William Shaw," *Select Committee on Aborigines*, August 7, 1835.

84. Fast, *Journal and Selected Letters*, 34, 35, 72, 137; "Testimony of William Shaw," *Select Committee on Aborigines*, August 7, 1835; Young, *A Missionary Narrative of the Triumphs of Grace*, 74–75.

85. Shaw, *Story of My Mission*, 330–331, emphasis mine.

86. Fast, *Journal and Selected Letters*, 44.

87. Calderwood, *Caffres and Caffre Missions*, 81.

88. In *Caffres and Caffre Missions*, Calderwood of the LMS declared these periods of inquiry as "fatiguing, sometimes very trying, at other times delightful, but always instructive," 76.

89. Shaw, *Story of My Mission*, 330.

90. "Testimony of Stephen Kay before the House of Commons," *Select Committee on Aborigines*, March 22, 1837.

91. Hammond-Tooke, *Journal of William Shaw*, 123.

92. Fast, *Journal and Selected Letters*, 74; Similar incidents occurred at Scottish missions. In the pioneer era of the 1820s and 1830s Robert Young wrote, "[T]he natives would come to church with their bodies and karosses besmeared with red clay, and, slipping off the wooden slab benches, would squat on the ground and take out their pipes and have a smoke. They knew no better. Church services to them were quite a novelty," *African Wastes Reclaimed*, 142.

93. Fast, *Journal and Selected Letters*, 29.

94. Steedman, *Wanderings and Adventures in the Interior of Southern Africa*, 1: 34.

95. John W. D. Moodie, *Ten Years in South Africa: Including a Particular Description of the Wild Sports of that Country*, 2 vols (London: Richard Bentley, 1835), 262.

96. Shaw, *Story of My Mission*, 392–393; Backhouse, *A Narrative of a Visit to Maritius and South Africa*, 261.

97. Robert Gray, *A Journal of the Bishop's Visitation Tour through the Cape Colony in 1848* (London: Society for the Propagation of the Gospel, 1851), 100–101; Backhouse, *A Narrative of a Visit to Maritius and South Africa*, 257.

98. Fast, "Introduction," in *Journal and Selected Letters*, 12.

99. Fast, *Journal and Selected Letters*, 72, 75, italics in original.

100. Fast, *Journal and Selected Letters*, 125.

101. Moodie, *Ten Years in South Africa*, 2: 280.

102. Fast, *Journal and Selected Letters*, 72, italics in original.

103. Fast, *Journal and Selected Letters*, 74.

104. Sanneh, *Translating the Message*. Not all missionaries in South Africa shared the same opinion about the vernacular, however. In his monograph *Caffres and Caffre Missions*, Henry Calderwood declared in a rather condescending tone that while he would rejoice that Africans could read the Bible in the vernacular, their languages had some shortcomings. English was the best means to facilitate the civilizing mission. The local vernacular, he asserted, were languages of "a savage people having little knowledge and few wants. Their ideas are not only few, but wholly confined to objects of sense . . . their language is not a very efficient medium through which to convey accurate views of spiritual and abstract truth to such minds," 233.

105. On missionary proficiency in African languages, see Mesthrie, "Words Across Worlds: Aspects of Language Contact and Language Learning in the Eastern Cape, 1800–1850"; John Frye, ed., *The War of the Axe and the Xosa Bible: The Journal of Reverend J. W. Appleyard* (Cape Town: C. Struik, 1971).

106. Monica Wilson, *The Interpreters*, (Grahamstown: 1820 Settlers, National Monument Foundation, 1972), 8; Williams, "The Missionaries on the Eastern Frontier," 198.

107. Fast, *Journal and Selected Letters*, 129.

108. Moodie, *Ten Years in South Africa*, 2: 256–257, emphasis his.

109. Fast, *Journal and Selected Letters*, 129, emphasis in original.

110. See, for example, Gibson, *Eight Years in Kaffraria*, 54, emphasis mine.

111. Callaway, *Sketches of Kafir Life*, 103.

112. Gray, *A Journal of the Bishop's Visitation Tour*, 100–101; Backhouse, *A Narrative of a Visit to Maritius and South Africa*, 257.

113. Fast, *Journal and Selected Letters*, 125.

114. Fast, *Journal and Selected Letters*, 124.

115. James Perrigo, *Recollections of a Visit to Kaffraria* (London: SPCK, 1866), 78.

116. Fast, *Journal and Selected Letters*, 105.

117. Fast, *Journal and Selected Letters*, 105.

118. Fast, *Journal and Selected Letters*, 95.

119. Fast, *Journal and Selected Letters*, 99.

120. Fast, *Journal and Selected Letters*, 152.

121. Fast, *Journal and Selected Letters*, 44.

122. Fast, *Journal and Selected Letters*, 29. What did this process entail? It is interesting that the Methodists seem so desperate for converts yet insist on being so exclusive.

123. Shaw, *Story of My Mission*, 380, 381.

124. Perrigo, *Recollections of a Visit to British Kaffraria*, 78.

125. Fast, Shrewsbury, *Journal and Selected Letters*, 125.

126. Williams, *The Missionaries on the Eastern Frontier*; Norman Etherington, *Preachers, Peasants and Politics in Southeast Africa, 1835–1880: African Christian Communities in Natal, Pondoland, and Zululand* (London: Royal Historical Society, 1978); and Erlank, "Gender and Christianity among Africans Attached to Scottish Missions in Xhosaland."

127. Young, *A Missionary Narrative*, 86.

128. Young, *A Missionary Narrative*, 120.

129. Young, *A Missionary Narrative*, 119.

130. Young, *A Missionary Narrative*, 120.

131. Young, *A Missionary Narrative*, 121.

132. Young, *A Missionary Narrative*, 121.

133. Etherington, *Preachers, Peasants and Politics in Southeast Africa*, 87; Erlank, "Gender and Christianity among Africans Attached to Scottish Missions in Xhosaland," 83.

134. Fast, *Journal and Selected Letters*, 78–80.

135. Fast, "Introduction," *Journal and Selected Letters*, 17–18.

Chapter 3

1. Keith Hunt, "The Development of Municipal Government in the Eastern Province of the Cape of Good Hope with reference to Grahamstown, 1827–1862" (Rhodes University: M.A. thesis, 1961; reprint, *Archives Yearbook for South African History* 61 (Cape Town: Office of the Director of Archives, 1963), 205, 206.

2. Shaw, *Story of My Mission*, 290.

3. The Zuurveld: sour veld, a characteristic that means the Zuurveld provides suitable pasture only for about six months out of the year. As a result cattle belonging to whites and Africans have to migrate seasonally, creating protracted disputes over land and water access.

4. For an historiographical treatment of frontiers in South Africa including the Eastern Cape frontier, see Martin Legassick, "The Frontier Tradition in South African Historiography," 44–79; for a comparative perspective on the frontier, see Lamar and Thompson, *The Frontier in History*; on the historiographical treatment of the Eastern Cape frontier, see note in the Introduction.

5. Giliomee, "The Eastern Frontier," 433.

6. Giliomee, "The Eastern Frontier," 432.

7. Maclennan, *A Proper Degree of Terror*, 148.

8. "Report from the Landdrost and Hemraaden of Swellendam to Governor Plettenberg, and Council," in Moodie, *The Record*, 3: 47–48.

9. Moodie, *The Record* 5: 9–10; For further reinforcement among Cape colonial officials that the Fish River was the boundary of the Colony as well as the difficulties of maintaining and policing this border, see Moodie, *The Record* 3: 93, 94, 100, 101; 5: 14, 58.

10. John Campbell, *Travels in South Africa, 2nd ed.* (1815; reprint, Cape Town: Struik, 1974), 100–101.

11. On the 1820 Settlers, see A. E. Makin, *The 1820 Settlers of Salem* (Wynberg, South Africa: Juta 1971).

12. A. Stockenström to Colonel Bell, December 13, 1828, in Hutton, *Autobiography of the Late Sir Andries Stockenström*, 352.

13. Moodie, *The Record*, 5: 18–19.

14. Le Cordeur, *The Politics of Eastern Cape Separatism*, 281.

15. Keegan, *Colonial South Africa and the Origins of the Racial Order*, 156.

16. Cowper Rose, *Four Years in Southern Africa* (London: Henry Colburn and Richard Bentley, 1829), 54, 55.

17. Rose, *Four Years in Southern Africa*, 45.

18. Rose, *Four Years in Southern Africa*, 45.

19. The 1820 Settlers suffered many material hardships for the first few years of their settlement. Obstacles such as crop failures, heavy rain, and unfamiliarity with the appropriate farming methods and the terrain caused many to leave the lands allocated in search of more suitable employment. For first-hand account of these hardships, see: Una Long, ed., *The Chronicle of Jeremiah Goldswain, Albany Settler of 1820*, vol. 1 (Cape Town: The Van Riebeeck Society, 1946); Margaret Rainier, *The Journals of Sophia Pigot* (Cape Town: A. A. Balkema, 1974); Hinchliff, *The Journal of John Ayliff*; W. A. Maxwell and R. T. McGeogh, eds., *The Reminiscence of Thomas Stubbs* (Cape Town: A. A. Balkema, 1978); Thomas Pringle, *Narrative of a Residence in South Africa* (Cape Town: C. Struik, 1966).

20. Long, *The Chronicle of Jeremiah Goldswain, Albany Settler of 1820*, 24. The spelling errors are in the original journal.

21. Arthur Keppel-Jones, ed., *Philips, 1820 Settler, His Letters* (Pietermaritzburg: Shuter and Shooter, 1960), 51.

22. Hammond-Tooke, *Journal of William Shaw*, 43.

23. Hinchliff, *The Journal of John Ayliff*, 27, 31, 40.

24. "The Village That Came Alive Again," *Sunday Times Magazine*, July 4, 1976.

25. Crais, *White Supremacy and Black Resistance*, 88–93; Lester, *Imperial Networks*, 48–53.

26. Lester, *Imperial Networks*, 53–54.

27. Deborah Gaitskell, "Rethinking Gender Roles: The Field Experience of Women Missionaries in South Africa," in *The Imperial Horizons of British Protestant Missions* (Grand Rapids, William B. Eerdmans, Publishing, 2003), 134, 136; 138; Patricia Grimshaw and Peter Sherlock, "Women and Cultural Exchange," in *Oxford History of the British Empire: Missions and Empire*, ed. Norman Etherington (New York: Oxford University Press, 2005), 180–182.

28. Lester, *Imperial Networks*, 54; Keegan, *Colonial South Africa and the Origins of the Racial Order*, 131.

29. [Henry Ellis, Dep. Colonial Secretary], "Circular No. 7," Grahamstown, May 23, 1820, cited in William Wilberforce Bird, *State of the Cape of Good Hope in 1822* (1823; reprint, Cape Town: C. Struik, 1966), 201–202.

30. "Inventory of the estate of the late P. Amm of Lindale," *GTJ*, May 3, 1873.

31. Thompson, *Travels and Adventures in Southern Africa: Comprising a View of the Present State of the Cape Colony with Observation on the Progress and Prospects of the British Emigrants*, 2 vols (London: Henry Colburn, 1827), 1: 26.

32. Fast, *Journal and Selected Letters*, 27.

33. Fast, *Journal and Selected Letters*, 27; see also Margot Winer and James Deetz, "The Transformation of British Culture in the Eastern Cape, 1820-1860," *Social Dynamics* 16 (1) (1990): 55–75; Jill Payne, "Re-creating Home: British Colonialism, Culture and The Zuurveld Environment in the 19th Century (MA thesis, Rhodes University, 1998), 13.

34. "Memorial of Uitenhage Agricultural and Horticultural Society," (with annexures on the Eastern Division of the Cape Colony), Theal, *RCC* 28: 366–367.

35. Backhouse, *A Narrative of a Visit to Mauritius and South Africa*, 174.

36. Backhouse, *A Narrative of a Visit to Mauritius and South Africa*, 174.

37. Shaw, *Story of My Mission*, 76.

38. Hammond-Tooke, *Journal of William Shaw*, 38; Shaw, *Story of My Mission*, 115.

39. Chase, *The Cape of Good Hope*; Godlonton, *Sketches of the Eastern Districts of the Cape of Good Hope*.

40. "Cursory Remarks on a Letter from Sir Rufane Shawe Donkin to Earl Bathurst, April 6, 1827," in Theal, comp., *RCC* 32: 453; Backhouse, *A Narrative of a Visit to Mauritius and South Africa*, 174.

41. "Directory of Grahamstown, 1843," in Chase, *The Cape of Good Hope*, 287–294.

42. CL, MS 15 899/1, Grahamstown Baptismal Registry.

43. Shaw, *Story of My Mission*, 117, 280; Hinchliff, *Journal of John Ayliff*, 34. On "Prize Negroes," see Christopher Saunders, "Free Yet Slaves: Prize Negroes at the Cape Revisited," in *Breaking the Chains*, eds. Nigel Worden and Clifton Crais (Johannesburg: Witwatersrand University Press, 1994), 99–115; "Liberated Africans in the Cape Colony in the First Half of the Nineteenth Century," *IJAS* 18 (1985): 223–239; "Between Slavery and Freedom," *Kronos* 9 (1984): 36–43.

44. Hammond-Tooke, *The Journal of William Shaw*, 61.

45. Peires, *The House of Phalo*, 106

46. Keppel-Jones, *Philipps, 1820 Settler*, 322; Hammond-Tooke, *The Journal of William Shaw*, 43; Backhouse, *A Narrative of a Visit to Mauritius and South Africa*, 174.

47. Backhouse, *A Narrative of a Visit to Mauritius and South Africa*, 309.

48. Shaw, *Story of My Mission*, 78; Backhouse, *A Narrative of a Visit to Mauritius and South Africa*, 309.

49. [Communication from the Landdrost of Somerset February 20, 1827], in Theal, *RCC*, 34: 371–372.

50. Susan Newton-King, "The Labor Market of the Cape Colony 1807–1828," in *Economy and Society in Pre-Industrial South Africa*, eds. Shula Marks and Anthony Atmore (London: Longman, 1980), 171–207.

51. [Council Meeting, March 6, 1827,] *RCC*, vol. 34: 367.

52. [Communication from the Landdrost of Somerset, February 20, 1827] in Theal, *RCC* 34: 370.

53. Crais, *White Supremacy and Black Resistance in South Africa*, 76–79.

54. Crais, *White Supremacy and Black Resistance in South Africa*, 79.

55. [Communication from the Landdrost of Somerset] in Theal, *RCC*, 34:371.

56. Maxwell and McGeogh, *The Reminiscences of Thomas Stubbs*, 93; Hutton, *The Autobiography of the Late Sir Andries Stockenström*, 1: 353–365. For rumors in the 1820s, see also Hinchliff, *Journal of John Ayliff*, 20–21.

57. Hutton, *The Autobiography of the Late Sir Andries Stockenström*, 1:353.

58. Keppel-Jones, *Philipps, 1820 Settler*, 321, 323; for Philipps's discussion of the unfaithfulness of the regiment, see also 108–108; 213–214.

59. "Meeting at Uitenhage," February 19, 1827, Theal, *RCC*. 34: 369.

60. "Mrs. Philipps to My Dear Sister," July 14, 1825, in Keppel-Jones, *Philipps, 1820 Settler*, 250.

61. "Hottentot Institutions," *South African Commercial Advertiser*, March 10, 1824.

62. [Council Meeting, March 6, 1827] in Theal, *RCC* 34: 367, 372.

63. "Extract of a Letter from Mrs. Phillips [to her sister in law Catherine]" October 9, 1826, in Keppel-Jones, *Philipps, 1820 Settler*, 314.

64. "Extract of a letter from Mrs. Philips to Mrs. Lee," November 27, 1825, in Keppel-Jones, *Philipps, 1820 Settler*, 252.

65. "Mrs. Philipps to Mrs. R," July 14, 1825, in Keppel-Jones, *Philipps, 1820 Settler*, 251.

66. Keppel-Jones, *Philipps, 1820 Settler*, 323.

67. Moyer, "The Mfengu, Self Defense and the Cape Frontier War," 101.

68. "Extract of a Letter from Mrs. Philipps to Mrs. Lee," November 27, 1825, in Keppel-Jones, *Philipps, 1820 Settler*, 251.

69. Crais, *White Supremacy and Black Resistance in South Africa*, 77.

70. "Mrs. Philipps to Mrs. R." in Keppel-Jones, *Philipps, 1820 Settler*, 250; her husband found little to endear him to Theopolis and he subjected the mission to quite a verbal shellacking; see Payne, "Re-creating Home," 70.

71. Robert Ross, "Congregations, Missionaries and the Grahamstown Schism of 1842–43" in *The London Missionary Society in Southern Africa: Historical Essays in Celebration of the LMS in Southern Africa*, ed. John De Gruchy (Cape Town: David Philip, 1999), 124.

72. CAR, MS 17 044, Letter from John Montagu to Chas. L. Stretch, diplomatic agent, re memorial of certain missionaries respecting Kaffir laws, December 4, 1844.

73. CAR, BK 90, John Maclean to Reverend E. Clay, October 4, 1850.

74. CAR, CO 465, William Shaw to Colonel Bell, April 2, 1839.

75. CAR, CO 465, William Shaw to Colonel Bell, April 2, 1839.

76. CL, WMMS, *Annual Report*, Grahamstown, 1838.

77. "Isi-milo sika-Pato gayo i-Sabbata," *Umshumayeli Wendaba*, 3 (1837): 1–4; "Indaba za kwa-Kma," *Umshumayeli Wendaba* (October 1840): 3–6; "Imbali zabantu ba kudala: U-Adame," *Umshumayeli Wendaba* (1840): 1–4; "Imbali zabantu ba kudala: U-Eva," *Umshumayeli Wendaba*, 3 (October 1840): 1–3.

78. CAR, CO 465 William Shaw to Colonel Bell, April 2, 1839.

79. Shaw, *Story of My Mission*, 291.

80. Shaw, *Story of My Mission*, 65.

81. Shaw, *Story of My Mission*, 34–35.

82. "A Letter to the Right Hon. The Earl of Aberdeen," in Sadler, *Never A Young Man*, 157.

83. CAR, CO 465, William Shaw to Colonel Bell, April 2, 1839.

84. Hutton, *The Autobiography of the Late Sir Andries Stockenström*, 1: 353–354.

85. *GTJ*, June 8, 1832.

86. *GTJ*, June 8, 1832.

87. *GTJ*, August 10, 1832; December 13, 1832.

88. *GTJ*, June 29, 1832.

89. *GTJ*, June 6, 1833.

90. CAR, CO 465, William Shaw to Colonel Bell, April 2, 1839.

91. Crais, *White Supremacy and Black Resistance in South Africa*, 78.

92. CAR, CO 465, William Shaw to Colonel Bell, April 2, 1839.

93. CAR, CO 465, William Shaw to Colonel Bell, April 2, 1839; Shaw, *Story of My Mission*, 290–292; for a discussion of mission and labor see Patrick Wilkinson, *Church Clothes:*

Land, Mission, and the End of Apartheid in South Africa in South Africa (Washington, DC: *Maisonneuve Press*, 2004), 35, 169.

94. "Return of the Residents and their Families, and Property at the Wesleyan Mission Institution at Farmerfield," 7 and February 8, 1849, in Cape of Good Hope, *Master and Servant, Addenda to the Documents on the Working Order in Council,* July 21, 1846. Figure extrapolated from the total number of household heads listed at Farmerfield in 1849.

95. Shaw, *Story of My Mission*, 293.

96. Shaw, *Story of My Mission*, 293.

97. CL, MS 15 034, Deed of Transfer [Kliphuevel/Farmerfield], May 28, 1839.

98. Shaw, *Story of My Mission*, 293.

Chapter 4

1. William Shaw, *Story of My Mission*, 291.

2. CL, Cameron, *Journal*, June 14, 1839.

3. Godlonton, comp., *Sketches of the Eastern Districts*, 116–117; Stubbs, *Reminiscences*, 74.

4. Of course, the old, the infirm, or otherwise disabled probably faced little opposition from their former owners as they were considered a liability. On apprenticeship and emancipation, see Nigel Worden, "Between Slavery and Freedom: The Apprenticeship Period, 1834–1838," in *Breaking the Chains*, Worden and Crais, eds., 117–144; Robert Shell, *Children of Bondage*; John Mason, "'Fit for Freedom:' The Slaves, Slavery, and Emancipation in the Cape Colony, South Africa, 1806–1842" (Ph.D. diss., Yale University, 1992) and *Social Death and Resurrection* (Charlottesville: University Press of Virginia, 2003).

5. CAR, CO 485, William Shaw to Colonel Bell, April 2, 1839.

6. CL, WMMS, "The Report of the Wesleyan Methodist Missionary Society," 1840, 59–60; Robert Godlonton, comp., *Sketches of the Eastern Districts*, 53.

7. On the creation of Colored identity, see the classic works: W. M. Macmillan, *The Cape Colour Question, A Historical Survey* (Cape Town: A. A. Balkema, 1968); J. S. Marais, *The Cape Coloured People* (London: Longmans, 1939).

8. CAR, CO 465, H. P. Halbeck to Colonel Bell, April 8, 1839, Enon, Genadendal and Elim; Edna Bradlow, "Capitalists and Laborers in the Post-Emancipation Rural Cape—I" *Historia* 31 (September 1985): 49–62; "Capitalist and Laborers in the Post-Emancipation Rural Cape—II" *Historia* 31 (May 1986): 57–67; *Graham's Town Journal* April 18, 1839; E. H. Ludlow, "Missions and Emancipation in the South-West Cape: A Case Study of Groenekloof (Mamre), 1838–52" (M.A. thesis, University of Cape Town, 1992), and "Groenkloof after the Emancipation of Slaves, 1838–1852: Leavers, Soldiers and Rebels," in Bredekamp and Ross, *Missions and Christianity in South African History*, 113–133.

9. The circular, dated March 12, 1839, asked "Are the late Apprenticed laborers solicited or encouraged by the missionaries to quit the employment of the farmers and repair to the institution [mission stations]?"

10. CAR, CO 485, William Shaw to Colonel Bell, April 2, 1839.

11. [Rules and Regulations of the Farmerfield Estate], in Farmerfield Estate Trust Committee, Report to the Grahamstown District Synod, (n. d).

12. [Rules and Regulations of the Farmerfield Estate], Farmerfield Estate Trust Committee, Report to the Grahamstown District Synod (n. d.).

13. "Henry H. Dugmore, Wesleyan Missionary to Col. McKinnon, Chief Commissioner," June 30, 1848, in Andre Du Toit, *The Earliest South African Documents on the Education and Civilization of the Bantu*, (Pretoria: Communications of the University of South Africa, 1963), 73, emphasis in original.

14. "Henry H. Dugmore, Wesleyan Missionary to Col. McKinnon, Chief Commissioner," in Du Toit, *Earliest South African Documents*, 73.

15. CAR, CO 486, William Shaw to Colonel Bell, April 2, 1839.

16. Backhouse, *Narrative*, 305; Shaw, *Story of My Mission*, 294.

17. See Christopher Saunders, "Liberated Africans in the Cape Colony on the First Half of the Nineteenth Century," *International Journal of African Historical Studies* 18 (1985): 223–239; and "Free Yet Slaves: Prize Negroes at the Cape Revisited," in *Breaking the Chains: Slavery and Its Legacy in the Nineteenth-Century Cape Colony*, Nigel Worden and Clifton Crais, eds., (Johannesburg: Witwatersrand University Press, 1994), 99–115.

18. "Testimony of William Shaw," *Select Committee on Aborigines*, August 7, 1835.

19. Michael Ashley, "African Education and Society in the Nineteenth Century Eastern Cape," in *Beyond the Cape Frontier: Studies in the History of the Transkei and Ciskei*, Christopher Saunders and Robin Derricourt, eds., (London: Longman, 1974) 201.

20. For similar discussion about isolating African youth from their homes in an attempt to limit "heathen" influences, see also Gibson, *Eight Years in Kaffraria*, 88.

21. Fast, ed., *Journal and Selected Letters, 1826–1835* (Johannesburg: Witwatersrand University Press, 1994), 63.

22. CL, WMMS, *Annual Report, 1826*, 42.

23. Shaw, *Story of My Mission*, 292; CL, MS 15 023/1[1830–1839], Minute Book for the Albany District, Minutes of the Fifteenth Annual District Meeting, Grahamstown, March 7, 1839.

24. Backhouse, *Narrative*, 304; see also Barnabas Shaw, *Memorials of South Africa* (London: J. Mason, 1841), 249.

25. Backhouse, *Narrative*, 305.

26. See Backhouse, *Narrative*, 393, for a description of one of the chiefs whose son was a pupil of the Watson Institute at Farmerfield; Baron Frederick John Dealtry Lugard, *The Rise of Our East African Empire: Early Efforts in Nyasaland and Uganda* (London: W. Blackwood, 1893), 71.

27. Various individuals at the Cape tried to implement similar plans for changing African societies through the influence of young people. This was Governor George Grey's motivation, for example, in creating a college for the children of African chiefs and other influential individuals in African societies. For a detailed example of a chief's daughter who was subjected to such intervention through schooling and her choice of marriage partners see Janet Hodgson, *Princess Emma* (Craighall, South Africa: A.D. Donker, 1987). On George Grey, see J. Rutherford, *Sir George Grey* (London: 1961).

28. Shaw, *Story of My Mission*, 292.

29. "Wesleyan Mission at Farmerfield, South Africa," *Papers Relative to the Wesleyan Missions and to the State of "Heathen" Countries*, (December 1847), 207; Fast, ed., *Journal and Selected Letters*, 63; Smith, *South Africa Delineated*, 119.

30. CL, MS 15 023/3: 1845–1858, Report of the Salem and Farmerfield Circuit, 1848, appendix 2; SAL, WMS, *Annual Report*, 1844; *Annual Report*, 1850.

31. See the responses that the following missionaries of the Wesleyan Missionary Society, Berlin Missionary Society, London Missionary Society, Glasgow Missionary Society, United Brethren (Moravians) made to the colonial government in 1848 for the best way to educate, civilize, and uplift the African population newly subdued and absorbed into the Cape Colony after the Frontier War of 1846–1847: Adolphus Schaller, A. Kropf, F. G. Kayers, John Ross, J. Schultheiss, J. C. Warner, James Laing, James Weir, A. Bonatz, James Read, Sr., James Read, Jr., Henry H. Dugmore, Robert Niven, and William Impey in Du Toit, *Earliest South African Documents*, 37–91.

32. "Adolphus Schaller to His Excellency," March 18, 1848; Du Toit, *Earliest South African Documents*, 39.

33. "A. Bonatz to His Excellency," in Du Toit, *Earliest South African Documents*, 65.

34. "J. Schultheiss to the High Commissioner," May 10, 1848, in Du Toit, *Earliest South African Documents*, 48.

35. Robert Young, *African Wastes Reclaimed, Illustrated in the Story of the Lovedale Mission* (London: J. M. Dent, 1902); Robert Shepherd, *Lovedale, South Africa: The Story of a Century* (Lovedale: The Lovedale Press, 1931); Henry Calderwood, *Caffres and Caffre Missions*, 134–136; 140–141, 143.

36. CL, MS 15 023: 3 1845–1858, Report of the Salem and Farmerfield Circuit, Appendix 2; CAR, BK 90 "Report of the Training and Day School at Mount Coke," 1853; Shaw, *Story of My Mission*, 477; Calderwood, *Caffres and Caffre Missions*, 140–141.

37. Shaw, *Story of My Mission*, 294.

38. "Wesleyan Mission at Farmerfield, South Africa," *Papers Relative to the Wesleyan Missions*, frontispiece.

39. "Wesleyan Mission at Farmerfield, South Africa," *Papers Relative to the Wesleyan Missions*, 207.

40. CAR, CO 485, William Shaw to Colonel Bell, April 2, 1839.

41. Chase, *The Cape of Good Hope*, 37; Godlonton, *Sketches of the Eastern Districts of the Cape of Good Hope*, 7.

42. Jane Sales, *Mission Stations and the Coloured Communities of the Eastern Cape, 1800–1852* (Cape Town: A. A. Balkema, 1975) 67–68; Backhouse, *Narrative*, 297; Marion Rose Currie. "The History of Theopolis Mission Station, 1814–1857," 2 vols. (M. A., Rhodes University, 1983), 1: 211, 222.

43. Sales, *Mission Stations*, 80, 84–90.

44. Peires, *House of Phalo*, 107.

45. "J. Schultheiss to the High Commissioner," May 17, 1848, in Du Toit, *Earliest South African Documents*, 48; Robert H. W. Shepherd, *Lovedale, South Africa, The Story of a Century, 1841–1941* (Lovedale: The Lovedale Press, 1931) v 36.

46. Peires, *House of Phalo*, 107.

47. "A Kropf to the High Commissioner," May 8, 1848, in Du Toit, *Earliest South African Documents*, 40.

48. "J.C. Warner to Chief Commissioner, Col. Mackinnon," May 17, 1848; " A Bonatz to the Commissioner," June 15, 1848, in Du Toit, *Earliest South African Documents*, 52, 64; Calderwood, *Caffres and Caffre Missions*, 198, 199.

49. William Holden, *The Past and Future of Kaffir Races* (Cape Town: C. Struik), 180, 202–217.

50. Smith, *South Africa Delineated*, 88.

51. Smith, *South Africa Delineated*, 88; Shaw expressed the same sentiments about the lot of African women: "They are hewers of wood and drawers of water. They are also architects and builders, who must bring all the materials to the spot, and therewith construct the dwelling. . . . To them it belonged to sow the seed, to weed the ground, to protect the growing crops from the animals and birds; to reap the harvest, and to carry it home in large bundles on their heads to the threshing-floor, where they used to beat out the grain with sticks [.]" Shaw, *Story of My Mission*, 418.

52. Smith, *South Africa Delineated*, 88.

53. Smith, *South Africa Delineated*, 88.

54. For similar sentiments about the Tswana household, see John and Jean Comaroff, "Home-Made Hegemony," 41–43.

55. Calderwood, *Caffres and Caffre Missions*, 198.

56. Calderwood, *Caffres and Caffre Missions*, 208.

57. *Missionary Notices*, "Extract of a letter from the Rev. W. J. Davis," 1840, 785–786; Robert Gray, *Journal of the Bishop's Visitation Tour throughout the Cape Colony in 1850* (London: SPCK, 1851); D. H. Varley and H. M. Matthew, eds., Nathaniel James Merriman, *The Cape Journals of Archdeacon N.J. Merriman, 1848–1855* (Cape Town: The Van Riebeeck Society, 1957), 124–125.

58. Shaw, *Story of My Mission*, 294.

59. CL, WMMS, "The Report of the Wesleyan-Methodist Missionary Society, Salem and Farmerfield Circuit Report" 1842.

60. "Wesleyan Mission at Farmerfield, South Africa," *Papers Relative to the Wesleyan Missions*, 207.

61. Newton-King, "The Labor Market of the Cape Colony," 182–200; Crais, *White Supremacy and Black Resistance*, 106, 114–115.

62. Crais, *White Supremacy and Black Resistance*, 114–115, 121, 129–131.

63. CAR, CO 485, William Shaw to Colonel Bell, April 2, 1839.

64. CAR, CO 485, William Shaw Colonel Bell, April 2, 1839; Boyce, *Notes on South African* Affairs, 134; Backhouse, *Narrative*, 305.

65. Backhouse, *Narrative*, 305.

66. Boyce, *Notes on South African Affairs*, 134.

67. William Shaw, *A Defence of the Wesleyan Missionaries in Southern Africa* (1839; reprint, Pretoria: State Library, 1976).

68. CAR, CO 485, William Shaw to Colonel Bell, April 2, 1839; for similar sentiments on awakening new needs and desires, see Thornley Smith, *South Africa Delineated*, 110, and Calderwood, *Caffres and Caffre Missions*, 137.

69. CAR, CO 485, William Shaw to Colonel Bell, April 2, 1839.

70. CAR, CO 485, William Shaw to Colonel Bell, April 2, 1839.

71. This appellation applied to Africans living beyond the colonial boundaries of the Cape Colony. The sources for the population figures are Chase, *The Cape of Good Hope*, 37; Godlonton, *Sketches of the Eastern Districts of the Cape of Good Hope*, 7.

72. CL, WMMS, Synod Minutes, *Report of the Salem Circuit* 1840.

73. Chase, *The Cape of Good Hope*, 37; Godlonton, *Sketches of the Eastern Districts of the Cape of Good Hope*, 7.

74. Bundy, *The Rise and Fall of a South African Peasantry*, 2nd edition (Cape Town and Johannesburg: David Philip, 1988).

75. Helen Bradford, "Peasants, Historians and Gender: A South African Case Study Revisited," *History and Theory* 39 (December 2000): 86–110.

76. *Master and Servant Addenda*, "Return of Residents . . . Farmerfield, 1849."

77. Hammond-Tooke, ed., Journal of William Shaw, 179; CL, MS 15 871 [Salem and Farmerfield] Marriage Registry, 1840–1923, entry #30.

78. SAL, WMMS, "The Report of the Wesleyan Methodist Missionary Society," 1845, 1847, 1848, 1851, 1852, 1853.

79. Pringle, *Narrative of a Residence in South Africa*, 24.

80. Pringle, *Narrative of a Residence in South Africa*, 25.

81. Gray, *Journal of the Bishops Visitation Tour . . . 1850*, 128.

82. Cape of Good Hope, *Master and Servant, Addenda to the Documents on the Working Order in Council, July 21, 1846*, "Return of the Residents and their families, and Property at the Wesleyan Mission Institution at Farmerfield," 7 and February 8, 1849.

83. CL, MS 16 582/2, March 25, 1853, and March 28, 1853.

84. Godlonton, *Sketches*, 7.

85. Bradford, "Peasants, Historians and Gender," 86.

86. CL, MS 15 871/1 Marriage Registry, Salem and Farmerfield, 1840.

87. Cape of Good Hope, *Master and Servant, Addenda*, "Return of the Residents . . . Farmerfield," 7 and February 8, 1849.

88. Cape of Good Hope, *Master and Servant, Addenda*, "Return of the Residents . . . Farmerfield," 7 and February 8, 1849.

89. E. P. Thompson, *The Making of the English Working Class*, 230–231.

90. CL, MS 16 582/2 March 25, 1853, and March 28, 1853.

91. Boyce, *Notes on South African Affairs*, 132.

92. SAL, WMMS, *Annual Report*, 1843.

93. CL, MS 15 023/3: 1845–1858, Report of the Salem and Farmerfield Circuit for 1846, Report of the Salem, and Farmerfield Circuit, 1847.

94. SAL, WMMS, *Annual Report*, 1844.

95. SAL, WMMS, *Annual Report*, 1850.

96. CL, MS 5 023/3: 1845–1858, Report of the Salem and Farmerfield Circuit, 1849.

97. Godlonton and Edward Irving, *Narrative of the Kaffir War, 1850–1852*, 2 vols. (1851; reprint., Cape Town: C. Struik, 1962), 1:338.

98. Godlonton and Irving, *Narrative of the Kaffir War*, 2: 30, 34, 47.

99. SAL, WMMS, Synod Minutes, 1854; Synod Minutes, 1856.

100. SAL, WMMS, Synod Minutes, 1856.

Chapter 5

1. SAL, WMMS, *Annual Report*, 1851.

2. Crais, *White Supremacy and Black Supremacy*, 76–82.

3. Boyce, *Notes on South African Affairs*, 133; Boyce made it clear that he included "Kaffers, Bechuanas, Fingoes, emancipated prize slaves," in his definition of "Colored."

<ol start="4">
<li>Boyce, Notes on South African Affairs, 132.</li>
<li>Hildegarde H. Fast. "'In at One Ear and Out at the Other': African Responses to the Wesleyan Message in Xhosaland, 1825–1835," Journal of Religion in Africa 23 (1993): 47–74. Williams, "The Missionaries on the Eastern Frontier of the Cape Colony"; Etherington, Preachers, Peasants, and Politics; Comaroff, Of Revelation and Revolution;</li>
<li>Godfrey Callaway, Sketches of Kafir, 91.</li>
<li>Mills, "The Role of African Clergy," 90–94.</li>
<li>The following two narratives are drawn from the journals of the Methodist missionaries James Cameron, William Shaw, and Samuel Young, and an official government survey of mission institutions: W. D. Hammond-Tooke, ed., Journal of William Shaw (Cape Town: A. A. Balkema, 1972); Samuel Young, A Missionary Narrative of the Triumphs of Grace as Seen in the Conversion of Kafirs, Hottentots, Fingoes and Other Natives of South Africa (New York: G. Lande and P. P. Stanford, 1843); James Cameron, Journal containing an Account of Incidents and Occurrences from 1836 to 1841 in Kaffirland, Albany, and Bechuanaland (unpublished manuscript, Cory Library); Cape of Good Hope, Master and Servant, Addenda to the Documents on the Working Order in Council, July 21, 1846, "Return of the Residents and their families, and Property at the Wesleyan Mission Institution at Farmerfield," 7 and February 8, 1849.</li>
<li>For a description of some of these "depredations," see Graham's Town Journal, hereafter GTJ, March 23, 1832, July 20, 1832, September 7, 1832, October 18, 1832, October 25, 1832, November 11, 1832, November 15, 1832; the newspaper is particularly rife with news of these "depredations" between the outbreak of the war in 1834 and 1835. For earlier "depredations," see, for example, "Abstract of the Returns of Cattle Stolen by the Caffres from the Inhabitants of the Uitenhage and Albany Districts, and of Those Recovered During the Years 1817, 1818, 1819, 1820, 1821, 1822, 1823 and 1824," in Papers Relative to the Condition and Treatment of the Native Inhabitants of Southern Africa within the Colony of the Cape of Good Hope (Great Britain, House of Commons, March 18, 1835), 183.</li>
<li>"Extracts from the Report of the Commissioners of Inquiry at the Cape of Good Hope, May 25, 1825," in Papers Relative to the Condition and Treatment of the Native Inhabitants of Southern Africa, 194–200; Justus [Mackenzie Beverley] The Wrongs of the Caffre Nation: A Narrative by Justus (London: James Duncan, 1837); John Mitford Bowker, Speeches, Letters, and Selections from the Important Papers of the Late John Mitford Bowker (Grahamstown: Godlonton and Richards, 1864); John S. Galbraith, Reluctant Empire: British Policy on the South African Frontier (Berkeley and Los Angeles: University of California Press, 1963) 49–50. On an infamous botched commando, see "Extract of Letter from Mr. Thomas Pringle to the Commissioners of Inquiry, dated Grahamstown, January 12, 1826," and "Extract of a letter from Mr. H. Huntley to the Commissioners of Inquiry dated Uitenhage, January 17, 1826" in Papers Relative to the Condition and Treatment of Native Inhabitants of Southern Africa, 183–185.</li>
<li>On the use of beads, buttons, and brass wire as a medium of trade between whites and Africans, see "Evidence of Mr. [William] Fleming . . . relative to Caffre Fairs," and "Letter from Mr. Thomson," Chumie [Tyhume Mission Station], April 30, 1835, and in Papers Relative to the Condition and Treatment of Native Inhabitants of Southern Africa within the Colony of the Cape of Good Hope (Great Britain, House of Commons,</li>
</ol>

March 18, 1835) 189 and 190; Roger Beck "Bible and Beads: Missionaries as Traders in Southern Africa in the Early Nineteenth Century," *JAH* 30 (2) (1989): 211–225; W. D. Hammond-Tooke, ed., *The Journal of William Shaw*, 82; Peires, *House of Phalo*, 100; Dugmore, *Reminiscences*, 34–35; Andrew Steedman, *Wanderings and Adventures in the Interior of Southern Africa*, 1: 7, 8, 16–17.

12. CL, WMMS, *Annual Report*, Wesleyville, 1824, 53.

13. Hammond-Tooke, ed., *The Journal of William Shaw*, 82.

14. There is some discrepancy in the dates provided for Dubula's and Chief Kama's baptism. William Shaw indicated in his edited *Journal* that he instructed Chief Kama and other catechumens on October 4, 1829, that he should prepare for baptism the following Sabbath. On October 11, 1829, Shaw indicated that this baptism did indeed take place as scheduled (Pages 180, 182). William Holden, in his monograph on Chief Kama, *British Rules in South Africa as Illustrated in the Story of Kama and his Tribe and the War in Zululand*, states that Shaw cites the baptismal dates as August 19, 1825 (*in his later journal, Story of My Mission*, page 391). Shaw did indeed say he baptized three individuals on that date. However, it is only in the next paragraph when he is discussing baptisms generally that he notes the significance of Kama's baptism, hence the room for discrepancy. Moreover, on October 11, 1829, Shaw indicated that Kama was one of four individuals baptized. I have taken the 1829 date as the more reliable one.

15. The other was Dyani Tshatshu [also Jan Tzatzoe; Jan Tshatshu], chief of the Amantinde, a Xhosa chiefdom that had a long association with the LMS missionaries from his early education at the Bethelsdorp mission under Van der Kemp to his historic visit in England to testify before the aborigines committee in 1836. For the most comprehensive treatment of Tzatzoe, see Roger Levine, *A Living Man from Africa*.

16. Hammond-Tooke, ed., *Journal of William Shaw*, 182.

17. Hammond-Tooke, ed., *Journal of William Shaw*, 182. On Chief Kama, see William Clifford Holden, *British Rule in South Africa*; Drusilla Siziwe Yekela "The Life and Times of Kama Chungwa, 1798–1875," (Rhodes University, M.A. thesis, 1988). Chief Kama Chungwa, who took on the English name of William upon his baptism, is not to be confused with the Tswana Chief Khama of Botswana whose conversion to Christianity was also heralded as a triumph by the [LMS] missionaries. On the history of this Tswana chief and his relationship with Christian missionaries, see John Charles Harris, *Khama, the Great African Chief* (London: The Livingstone Press, 1923) and Landau, *The Realm of the Word*.

18. CL, WMMS, *Annual Report*, Wesleyville, 1830.

19. Fast, ed., *Journal and Selected Letters*, 131.

20. Reverend J. Whiteside, *History of the Wesleyan Methodist Church of South Africa*, 199, 200; H. H. Dugmore, *The Reminiscences of an Albany Settler* (Grahamstown: Grocott and Sherry, 1958), 76.

21. SAL, WMMS, Great Britain, *Annual Report*, "The Albany and Kaffraria District," 1840, 59; Shaw, *Story of My Mission*, 291.

22. James Cameron, *Journal*, January 26, 1840 (unpublished manuscript).

23. James Cameron, *Journal*, January 26, 1840.

24. CL, MS 15 871/1, Farmerfield Marriage Registry, 1840–1943.

25. Cameron, *Journal*, January 26, 1840.

26. Etherington, *Preachers, Peasants and Politics*, 4.

27. CL, MS 15 023/2, Salem and Farmerfield Report, 1840.

28. CL, WMMS, *Annual Report*, Grahamstown, 1838.

29. Varley and Matthews ed., *The Cape Journal of Archdeacon N. J. Merriman*, 49; Ross, "The Grahamstown Schism," in *The London Missionary Society in Southern Africa*, 123–124.

30. CL, Cameron, *Journal*, September 8, 1839.

31. CL, WMMS, Synod Minutes, Albany District Meeting, 1833; *Annual Report*, Wesleyville, 1830.

32. CL, MS 15 023/1, Salem and Farmerfield report 1839, 1840.

33. CL, WMMS, Synod Minutes, Report of the Salem and Farmerfield Circuit, 1840.

34. CL, WMMS, Synod Minutes, Report of the Salem and Farmerfield Circuit, 1840; SAL, WMMS *Annual Report*, 1842.

35. CL, Cameron, *Journal*, April 21, 1839; for a missionary's keen sense of his *own* as opposed to his interpreter's shortcomings, see Callaway, *Sketches of Kafir Life*, 90.

36. CL, MS 15 127, Quarterly Meeting, January 5, 1883.

37. Backhouse, *Narrative*, 282.

38. SAL, WMMS, *Annual Report*, 1842.

39. SAL, WMMS, *Annual Report*, 1843.

40. CL, WMMS, Synod Minutes, 1838, *District Minutes*, 1838.

41. CL WMMS, *Annual Report*, 1826, 41.

42. Samuel Young, *Missionary Narrative*, 139; CL, WMMS, *Annual Report*, 1834, 45. While Shaw was stationed in the Leeds circuit (August 1833 to August 1836) during part of his leave from the Cape Colony, he had frequent opportunities to share his vision of the relationship between education and evangelism in southeastern Africa with other Methodists, who eventually provided the seed money for the Watson Institute.

43. "Testimony of William Shaw," *Select Committee on Aborigines*, August 7, 1835.

44. CL, WMMS, Synod Minutes, Albany and Kaffraria District, General Returns, Farmerfield, 1843.

45. CL, MS 15 871/1, Farmerfield Marriage Registry, February 10, 1840; MS 15 540 B, Quarterly Meeting, June 1841; MS 15 126, Circuit Book, Salem and Farmerfield, 1863–1866.

46. CL, DOC 82, Diary of Simon George Amm, January 1892. Albany Museum, Bowker Library, Diary of S. E. Amm.

47. On the history of Healdtown, see Leslie Hewson, "Healdtown: A Study of a Methodist Experiment in African Education," Ph.D. diss., Rhodes University, 1959.

48. William Eveleigh, ed., *The Story of a Century, 1823–1923* (Cape Town: Methodist Publishing Book House and Book Depot), 1923, 23.

49. Ross, "Congregations, Missionaries, and the Grahamstown Schism," 122.

50. Great Britain, WMMS, Annual Report, 1867, 1868.

51. Taylor, *Christian Adventures in South Africa*, 110; Mills, "The Role of African Clergy," 26–27.

52. Methodist Church of South Africa, *Minutes*, 1911, 1913, 1926, Death notices for Charles Lwana, Samuel Ntsiko, and Christopher Lubisi.

53. Eveleigh, *Story of a Century*, 25.

54. Deborah Gaitskell, "'Praying and Preaching': The Distinctive Spirituality of African Women's Church Organizations," and Norman Etherington, "Gender Issues in South-East African Missions" in Bredekamp and Ross, *Missions and Christianity in South African History*, 135–152 and 211–232; Deborah Gaitskell, "Power in Prayer and Service: Women's Christian Organizations," in *Christianity in South Africa: A Political, Social, and Cultural History*, Elphick and Davenport, eds., 253–267.

55. SAL, WMMS, *Annual Report*, 1844.

56. Eveleigh, ed., *Story of a Century*, 28.

57. Whiteside, *History of the Wesleyan Methodist Church of South Africa*, 281.

58. *Master and Servant Addenda*, "Return of Residents . . . Farmerfield, 1849."

59. SAL, WMMS, *Annual Report* 1840.

60. SAL, WMMS, *Annual Report*, "Albany and Kaffraria District," 1843.

61. CL, WMMS, Synod Minutes, Report of the Salem Circuit, 1840.

62. CL, MS 16 582/2, Case of John, October 14, 1851.

63. CL, MS 16 582/2, Case of P. Roman, July 22,1840.

64. CL, MS 16 582/2, Case of Jafta and James January, February 24, 1854.

65. CL, MS 16 582/2, Case of Lucas, March 31, 1858.

66. CL, MS 16 582/2, Case of Zwartboy, June 6, 1842.

67. CL, MS 16 582/2, Case of Jephtha and Noah Mozambiker, September 2, 1852, and September 17, 1852.

68. CL, MS 16 582/2, Case of Josiah Badi and Malgas April, January 20, 1852.

69. CL, MS 16 582/1, Case of the Widow Hlebikazi, July 4, 1839, and July 6, 1839.

70. CL, MS 16/582/1, Case of Kitje, Wife of Peter, October 25, 1839.

71. CL, MS 16/582/2, Case of J. Dicks, June 26, 184.

72. CL, MS 15 122, [Salem] November 12, 1862 [Meeting of W. H. Matthews, C. Penny, W. King, C. Hill, W. Garrett and C. Butt].

73. CL, MS 16 582/2, Case of Anna and John Pato, June 16, 1851.

74. CL, MS 16 582/2, Case of Sanna and Jacob, March 8, 1856.

75. CL, MS 16/582/2, Case of Sarah and Kunuck, January 11, 1860, January 12, 1860, May 24, 1860, May 26, 1860.

76. CL, MS 16 582/2, M. West Esq., Civil Commissioner to Magistrate, June 1843; CL, MS 15 023/3, Report of the Salem and Farmerfield Circuit, 1846; Penelope Silva, *The Albany Journal of Thomas Stone* (Cape Town: Maskew Miller Longman, 1992); "Conversation with Wedderburn," in Michael Berning, ed., *The Historical Conversations of Sir George Cory* (Cape Town: Maskew Miller Longman, 1989), 187.

77. CL, MS 15 124, Case of Pompey and Clara Bem, March 20, 1862, August 4, 1862, September 10, 1862, September 15, 1862, September 16, 1862.

78. CL, MS 15 582/2, Case of Gudula, Mechi, and Jonas, July 6–8, 1852, September 16, 1852, September 18, 1852, November 22, 1852, December 6, 1852.

79. Boyce, *Memoir of the Rev. William Shaw*, 208.

Chapter 6

1. Bowker, *Speeches, Letters and Selection*, "Extract of a letter" 1842, 109, 110.

2. J. Whiteside, *History of the Wesleyan-Methodist Church of South Africa* (London: Elliot Stock, 1906); Leslie Hewson, *Introduction to South African Methodists* (Cape Town:

Standard Press, 1950); William Clifford Holden, *A Brief History of Methodism, and of Methodist Missions in South Africa* (London: Wesleyan Conference Office, 1877).

3. J. Whiteside, *History of the Wesleyan Methodist Church*, 408; Leslie Hewson, *Introduction to South African Methodists*, 81.

4. CL, WMMS, Synod Minutes, South Africa, 1880–1881, Grahamstown District Resolution, RE: Formation of an Annual South African Conference.

5. CL WMMS, Synod Minutes, South Africa, 1880–1881, Summary Report by John Kilner, Deputation to South African Mission Field.

6. CL, Minutes of the First Conference of the Wesleyan Methodist Church of South Africa, April 10, 1883 (Cape Town, 1883).

7. CL, MS 15 880, Records of the Farmerfield Estate, Report of the Committee appointed by the Conference of 1884.

8. CL, WMMS, Correspondence, South Africa, "The first South African Conference, April 1883."

9. Etherington, *Preachers, Peasants and Politics*, 176–179.

10. G. 8 of 1883, Blue Book on Native Affairs, Report of the Civil Commissioner of Albany.

11. Bundy, *Rise and Fall of a South African Peasantry*; for the Eastern Cape, see Crais, *White Supremacy and Black Resistance* and Les Switzer, *Power and Resistance in an African Society*.

12. WMMS, Correspondence, South Africa, "The first South African Conference, April 1883, Conference authorizes the president to prepare a scheme for the sale of the Farmerfield estate and to take any action which may be necessary before the next Conference."

13. CL, MS 15 880, Records of the Farmerfield Estate, "Report of the Committee appointed by the Conference of 1884."

14. CL, WMMS, Synod Minutes, South Africa, "Grahamstown Minutes, January 15, 1868; Report of the Salem and Farmerfield Circuit, 1867."

15. Meintjes, "Family and Gender in the Christian Community at Edendale," 130.

16. CL, WMMS, South African Correspondence, "Reverend John Smith to Reverend Boyce," Salem, December 13, 1867.

17. CL, MS 15 880, Records of the Farmerfield Estate, Report of the Committee appointed by the Conference of 1884.

18. CAR 1 AY 1/8–1/14 [Albany Criminal Record Book].

19. CL, MS 15 450 "William Impey to Charles Brownlee, Secretary of Native Affairs," March 15, 1877.

20. CL, MS 15 880, Records of the Farmerfield Estate, Report of the Committee appointed by the Conference of 1884.

21. CL, MS 15 880, Records of the Farmerfield Estate.

22. Gibson, *Eight Years in Kaffraria*, 168.

23. Marais, *Cape Coloured People*, 155.

24. Jane Sales, *The Planting of the Churches in South Africa* (Michigan: William B. Eerdmans Publishing Company, 1971), 64.

25. Cape of Good Hope, *Report of the Select Committee appointed to considered and report on the Missionary Institutions Bill.* (Cape Town: Saul Solomon, 1872).

26. Marais, *Cape Coloured People*; Macmillan, *Cape Colour Question*.

27. Manona, "The Drift from Farms to Town," 72–75, 94–95.

28. See Gibson, *Eight Years in Kaffraria* for his interesting perspective on non-Christian residents at two local Wesleyan stations. Gibson's is an Anglican missionary commentary on some distinctions between Anglican and Methodist missions, 150.

29. Donavan Williams, "The Missionaries on the Eastern Frontier of the Cape Colony, 1799–1853" (Ph.D. (University of Witwatersrand, 1960).

30. Porter, *Religion versus Empire*, 225.

31. Porter, *Religion versus Empire*, 190.

32. Andrew Bank, "Losing Faith in the Civilising Mission, The Premature Decline of Humanitarian Liberalism at the Cape 1840–1860," in M. J. Daunton and Richard Halpern, *British Empire and Others: British Encounters with Indigenous Peoples* (Philadelphia: University of Pennsylvania Press, 1999), 364–383. Catherine Hall, *Civilising Subjects: Metropole and Colony in the Imperial Imagination, 1830–1867* (Chicago, 2002); Tim Keegan, *Colonial South Africa and the Origins of the Racial Order* (Charlottesville: University Press of Virginia, 1996).

33. Keegan, *Colonial South Africa and the Origins of the Racial Order*, 127.

34. Porter, *Religion versus Empire*, 40, 43.

35. Sensbach, *Rebecca's Revival*, 193, 194.

36. Gibson observed in *Eight Years in Kaffraria* the isolated life a priest had to live, a situation made even more difficult by his residence "among people of a lower moral standard, and no spiritual standard whatsoever." "Who is sufficient for these things, he queried? Only the man of God," 166; in his account of the Lovedale institution, *African Wastes Reclaimed*, Robert Young wrote that the missionaries who established Lovedale and their wives "in the exercise of a noble self-sacrificing faith, voluntarily exchanged the comforts of civilization for the manifold inconveniences and discomforts of barbarism—the society of the refined, virtuous, and educated for that of ignorant, degraded and blood thirsty "heathens," 4.

37. Gibson, *Eight Years in Kaffraria*, 8.

38. Janet Hodgson, *Princess Emma*, 18, 20.

39. Gibson, *Eight Years in Kaffraria*, 17.

40. William Boyce, *Statistics of Protestant Missionary Societies*, 56. Boyce glossed over Southern Africa and South Africa.

41. Boyce, *Statistics*, 59.

42. Samuel Broadbent, *A Narrative of the First Introduction of Christianity amongst the Barolong Tribe of Bechuanas, South Africa* (London: Wesleyan Mission House, 1865), 204.

43. Whiteside, *History of the Wesleyan Methodist Church of South Africa*, 322.

44. Hodgson, *Princess Emma*, 27.

45. WMMS, "Report of the Salem and Farmerfield Circuit, 1867."

46. It is difficult to calibrate all the numbers of the various missionary societies using the same metrics, as many are based on estimates, while others make distinctions between members, those on trial, and those undergoing catechism and so on.

47. Whiteside, *History of the Wesleyan Methodist Church of South Africa*, 321.

48. For important evaluations of missionary work from the Anglican perspective, see Callaway, *Sketches of Kafir Life*, especially the Appendix, "Work Among the Native Races of South Africa"; see also Alan Gibson, *Eight Years in Kaffraria*, especially

the two chapters entitled, "Review of Eight Years Extension of Work" and "Some Missionary Problems."

49. Gibson, *Eight Years in Kaffraria*, 55.
50. Whiteside, *History of the Wesleyan Methodist Church of South Africa*, 321.
51. SAL, "General Report of the work of the Wesleyan Missionary Society in South Africa," 1882.
52. At the Edendale mission, for example, Sheila Meintjes noted that second generation Christians, reared at the mission and fully immersed in Christian culture, often returned to practices like polygyny, "Family and Gender in the Christian Community at Edendale, 145.
53. Williams, "The Missionaries on the Eastern Frontier of the Cape Colony," 229.
54. Holden, *Past and Future of the Kaffir Races*, 486, 490.
55. Calderwood, *Caffres and Caffre Missions*, 137.
56. Holden, *Past and Future*, 487, emphasis in the original.
57. Callaway, *Sketches of Kafir Life*, 112.
58. Calderwood, *Caffres and Caffre Missions*, 198.
59. Young, *African Wastes Reclaimed*, 141.
60. Williams, "The Missionaries," 264; Gibson, *Eight Years in Kaffraria*, 167.
61. John Edwin Mason, "Fit for Freedom": The Slaves, Slavery and Emancipation in the Cape Colony, South Africa, 1806–1842 (Yale University Ph.D, 1992).
62. C. M. Maxeke, "The Progress of Native Womanhood," in *Christianity and the Natives of South Africa*, James Dextor Taylor, comp and ed., (Lovedale: General Missionary Conference of South Africa, 1929), 178.
63. "Testimony of William Shaw Kama and Others to the Commissioners," Cape of Good Hope, *Report and Proceedings of the Government Commission on Native Laws and Customs*, 1883 (1), 239–240.
64. Whiteside, *History of the Wesleyan Methodist Church of South Africa*, 275.
65. http://anglicanhistory.org/africa/kaffraria_gibson/01.html, September 21, 2007.
66. Gibson, *Eight Years in Kaffraria*, 14.
67. Callaway, *Sketches of Kafir Life*, 92.
68. Callaway, *Sketches of Kafir Life*, 64.
69. Williams, "The Missionaries," 230; Young, *African Wastes Reclaimed*, 142.
70. Gibson, *Eight Years in Kaffraria*, 90.
71. Whiteside, *History of the Wesleyan Methodist Church of South Africa*, 314.
72. Maurice Evans, *Black and White in Southeast Africa: A Study in Sociology* (London: Longmans, 1916), 84.
73. Meintjes, "Family and Gender in the Christian Community at Edendale," 131.
74. Gibson, *Eight Years in Kaffraria*, 172–173.
75. Gibson, *Eight Years in Kaffraria*, 74, 174–175.
76. Alan Gibson discussed the case of one headman who declined to join the Wesleyans because of the expense of the ticket monies and asked to be exempted from the ten-pound contribution toward the teacher and the preacher that the Anglicans asked in *Eight Years in Kaffraria*, 103. Similarly, Catherine Higgs has noted of the debt of J. T. Jabavu, *Ghost of Equality*, 59.
77. Backhouse, *Narrative, 285.*
78. Calderwood, *Caffres and Caffre Missions*, 145–146.

79. CL, WMMS, "Report of the Salem and Farmerfield Circuit, 1879."

80. Gibson, *Eight Years in Kaffraria*, 91.

81. Gibson, *Eight Years in Kaffraria*, 101.

82. Young, *African Wastes Reclaimed*, 144.

83. Young, *Eight Years in Kaffraria*, 90.

84. Holden, *Past and Future of the Kaffir Races*, 491.

85. Evans, *Black and White in South East Africa*, 28.

86. "W. C. Jeffrey, Evidence before the Commissioners, Kamastone location, Cape of Good Hope, Report and Proceedings of the Government Commission on Native Laws and Customs," 2: 1883.

87. Callaway, *Sketches of Kafir Life*, 39.

88. The term "Ethiopian" reflects the symbolism of the biblical verse, "Ethiopia shall soon stretch out her hands to God," Psalms 68:31, and its use to validate the idea that Africans themselves had a decisive role to play in the evangelization of Africa.

89. Bengt Sundkler, *Bantu Prophets in South Africa* (1948; reprint, Oxford University Press, 1961), 52, 53; on the rise of African separatist movements and various reactions to this phenomenon in South Africa, see B. A. Pauw, "The Influence of Christianity," in D. W. Hammond-Tooke, ed., *The Bantu Speaking Peoples of Southern Africa* (London: Routledge and Keegan Paul,) 415–440; B. A. Pauw, *Christianity and Xhosa Tradition: Belief and Ritual among Xhosa Speaking Christians* (Cape Town and London: Oxford University Press, 1975); "The Cave of Adullam: Missionary Reaction to Ethiopianism at Lovedale, 1898–1902," *Missionalia* 19 (1) (1991): 57–64.

90. Michael Mahoney, "The Millennium Comes to Mapumulo: Popular Christianity in Rural Natal, 1866–1906," *JSAS* 25 (3) (September 1999): 375–391.

91. Mahoney, "The Millennium Comes to Mapumulo," 376.

92. Callaway, *Sketches of Kafir Life*, 55.

93. Gibson, *Eight Years in Kaffraria*, 134.

94. Many thanks to Rodney Davenport, who steered me clear on the Matthews family genealogy when he read the dissertation, and Jeff Peires of the Cory Library and Fleur Way-Jones of the Albany Museum for tracking down the references; CL, Betty Davenport, "A History of the Matthews settler family of Salem and 'Woodstock', Alice, South Africa. 1820–1950" (privately published, Cape Town 2010), 40–41; Albany Museum, Bowker Library, Journal of Mrs. S. E. Amm.

95. CL, Simon George Amm, *Journal*, 1886 to 1957 [June 19, 1895, entry], Albany Museum, Bowker Library, Diary of S. Amm.

96. CL, Simon George Amm, *Journal*, 1886–1957.

97. CL, Simon George Amm, *Journal*, 1886–1957.

98. CL, MS 15 880, "Records of the Farmerfield Estate, Report of the Committee appointed by the Conference of 1884."

99. CL, MS 15 880, "Records of the Farmerfield Estate, Report of the Committee appointed by the Conference of 1884."

100. CL, MS, 15 880, "Records of the Farmerfield Estate, Report of the Committee appointed by the Conference of 1884."

101. CL, MS 15 880, "Records of the Farmerfield Estate, Report of the Committee appointed by the Conference of 1884."

102. CL, MS 15 880, "Records of the Farmerfield Estate, Report of the Committee appointed by the Conference of 1884"; CL, MS 467, *Report of the Committee on the Farmerfield Estate*, March 11, 1886.

103. CL, MS 15 467, Report of the Committee on the Farmerfield Estate, March 11, 1886.

Chapter 7

1. Cherryl Walker, *Landmarked: Land Claims and Restitution in South Africa* (Athens, OH: Ohio: University Press, 2008), 16–17.

2. CL, MS 15 128, Circuit Schedule Book, March 1882 to December 1885.

3. CL, MS 15 869, Baptismal Registry, Salem and Farmerfield.

4. CL, MS 15 126, Circuit Book, Salem and Farmerfield, 1858–1876; CL, MS 15 361, Local Preachers Meeting, July 8, 1909.

5. *Master and Servant Addenda*, "Return of Residents . . . Farmerfield, 1849 "Return of Residents—1849."

6. CL, MS 15 870, Baptismal Registry, Salem and Farmerfield.

7. CL, MS 15 361, Local Preachers Meeting, July 8, 1909.

8. SAL, General Report of the Work of the WMS, 1887.

9. SAL, General Report of the Work of the WMS, 1890.

10. SAL, General Report of the Work of the WMS, 1894.

11. CL, MS 15 127, Quarterly Meeting Salem, April 6, 1880; CL, MS 15 081/1, Native District Meeting, Grahamstown, January 9, 1884, and January 16, 1884.

12. CL, G7. 94 Report of the General Superintendent General of Education, 1893; G7. 95 Report of the General Superintendent for Education, 1895.

13. SAL, General Report of the Work of the WMS, 1892, 1896.

14. CL, G8. 95 Blue Book, Albany, 1895.

15. SAL, General Report of the Work of the WMS, 1895.

16. SAL, General Report of the WWS, 1897.

17. CL, G. 4 of '93, Blue Book on Native Affairs, [Albany]; G. 9 of '94, Blue Book on Native Affairs, [Albany], G. 8 of '95, Blue Book on Native Affairs, [Albany];G. 8 of '96 Blue Book on Native Affairs, [Albany], G. 5 of 1896; G. 19 of 97, Blue Book on Native Affairs [Albany]; G. 42 of '98, Blue Book on Native Affairs [Albany].

18. SAL, General Report of the WMS, 1899; General Report of the WMS, 1900; CL, G. 25 of '02, Blue Book on Native Affairs, [Albany], 1902.

19. "Report of Civil Commissioner, John Hemming, January 24, 1899," Blue Book on Native Affairs, [Albany], 1899.

20. CL, G. 29 of '03, Blue Book on Native Affairs [Albany], 1903.

21. CL, DOC 82, Diary of Simon George Amm, 1900.

22. Beinart, *Twentieth-Century South Africa* (Oxford: Oxford University Press, 1994), 14.

23. Beinart, *Twentieth-Century South Africa*, 9.

24. Keegan, *Facing the Storm*, 44.

25. CL, MS 312, *Farmerfield Mission Notebook*, 1906–1910.

26. CL, MS 312, *Farmerfield Mission Notebook*, 1906–1910.

27. CL, MS 15 880, "Memoranda on the Farmerfield Estate," June 30, 1915.

28. CL, MS 15 018/2, Grahamstown District Synod, January 15, 1908; Grahamstown District Synod, January 21, 1909.

29. CL, MS 15 018/1, Grahamstown District Synod, Native District Meeting, January 16, 1872; April 16, 1873.

30. MS 15 018/1, Grahamstown District Synod, Native District Meeting, January 15, 1908.

31. CL, MS 15 361, Quarterly Meeting, Salem, July 6, 1905.

32. CL, MS 15 871/1, Salem and Farmerfield Marriage Registry.

33. CL, MS 15 132, Local Preachers Meeting, January 6, 1916.

34. CL, MS 15 361, Local Preachers Meeting, July 5, 1906.

35. CL, MS 15 361, Quarterly Meeting, July 5, 1906; CL, MS 312, Farmerfield Mission Notebook [Resolution on Circumcision, rent day July 11, 1906].

36. CL, MS 312, Farmerfield Mission Notebook, August 3, 1907.

37. CL, MS 15 880, Minutes, Committee and Councilors, January 21, 1916.

38. CL, MS 15 018/4, Grahamstown District Synod, "Report of the Committee on the Farmerfield Estate, January 26, 1916;" CL, MS 15 880, Minutes, "Special Meeting appointed by Synod of 1916 to Consider Certain Matters relating to Farmerfield."

39. CL, MS 15 880, Minutes, Committee and Councilors, January 18, 1917.

40. CL, MS 15 132, Special Leaders Meeting, October 11, 1917; CL, MS 15 861A, Reverend H. Allen to the John Mitchell Watkinson, October 16, 1917; Reverend H. Allen to John Mitchell Watkinson, September 25, 1917.

41. CL, MS 15 880, Minutes, Committee and Councilors, July 23, 1915, and January 23, 1919.

42. CL, MS 15 880, Minutes, Committee and Councilors, January 23, 1919; Minutes, Committee, Councilors and Tenants, July 31, 1919.

43. CL, MS 15 861A, "Contributions to Mission Fund," 1918.

44. CL, MS 15 356 [Correspondence on the Influenza Epidemic of 1918], 1919; CL, MS 15 861A, Rev. H. Allen to Rev. John Mitchell Watkinson, November 25, 1918; CL, MS 15 880, report of the Farmerfield Estate, 1918.

45. CL, MS 15 880, Minutes, Committee, Councilors and Tenants, July 31, 1919.

46. CL, MS 15 880, Report "of the Farmerfield Estate, 1918," read at the Grahamstown Synod, January 27, 1919; "Minutes of Synod Committee held at Farmerfield," February 20, 1919; CL, MS 15 861A, Reverend Herbert Allen to John Mitchell Watkinson, February 5, 1919.

47. CL, MS 15 018/4, Grahamstown District Synod, "Report of the Committee on the Farmerfield Estate," January 25, 1918. CL, MS 15 356, J. Emslie to Reverend Herbert Allen, May 19, 1919; Frank Emslie to Revered H. Allen, May 19, 1919; J. Bertram Attwell to the Committee of Management of the Farmerfield Estate, June 12, 1919; W. Shepstone-Jeffrey to Rev. H. Allen, September 19, 1919, and October 2, 1919; Robert Harries to Rev. H. Allen, October 9, 1919; G. E Harper to Rev. Allen October 29, 1919; W. Shepstone Jeffrey to Rev. H. Allen, December 17, 1919; *The Methodist Churchman*, September 8, 1919; CL, MS 15 880 Minutes, Synod Committee of the Farmerfield Estate, December 3–5, 1919.

48. CL, MS 15 880, Minutes of Synod Committee held at Farmerfield, February 20, 1919; CL, MS 15 861A, Reverend Herbert Allen to John Mitchell Watkinson, February 21, 1919.

49. CL, MS 15 356, "The tenants of Farmerfield to the Synod Committee," April 19, 1919.

50. CL, MS 15 861A, "Solomon Kayser to John Mitchell Watkinson," March 29, 1920.

51. CL, MS 15 861A, "Reverend Herbert Allen to John Mitchell Watkinson," February 21, 1920.

52. CL, MS 15 880, "Report read at Synod," January 1920.

53. CL, MS 15 861A, "The Tenants of Farmerfield to John Mitchell Watkinson," March 16, 1920.

54. CL, MS 15 861A, "Reverend Herbert Allen to John Mitchell Watskinson," March 15, 1920.

55. CL, MS 15 356, "J. M. Watkinson to Solomon Kayser," March 23, 1920.

56. CL, MS 861A, "Reverend Herbert Allen to John Mitchell Watkinson," March 18, 1920.

57. CL, MS 15 861A, "Reverend Herbert Allen to John Mitchell Watkinson," March 18, 1920.

58. CL, MS 15 018/5, Grahamstown District Synod, Minutes, January 25, 1923; CL, MS 15 880, Report of the Farmerfield Estate, 1920, 1921, 1922, 1923.

59. CL, MS 15 861A, John Saunders to John Mitchell Watkinson, May 22, 1922.

60. CL, MS 15 875, Quarterly Meeting, July 12, 1920; Quarterly Meeting April 9, 1920; Quarterly Meeting December 1, 1920.

61. CL, MS 15 875, Minutes, Quarterly Meeting, October 7, 1922.

62. CL, MS 15 875, Quarterly Meeting, October 11, 1918.

63. CL, MS 15 880, Report of the Farmerfield Estate, 1923.

64. CL, MS 15 880, Report of the Farmerfield Estate, 1923–1929; CL, MS 15 861A, FJ Rhead Marsh to J. M. Watkinson, December 21, 1923, May 23, 1924.

65. CL, MS 15 735, M. D. Foley to Reverend F. J. Rhead Marsh, June 4, 1926.

66. CL, MS 15 735, F. J. Rhead Marsh to M. D. Foley, October 5, 1926; F. J. Rhead Marsh to J. M. Watkinson, October 5, 1926; May 23, 1927.

67. CL, MS 15 735, J. M. Watkinson to F. J. Rhead Marsh, September 14, 1926.

68. Robert Edgar, *Because they Chose the Plan of God: The Story of the Bulhoek Massacre* (Johannesburg: Ravan Press, 1988).

69. Karen Fields, *Revival and Rebellion in Colonial Central Africa* (Princeton: Princeton University Press, 1985).

70. CL, MS 15 735, "Watkinson to Rhead Marsh," September 14, 1926.

71. CL, MS 15 735, "F. P Long to Rhead Marsh," September 28, 1927.

72. CL, MS 15 735, "Simon George to F. J. Rhead Marsh," November 22, 1927.

73. CL, MS 15 018/5, Grahamstown District Synod, January 30, 1928.

74. CL, MS 15 735, "Reverend T. Curnick to Reverend F. J. Rhead Marsh," October 24, 1927; MS 15 880, "Minutes of the Connexional Committee," November 24, 1927.

75. CL, MS 15 735, "Reverend John Mitchell Watkinson to Reverend F. J. Rhead Marsh," May 20, 1928, emphasis in original.

76. CL, MS 15 735, "Rev William Flint to Reverend F. J. Rhead Marsh," July 25, 1928; CL, MS 15 880, "Rhead Marsh to members of the Conference Committee," November 29, 1928; CL, MS 15 018/5 Grahamstown District Synod, February 11, 1929.

77. CL, MS 15 735, "Reverend Benjamin Rwairwai to Reverend Rhead Marsh," September 21, 1928.

78. SAB, NTS 2598 102/305, "Reverend G. H. P. Jacques to the Resident Magistrate of Grahamstown," January 16, 1933.

79. CL, MS 15 880, "District Committee Meeting," December 2, 1930.

80. CL, MS 15 880, Report of the Farmerfield Estate, 1930.

81. CL, MS 15 880, Report of the Farmerfield Estate, 1930.

Chapter 8

1. CL, MS 15 735, "F. J. Rhead Marsh to John Mitchell Watkinson," October 5, 1926.

2. CL, MS 15 735, "John Mitchell Watkinson to F. J. Rhead Marsh," September 14, 1926.

3. Bundy, *The Rise and Fall of the South African Peasantry*, 235.

4. CL MS 15 450, "Reverend William Impey to Charles Brownlee, Secretary for Native Affairs," March 15, 1877; CL, MS 15 875, "Reverend Hebert Allen to John Mitchell Watkinson," July 20, 1918.

5. *Methodist Churchman*, "Native Land and Missions," March 13, 1939.

6. Saul Dubow, "The Elaboration of Segregation Ideology," in *Segregation and Apartheid in Twentieth Century*, William Beinart and Saul Dubow, eds. (London and New York: Routledge, 1995), 145–175.

7. Cherryl Walker, *Landmarked*, 16–17.

8. SAB, NTS 2598 102/305, "Farmerfield Mission Lands: Albany District," December 3, 1952.

9. SAB NTS 2598 102/305, "Farmerfield Mission Lands: Albany District," December 3, 1952.

10. SAB, NTS 2598 102/305, "Reverend George H. P. Jacques to the Magistrate of Grahamstown," November 15, 1938; "The Secretary for Native Affairs to the Chief Native Commissioner," October 4, 1938.

11. SAB, NTS 2598 102/305, "Reverend George H. P. Jacques the Magistrate of Grahamstown," November 15, 1938.

12. SAB, URU 1850/213; Transactions in terms of section 1 of the Natives Land Act, 1913, Renewal of Lease of Residential Rights on Mission Farm, Farmerfield, Albany to John Malakani and others, 1939; URU 1793/1360, Transactions . . . to John Malakani and others, 1940.

13. CL, MS 15 880, Owen R. Thompson to Native Commissioner, Grahamstown April 18, 1939.

14. Solomon Plaatje, *Native Life in South Africa Before and Since the European War and the Boer Rebellion* (1916; reprint, New York: Negro Universities Press, 1969), 17.

15. Union of South Africa, Natives Land Act, Act No. 27 of 1913, Pretoria: Government Printer, 1913; Union of South Africa, Native Trust and Land Act, Act No. 18 of 1936, Pretoria, Government Printer, 1936; Union of South Africa, Group Areas Act, Act No. 41 of 1950, Pretoria, Government Printer, 1950.

16. Timothy Keegan, *Rural Transformations in Industrializing South Africa: The Southern Highveld to 1914* (Braamfontein, South Africa: Ravan Press, 1986); Charles Van Onselen, *The Seed is Mine: The Life of Kas Maine, a South African Sharecropper* (New York: Hill and Wang, 1996). Belinda Bozzoli, *Women of Phokeng: Consciousness, Life Strategy and Migrancy in South Africa, 1900–1983* (Portsmouth, NH: Heinemann, 1991); Tim Keegan, *Facing the Storm: Portraits of Black Lives in Rural South Africa* (London: Zed Books, 1988).

17. Bozzoli, *Women of Phokeng*, 81–82. Keegan, *Facing the Storm*, 16, 19, 85.

18. CL, MS 15 874, Baptismal Registry, Salem and Farmerfield; CL, MS 15 870, Baptismal Registry, Salem and Farmerfield; CL, MS 15 871/1, Marriage Registry, Salem and Farmerfield.

19. Interview, Buyisile Budaza, March 7, 1999; while several members of the Budaza family place the date of migration around 1909, Farmerfield records indicate that the family had moved there as early as 1900.

20. Interview, Welsch Budaza, January 31, 1999.

21. CL, MS 15 880, Report of the Farmerfield Estate, Rent Day July 1, 1929; CL MS 15 879, "Mr. Wiggin to Reverend Thomas," Grahamstown, January 29, 1937.

22. Interview, Buyisile Budaza, March 7, 1999.

23. Interview, Tamsana Bangushe, February 28, 1999.

24. Interview, Anderson Budaza, March 7, 1999; Interview, Buyisile Budaza, March 7, 1999.

25. Interview, Mary Jane Maxegwana, February 28, 1999.

26. Interview, Nonyameko Mpati, May 2, 1999.

27. Interview, Sylvia Zweni, January 31, 1999.

28. Interview, Miriam Budaza, January 31, 1999.

29. Interview, Sylvia Zweni, January 31, 1999.

30. Interview, Florence Matini, January 31, 1999.

31. Interview, Daniel Matini, January 31, 1999.

32. Interview, Sylvia Zweni, January 31, 1999.

33. Interview, Florence Matini and Sylvia Zweni, January 31, 1999.

34. Interview, Mongameli Maxegwana, February 21, 1999.

35. Jacklyn Cock, "Domestic Service and Education for Domesticity: The Incorporation of Xhosa Women into Colonial Society," in *Women and Gender in Southern Africa to 1945*, Cherryl Walker, ed., 76–96.

36. Jacklyn Cock, *Maids and Madams: A Study of the Politics of Exploitation* (Cape Town: Ravan Press, 1980).

37. Interview, Murphy Mquqo, February 21, 1999.

38. Interview, Mavis Rasana, February 28, 1999; Interview, Cecil Nonqane, June 29, 2001.

39. Interview, Murphy Mquqo, February 21, 1999.

40. Interview, Nofelity Gaba, February 1, 1999.

41. Interview, Jayile Saki, May 1, 1999; Interview, Cecil Nonqane, June 29, 2001; Cecil Manona, "The Drift From Farms to Town: A Case Study of Migration From White Owned Farms in the Eastern Cape To Grahamstown," (Rhodes University, Ph.D. diss., 1988), 91–96.

42. Interview, Elsie Luzipho Mzizi, February 28, 1999. Mrs. Mzizi's statements are borne out by other studies of the socioeconomic position of farm workers in the Eastern Cape, most notably two studies that form part of a series (Xhosa in Town): Philip Mayer, *Townsmen or Tribesmen: Conservatism and the Process of Urbanization in a South African City* (Cape Town: Oxford University Press, 1961) and D. H. Reader, *The Black Man's Portion: History, Demography and Living Conditions in the Native Locations* (Cape Town: Oxford University Press, 1961) and by Cecil Manona, "The Drift From Farms to Town," 1988. For rural struggles elsewhere in South Africa,

see: Stanley Trapido, "Landlord and Tenant in a Colonial Economy: The Transvaal, 1880–1910" *JSAS* 5 (1)(1978): 26–58; Timothy Keegan, *Rural Transformations in Industrializing South Africa: The Southern Highveld to 1914* (Braamfontein: Ravan Press, 1986); Charles van Onselen, "Race and Class in a South African Countryside: Cultural Osmosis and Social Relations in the Sharecropping Economy of the South Western Transvaal, 1900–1950," AHR 95 (1) (1990): 99–123; Jeremy Krikler, *Revolution from Above, Rebellion from Below: The Agrarian Transvaal at the Turn of the Century* (Oxford: Clarendon Press, 1993); Van Onselen, *The Seed is Mine.*

43. Interview, Violet Ngqondi, May 2, 1999.

44. Manona, "The Drift from Farms to Town," 256; Philip Mayer, *Townsmen or Tribesmen,* 167.

45. Interview, Elsie Luzipho Mzizi, February 28, 1999.

46. Interview, Cecil Nonqane, June 29, 2001; Manona, "The Drift from Farms to Town," 111, 112.

47. Manona, "The Drift From Farms to Town," 95.

48. Interview, Jayile Saki, May 1, 1999.

49. Interview, Nonyameko Mpati, May 2, 1999.

50. Interview, Jayile Saki, May 1, 1999; Interview, Nimrod Plaatje, May 1, 1999.

51. Interview, Buyisile Budaza, March 7, 1999.

52. Interview, Michael Madinda, February 28, 1999.

53. Interview, Miriam Budaza, January 31, 1999.

54. Nelson Mandela, *Long Walk to Freedom: The Autobiography of Nelson Mandela* (New York: Little, Brown, 1994), 24.

55. Interview, Buyisile Budaza, March 7, 1999.

56. Interview, Setchaba May, February 21, 1999.

57. Interview, Napthali Mbozanani, June 16, 2001.

58. Interview, Miriam Budaza, January 31, 1999.

59. Melville Festenstein and Claire Pickard-Cambridge, *Land and Race: South Africa's Group Areas and Land Acts* (Johannesburg: SAIRR, 1987); Harvey Feinberg, "The 1913 Natives Land Act in South Africa: Politics, Race and Segregation in the Early Twentieth Century," *IJAHS* 26 (1): 65–109; T. R. H. Davenport, "Can Sacred Cows be Culled?: A Historical Review of Land Policy in South Africa with some Questions about the Future," *Development Southern Africa* 4 (3) (April 1987): 388–400; William Beinart and Saul Dubow, eds., *Segregation and Apartheid in Twentieth Century South Africa* (New York: Routledge, 1995), 164.

60. Higgs, *The Ghost of Equality,* 59.

61. Union of South Africa. U. G. 22 of 1932. Native Economic Commission, 1930–1932.

62. Bettina Schmidt, *Creating Order: Culture as Politics in 19th and 20th Century South Africa* (Nijmegen: Third World Center, University of Nijmegen, 1996), 142; Saul Dubow, "The Elaboration of Segregationist Ideology," 164, 166; Beinart, *Twentieth Century South Africa,* 84–108.

63. Schmidt, *Creating Order,* 164.

64. Beinart, *Twentieth Century South Africa,* 107.

65. Gilbert Marcus, "Section 5 of the Black Administration Act: The Case of the Bakwena ba Magopa," in Christina Murray and Catherine O'Regan, eds. *No Place to Rest: Forced*

Removals and the Law in South Africa (Cape Town: Oxford University Press, 1990), 13, 18.

66. Gerry Mare, *African Population Relocation in South Africa* (Johannesburg: SAIRR, 1980); Elaine Hunterhalter, *Forced Removal: The Division, Segregation and Control of the People of South Africa*, 1987 (International Defense and Aid Fund for Southern Africa, 1987); *Removals and the Law*, Transcript of a Workshop held in Grahamstown (Cape Town: SPP; Pietermaritzburg: AFRA), 1984.

67. Interview, Buyisile Budaza, March 7, 1999.

68. 10411 30/447/1, "Chief Native Commissioner, Eastern Cape to Secretary of Native Affairs, Pretoria," February 24, 1958.

69. SAB, NTS 10411 30/447/1, "Lys van plakkers en hulle gesinne op Farmerfield asook hulle lewendehawe en aan watter stam hulle behoort en voorwaardes wat hulle daar woon."

70. SAB, NTS 10411 30/447/1, "Lys van plakkers en hulle gesinne op Farmerfield."

71. SAB NTS 10411 30/447/1, "Chief Native Commissioner, Eastern Cape to Secretary of Native Affairs, Pretoria," February 24, 1958.

72. SAB NTS 10411 30/447/1, "Chief Native Commissioner to the Secretary for Native Affairs," June 10, 1958.

73. SAB NTS 10411 30/447/1, "Chief Native Commissioner to the Secretary for Native Affairs," June 10, 1958.

74. SAB NTS 10411 30/447/1, "J.B. Smith, Magistrate to Secretary of Native Affairs, Pretoria," November 10, 1958.

75. SAB NTS 7186 974/323/129 Secretary for Bantu Administration and Development to the Chief Native Commissioner, 1959; NTS 10411/30/447/1, Secretary of Native Affairs to the Chief Native Commissioner, Eastern Cape, June 3, 1958; "Lys van plakkers en hulle gesinne op Farmerfield."

76. SAB NTS 2598 102/305, "Memo, Urban Areas Section, November 5, 1941.

77. Interview, Buyisile Budaza, March 7, 1999; Interview, Patrick Hewana, January 29, 1999; Interview Solomon Mzizi, February 23, 1999.

78. Interview, Solomon Mzizi, February 23, 1999.

79. Interview, Miriam Budaza, January 31, 1999.

80. Laurine Platzky and Cherryl Walker, *The Surplus People: Forced Removals in South Africa* (Johannesburg: Ravan Press, 1985), 253.

81. Interview, Napthali Mbozanani, May 1, 1999.

82. DLA, *Report 108/96*.

83. Interview, Elsie Luzipho Mzizi, February 28, 1999.

84. Laurine Platzky and Cherryl Walker, *The Surplus People: Forced Removals in South Africa* (Johannesburg: Ravan Press, 1985), 10; Roger Omond, *The Apartheid Handbook: A Guide to South Africa's Everyday Racial Policies* (1985; reprint, Penguin Books, 1986); Desmond Cosmas, *The Discarded People: An Account of African Resettlement in South Africa* (Harmondsworth: Penguin Books, 1970).

85. Interview, Sylvia Zweni, January 31, 1999, DLA, Report 108/96.

86. Interview, Daniel Matini, January 31, 1999; Interview, Msewu May, February 1999.

87. Interview, Solomon Mzizi, February 23, 1999.

88. Laurine Platzky and Cherryl Walker, *The Surplus People*, 88.

89. Interview, Buyisile Budaza, March 7, 1999.

90. Interview, Sylvia Zweni, January 31, 1999.

91. Interview, Florence Matini, January 31, 1999.

92. Interview, Petrus Zatu, June 16, 2001.

93. Interview, Mbulelo Mquqo, February 21, 1999.

94. Interview, Mbulelo Mquqo, February 21, 1999.

95. Interview, Nonyameko Mpati, May 2, 1999; Interview Buyisile Budaza, March 7, 1999; Interview, Mbulelo Mquqo, February 21, 1999.

96. Interview, Mongameli Maxegwana, February 21, 1999; Interview Mary Jane Maxegwana, February 28, 1999.

97. Interview, Daniel Matini, January 31, 1999.

98. Interview, Sylvia Zweni, January 31, 1999.

99. Interview, Sylvia Zweni, January 31, 1999.

100. Interview, Mr. Mbulelo Mquqo, February 21, 1999.

101. Interview, Mr. Mbulelo Mquqo, February 21, 1999.

102. Interview Nofelity Gaba, February 1, 1999.

103. Interview, Buyisile Ivan Budaza, March 7, 1999.

104. Interview, Daniel Matini, January 31, 1999.

105. Interview, Msewu May, February 21, 1999.

106. CL, PR 7700, "Farmerfield Notes."

107. CL, PR 7700, "Farmerfield Notes."

108. CL PR 7700, "Letter from A.M. Mamase, Circuit Steward, Uitenhage," June 16, 1981.

109. CL PR 7700, "Farmerfield Notes."

110. Interview, Nofelity Gaba, February 1, 1999.

111. Interview, Mongameli Maxegwana, February 21, 1999.

112. Interview, Miriam Budaza, January 31, 1999.

113. Interview, Mongameli Maxegwana, February 21, 1999.

114. Colin Bundy, "Comparatively Speaking: Kas Maine and South African Agrarian History," review of *The Seed is Mine* by Charles Van Onselen, *JSAS* 23 (June 1997) (2), 8.

Chapter 9

1. Interview, Elsie Luzipho Mzizi, February 28, 1999.

2. Mandela, *Long Walk to Freedom*, 556, 561.

3. Anthony Minaar, ed., *Access to and Affordability of Land in South Africa: The Challenge of Land Reform in the 1990s* (Pretoria: HSRC, 1994); Lala Steyn, *Closing the Door: The Implication and Implementation of the 1993 Land Legislation* (Braamfontein: National Land Committee and Athlone: Surplus People's Project, 1994); Marlene Winberg, *Voices from the Land: Experiences of Land Reform in South Africa* (Kenwyn, South Africa: Juta 1998); Richard Levin and Daniel Weiner, eds., *No More Tears: Struggles for Land in Mpumalanga, South Africa* (Trenton: Africa World Press, 1997); Michael Aliber and Rueben Mokoena, *Interaction Between the Land Redistribution Program and the Land Market in South Africa: A Perspective on the Willing-Buyer/Willing-Seller Approach* (Cape Town: Program for Land and Agrarian Studies, School of Government, University of the Western Cape, 2002); Michael Aliber and Deborah Johnston, *Land Reform in South Africa: Micro and Macro-Economic Perspectives*

(Johannesburg: L &APC), 1998; Ben Cousins, ed., "At the Crossroads: Land and Agrarian Reform in South Africa into the 21st Century," Papers from a conference held in Pretoria, July 26–28, 1999 (Braamfontein, South Africa: National Land Committee, 2000); Ben Cousins, *Issues and Options for Institutional Change for Rural Development* (Johannesburg: Land and Agriculture Policy Center, 1994). Johann Kirsten Johan Van Zyl and Nick Vink, *Agricultural Democratization* (Cape Town: AIPA, 1998); Tessa Marcus, Kathy Eales and Adele Wildschut, *Down to Earth: Land Demands in the New South Africa* (Johannesburg: Land and Agriculture Policy Center, 1996); Ntsebeza Lungisile, *Land Tenure Reform, Traditional Authorities and Rural Local Government in Post-Apartheid South Africa: Case Studies from the Eastern Cape* (Belville: Program for Land and Agrarian Studies, University of the Western Cape, 1999); Stephen Turner and Hilde Ibsen, *Land and Agrarian Reform in South Africa: A Status Report* (Belville, Program for Land and Agrarian Studies, 2000); Annette Fox, *Land Reform and Gender in South Africa* (Ottawa: National Association of Women and the Law); Shamin Meer, ed., *Women, Land and Authority: Perspectives from South Africa* (Cape Town: David Philip, 1997); Fiona Archer and Shamim Meer, *Woman's Work is Only Recognized When It Is Not Done* (Athlone: Surplus People's Project, 1995); Catherine Cross and Donna Hornby, *Opportunities and Obstacles to Women's Land Access in South Africa* (National Land Committee, Department of Land Affairs, South Africa, 2002); and On Economic Development on the eve of land reform in the Eastern Cape, see W. J. Davies, *Black Non-Urban Economic Employment Prospects in the Albany and Bathurst Districts of the Eastern Cape* (Rhodes University: Institute of Social and Economic Research, 1989); Andre Roux and David Gilmour, *Economic Conditions Among Black in Rural Ciskei* (Rhodes University: Institute of Social and Economic Research, 1991).

4. Walker, *Landmarked*, 21, 22.

5. *Land Info*, December 1998–February 1999.

6. *The Economist* cited 10,000 attacks and 1,650 deaths involving mostly white farmers and their families since 1991. "Land Reform in South Africa: Hurry Up, "December 3, 2009; Marian L. Tupy and Michael Kransdorff, "The Zimbabwe-ification of South Africa?, *Wall Street Europe*, July 15, 2009.

7. *Constitution of the Republic of South Africa*, Act No. 22, 1994.

8. DLA, *Annual Report*, 1994, 15

9. DLA, *Annual Report*, 1999.

10. DLA, *Annual Report*, April 1, 2006–March 31, 2007, 18.

11. Department of Rural Development and Land Reform (formerly Department of Land Affairs), *Annual Report*, April 1, 2009–March 2010.

12. http://www.info.gov.za/speeches/2006/06013012451001.htm (March 23, 2011).

13. Ruth Hall, "Land, Restitution in South Africa: Rights, Development and the Restrained State," *CJAS*, 38 (3) (2004), 659.

14. DLA, *Annual Report*, April 1, 2006–March 31, 2007, 9.

15. DLA, *Annual Report*, April 1, 2006–March 31, 2007, 9.

16. The NLC comprises: The Association for Rural Advancement (AFRA), The Border Rural Committee (BRC), East Cape Land Committee (ECLC), Farmworkers Research and Resource Project (FRRP), Orange Free State Rural Committee (OFSRUC), The Southern Cape Land Committee (SCLC), Surplus People Project (SPP), Transvaal

Rural Action Committee (TRAC), and Transkei Land Service Organization (TRALSO).

17. "The Elandsklowers Return at Last," *Land Update* 55 (December 1996), 5.

18. Dumisani Deliwe, "Forced Removal and Land Restitution in South Africa: A Case Study of the Mfengu of Tsistsikamma," in *From Reserve to Region: Apartheid and Social Change in the Keiskammahoek District of (former) Ciskei; 1950–1990*, Chris de Wet and Michael Whisson, eds. (Grahamstown: Institute for Social and Economic Research, Rhodes University, 1997), 267–296; Patrick McCartan, "Tsitsikamma Reserves (Eastern Cape)" in *Removals and the Law*, 122–131.

19. Department of Land Affairs, Report 108/96; Land Claims Commission, Eastern Cape [Application Form].

20. Hall, "Land Restitution in South Africa," 661–662.

21. Notice 268 of 1996: "Notice is hereby given in terms of section 11 (1) of the Restitution of Land Rights Act (Act No. 22 of 1994), that a claim for the restitution of land rights on Remaining Extent and Portion 7 of farm Klipheuvel 549, commonly known as Farmerfield in the District of Albany being 759,4919 has in extent (formerly 886,7059 morgen), held by T30584/1986 AND T92311/1994 (formerly T2173/1963), currently owned by Mr. Lawrence Raymond Riddin and Mr. John Michael Mullins, has been submitted on February 15, 1996, by Mr. S. Mzizi on behalf of Farmerfield community to the Regional Land Claims Commissioner (RLCC), Eastern Cape and Free State, and that the Commission on Restitution of Land Rights will investigate the claim in terms of the provisions of the Act in due course." *Government Gazette*, 17017, March 8, 1996.

22. Interview, Solomon Mzizi, February 23, 1999; Interview, Patrick Hewana, January 29, 1999.

23. Zingisile Mapazi, "Albany Farm Lands Restored to 20 Families," *Dispatch*, December 23, 1997.

24. *Farmerfield Communal Property Trust v. Remaining Extent of Portion 7 of the Farm Klipheuvel No. 459*, Land Claims Court of South Africa, Judgment of November 23, 1998.

25. Marian L. Tupy, "South Africa's Land Woes," *Washington Times*, March 6, 2006.

26. Department of Land Affairs, "Report 108/96, 1996; Interview, Patrick Hewana January 29, 1999; Interview, Solomon Mzizi, February 23, 1999.

27. Crystal Jannecke, "Constituting Community: The Contested Rural Land Claim of the Tsitsikamma 'Fingo/Mfengu' and Clarkson Moravian Mission in South Africa," *Kronos: Journal of Cape History*, 32 (2006): 192–215.

28. Walker, *Landmarked*, 34–36; Deborah James, *Gaining Ground? "Rights and Property" in South African Land Reform* (Abingdon: Routledge-Cavendish, 2007), 54–55.

29. James, *Gaining Ground*, 54.

30. Interview, Murphy Mquqo, February 21, 1999.

31. Interview, Mongameli Maxegwana, February 21, 1999.

32. Interview, Florence Matini, January 31, 1999.

33. Interview, Mary Jane Maxegwana, February 28, 1999.

34. Interview, Miriam Budaza, January 31, 1999.

35. Interview, Nonyameko Mpati, May 2, 1999.

36. Interview, Miriam Budaza, January 31, 1999.

37. Interview, Miriam Budaza, January 31, 1999.

38. Interview, Anderson Budaza, March 7, 1999.

39. Interview, Mary Jane Maxegwana, February 28, 1999.

40. Interview, Nofelity Gaba, February 1, 1999.

41. Interview, Petrus Zatu, May 1, 1999; Interview, Mbulelo Mquqo, February 21, 1999.

42. Interview, Nonyameko Mpati, May 2, 1999.

43. Interview, Patrick Hewana, January 29, 1999.

44. Thembela Kepe, "The Problem of Defining 'Community:' Challenges for the Land Reform Program in Rural South Africa," *Development Southern Africa* 16 (3) (Spring 1999), 417–422.

45. Department of Rural Development and Land Reform, *Annual Report*, April 1, 2009 to March 31, 2010, 6.

46. Community Survey, 2007 Eastern Cape, http://www.statssa.gov.za/publications/Report-03-01-32/Report-03-01-322007.pdf (March 20, 2010).

47. Elne Jacobs and Cecilia Punt, Western Cape Department of Agriculture, "A Profile of the Eastern Cape Province: Demographics, Poverty, Income, Inequality and Unemployment from 2000 till 2007," (Background Paper, 2009: 1 (2) Provincial Decision Making Enabling Project), www. elsenburg.com/provide/ . . . /BP2009 _1_2_% 20EC%20 Demographics.pdf (March 21, 23, 2011). Note that this report uses the figures of 47.7 and 7 million to represent South Africa's and the Eastern Cape's populations, respectively.

48. Adrienne Carlisle, "56 Families Stranded as Land Deal Stalls," *Dispatch*, June 6, 2000.

49. Interview, Mongameli Maxegwana, February 21, 1999.

50. Cooperative Housing Foundation International, "Road to Sustainability (RTF) Program, Semi-Annual Performance Report," April 2001–September 2001, http://pdf.usaid.gov/pdf_docs/PDABU235.pdf (March 23, 2011).

51. Interview, Miriam Budaza, January 31, 1999.

52. Hall, "Land Restitution in South Africa," 658.

53. Interview, Mongameli Maxegwana, February 21, 1999.

54. Hall, "Land Restitution in South Africa," 664.

55. Jannecke, "Constituting Community," 214.

56. Jannecke, "Constituting Community," 213, 214.

57. Interview, Daniel Matini and Florence Matini, August 1, 2007; Sylvia Zweni, Patrica Zweni, and Mina Nothemba Nonzube, August 3, 2007.

58. James, *Gaining Ground*, 57.

59. Walker, *Landmarked*, 78, 79.

60. Walker, *Landmarked*, 77–79.

61. James, *Gaining Ground*, 57, 64–77.

62. Wessel Visser, "'Shifting RDP into GEAR:' The ANC Government's Dilemma in Providing an Equitable System of Social Security for the 'New' South Africa," Paper presented at the 40th ITH Linzer Konferenz (University of Stellenbosch, South Africa, September 17, 2004).

63. *South Africa Millennium Development Goals, Mid-Term Country Report, 2007*, http://planipolis.iiep.unesco.org/upload/South%20Africa/SouthAfricaMDGmidterm.pdf. (March 21, 2011).

64. Interview, Florence Matini; Interview, Daniel Matini, July 31, 2007; Sylvia Zweni, Patrica Zweni, and Mina Nothemba Nonzube, August 3, 2007.

65. *South African Yearbook* 2009/2010, 131.

66. Interview, Florence Matini; Interview, Daniel Matini, July 31, 2007.

67. Cooperative Housing Foundation International, "Road to Sustainability (RTF) Program, Final Performance Report," Port Elizabeth, South Africa, May 22, 2002, http://pdf.usaid.gov/pdf_docs/PDABZ002.pdf (June 20, 2010; March 23, 2011).

68. Department of Land Affairs, "Progress on Restitution," January 27, 2006, http://www.info.gov.za/speeches/2006/06013012451001.htm. (March 23, 2011).

69. Interview, Patricia Zweni, August 3, 2007.

70. Interview, Solomon Mzizi, August 1, 2007.

71. Interview, Patricia Zweni; Interview, Sylvia Zweni, August 3, 2007.

72. Interview, Sylvia Zweni, August 3, 2007.

BIBLIOGRAPHY

Primary Sources

CORY LIBRARY FOR HISTORICAL RESEARCH, GRAHAMSTOWN, SOUTH AFRICA

ARCHIVAL RECORDS

MS 15 1188, Anonymous, n. d.

MS 15 034: Deed of Transfer [Klipheuvel/Farmerfield], May 28, 1839

MS 15 137: Book of Stubs, 1877–1896; 1932–1933

MS 15 173: John Kilner to John Walton, February 28, 1881

MS 15 312: Farmerfield Mission Notebook, 1906–1910

MS 15 356: Miscellaneous Papers, Letters, Accounts and Rules [Farmerfield]

MS 866: Letters from George and Mary Anne Impey, 1845

PR 3548: James Cameron, Journal Containing an Account of Incidents and Occurrences from 1836–1841 in Kaffirland

MS 15 402: Document whereby John Pato and Noah Mosambeker agree to accept the arbitration of William Henry Matthews

MS 15 450: William Impey to Charles Brownlee, Secretary for Native Affairs re Farmerfield and the Native Locations Act, March 15, 1877

MS 18 120: Peter Eyre, Diaries, 1900–1917

MS 15 093: Journal of William Impey

MS 15 056: Memo on Farmerfield, House Duties, 1887

MS 15 467: Report of the Committee on the Farmerfield Estate, March 11, 1886

MS 15 869: Farmerfield Baptismal Registry, 1841–1858

MS 15 870: Farmerfield Baptismal Registry, 1859–1899

MS 15 874: Farmerfield Baptismal Registry, 1844–1877

MS 16 582/1: Record Book kept by W. H. Matthews, 1839–1861

MS 16 582/2: Record Book kept by W. H. Matthews, 1839–1861

MS 17 212/1–6: Farmerfield Baptismal Registry, 1899–1955

MS 15 871/1–4: Farmerfield Marriage Registry, 1840–1949

MS 17 213: Farmerfield Marriage Registry, 1948–1955

MS 15 872: Farmerfield Burial Registry, 1864–1964

MS 15 880: Record Book [Bound Volume]
MS 15 880: Record Book [2 Unbound Volumes]
MS 15 128: Circuit Schedule Book, Salem and Farmerfield Circuit, March 1876–June 1893
MS 15 129: Circuit Schedule Book, Salem and Farmerfield Circuit, September 1893–December
    1916
MS 15 023/1–4: Minute Book, Albany and Kaffraria District, 1838–1871
MS 15 024: Minute Book, Albany and Kaffraria District, 1859–1870
MS 15 025: Minute Book, Albany and Kaffraria District, 1871–1884
MS 5 850: Miscellaneous Farmerfield Files, 1938
MS 15 879: Income and Expenditure Journal, Farmerfield
MS 17/127: Minutes, Quarterly Meeting, 1876–1887
MS 17 032: Minutes, Quarterly Meetings, 1888–1908
MS 15 875: Minutes, Quarterly Meetings, 1908–1922; 1922–1969
MS 15 361: Minutes, Quarterly Meetings and Local Preachers Meetings, 1903–1914
MS 15 132: Minutes, Quarterly Meetings and Local Preachers Meetings, 1914–1920
MS 15 018/1–10: Minutes, Grahamstown District Synod, 1872–1962
MS 15 735 F. J. Rhead Marsh to John Mitchell Watkinson, October 5, 1926
MS 15 735 John Mitchell Watkinson to F. J. Rhead Marsh, September 14, 1926
DOC 82: Journal of Simon George Amm 1886–1957
PR 7700: Farmerfield Notes
PR 7700, Letter from A. M. Mamase, Circuit Steward, Uitenhage, June 16, 1981

ALBANY MUSEUM, BOWKER LIBRARY

Klipheuvel File
Journal of Mrs. S. E. Amm

CAR: CAPE ARCHIVES REPOSITORY, CAPE TOWN, SOUTH AFRICA

British Kaffraria BK 90
1 AY 1/8–1/16 [Albany Criminal Record Book]
CO 465 Missionaries
CO 486 William Shaw to Colonel Bell, April 2, 1839
MS 17 044, Letter from John Montagu to Charles. L. Stretch, diplomatic agent, re memorial
    of certain missionaries respecting Kaffir laws, December 4, 1844.

SAB: PRETORIA ARCHIVES, PRETORIA

NTS (Secretary of Native Affairs) 10411 30/447/1
Chief Native Commissioner, Eastern Cape to Secretary of Native Affairs, Pretoria, 24 February
    1958.
Chief Native Commissioner to the Secretary for Native Affairs, June 10, 1958.
J. B. Smith, Magistrate to Secretary of Native Affairs, Pretoria, November 10, 1958.
Lys van plakkers en hulle gesinne op Farmerfield asook hulle lewendehawe en aan watter
    stam hulle behoort en voorwaardes wat hulle daar woon
NTS (Secretary of Native Affairs) 2598 102/305
Farmerfield Mission Lands: Albany District, December 3,1952.
Reverend George H. P. Jacques to the Magistrate of Grahamstown, November 15, 1938;
    The Secretary for Native Affairs to the Chief Native Commissioner, October 4, 1938.
Memo, Urban Areas Section, November 5, 1941.

NTS (Secretary of Native Affairs) 7186 /974/323/129

Secretary for Bantu Administration and Development to the Chief Native Commissioner, 1959

URU (Decisions of the Executive Council) 1850/213

Transactions in terms of section 1 of the Natives Land Act, 1913, Renewal of Lease of Residential Rights on Mission Farm, Farmerfield, Albany to John Malakane and others, 1939

URU (Decisions of the Executive Council) 1793/1360

Transactions in terms of section 1 of the Natives Land Act, 1913, Renewal of Lease of Residential Rights on Mission Farm, Farmerfield, Albany to John Malakane and others, 1940

SOUTH AFRICAN LIBRARY (SAL)

Report of the Wesleyan Missionary Society for the Albany and Kaffraria District for the Year ending 1853.

GOVERNMENT SOURCES

Blue Book on Native Affairs, Albany, G. 4 of 1893

Blue Book on Native Affairs, Albany, G. 9 of 1894

Blue Book on Native Affairs, Albany, G. 8 of 1895

Blue Book on Native Affairs, Albany, G. 5 of 1896

Blue Book on Native Affairs, Albany, G. 19 of 1897

Blue Book on Native Affairs, Albany, G. 42 of 1898

Blue Book on Native Affairs, Albany, G. 25 of 1902

Blue Book on Native Affairs, Albany, G. 29 of 1903

Cape of Good Hope. Master and Servant, Addenda to the Documents on the Working Order in Council, July 21, 1846.

Cape of Good Hope. Commission on Native laws and Customs. *Report and Proceedings of the Government Commission on Native Laws and Customs.* 2 vols. C. Struik, 1883.

Department of Land Affairs. *Annual Report*, 1994

Department of Land Affairs. *Report 108/96* [Farmerfield], 1996

Department of Land Affairs. *Annual Report*, 1999

Department of Land Affairs. *Annual Report*, April 1, 2006–March 31, 2007

Department of Rural Development and Land Reform, (formerly Department of Land Affairs). *Annual Report*, April 1, 2009–March 2010.

Department of Rural Development and Land Reform. *Annual Report*, April 1, 2009–March 31, 2010.

Great Britain. House of Commons. Papers Relative to the Condition and Treatment of Native Inhabitants of Southern Africa within the Colony of the Cape of Good Hope. March 18, 1835.

———. Select Committee. Report of the Select Committee on Aborigines, 1836–1837.

———. Select Committee. Report of the Select Committee on the Kafir Tribes, 635 of 1851.

Notice 268 of 1996. *Government Gazette*, March 8, 1996. [Claim for Restitution of Land Rights, Farmerfield]

Regional Land Claims Commission, (RLCC) Eastern Cape. [Application Form].

Republic of South Africa. Constitution of the Republic of South Africa. Restitution of Land Rights Act. Act No. 22 of 1994.Pretoria: Government Printer, 1994.

Republic of South Africa. *South African Yearbook 2009/2010.* Government Communication and Information System, 2010.

Union of South Africa. *Natives Land Act, Act No.27 of 1913*. Pretoria: Government Printer, 1913.

Union of South Africa. U.G. 22 of 1932. Native Economic Commission, 1930–1932.

Union of South Africa. *Natives Land Act, Act No.18 of 1936*. Pretoria: Government Printer, 1936.

Union of South Africa. *Group Areas Act. Act No. 41 of 1950*. Pretoria: Government Printer, 1950.

NEWSPAPERS AND PERIODICAL LITERATURE

Black Sash
Cape Frontier Times
Dispatch
General Report of the WMS
Graham's Town Journal
Land Info
Land Update
Mail & Guardian
Methodist Churchman
Papers Relative to the Wesleyan Missions and to the State of "Heathen" Countries,
South African Christian Watchman and Missionary Magazine
South African Commercial Advertiser
South African Yearbook
Sunday Times Magazine
Wesleyan Missionary Notices
Umshumayeli Wendaba
Wall Street Journal Europe
Washington Times

Printed Primary Sources

Alberti, Ludwig. *Alberti's Account of the Xhosa in 1807*. Translated by W. Fehr. Cape Town: A.A. Balkema, 1968.

Appleyard, John. *The War of the Axe and the Xosa Bible*. Cape Town: C. Struik, 1971.

Backhouse, James. *A Narrative of a Visit to Mauritius and South Africa*. London: Hamilton, Adams, 1844.

Bird, William Wilberforce. *State of the Cape of Good Hope in 1822*. London: John Murray, 1823. Reprint, Cape Town: C. Struik, 1966.

Bowker, John Mitford. *Speeches, Letters, and Selections from Important Papers*. Grahamstown: Godlonton and Richards, 1864. Reprint, Cape Town: C. Struik, 1962.

Boyce, William B. *Notes on South African Affairs*. London: Mason, 1839.

Bredekamp, H. C. and H. E. F. Plüddemann, eds. *Genadendal Diaries: Diaries of the Herrnhut Missionaries, H. Marsveld, D. Schwinn and J.C. Kühnel*. 2 vols. Trans. A.B.L. Flegg. Bellville: University of the Western Cape Institute for Historical Research, 1992–1999.

Broadbent, Samuel. *A Narrative of the First Introduction of Christianity among the Barolong Tribe of Bechuanas, South Africa*. London: Wesleyan Mission Press, 1865.

Brownlee, Charles. *Reminiscences of Kaffir Life and History*. 2nd ed. Lovedale: Lovedale Mission Press, 1916.

Calderwood, Henry. *Caffres and Caffre Missions*. London: Nisbet, 1858.

Callaway, Godfrey. *Sketches of Kafir Life*. London: A.R. Mowbray, 1905. Reprint, New York: Negro Universities Press, 1969.

———. *South Africa from within made Known in the Letters of a Magistrate*. London: SPCK, 1930.

Callaway, Henry. *Polygamy, A Bar to Admission into the Christian Church*. Durban: John Brown, 1862.

Campbell, John. *Travels in South Africa*. London: Black and Parry, 1815. Reprint, Cape Town: C. Struik, 1974.

Chase, John Centlivres. *The Cape of Good Hope and the Eastern Province of Algoa Bay*. 1843. Reprint, Cape Town: C. Struik, 1967.

Conference of the Wesleyan Methodist Church of South Africa. *A Manual of the Laws and Discipline of the Wesleyan Methodist Church of South Africa*. Queenstown: Wesleyan Book Room, 1898.

Dugmore, Henry. *Reminiscences of an Albany Settler*. Grahamstown: Grocott and Sherry, 1958.

Fast, Hildegard, ed. *The Journal and Selected Letters of Rev. William J. Shrewsbury, 1826–1835*. Johannesburg: Witwatersrand University Press, 1994.

Gibson, Alan. *Eight Years in Kaffraria, 1882–1890*. London: Wells, Gardner, Darton, 1891. Reprint, New York: Negro Universities Press, 1969.

Godlonton, Robert. *A Narrative of the Kaffir War of 1850–51*. Grahamstown: Godlonton and White, 1852.

———. *Sketches of the Eastern Districts of the Cape of Good Hope*. Grahamstown: Office of the Graham's Town Journal, 1842.

Gray, Robert. *A Journal of the Bishop's Visitation Tour through the Cape Colony in 1848*. London: Society for the Propagation of the Gospel, 1851.

Hammond-Tooke, D. W., ed. *Journal of William Shaw*. Cape Town: A. A. Balkema, 1972.

Hinchliff, Peter, ed. *The Journal of John Ayliff*. Cape Town: A. A. Balkema, 1971.

Hutton. C. W., ed. *The Autobiography of the Late Sir Andries Stockenström*. 2 vols. 1887. Reprint. Cape Town: C. Struik, 1964.

'Justus.' *The Wrongs of the Caffre Nation*. London: James Duncan, 1837.

Kay, Stephen. *Travels and Researches in Caffraria: Describing the Character, Customs, and Moral Condition of the Tribes Inhabiting that portion of Southern Africa*. London: John Mason, 1833.

Keppel-Jones, Arthur. *Philips, 1820 Settler, His Letters*. Pietermaritzburg, South Africa: Shuter and Shooter, 1960.

Kingsley, Mary. *Travels in West Africa*. London: Macmillan, 1897. Reprint, London: Dent/Everyman, 1993.

Land Claims Court. *Farmerfield Communal Property Trust v. The Remaining Extent of Portion 7 of the Farm Klipheuvel No 459*. Case no. LCC35/97, November 23, 1998.

Le Cordeur, Basil and Christopher Saunders. *The Kitchingman Papers: Missionary Letters and Journals, 1817–1848 from the Brenthurst Collection, Johannesburg*. Johannesburg: Brenthurst, 1976.

Livingstone, David. *Missionary Travels and Research in Africa*. London: Murray, 1857.

Long, Una, ed. *The Chronicle of Jeremiah Goldswain, Albany Settler of 1820*. 2 vols. Cape Town: The Van Riebeeck Society, 1946–1948.

Lugard, Frederick John Dealtry, Baron. *The Rise of Our East African Empire: Early Efforts in Nyasaland and Uganda*. London: William Blackwood, 1893.

Maclean, John, ed. *A Compendium of Kafir Laws and Customs*. Mount Coke, South Africa: Wesleyan Mission Press, 1858.

Maxwell, W. A. and R. T. McGeogh, eds. *The Reminiscences of Thomas Stubbs*. Cape Town: A. A. Balkema, 1978.

Mayhew, Henry. *London Labor and the London Poor*. London: Penguin Books, 1985.

Moodie, Donald. *The Record, or a Series of Official Papers Relative to the Condition and Treatment of the Native Races of South Africa*. Cape Town: A. A. Balkema, 1960.

Moodie, John W. D. *Ten Years in South Africa: Including a Particular Description of the Wild Sports of That Country*. 2 vols. London: Richard Bentley, 1835.

Moffat, Robert. *Missionary Labours and Scenes in Southern Africa*. London: Snow, 1846.

Perrigo, James. *Recollections of a Visit to Kaffraria*. London: SPCK, 1866.

Philip, John. *Researches in South Africa: Illustrating the Civil, Moral, and Religious Condition of Native Tribes*. 2 vols. London: James Duncan, 1828.

Philipps, Thomas. *Scenes and Occurrences in Albany and Caffreland, South Africa*. London: William Marsh, 1827.

Plaatje, Solomon. *Native Life in South Africa and since the European War and Boer Rebellions*. London: P. S. King and Son, 1916. Reprint, New York: Negro Universities Press, 1969.

Pringle, Thomas. *Narrative of a Residence in South Africa*. London: Moxon, 1835.

Rose, Cowper. *Four Years in Southern Africa*. London: Henry Colburn and Richard Bentley, 1829.

Sadler, *Celia, comp. Never a Young Man: Extracts from the Letters and Journals of the Rev. William Shaw*. Cape Town: HAUM, 1967.

Schwar J. F., and R. W. Jardine, ed. and transl. *The Letters and Journal of Gustav Steinbert*. 2 vols. Port Elizabeth: University of Port Elizabeth, 1975.

Shaw, Barnabas. *Memorials of South Africa*. London: J. Mason, 1841.

Shaw, William. *A Defence of Wesleyan Missionaries in Southern Africa comprising Copies of a Correspondence with the Reverend John Philip D. D.* London: J. Mason, 1839.

———. *The Story of my Mission in South-eastern Africa*. London: Hamilton, 1860.

Steedman, Andrew. *Wanderings and Adventures in the Interior of Southern Africa*. 2 vols. London: Longman, 1835.

Theal, George McCall, comp. *Records of the Cape Colony*. 36 vols. London: Government of the Cape, 1897–1905.

———. *Documents Relating to the Kaffir War of 1835*. London: Clowes, 1912.

Thompson, George. *Travels and Adventures in Southern Africa: Comprising a View of the Present State of the Cape Colony with Observation on the Progress and Prospects of the British Emigrants*. 2 vols. London: Henry Colburn, 1827.

Wilberforce, William. *An Appeal to the Religion, Justice and Humanity of the Inhabitants of the British Empire on Behalf of the Negro Slaves in the West Indies*. London: J Hatchard and Sons, 1823.

Young, Samuel. *A Missionary Narrative of the Triumphs of Grace as Seen in the Conversion of Kafirs, Hottentots, Fingoes and other Natives of South Africa*. New York: G. Lande and P. P. Stanford, 1843.

Secondary Sources

Adas, Michael. *Machines as the Measure of Men: Science, Technology and Ideologies of Western Dominance*. Ithaca: Cornell University Press, 1989.

Ajayi, Jacob. *Christian Missions in Nigeria, 1841–1891: The Making of a New Elite*. London: Longman, 1965.

Antsey, Roger. *The Atlantic Slave Trade and Abolition, 1760–1810*. London: Macmillan, 1975.

Axtell, James. *The European and the Indian, Essays in the Ethnohistory of Colonial America*. Oxford: Oxford University Press, 1981.

Ayandele, Emmanuel. *The Missionary Impact on Modern Nigeria, 1842–1914: A Political and Social Analysis*. New York: Humanities Press, 1966.

Bank, Andrew. "Losing Faith in the Civilising Mission: The Premature Decline of Humanitarian Liberalism at the Cape, 1840–1860." In *British Empire and Others: British Encounters with Indigenous Peoples*, eds. M.J. Daunton and Richard Halpern, 364–383. Philadelphia: University of Pennsylvania Press, 1999.

Bayly, C. A. *Imperial Meridian: The British Empire and the World, 1780–1830*. Essex: Longman, 1989.

Bebbington, D. W. *Evangelicalism in Modern Britain: A History from the 1730s to the 1980s*. London: Unwin Wyman, 1989.

Beck, Roger. "Bible and Beads: Missionaries as Traders in Southern Africa in the Early Nineteenth Century," *JAH* 30(2) (1989): 211–225.

Beidelman, Thomas. *Colonial Evangelism: A Socio-Historical Study of an East African Mission at the Grassroots*. Bloomington, IN: Indiana University Press, 1982.

Beinart, William. *Twentieth Century South Africa*. Oxford: Oxford University Press, 1994.

——— and Saul Dubow, eds. *Segregation and Apartheid in Twentieth Century South Africa*. London: Routledge, 1995.

Bergh, J. S., and Visagie, J. C. *The Eastern Cape Frontier Zone, 1660–1980: A Cartographical Guide for Historical Research*. Durban: Butterworths, 1985.

Berning, Michael, ed. *The Historical "Conversations" of Sir George Cory*. Cape Town: Maskew Miller Longman, 1989.

Blackburn, Robin. *The Overthrow of Colonial Slavery, 1776–1848*. London: Verso, 1988.

Botha, Colin Graham. *The French Refugees at the Cape*, 3rd ed. Cape Town: C. Struik, 1970.

Bozzoli, Belinda. *Women of Phokeng: Consciousness, Life Strategy, and Migrancy in South Africa, 1900–1983*. Portsmouth, NH: Heinemann, 1991.

Bradford, Helen. "Peasants, Historians and Gender: A South African Case Study Revisited." *History and Theory* 39 (December 2000): 86–110.

Bradley, Ian. *The Call to Seriousness*. London: Jonathan Cape, 1976.

Bradlow, Edna. "Capitalists and Laborers in the Post-Emancipation Rural Cape, Part 1." *Historia* 31 (September 1985): 49–62.

———. "Capitalist and Laborers in the Post-Emancipation Rural Cape, Part 2." *Historia* 31 (May 1986): 57–67.

Bredekamp, Henry and Robert Ross, eds. *Missions and Christianity in South African History*. Johannesburg: Witwatersrand University Press, 1995.

Bundy, Colin. *The Rise and Fall of the South African Peasantry*. Berkeley: University of California Press, 1979.

———. "Comparatively Speaking: Kas Maine and South African Agrarian History." Review of *The Seed is Mine* by Charles Van Onselen, *JSAS* 23(2) (June 1997): 363–371.

Butler, Guy. *The 1820 Settlers: An Illustrated Commentary*. Cape Town: Human and Rousseau, 1974.

Butler, Jon. *Awash in a Sea of Faith, Christianizing the American People*. Cambridge: Harvard University Press, 1990.

———. *The Huguenots in America: A Refugee People in a New World Society*. Cambridge: Harvard University Press, 1983.

Bryer, Lynne with Keith Hunt, *1820 Settlers*. Cape Town: Don Nelson, 1984.

Carlisle, Adrienne. "56 Families Stranded as Land Deal Stalls." *Dispatch*, June 6, 2000.

Chidester, David. *Religions of South Africa*. London: Routledge, 1992.

———. *Savage Systems: Colonial and Comparative Religion in Southern Africa*. Charlottesville: University Press of Virginia, 1996.

Chimundu, Herbert. "Early Missionaries and the Ethnolinguistic Factor During the Invention of Tribalism in Zimbabwe." *JAH* 33 (1992): 87–109.

Cliff, Philip. *The Rise and Development of the Sunday School Movement in England, 1780–1980*. Nutfield, England: National Christian Education Council, 1986.

Cock, Jaclyn. "Domestic Service and Education for Domesticity: The Incorporation of Xhosa Women into Colonial Society." In *Women and Gender in Southern Africa to 1945*, ed. Cherryl Walker, 76–96. Cape Town: David Philip, 1990.

———. *Maids and Madams: A Study in the Politics of Exploitation*. Cape Town: Ravan Press, 1980.

Colley, Linda. *Britons: Forging the Nation, 1707–1837*. New Haven: Yale University Press, 1992.

Comaroff, Jean and John. *Of Revelation and Revolution: Christianity, Colonialism, and Consciousness in South Africa*. Vol 1. Chicago: University of Chicago Press, 1991.

———. "Home-Made Hegemony: Modernity, Domesticity, and Colonialism in South Africa." In *African Encounters with Domesticity*, ed. Karen Tranberg Hansen, 37–74. New Brunswick, NJ: Rutgers University Press, 1992.

———. *Of Revelation and Revolution: Christianity, Colonialism, and Consciousness in South Africa*. Vol. 2. Chicago: University of Chicago Press, 1997.

Cosmas, Desmond. *The Discarded People: An Account of African Resettlement in South Africa*. Harmondsworth: Penguin Books, 1970.

Crais, Clifton. "The Vacant Land: The Political Mythology of British Expansion in the Eastern Cape, South Africa." *Journal of Social History* 25 (1991): 255–75.

———. *White Supremacy and Black Resistance in Pre-Industrial South Africa: The Making of the Colonial Order in the Eastern Cape, 1770–1865*. Cambridge: Cambridge University Press, 1972.

———. *The Politics of Evil: Magic, State Power, and the Political Imagination in South Africa*. Cambridge: Cambridge University Press, 2002.

Currie, Marion Rose. "The History of Theopolis Mission Station, 1814–1857." 2 vols. M. A. Rhodes University, 1983.

Curtin, Philip. *The Atlantic Slave Trade: A Census*. Madison: The University of Wisconsin Press, 1969.

Dachs, Anthony. "Functional Aspects of Religious Conversion among the Sotho-Tswana." In *Christianity South of the Zambezi*. 2 vols. ed. A. J. Dachs and M. F. C. Bourdillon, 147–158. Gwelo, Rhodesia: Mambo Press, 1977.

Da Costa, Emilia Viotta. *Crown of Glory, Tears of Blood: The Demerara Slave Rebellion of 1823*. New York: Oxford University Press, 1994.

Davenport, Betty. "A History of the Matthews settler family of Salem and 'Woodstock', Alice, South Africa. 1820–1950." Cape Town: Privately Published, 2010.

Davenport, T. R. H. "Land Legislation: Determining the Present Racial Allocation of Land." *Development Southern Africa* 7 (3) (October): 431–440.

——— and K. S. Hunt. *The Right to the Land*. Cape Town: David Philip, 1974.

Davies, Horton. *Great South African Christians*. Oxford: Oxford University Press, 1951.

Davis, David Brion. *The Problem of Slavery in the Age of Revolution, 1770–1823*. Ithaca, NY: Cornell University Press, 1975.

——. *Slavery and Human Progress*. New York: Oxford University Press, 1984.

De Kock, Leon. *Civilising Barbarians Missionary Narrative and African Textual Response in Nineteenth-Century South Africa*. Johannesburg: Witwatersrand University Press, 1996.

Deliwe, Dumisani. "Forced Removal and Land Restitution in South Africa: A Case Study of the Mfengu of Tsitsikamma." In *From Reserve to Region: Apartheid and Social Change in the Keiskammahoek District of (former) Ciskei, 1950–1990*, eds. Chris de Wet and Michael Whisson, 267–296. Grahamstown: Institute for Social and Economic Research, Rhodes University, 1999.

Ditchfield, G. M. *The Evangelical Revival*. London: UCL Press, 1998.

Dooling, Wayne. "The Making of a Colonial Elite: Property, Family and Landed Stability in the Cape Colony, c. 1750–1834," *JSAS* 31 (1) (March, 2005): 147–162.

Dubow, Saul. "The Elaboration of Segregation Ideology." In *Segregation and Apartheid in Twentieth Century South Africa*, eds., William Beinart and Saul Dubow, 145–175. London: Routledge, 1995.

Du Plessis, Johannes. *A History of Christian Missions in South Africa*. London: Longmans, Green, 1911.

Du Toit, Andre. *The Earliest South African Documents on the Education and Civilization of the Bantu*. Pretoria: University of South Africa, 1963.

——. "No Chosen People: The Myth of the Calvinist Origins of Afrikaner Nationalism and Racial Ideology." *AHR* 88(4) (October 1983): 920–53.

Edgar, Robert. *Because they Chose the Plan of God: The Story of the Bulhoek Massacre*. Johannesburg: Ravan Press, 1988.

——. New Religious Movements, in Missions and Empire. In *Missions and Empire*, ed. Norman Etherington, 216–237. Oxford: Oxford University Press, 2005.

Edwards, Isobel. *The 1820 Settlers: A Study in British Colonial Policy*. London: Longmans and Green, 1934.

"The Elandsklowers Return at Last." *Land Update* 55 (December 1996).

Elbourne, Elizabeth. "Concerning Missionaries: The Case of Van der Kemp." *JSAS* 17 (1991): 153–64.

——. "'To Colonize the Mind': Evangelical Missionaries in Britain and the Eastern Cape, 1790–1837." Ph.D. diss., Oxford University, 1992.

——. *Blood Ground: Colonialism, Missions and the Contest for Christianity in the Cape Colony and Britain, 1799–1853*. Montreal: McGill-Queens University Press, 2002.

Elphick, Richard. *Kraal and Castle: Khoikhoi and the Making of White South Africa*. New Haven: Yale University Press, 1977.

——. "Africans and the Christian Campaign in Southern Africa." In *The Frontier in History, North America and Southern Africa Compared*, ed. Howard Lamar and Leonard Thompson, 270–308. New Haven: Yale University Press, 1981.

——. "Writing Religion into History." In *Missions and Christianity in South African History*, eds. Henry Bredekamp and Robert Ross, 11–26. Johannesburg: Witwatersrand University Press, 1995.

—— and Anna Boeseken, "The Meaning, Origin and Use of the Term Khoi San and Khoesan," *CABO*: Historical Society of Cape Town, 1(1) (August 1972): 5–10; *CABO* 2(2) (Jan 1974): 2–9; and 2(3) (November 1975): 12–18.

—— and Rodney Davenport, eds. *Christianity in South Africa: A Political, Social, and Cultural History*. Claremont, South Africa: David Philip, 1997.

———— and V. C. Malherbe. "The Khoesan to 1828" in *The Shaping of South African Society, 1652–1840*, eds. Richard Elphick and Hermann Giliomee, 4. Middletown, CT: Wesleyan University Press, 1979.

Enklaar, Ido H. *Life and Work of Dr. J. Th. Van Der Kemp 1747–1811: Missionary Pioneer and Protagonist of Racial Equality in South Africa*. Cape Town: A. A. Balkema, 1988.

Erlank, Natasha. "Gender and Christianity among Africans Attached to Scottish Mission Stations in Xhosaland in the Nineteenth Century." Ph.D. diss., St. Johns College, Cambridge University, 1998.

————. "Gendered Reactions to Social Dislocation and Missionary Activity in Xhosaland, 1836–1847." *African Studies*, 59(2) (2000): 205–227.

————. "'Raising up the Degraded Daughters of Africa:' The Provision of Education for Xhosa Women in the Mid-Nineteenth Century." *SAHJ* 43(2000): 24–38.

Etherington, Norman. "Mission Station Melting Pots as a Factor in the Rise of South African Black Nationalism." *IJAS* 9(4) (1976): 592–605.

————. *Preachers, Peasants and Politics in Southeast Africa, 1835–1880: African Christian Communities in Natal, Pondoland, and Zululand*. London: Royal Historical Society, 1978.

————. "Missionaries and the Intellectual History of Africa: A Historical Survey." *Itinerario* (7) (1983): 116–143.

————. "Recent Trends in the Historiography of Christianity in Southern Africa." *JSAS* 22 (1996): 201–219.

————. "Review of Alan Lester, *Imperial Networks*." *International Historical Review* 24(3) (2002): 646–647.

Evans, Maurice. *Black and White in South East Africa: A Study in Sociology*. London: Longmans, 1916.

Fast, Hildegarde H. "'In at One Ear and Out at the Other': African Responses to the Wesleyan Message in Xhosaland, 1825–1835." *Journal of Religion in Africa* 23 (1993): 47–74.

————, ed. *The Journal and Selected Letters of Rev. William J. Shrewsbury, 1826–1835*. Johannesburg: Witwatersrand University Press, 1994.

Festenstein, Melville and Claire Pickard-Cambridge. *Land and Race: South Africa's Group Areas and Land Acts*. Johannesburg: SAIRR, 1987.

Fields, Karen. *Revival and Rebellion in Central Africa*. Princeton: Princeton University Press, 1985.

Findlay, George and W. W. Holdsworth. *The History of the Wesleyan Methodist Missionary Society*. Vol. 1. London: Epworth Press, 1921.

Freund, William. "The Career of Johannes Theodorus Van Der Kemp and his Role in the History of South Africa." *Tijdschrift voor Geschiedenis* 86(3): 376–390.

Frye, John, ed. *The War of the Axe and the Xosa Bible: The Journal of Reverend J. W. Appleyard*. Cape Town: C. Struik, 1971.

Fyfe, Christopher. *A History of Sierra Leone*. Oxford: Oxford University Press, 1962.

Galbraith, J. S. *Reluctant Empire: British Policy on the South African Frontier, 1834–1854*. Berkeley: University of California Press, 1963.

Gaitskell, Deborah. "'Praying and Preaching:' The Distinctive Spirituality of African Women's Church Organizations," in *Missions and Christianity in South African History*, eds. Henry Bredekamp and Robert Ross, 135–152. Johannesburg: Witwatersrand University Press, 1995.

———. "Power in Prayer and Service: Women's Christian Organizations." In *Christianity in South Africa: A Political, Social and Cultural History*, Richard Elphick and Rodney Davenport, eds., 253–267. Berkeley: University of California Press, 1997.

———. "Rethinking Gender Roles: The Field Experience of Women Missionaries in South Africa," in *The Imperial Horizons of British Protestant Missions*. Grand Rapids: William B. Eerdmans, Publishing, 2003.

Gerstner, Jonathan. *The Thousand Generation Covenant: Dutch Reformed Covenant Theology and Group Identity in Colonial South Africa*. Leiden: E. J. Brill, 1991.

———. "A Christian Monopoly: The Reformed Church and Colonial Society under Dutch Rule." In *Christianity in South Africa: A Political, Social, and Cultural History*, eds. Richard Elphick and Rodney Davenport. Claremont, South Africa: David Philip, 1997.

Giliomee, Hermann. "The Eastern Frontier, 1770–1812." In *The Shaping of South African Society, 1652–1840*, eds. Richard Elphick and Hermann Giliomee, 421–471. Middletown, CT: Wesleyan University Press, 1979.

Goitein, S. D. *A Mediterranean Society: The Jewish Communities of the Arab World as Portrayed in the Documents of the Cairo Geniza. Vol. 5*. Berkeley: University of California Press, 1988.

Gordon, Robert. *The Bushman Myth: The Making of a Namibian Underclass*. Boulder, CO: Westview Press, 1992.

Grimshaw, Patricia and Peter Sherlock, "Women and Cultural Exchange," in *Oxford History of the British Empire: Missions and Empire*, ed. Norman Etherington. New York: Oxford University Press, 2005.

Guelke, Leonard. "Freehold Farmers and Frontier Settlers, 1657–1780." In *The Shaping of South African Society, 1652–1840*, eds. Richard Elphick and Herman Giliomee, 66–108. Middletown, CT: Wesleyan University Press, 1979.

——— and Robert Shell. "Landscape of Conquest: Frontier, Water Alienation and Khoikhoi Strategies of Survival, 1652–1780," *JSAS* 18(4) (1992): 803–824.

Guy, Jeff. *The Heretic: A Study of the Life of John William Colenso, 1814–1883*. Johannesburg: Ravan Press, 1983.

———. "Gender Oppression in Southern Africa's Pre-Capitalist Societies." In *Women and Gender in Southern Africa to 1945*, ed. Cherryl Walker, 33–47. Cape Town: David. Philip, 1990.

Hall, Catherine. *Civilising Subjects: Metropole and Colony in the Imperial Imagination, 1830–1867*. Chicago: University of Chicago Press, 2002.

Hall, Ruth. "Land, Restitution in South Africa: Rights, Development and the Restrained State," *Canadian Journal of African Studies*, 38(3) (2004): 654–671.

Hamilton, Carolyn ed. *The Mfecane Aftermath: Reconstructive Debates in Southern African History: Reconstructive Debates in Southern African History*, Carolyn Hamilton, ed. 241–276. Johannesburg: Witwatersrand University Press, 1995.

Hammond-Tooke, D. W. "The Symbolic Structure of Cape-Nguni Cosmology." In *Religion and Social Change in Southern Africa*, eds. Michael Whisson and Martin West. Cape Town: David Philip, 1975.

Harries, Patrick. *Butterflies and Barbarians: Swiss Missionaries and Systems of Knowledge in South East Africa*. Oxford: James Currey, 2007.

Harris, John Charles. *Khama, the Great African Chief*. London: The Livingstone Press, 1923.

Haskins, James. *The Methodists*. New York: Hippocrene Books, 1992.

Hastings, Adrian. *The Church in Africa, 1450–1950*. Oxford: Clarendon Press, 1994.

Henriques, Ursula. *Religious Toleration in England, 1787–1833*. Toronto: University of Toronto Press, 1961.

Hewson, Leslie. "Healdtown: A Study of a Methodist Experiment in African Education." Ph.D. diss., Rhodes University, 1959.

———. "History of Farmerfield: The Idea and the Place." *Annals of the Grahamstown Historical Society* 18 (1988): 60–62.

Higgs, Catherine. *The Ghost of Equality: The Public Lives of D. D. T. Jabavu of South Africa, 1885–1959*. Athens, OH: Ohio University Press, 1997.

Hilton, Boyd. *The Age of Atonement: The Influence of Evangelicalism on Social and Economic Thought, 1795–1865*. Oxford: Clarendon Press, 1988.

Hobsbawm, Eric. *Age of Revolution: 1789–1848*. New York: New American Library, 1962.

Hodgson, Janet. *God of the Xhosa: A Study of the Origins and Development of the Traditional Concepts of the Supreme Being*. Cape Town: Oxford University Press, 1982.

———. *Princess Emma*. Craighall, South Africa: Ad. Donker, 1987.

Holden, William Clifford. *British Rule in South Africa Illustrated in the Story of Kama and his Tribe and of the War in Zululand*. 1879. Reprint, Pretoria: State Library, 1969.

———. *The Past and Future of the Kaffir Races*. 1866. Reprint, Cape Town: C. Struik, 1963.

Holst-Petersen, Karen, ed., *Religion, Development and African Identity*. Uppsala: Scandinavian Institute of African Studies, 1987.

Horton, Robin. *Patterns of Thought in Africa and the West*. Cambridge: Cambridge University Press 1993.

———. "African Traditional Thought and Western Science." *Africa* 37 (1967): 50–71.

———. "African Conversion." *Africa: Journal of International African Institute* 41 (1971): 85–108.

———. "On the Rationality of Conversion." Part 1. *Africa: Journal of the International African Institute* 45(3) (1975): 219–35.

———. "On the Rationality of Conversion." Part 2. *Africa: Journal of the International African Institute* 45(4) (1975): 373–99.

Hunt, Keith. "The Development of Municipal Government in the Eastern Province of the Cape of Good Hope with reference to Grahamstown, 1827–1862." M.A. thesis, Rhodes University, 1961. Reprint, *Archives Yearbook for South African History* 61. Cape Town: Office of the Director of Archives, 1963.

Hunterhalter, Elaine. *Forced Removal: The Division, Segregation and Control of the People of South Africa*. London: International Defense and Aid Fund for Southern Africa, 1987.

Jacobs, Elne and Cecilia Punt. Western Cape Department of Agriculture. "A Profile of the Eastern Cape Province: Demographics, Poverty, Income, Inequality and Unemployment from 2000 till 2007." Background Paper, 2009: 1 (2) Provincial Decision-Making Enabling Project.

James, Deborah. *Gaining Ground? 'Rights and 'Property' in South African Land Reform*. Abingdon: Routledge-Cavendish, 2007.

Jannecke, Crystal. "Constituting Community: The Contested Rural Land Claim of the Tsitsikamma 'Fingo/Mfengu' and Clarkson Moravian Mission in South Africa." *Kronos: Journal of Cape History* 32 (2006): 192–215.

Jennings, Francis. *The Invasion of America: Indians, Colonialism and the Cant of Conquest.* Chapel Hill: University of North Carolina Press, 1975.

Keegan, *Tim Facing the Storm: Portraits of Black Lives in Rural South Africa.* London: Zed Books, 1988.

———. *Colonial South Africa and the Origins of the Racial Order.* Charlottesville: University Press of Virginia, 1996.

Kepe, Thembela. "The Problem of Defining 'Community:' Challenges for the land Reform Program in Rural South Africa." *Development Southern Africa* 16(3) (Spring 1999): 415–433.

Kirk, Tony. "Progress and Decline in the Kat River Settlement." *JAH* 14 (1973): 411–28.

Kirkaldy, Alan. *Capturing the Soul: The VhaVenda and the Missionaries, 1870–1900.* Pretoria: Protea Book House, 2005.

Klein, Herbert. *The Middle Passage: Comparative Studies in the Atlantic Slave Trade.* Princeton: Princeton University Press, 1978.

Krüger, Bernhard. *The Pear Tree Blossoms: A History of the Moravian Mission Stations in South Africa, 1737–1869.* Genadendal, South Africa: Moravian Book Depot, 1966.

Lamar, Howard and Leonard Thompson, eds. *The Frontier in History: North America and Southern Africa Compared.* New Haven: Yale University Press, 1981.

Lambourne, Bridget. "Methods of Mission: The Ordering of Space of Time, Land and Labor on Methodist Mission Stations in Caffraria, 1823–1835." Seminar, African Studies Institute, University of the Witwatersrand, 1992.

"Land Reform in South Africa: Hurry Up." *Economist.* December 3, 2009.

Landau, Paul. *The Realm of the Word: Language, Gender, and Christianity in a Southern African Kingdom.* Portsmouth, NH: Heinemann and London: James Currey, 1995.

———. *Popular Politics in the History of South Africa, 1400–1948.* New York: Cambridge University Press, 2010.

Laquer, Thomas Walter. *Religion and Respectability: Sunday Schools and Working Class Culture: 1780–1850.* New Haven: Yale University Press, 1976.

Le Cordeur, Basil. *The Politics of Eastern Cape Separatism, 1820–1854.* Cape Town: Oxford University Press, 1981.

———. and Christopher Saunders. *The Kitchingman Papers: Missionary Letters and Journals, 1817–1848 from the Brenthurst Collection, Johannesburg.* Johannesburg: Brenthurst Press, 1976.

Ledger-Lomas, Michael. "Glimpses of the Great Conflict": English Congregationalists and the European Crisis of Faith, 1840–1875." *Journal of British Studies* 46(4) (October 2007): 826–860.

———. "Mass Markets: Religion." In *Cambridge History of the Book in Britain: 1830–1914.* David McKitterick, ed. 324–358. Cambridge: Cambridge University Press, 2009.

Lee, Richard B. *The !Kung San: Men, Women, and Work in a Foraging Society.* Cambridge: Cambridge University Press, 1979.

Legassick, Martin. *The Sotho-Tswana People before 1800.* New York: Praeger Publishers 1969.

———. "The Northern Frontier to C. 1840: The Rise and Decline of the Griqua People." In *The Shaping of South African Society, 1652–1840,* eds. Elphick and Giliomee, 358–420. Middletown, CT: Wesleyan University Press, 1979.

———. "The Frontier Tradition in South African Historiography." In Shula Marks and Anthony Atmore, eds., *Economy and Society in Pre-Industrial South Africa*, 44–79. London: Longman, 1980.

Lester, Alan. *Imperial Network: Creating Identities in Nineteenth-Century South Africa and Britain*. London: Routledge, 2001.

Levine, Roger. *A Living Man from Africa: Jan Tzatzoe, Xhosa Chief and Missionary, and the Making of Nineteenth-Century South Africa*. New Haven: Yale University Press, 2010.

Lewis, Donald. *Lighten their Darkness: The Evangelical Mission to Working-Class London*. New York: Greenwood Press, 1986.

Lewis, Jack. "The Rise and Fall of a South African Peasantry: A Critique and Reassessment." *JSAS* 11(1) (1984): 1–24.

Long, Una. ed., *The Chronicle of Jeremiah Goldswain, Albany Settler of 1820*. 2 vols. Cape Town: The Van Riebeeck Society, 1946.

Lovegrove, Deryck W. *Established Church, Sectarian People: Itinerancy and the Transformation of English Dissent*. Cambridge: Cambridge University Press, 1988.

Lovejoy, Paul. *Transformations in Slavery*. Cambridge: Cambridge University Press, 1983.

Lowenthal, David. *The Past is a Foreign Country*. Cambridge: Cambridge University Press, 1985.

Ludlow, E. H. "Missions and Emancipation in the South-West Cape: A Case Study of Groenekloof (Mamre), 1838–52." M.A. thesis, University of Cape Town, 1992.

———. "Groenekloof after the Emancipation of Slaves, 1838–1852: Leavers, Soldiers and Rebels." In *Missions and Christianity in South African History*, eds. Henry Bredekamp and Robert Ross, 113–133. Johannesburg: Witwatersrand University Press, 1995.

Maclennan, Ben. *A Proper Degree of Terror: John Graham and the Cape's Eastern Frontier*. Braamfontien, South Africa: Ravan Press, 1986.

Macmillan, William. *The Cape Colour Question: A Historical Survey*. London: Faber and Gwyer, 1927.

Mafeje, Archie. "Religion, Class and Ideology in South Africa." In *Religion and Social Change in Southern Africa*, ed. Michael Whisson and Martin West, 164–184. Cape Town: David Philip, 1975.

Malherbe, V. C. "Testing the 'Burgher Right' to the Land: Khoesan, Colonist and Government in the Eastern Cape after Ordinance 50 of 1828." *SAHJ* 40 (May 1999): 1–20.

Makin, A. E. *The 1820 Settlers of Salem*. Wynberg, South Africa: Juta, 1971.

Mandela, Nelson. *Long Walk to Freedom: The Autobiography of Nelson Mandela*. New York: Little, Brown, 1994.

Manona, Cecil. "The Drift from Farms to Town: A Case Study of Migration from White-Owned Farms in the Eastern Cape to Grahamstown." Ph.D. diss., Rhodes University, 1988.

Mapazi, Zingisile. "Albany Farm Lands Restored to 20 Families." *Dispatch*, December 23, 1997.

Marais, Johannes Stephanus. *The Cape Coloured People, 1652–1937*. London: Longmans, 1939.

Mare, Gerry. *African Population Relocation in South Africa*. Johannesburg: SAIRR, 1980.

Martin, Roger. *Evangelicals United: Ecumenical Stirrings in Pre-Victorian Britain, 1795–1830*. Metuchen, NJ: Scarecrow Press, 1983.

Mason, John. "'Fit for Freedom:' The Slaves, Slavery, and Emancipation in the Cape Colony, South Africa, 1806–1842." Ph.D. diss., Yale University, 1992.

———. *Social Death and Resurrection*. Charlottesville: University Press of Virginia, 2003.

Maxeke, Charlotte. "The Progress of Native Womanhood." In *Christianity and the Natives of South Africa, compiled* and ed. James Dextor Taylor. Lovedale: General Missionary Conference of South Africa, 1929.

Maxwell, W. A. and R. T. McGeogh, eds. *The Reminiscences of Thomas Stubbs*. Cape Town: A. A. Balkema, 1978.

Mayer, Philip. *Townsmen or Tribesmen: Conservatism and the Process of Urbanization in a South African City*. Cape Town: Oxford University Press, 1961.

Mbiti, John S. *African Religions and Philosophy, 2nd ed.* Oxford: Heinemann, 1990.

McCartan, Patrick. "Tsitsikamma Reserves (Eastern Cape)." In *Removals and the Law: Transcript of a Workshop Held in Grahamstown, July 1982*, 122–131. Cape Town: Surplus People's Project, 1984.

Meintjes, Sheila. "Family and Gender in the Christian Community at Edendale, Natal, in Colonial Times." In *Women and Gender in Southern Africa*, ed. Cherryl Walker, 125–145. Cape Town: David Philip, 1990.

Mesthrie, Rajend. "Words Across Worlds: Aspects of Language Contact and Language Learning in the Eastern Cape, 1800–1850." *African Studies* 57(1) (1998): 5–26.

Miers Suzanne and Igor Kopytoff, eds. *Slavery in Africa*. Madison, WI: University of Wisconsin Press, 1977.

——— and *Richard Roberts. The End of Slavery in Africa*. Madison, WI: University of Wisconsin Press, 1988.

Mills, Wallace George. "The Role of African Clergy in the Reorientation of Xhosa Society to the Plural Society in the Cape Colony, 1850–1915." Ph. D. diss., University of California, Los Angeles, 1975.

Milton, John. *The Edges of War: A History of Frontier Wars, 1702–1878*. Cape Town: Juta, 1983.

Mostert, Noël. *Frontiers: The Epic of South Africa's Creation and the Tragedy of the Xhosa People*. New York: Knopf, 1992.

Moyer, Richard. "The Mfengu, Self Defense and the Cape Frontier War." In *Beyond the Cape Frontier: Studies in the History of the Transkei and Ciskei*, ed. Christopher Saunders and Robin Derricourt, 101–126. London: Longman, 1974.

———. "A History of the Mfengu of the Eastern Cape." Ph.D. University of London, 1976.

Murray, Christina and Catherine O'Regan, eds. *No Place to Rest: Forced Removals and the Law in South Africa*. Cape Town and New York: Oxford University Press in association with the Labor Law Unit, University of Cape Town, 1990.

Nash, M., and N. Charton. *An Empty Table? Churches and the Ciskei Future, Report on a Churches'[sic] Consultation on Resettlement in the Ciskei held in Grahamstown, 29–30 Grahamstown, August 1980*. Johannesburg: South African Council of Churches, 1981.

Newton-King, Susan. "The Labor Market of the Cape Colony, 1807–1828." In *Economy and Society in Pre-Industrial South Africa*, eds., Shula Marks and Anthony Atmore, 171–207. London: Longman, 1980.

———. *Masters and Servants in the Cape Eastern Frontier*. Cambridge: Cambridge University Press, 1999.

Omond, Roger. *The Apartheid Handbook: A Guide to South Africa's Everyday Racial Policies*. Middlesex, England: Penguin Books, 1985 repr. 1986.

Pachai, Bridglal, ed. *Livingstone: Man of Africa*. London: Longman, 1973.

Paton, Alan. *Cry the Beloved Country.* New York: Scribner, 1948.

Pauw, B. A. "Universalism and Particularism in the Beliefs of Xhosa-Speaking Christians." In *Religion and Social Change in Southern Africa*, eds., Michael Whisson and Martin West, 153–63. Cape Town: David Philip, 1975.

———. "The Influence of Christianity." In *The Bantu-Speaking Peoples of Southern Africa*. D. W. Hammond-Tooke, ed. 415–440. London: Routledge and Keegan Paul, 1980.

———. *Christianity and Xhosa Tradition: Belief and Ritual among Xhosa-Speaking Christians.* Cape Town: Oxford University Press, 1975.

———. "The Cave of Adullam: Missionary Reaction to Ethiopianism at Lovedale, 1898–1902." *Missionalia* 19(1) (1991): 57–64.

Payne, Jill. "Re-creating Home: British Colonialism, Culture and the Zuurveld Environment in the 19th Century." M.A. thesis, Rhodes University, 1998.

Peel, J. D. Y. *Religious Encounter and the Making of the Yoruba.* Bloomington, IN: Indiana University Press, 2000.

Peires, J. B. "Nxele, Ntsikana and the Origins of the Xhosa Religious Reaction." *JAH* 20 (1979): 51–62.

———. *House of Phalo: A History of the Xhosa People in the Days of Their Independence.* Berkeley: University of California Press, 1982.

———. *The Dead Will Arise: Nongqawuse and the Great Xhosa Cattle-Killing Movement of 1856–7.* Johannesburg: Ravan Press, 1989.

Peterson, Derek and Jean Allman, "Introduction: New Directions in the History of Missions in Africa." *The Journal of Religious History* 23(1) (1999):1–7.

Peterson, J. *Province of Freedom: A History of Sierra Leone, 1787–1870.* London: Faber, 1969.

Plaatje, Solomon. *Native Life in South Africa and since the European War and Boer Rebellions.* London: P. S. King and Son, 1916. Reprint, New York: Negro Universities Press, 1969.

Platzky, Laurine and Cherryl Walker. *The Surplus People: Forced Removals in South Africa.* Johannesburg: Ravan Press, 1985.

Porter, Andrew. "Religion, Missionary Enthusiasm, and Empire." In *The Oxford History of the British Empire: Volume 3: The Nineteenth Century*, ed. Andrew Porter, 222–246. 5 vols. Oxford: Oxford University Press, 1999.

———."Trusteeship, Anti-Slavery and Humanitarianism." In *The Oxford History of the British Empire: Volume 3: The Nineteenth Century*, ed. Andrew Porter, 198–221. Oxford: Oxford University Press, 1999.

———, ed. *Religion versus Empire? British Protestant Missionaries and Overseas Expansion, 1700–1914.* Manchester: Manchester University Press, 2004.

Prevost, Elizabeth. "Assessing Women, Gender, and Empire in Britain's Nineteenth-Century Protestant Missionary Movement." *History Compass* 7(3) (2009): 765–799.

Price, Richard. *Making Empire: Colonial Encounters and the Creation of Imperial Rule in Nineteenth-Century Africa.* Cambridge: Cambridge University Press, 2008.

Pringle, Thomas. *Narrative of a Residence in South Africa.* Cape Town: C. Struik, 1966.

Raboteau, Albert. *Slave Religion.* Oxford: Oxford University Press, 1980.

Ranger, Terence and Isaria Kimambo, eds. *The Historical Study of African Religion.* London: Heinemann Educational, 1972.

Ranger, Terence. *Peasant Consciousness and Guerilla War in Zimbabwe.* London: James Currey, 1985.

———. "Religion, Development and African Christian Identity." In *Religion, Development and African Identity*, ed., Karen Holst-Petersen, 29–57. Uppsala: Scandinavian Institute of African Studies, 1987.

———. "Religious Movements and Politics in Sub-Saharan Africa." *African Studies Review* 29 (2) (June 1986):1–69.

———. "The Local and the Global in Southern African Religious History." In *Conversion to Christianity*, ed., Robert W. Hefner, ed, 65–98. Berkeley: University of California Press, 1993.

———. "Missionaries, Migrants and the Manyika: The Invention of Ethnicity in Zimbabwe," in *The Creation of Tribalism in Southern Africa*, ed. Leroy Vail, 118–150. Berkeley: University of California Press, 1989.

———. *Are We Not Also Men? The Samkange Family and African Politics in Zimbabwe 1920–1964*. London: James Currey, 1995.

Rainier, Margaret. *The Journals of Sophia Pigot*. Cape Town: A. A. Balkema, 1974.

Ross, Andrew. "The Origins and Development of the Church of Scotland Mission, Blantyre, Nyasaland, 1875–1926." Ph.D diss., University of Edinburgh, 1968.

———. *John Philip (1775–1851): Missions, Race and Politics in South Africa*. Aberdeen: Aberdeen University Press, 1986.

Ross, Kenneth. "Vernacular Translation in Christian Mission: The Case of David Clement Scott and the Blantyre Mission, 1888–1898." *Missionalia* 21(1) (April 1993): 5–18.

Ross, Robert. "The Cape of Good Hope and the World Economy, 1652–1835." In *The Shaping of South African Society, 1652–1840*, eds. Richard Elphick and Hermann Giliomee, 243–280. Middletown, CT: Wesleyan University Press, 1979.

———. *Status and Respectability in the Cape Colony, 1750–1870: A Tragedy of Manners*. Cambridge: Cambridge University Press, 1999.

———. "The Grahamstown Schism." In *The London Missionary Society in Southern Africa, 1799–1999: Historical essays in celebration of the bicentenary of the LMS in Southern Africa*. John de Gruchy, ed. 120–131. Athens, Ohio: University Press, 2000.

———. "Congregations, Missionaries and the Grahamstown Schism of 1842–43." In *The London Missionary Society in Southern Africa: Historical essays in Celebration of the LMS in Southern Africa*, ed. John De Gruchy. Cape Town: David Philip, 1999.

Rutherford, J. *Sir George Grey, K. C. B., 1812–1898: A Study in Colonial Government*. London: Cassell, 1961.

Rupp, E. Gordon. *Religion in England, 1688–1791*. Oxford: Clarendon Press, 1986.

Sales, Jane. *Mission Stations and the Coloured Communities of the Eastern Cape, 1880–1852*. Cape Town: A. A. Balkema, 1975.

———. *The Planting of the Churches in South Africa*. Grand Rapids, MI: Eerdmans, 1971.

Sanneh, Lamin. *West African Christianity: The Religious Impact*. Maryknoll, NY: Orbis Books, 1983.

———. *Translating the Message: The Missionary Impact on Culture*. Maryknoll, NY: Orbis Books, 1989.

———. *Encountering the West: Christianity and the Global Impact on the Global Cultural Process: The African Dimension*. Maryknoll, NY: Orbis Books, 1993.

———. *Abolitionists Abroad: American Blacks and the Making of Modern West Africa*. Cambridge, MA: Harvard University Press, 1999.

Saunders, Christopher and Robin Derricourt. *Beyond the Cape Frontier: Studies in the History of the Transkei and Ciskei*. London: Longman, 1974.

Saunders, Christopher. "'The Hundred Years War': Some Reflections on African Resistance on the Cape-Xhosa Frontier." In *Profiles of Self-Determination*, ed. David Chanaiwa, 55–77. Northridge: California State University Foundation, 1976.

———. "Between Slavery and Freedom." *Kronos* 9 (1984): 36–43.

———. "Liberated Africans in the Cape Colony on the First Half of the Nineteenth Century." *International Journal of African Historical Studies* 18 (1985): 223–239.

———. "Free Yet Slaves: Prize Negroes at the Cape Revisited." In *Breaking the Chains: Slavery and Its Legacy in the Nineteenth-Century Cape Colony*, Nigel Worden and Clifton Crais, eds., 99–115. Johannesburg: Witwatersrand University Press, 1994.

Schmidt, Bettina. *Creating Order: Culture as Politics in 19th and 20th Century South Africa*. Nijmegen: Third World Center, University of Nijmegen, 1996.

Semmel, Bernard. *The Methodist Revolution*. New York: Basic Books, 1973.

Sensbach, Jon F. *Rebecca's Revival: Creating Black Christianity in the Atlantic World*. Cambridge: Harvard University Press, 2005.

Seton. B. E. "Wesleyan Missionaries and the Sixth Frontier War, 1834–1835." Ph.D. diss., University of Cape Town, 1962.

Shapin, Steven. *A Social History of Truth. Chicago: Civility and Science in Seventeenth-Century England*. Chicago: University of Chicago Press, 1994.

Shell, Robert. *Children of Bondage: A Social History of the Slave Society at the Cape of Good Hope, 1652–1838*. Hanover, NH: University Press of New England, 1994.

Silva, Penelope. *The Albany Journal of Thomas Stone*. Cape Town: Maskew Miller, 1992.

Spielvogel, Jackson. *Western Civilization*, 2nd ed., 2 vols. New York: West Publishing, 1994.

SPP and AFRA. *Removals and the Law, Transcript of a Workshop held in Grahamstown*. Cape Town: SPP; Pietermaritzburg: AFRA, 1984.

Stapleton, Timothy. *Maqoma: Xhosa Resistance to Colonial Advance, 1798–1873*. Johannesburg: J. Ball, 1994.

———. "The Expansion of a Pseudo Ethnicity on the Eastern Cape: Reconsidering the Fingo Exodus of 1865." *IJAS* 29(2): 233–250.

Stuart, Doug. "'The Wicked Christians' and the 'Children of the Mist:' Missionary and Khoi Interactions at the Cape in the Early Nineteenth Century." In *Societies of Southern Africa in the 19th and 20th Centuries: Collected Seminar Papers*. University of London, Institute of Commonwealth Studies, 18 (1992).

Sundkler, Bengt. *Bantu Prophets in South Africa*. 1948. Reprint, London: Oxford University Press, 1961.

Switzer, Les. *Power and Resistance in an African Society: The Ciskei Xhosa and the Making of South Africa*. Madison: University of Wisconsin Press, 1993.

Temperley, Howard. *White Dreams, Black Africa: The British Antislavery Expedition to the River Niger, 1841–1842*. New Haven: Yale University Press, 1991.

Theal, George McCall. Comp. *Records of the Cape Colony*, 36 vols. London: Government of the Cape Colony, 1897–1905.

———. *Documents Relating to the Kaffir War of 1835*. London: Clowes, 1912.

Thompson, E. P. *The Making of the English Working Class*. New York: Vintage Books, 1966.

Thompson, Leonard. *Survival in Two Worlds: Moshoeshoe of Lesotho, 1786–1870*. Oxford: Clarendon Press, 1975.

————. *Political Mythology of Apartheid*. New Haven: Yale University Press, 1985.

Thorne, Susan. "The Conversion of Englishmen and the Conversion of the World Insepara-ble." In *Tensions of Empire: Colonial Cultures in a Bourgeois World*, eds., Frederick Cooper and Ann Laura Stoler, 238–262. Berkeley: University of California Press, 1997.

————. *Congregational Missions and the Making of an Imperial Culture in Nineteenth-Century England*. Stanford: Stanford University Press, 1999.

Thornton, John. *Africa and Africans in the Making of the Atlantic World, 1400–1680*, 2nd edn. Cambridge: Cambridge University Press, 1998.

Tupy, Marian L. "South Africa's Land Woes." *Washington Times*, March 6, 2006.

———— and Michael Kransdorff. "The Zimbabwe-ification of South Africa?" *Wall Street Europe*, July 15, 2009.

Turner, Mary. *Slaves and Missionaries: The Disintegration of Jamaican Slave Society, 1787–1834*. Urbana: University of Illinois Press, 1982.

Van der Merwe, P. J. *The Migrant Farmer in the History of the Cape Colony*. Transl. Roger Beck. Athens: Ohio University Press, 1995.

Vassady Jr., Bela. "The Role of the Black West Indian Missionary in West Africa, 1840–1890." Ph.D, diss.,Temple University, 1972.

Viljoen, Russel. "Moravian Missionaries, Khoisan Labour and the Overberg Colonists." In *Missions and Christianity in South African History*, eds. Henry Bredekamp and Robert Ross, 49–64. Johannesburg: Witwatersrand University Press, 1995.

Visser, Wessel. "'Shifting RDP into GEAR:' The ANC Government's Dilemma in Providing an Equitable System of Social Security for the 'New' South Africa." Paper presented at the 40th ITH Linzer Konferenz. University of Stellenbosch, South Africa, September 17, 2004.

Walls, Andrew F. *The Missionary Movement in Christian History: Studies in the Transmission of Faith*. Maryknoll, NY: Orbis Books, 1996.

Walker, Cherryl, ed. *Women and Gender in Southern Africa to 1945*. Cape Town: D. Philip, 1990.

————. *Landmarked: Land Claims and Restitution in South Africa*. Athens, OH: Ohio University Press, 2008.

Walvin, James. *England, Slaves and Freedom, 1776–1838*. Jackson: University Press of Mississippi, 1986.

Ward, W. R. *Religion and Society in England, 1790–1850*. London: Batsford, 1972.

Watts, Michael. *The Dissenters: The Expansion of Evangelical Nonconformity*. Vol 2. Oxford: Oxford University Press, 1995.

Webster, Alan. "Land Expropriation and Labor Extraction under Cape Colonial Rule: The War of 1835 and the Emancipation of the Fingo." M.A. thesis, Rhodes University, 1991.

————. "Unmasking the Fingo: The War of 1835 Revisited." In *The Mfecane Aftermath: Reconstructive Debates in Southern African History*, Carolyn Hamilton, ed. 241–276. Johannesburg: Witwatersrand University Press, 1995.

Wells, Julia. "The Scandal of Rev James Read and the Taming of the London Missionary Society by 1820." *SAHJ* 42 (May 2000): 136–160.

Whisson, Michael and Martin West, eds. *Religion and Social Change in Southern Africa: Anthropological Essays in Honor of Monica Wilson*. Cape Town: David Philip, 1975.

White, Landeg. *Magomero: Portrait of an African Village*. Cambridge: Cambridge University Press, 1987.

Whiteside, Joseph. *History of the Wesleyan Methodist Church of South Africa*. London: Elliot Stock, 1906.

Wilkinson, Patrick. *Church Clothes: Land, Mission, and the End of Apartheid in South Africa*. Washington, DC: Maisonneuve Press, 2004.

Williams, Donavan. "The Missionaries on the Eastern Frontier of the Cape Colony, 1799–1853." Ph.D, University of Witwatersrand, 1959.

———. *Umfundisi: A Biography of Tiyo Soga, 1829–1871*. Lovedale: Lovedale Press, 1978.

———, ed. *The Journal and Selected Writings of the Reverend Tiyo Soga*. Cape Town: A. A. Balkema, 1983.

Williams, Walter L. *Black Americans and the Evangelization of Africa, 1877–1900*. Madison: University of Wisconsin Press, 1982.

Wilson, Monica. *The Interpreters*. Grahamstown: 1820 Settlers, National Monument Foundation, 1972.

Wilmsen, Edwin. *Land Filled With Flies*. Chicago: University of Chicago Press, 1989.

Wineburg, Sam. *Historical Thinking and Other Unnatural Acts: Charting the Future of Teaching the Past*. Philadelphia: Temple University Press, 2001.

Winer, Margot and James Deetz. "The Transformation of British Culture in the Eastern Cape, 1820–1860." *Social Dynamics* 16 (1) (1990): 55–75

Worden, Nigel. *Slavery in Dutch South Africa*. Cambridge: Cambridge University Press, 1985.

———. "Between Slavery and Freedom: The Apprenticeship Period, 1834–1838." In *Breaking the Chains: Slavery and its Legacy in Nineteenth-Century Cape Colony*. Worden and Crais, eds., 117–144. Johannesburg: Witwatersrand University Press, 1994.

———. and Clifton Crais, eds. *Breaking the Chains: Slavery and its Legacy in Nineteenth-Century Cape Colony*. Johannesburg: Witwatersrand University Press, 1994.

Yekela, Drusilla. "The Life and Times of Kama Chungwa (1778–1875)." M.A. thesis, Rhodes University, 1988.

Young, Robert. *African Wastes Reclaimed: Illustrated in the Story of the Lovedale Mission*. London: Dent/Everyman, 1902.

Internet Sources

Community Survey, 2007 Eastern Cape. Online. Available: http://www.statssa.gov.za/publications/Report-03-01-32/Report-03-01-322007.pdf. March 20, 2010.

Department of Land Affairs. "Progress on Restitution." January 27, 2006. Online. Available: http://www.info.gov.za/speeches/2006/06013012451001.htm. March 23, 2011.

Cooperative Housing Foundation International. "Road to Sustainability (RTF) Program, Final Performance Report." Port Elizabeth South Africa, May 22, 2002. Online. Available: http://pdf.usaid.gov/pdf_docs/PDABZ002.pdf. June 20, 2010; March 23, 2011.

———. "Road to Sustainability (RTF) Program, Semi-Annual Performance Report." April 2001–September 2001. Online. Available: http://pdf.usaid.gov/pdf_docs/PDABU235.pdf. March 23, 2011.

Elne Jacobs and Cecilia Punt, Western Cape Department of Agriculture, "A Profile of the Eastern Cape Province: Demographics, Poverty, Income, Inequality and Unemployment from 2000 till 2007." [Background Paper, 2009: 1 (2) Provincial Decision-Making Enabling Project]. Online. Available: www.elsenburg.com/provide/.../BP2009_1_2_%20EC%20Demographics.pdf. 21, March 23, 2011.

South Africa Millennium Development Goals, Mid-Term Country Report, 2007. Online. Available: http://planipolis.iiep.unesco.org/upload/South%20Africa/SouthAfrica MDGmidterm.pdf. March 21, 2011.

Interviews

All 1999 interviews conducted by Fiona Vernal and Cecil Nonqane; translations Cecil Nonqane and Stella Dhlomo; all 2007 interviews conducted by Fiona Vernal and Sabata Mageza; translations, Sabata Mageza

*unrecorded; + via telephone

Johnson Tamsana Bangushe, Grahamstown, February 28, 1999

+ Puleng Bennie, via phone, August 12, 1999

Anderson Budaza, Mimosa Park, March 7, 1999

Miriam Budaza, Mimosa Park, January 31, 1999

Ivan Buysile Budaza, Mimosa Park, March 7, 1999

[Koko] Welsch Budaza, Mimosa Park, January 31, 1999

Nofelity Gaba, Grahamstown February 1, 1999

Patrick Hewana, Grahamstown, January 29, 1999

Michael Madinda, Grahamstown, February 28, 1999

Daniel Matini, Mimosa Park, January 31, 1999; July 31, 2007

Florence Matini, Mimosa Park, January 31, 1999; July 31, 2007

*Beldin Msimoti Matini, Mimosa Park, March 7, 1999

Mary Jane Maxegwana, Grahamstown, February 28, 1999

Mongameli Maxegwana, Mimosa Park, February 1, 1999

Msewu May, Mimosa Park, February 21, 1999

Setchaba May, Mimosa Park, February 21, 1999

Napthali Mbozanani, Salem, May 1, 1999; June 16, 2001

Robert Mbulelo Mquqo, Mimosa Park, February 21, 1999

Nonyameko Mpati, May 2, 1999, Ginsburg, King Williams Town

Murphy Mquqo, Mimosa Park, February 21, 1999

*Tommy Mquqo, Mimosa Park, February 21, 1999

Elsie Luzipho Mzizi, Grahamstown, February 28, 1999

Mbali Solomon Mzizi, February 23, 1999, Grahamstown, August 1, 2007

Arthur Ngqondi, Zwelitsha, King Williams Town, May 2, 1999

Ernest [Ou Baas] Ngqondi, Zwelitsha, King Williams Town, May 2, 1999

Miriam Nombala Ngqondi, Port Elizabeth, March 14, 1999

Nomfundo Albertina Ngqondi, Port Elizabeth, March 14, 1999

Violet Ngqondi, Zwelitsha, King Williams Town, May 2, 1999

Cecil Nonqane, Grahamstown, June 29, 2001

Mina Nothemba Nonzube, Farmerfield, August 3, 2007

Nimrod Plaatjie, Southwell, May 1, 1999

Mavis Rasana, Grahamstown, February 28, 1999

*Jayile Saki, May 1, 1999, Riddin Farm, near Farmerfield, May 1, 1999

Petrus Zatu, Farmerfield, May 1, 1999 and June 16, 2001

Sylvia Zweni, Mimosa Park, January 31, 1999; Farmerfield, August 3, 2007

Patricia Zweni, Farmerfield, August 3, 2007

INDEX